The Gospel of Church

The Gospel of Church

How Mainline Protestants Vilified Christian Socialism and Fractured the Labor Movement

JANINE GIORDANO DRAKE

OXFORD
UNIVERSITY PRESS

OXFORD
UNIVERSITY PRESS

Oxford University Press is a department of the University of Oxford. It furthers
the University's objective of excellence in research, scholarship, and education
by publishing worldwide. Oxford is a registered trade mark of Oxford University
Press in the UK and certain other countries.

Published in the United States of America by Oxford University Press
198 Madison Avenue, New York, NY 10016, United States of America.

© Oxford University Press 2024

Library of Congress Cataloging-in-Publication Data
Names: Drake, Janine Giordano, author.
Title: the gospel of church: how mainline protestants vilified christian
socialism and fractured the labor movement / Janine Giordano Drake.
Description: New York, NY, United States of America : Oxford University Press, [2024] |
Includes bibliographical references and index.
Identifiers: LCCN 2023019541 (print) | LCCN 2023019542 (ebook) |
ISBN 9780197614303 (c/p) | ISBN 9780197614327 (epub) | ISBN 9780197614334
Subjects: LCSH: United States—Church history. | Christian socialism—United States. |
Church growth—United States. | Communities—Religious aspects—Christianity. |
Christianity and politics—United States.
Classification: LCC BR526 .D733 2023 (print) | LCC BR526 (ebook) |
DDC 277.308/3—dc23/eng/20230703
LC record available at https://lccn.loc.gov/2023019541
LC ebook record available at https://lccn.loc.gov/2023019542

DOI: 10.1093/oso/9780197614303.001.0001

Printed by Sheridan Books, Inc., United States of America

For IVCF,
And for Noelle, Julianna, and Nathalie

Contents

Acknowledgments

This project began early in the George W. Bush administration, when evangelical pastor Rick Warren, author of the best-selling *The Purpose Driven Church* (1995), told Americans to read the Bible with "church-growth eyes."[1] As a college student and curious new member of an evangelical church, I was intrigued by the way my new friends counted my church participation as evidence of their prayerful outreach. I was especially intrigued by how many of my new friends believed that churches' "faith-based initiatives" ought to grow to replace publicly-funded education and social services. As a child of the 1990s in suburban New York, I believed in the almost salvific value of municipal services. I spent many hours per week winding through diverse neighborhoods on a big yellow school bus while I marveled at the wonders of well-funded public libraries, public schools, Head Start, public afterschool programs, and public summer camps to build cross-class solidarities and a fundamental social safety net. My mother taught me to appreciate every one of these "municipalities," as she called them, as the foundation of a just society. Why did my new church friends think that "faith-based initiatives" could provide for the needs of their communities better than elected city governments? My new friends were not wealthy business leaders in search of tax shelters for their excess income. They were ordinary Christians who earnestly sought after what they called "biblical principles" as a guide for their civic participation.

This book, a chronicle of the great American rivalry between church growth and social democracy, is dedicated to those friends whose faithful support for growing "the Church" makes curiously little room for the state. I know some of these folks through Intervarsity Christian Fellowship at SUNY Geneseo or the University of Illinois. I know others through the Conference on Faith and History, the Great Falls Young Catholics, or St. Thomas Lutheran Church. Friends within these various communities have modeled respectful conversation on hard questions at the intersection of theology, ecclesiology, and politics. It is because of all these generous friends and colleagues, and the many life-giving communities we built together, that I grew convinced this book was worth writing.

Like any project that has occupied half one's life, this project has amassed uncountable debts. Because my dissertation "research year" coincided with the Great Recession of 2009–2010, I had to lean on the generosity of friends, family, and complete strangers to complete archival research in cities and towns across the country. My sister and brother-in-law, Regine and Josh Brady, shared their home with me and supported this project in numerous ways. Sherri Gall and Valerie Martin opened their homes to a complete stranger doing archival research in their small towns. As a graduate student, I benefited from the Everett Helm fellowship (Indiana University) and the Cushwa Center research fellowship (University of Notre Dame).

I completed the dissertation under the tutelage Jim Barrett, Dave Roediger, and Kathy Oberdeck, a dream team of both labor historians and specialists in the history of American socialism. Jim Barrett supported this project, despite its many challenges, from the start. I am thankful to my many graduate school colleagues, especially Ian Hartman, Kerry Pimblott, Jason Koslowski, and Tom Mackaman, for offering critical feedback on this project as a dissertation and after. My training in historical theology, religious studies, and American religious history has been less formal. I am grateful to Jonathan Ebel and Jacob Dorn for agreeing to serve on my dissertation committee at the final stage of the project. I am especially thankful to Paul Harvey—who gave me a chance as a blogger for Religion in American History—for introducing me to the broad field of American religious history. I am also thankful to Phil Goff, Laura Levitt and Jim Bennett for giving me the opportunity to join the Young Scholars in American Religion pandemic cohort. Tim Gloege, Elesha Coffman, Brian Ingrassia, Doug Thompson, and Mark Edwards deserve special thanks for reading all or parts of the manuscript.

When I joined the faculty at a small Catholic college in Montana, I had only a faint understanding of the extent to which I was being asked to carry on the complicated legacy of a twentieth-century initiative in Christian social service. I am grateful to colleagues Rachel Morgan, Matt Morgan, Brendan Palla, Sarah Spangler, and Angel Turoski for teaching me about the historic mission of a Catholic school in the United States.

Since arriving at Indiana University in 2019, I have been thankful to colleagues and friends who have helped me revisit an old project with new eyes. I have studied the multiple crises of the year 1919 for almost two decades, but the year 2020 taught me to see 1919 as I never had before. Tina Irvine, Sarah Knott, Chris Arnold, Carl Weinberg, Lacy Hawkins, Anna Poore, Leigh Ann Ruggiero, and Kalani Craig have been terrific friends.

The teachers I work with in the Advance College Project continue to mentor me in the sacrifices and joys built into the vocation of teaching as a public servant.

Most of all, my family has sacrificed for this project in ways I will never be able to repay. This book is only possible because of their unflagging willingness to support me and all that I do. My husband, Josh Drake, lived with this project for almost fifteen years. Our three daughters each remind me daily that I am blessed beyond comprehension to be their mother. While eight years of pregnancy and nursing may have extended the wait for this book a little bit, my curious daughters also remind me daily why books are worth writing.

Introduction

After finally knocking himself out with a sleep aid, Julian West accidentally overslept by 113 years. He awoke in the year 2000 in a pleasant, clean Boston that had abolished the wage system and nationalized all production. Everyone now worked for government scrip and slept in clean government homes. Children of the nineteenth-century poor now enjoyed access to the highest-quality education and art. But perhaps most remarkably, social equality had rendered churches obsolete.

In this best-selling Gilded Age fantasy, *Looking Backward: 2000–1887*, the rise of a Cooperative Commonwealth in the United States had relocated Christianity from the churches to the central fabric of society. Ministers found themselves relieved of the responsibility to cultivate wealthy donors whose "charity" would rationalize both the continuity of private capital and the dependence of the poor. Instead, Christians were elected to public office and served in various facets of social service. As Dr. Leete, Edward Bellamy's main character, explained the transition of the previous century, "Just as the abolition of royalty was the beginning of decent government, just as the abolition of private capitalism was the beginning of effective wealth production, so the disappearance of church organization and machinery, or ecclesiastical capitalism, was the beginning of a world-awakening of impassioned interest in the vast concerns covered by the word religion."[1]

This third-largest bestseller of the nineteenth century had struck a nerve. Gilded Age churches were small institutions that primarily served the wealthy. Many churches also ran missions or charities to serve the poor, but worship experiences were deeply segmented by race, class, and ethnicity. Fewer than 22 percent of Americans were members of any church, and likely only a small fraction of those members attended weekly services. As European Scripture scholars raised serious questions on the historicity of both the Old and New Testaments, working-class Americans largely avoided conventional, denominational churches. Wealthy churchgoers, with their ministers in fine robes, pews for rent, and expensive altars and chalices, seemed to symbolize the old, European world of kings and queens, gentry

The Gospel of Church. Janine Giordano Drake, Oxford University Press. © Oxford University Press 2024.
DOI: 10.1093/oso/9780197614303.003.0001

and peasants, all of which was quickly passing away. For many working-class Americans, church was incompatible with modernity.

Christianity, on the other hand, was only growing more popular in the United States. Many working-class Americans participated in an imagined Christian community made possible by a massive socialist print culture and a network of labor churches. Working people imagined Jesus as a poor carpenter who rejected traditional religious rituals and encouraged his followers to pour their faith into making a better world. This message was loud and clear in Bellamy's *Looking Backward* (1887) and its sequel, *Equality* (1898), which together sold more than one million copies. By 1895, Charles Sheldon's *In His Steps: What Would Jesus Do?*, became one of the best-selling books of all time. By the year 1906, it had sold more copies than the number of registered church members in the entire United States. Sheldon coined the term "Churchianity" to describe the worship of respectability and the trappings of "church" in place of the man Jesus Christ.[2]

In both Europe and the United States, the combination of industrialization, urbanization, and the rise of socialism seemed to foreshadow a future in secular democracies. A number of commentators described "socialism" as "Christianity's most formidable rival" in the world. Many suggested that theological schools should modernize to produce not only professional preachers, trained in ecclesiology, but also revivalists modeled on labor leaders. One minister reflected in 1907, "The present writer has heard a dozen impassioned Socialists, addressing audiences aggregating ten thousand people, make a finer, a more effective, a more dramatic, and a more moral use of the figures, the illustrations, and the moral teachings of the Gospels, in a single evening, than he has heard from any dozen preachers in a month in the last twenty years."[3]

These commentators were not wrong about the vitality of Christian imagery, Scripture study, and Christian fellowship within the growing labor movement. Eugene Debs, one of the chief organizers for the Socialist Party of America, endorsed the mission of the Christian Socialist Fellowship (CSF) when it was still in its infancy. He hoped that by drawing together socialist ministers within a larger network, he could make social democratic ideas more tenable to Christians in power and use churches as continued loci of socialist organizing. Starting in 1907, the CSF functioned as a veritable department of the Socialist Party of America. The group published dozens of books and maintained speakers' bureaus to present "the Socialist economic doctrine in any church, YMCA, or in any other organization which is closed to Socialist propaganda that does not come under the name 'Christian.' "[4] The CSF made significant inroads to winning well-respected, denominational preachers to their view of political economy. The prominent theologian Walter Rauschenbusch gave credit to Christian Socialists for his own social education in his 1912 *Christianizing the Social Order*. He wrote, "God had to raise up Socialism because the organized Church was too blind, or too slow, to realize God's ends."[5] By 1912, the Socialist Party had convinced several million Americans that municipal socialism, the cooperative ownership and management of utilities, in combination with a welfare state and collective bargaining rights, was the sincerest expression of the Kingdom of God on earth.[6] By 1916, the Socialist Party had won dozens of state and local elections and had more than three hundred affiliated newspapers in virtually every city in the United States. Socialists had built a powerful, grassroots movement that seemed invulnerable by 1917.

And yet, by the end of the Great War, it was socialism that had become nearly obsolete in the United States. Socialist print culture became borderline criminal activity under the terms of the 1918 Sedition Act, and many newspapers had to shut down. Socialist Christians frequently came under state and federal scrutiny for obstructing the war effort because of their rejection of nationalism and embrace of religious pluralism. While the process of rendering socialism anathema to Christian values had rapidly accelerated during the Great War, the conservative Christian battle against socialism and Christian Socialism had begun much earlier.

The Federal Council of Churches, formed as a federation of more than two dozen Protestant denominations in 1908, defined their vision of "social welfare" around the rejection of socialism. In his run for president and throughout his two terms, President Woodrow Wilson endorsed the mission of the Federal Council and encouraged the clergy at the leadership of this coalition to adopt his domestic and international foreign policy goals. It was the modern Social Gospel movement, a constellation of interests shared by ministers, lawmakers, and their corporate benefactors, that successfully thwarted socialism and encouraged Americans to see the Church as the foundation of the modern nation.

Why did the ministers of the Federal Council of Churches emerge as national authorities in a world where they were rapidly becoming cultural and religious minorities? Most scholars address this question by emphasizing the broad coalition of Catholic, Protestant and Jewish clergy and civic leaders who built a broad consensus around the mission to reform exploitative workplaces in the name of humanitarian justice.[7] We usually refer to this religiously-infused social reform coalition as the Social Gospel movement. More recently, historians have begun to query the role of wage earners in this story. Ken Fones-Wolf, Elizabeth Fones-Wolf, and Heath Carter, for example, have each shown that the early twentieth-century Social Gospel movement was the product of close collaboration between the trade union locals of the American Federation of Labor and supportive clergy within their communities. The Social Gospel was "union made," Carter argued, because it was trade union leaders who gave Protestant ministers their authority and respect.[8]

While it is true that the Social Gospel was "union made," this observation tells only part of the story. The white, male, skilled artisans at the head of the AFL did not speak on behalf of all wage earners in North America, especially after 1910. The growing majority of the industrial workforce in the early twentieth century were racially "in between" and semi-literate. They included migrants from the American South and overseas who took the most dangerous and lowest-paying jobs to escape systematic violence, war, and economic dislocation. Trade union leaders' rejection of socialism and early support for Woodrow Wilson made the trade union movement conservative, and even reactionary, by the standards of international labor at the start of the Great War. By 1917, a diminishing faction of the industrial working classes had access to the prestigious craft union membership that the had long AFL represented. In fact, employers were mechanizing production so quickly that craft-union skills themselves were becoming less and less valuable, a factor that was leading to the massive leveling of the working classes.

The growing ranks of labor were frustrated with the executive leadership of the American Federation of Labor and demanding a different kind of labor movement. Few recognized white American Protestant ministers, especially those within the most well-resourced denominations, as the nation's cultural or spiritual authorities. We need to recognize the alliances built between trade union executives and clergy as a curious coalition formed by a shared desire to preserve an older social order, a regime where aspirant-class white Protestant men in the North acted as foremen and supervisors over women, brown-skinned and racially "inbetween" people. To the extent the Social Gospel was "union made," this alliance between trade union leaders and clergy was also profoundly conservative.

The Gospel of Church traces the early twentieth-century debate over what it meant to be a Christian nation and who ought lead that country in moral and spiritual leadership. Many working people in the US, like their counterparts abroad, wanted to redeem the republic from the oppressive systems of patriarchy, white supremacy, and colonialism. Socialists, equipped with an early concept of human rights, were committed to universal suffrage, public works programs, collective bargaining, disability and old age insurance, and publicly funded social services across the domains of education and healthcare. They believed that a morally just state found ways to provide public services through taxation and profit-sharing initiatives, even if that meant forcibly nationalizing private transit systems, mines, and factories.

Protestant ministers within the Federal Council of Churches interpreted this socialist agenda an assault on the place of Christianity in the nation. Nineteenth century churches ran social programs for every stage of life, including nurseries, orphanages, grade schools, schools for the deaf and blind, seminaries, colleges, hospitals, rehabilitation facilities, and nursing homes. Church recreation halls and gymnasia, new in the early twentieth century, furnished the public spaces that built community around the shared experiences of courtship, marriage, childrearing, activism, and grief. In their narrative, Christian missionaries had almost entirely built the nation's social infrastructure for the poor. They believed they could rise to the occasion to meet the present industrial crisis. To many of these ministers, the suggestion that the nation should steward a new, public, secular infrastructure to replace that of Christian missionaries was to remove Christian leadership from regular contact with the laboring classes and threaten the future of the Christian republic. Most white clergy saw the hierarchies of Christians over non-Christians, whites over nonwhites, and men over women as natural and even central to the God-given social order.

This is a book about the conservative Christian takeover of both the churches and the labor movement in the early twentieth century. Conservatives usually described their goals as primarily ideological: they wanted to defend unions' independent and apolitical voice, and they supported the growth of church membership as a bulwark against vice, theological heresy, wayward women, and disloyalty to the nation. However, we also must also reckon with the unspoken ambitions of this conservative alliance. In a white supremacist nation thinly held together by widespread voter suppression, this conservative labor-religious alliance solidified the cultural authority of white men in the urban North. The Protestant ministers of the Federal Council like Worth Tippy, Charles Stelzle and Frank Mason North endorsed one version of democracy, Christianity, and labor justice against the many more egalitarian alternatives popular within the labor movement. They provided the ideological rationale for welfare capitalism, a new labor regime that placed white male foremen over the immigrants, African Americans, and women who not only clamored for universal suffrage, but also aspired to join the ranks of equality with white male counterparts in respectable, well-paying union jobs.

The book makes three main arguments. First, it shows that the social democratic labor movement directly competed with conservative church leaders for the authority to set the terms of social justice for the twentieth century. Wage earners utilized a variety of forums, including churches, socialist fellowships, unions, revivals, and print culture, to build momentum behind a new kind of Christian commonwealth.[9] Many imagined a nation built on a new social contract among businesses, workers, and the state, where social and economic relationships would be governed by the "service motive" instead of the "profit motive." Companies would share profits with employees, and the state would invest heavily in infrastructure to provide both employment and social services, enabling social mobility. Sunday morning worship services would play only a minor role in a society based in Christian principles.

Second, the book illustrates that Protestant ministers' work with the labor movement, roughly between 1908 and 1919, was always part and parcel of an effort to win wage earners' favor, reverence, and church membership—and to co-opt the moral authority of the Christian Socialist movement. Through their nationwide shop-floor organizing campaign, their widely circulated *Social Creed of the Churches*, and their heavy involvement in strike arbitration and reporting, ministers tried to prove their own expertise on industrial relations. However, their self-congratulatory strike reports always arrived too late to be helpful at the bargaining table. These reports constructed a narrative of the working classes as morally aimless and in need of ministers, foremen, and clerks to lead workers in healthy attitudes and opportunities for education and recreation. Protestant ministries for wage earners, including film discussions, afterschool programs, and adult classes in English, history, and philosophy, had similar goals. They sought to mimic but also replace the intellectual communities of "labor churches" and "people's churches" of the Gilded Age. Perhaps most of all, these ministries sought to convince middle-class and middling-class whites to trust them, rather than the labor movement, as true mouthpieces of Christian justice. Federal Council ministers claimed that working people deserved better wages and working conditions, but they used their cloak of well-trained, ministerial authority—inseparable from their whiteness and maleness—to claim that they were the only trust-worthy agents of Christian reform.

Third, in forming the Federal Council of Churches in 1908, white Protestant ministers effectively formed a trust (a noncompete agreement) on Christian ideals in order to keep the labor movement from drawing on the Christian tradition with its political demands. That is, they used their exper-tise as ministers to define the parameters of orthodox Christian worship and civic participation such that socialist belief and advocacy was political and did not deserve the protections of religious freedom. Protestant leaders held that "the Church" (the universal body, with a capital C) was not, as socialists claimed it to be, a community of social equals, seeking to redeem sin in the world. Rather, they claimed that the Church was a stable institution, existing outside politics and economics, for the primary purpose of personal spiritual renewal. American businessmen and politicians applauded the prospect of a new Christian orthodoxy that harbored no political or economic critiques. Many businessmen, but especially John D. Rockefeller, funded the Federal Council's project to plant these "apolitical," conservative churches every-where that radical working-class communities existed.

This new, conservative Christian orthodoxy changed the balance of power within both the labor movement and the wider culture. Socialists were quickly infiltrating the ranks of the AFL in the early decades of the twen-tieth century. When Protestant ministers partnered with the trade union movement to organize more apolitical trade unions, they threw money and authority behind the minority of antisocialist labor leaders on the executive council of the AFL. The Federal Council thus diluted the power of the so-cialist rank and file and painted socialists as both radical and theologically heterodox. If the fundamental mission of the Socialist Party was to garner moral authority for the labor movement in service of establishing a coopera-tive commonwealth, the ministers of the Federal Council were their greatest opponents.

The ministers' claims to Christian orthodoxy also allowed white Protestant clergy and their congregations, a cultural minority in the Gilded Age, to unite a cross-class coalition of white men around the identity of a theologically or-thodox "Christian." By 1916, weekly church attendance swelled by a factor of six, but this increase came almost entirely from the growing middling classes of clerks and foremen who now staffed factories and mines. Protestant church leaders claimed that these predominantly white, male, and Protestant clerks and foremen—industrial bosses—were the real representatives of the nation's wage earners. In this respect, the formation of the Federal Council of Churches was crucial to defining and protecting a white Protestant leadership over a rapidly diversifying United States.

This journey into the history of working-class Christianity in the industrial age reveals that the rivalry between Protestant clergy and the radical labor movement was really an argument about how to tell the story of Christian missionaries for the modern era. Protestant Social Gospel leaders within the Federal Council of Churches wanted to foreground the heroic story of the American missionary as "healer" of racial, gendered, and sectional divisions.[10] They explained their foreign and home missions work as supportive of marginalized peoples wherever they could be found. By 1920, these Social Gospel leaders pointed to the wage increases and ameliorated working conditions of the new welfare capitalist era as evidence of their consistent solidarity with the nation's most marginalized. This heroic narrative of Social Gospel ministers, which continues to resonate in churches to this day, won these ministers so much praise from the public that few questioned their credibility as "social service" experts, even after the Federal Council withdrew support from the AFL. In the long run, the clergy-led Social Gospel movement offered only short-lived and partial support for the demands of wage workers. What the Social Gospel really accomplished was to restore churches and church-based charities to that coveted role in American culture as the primary purveyors of education, health, and social services.

Defining Scope and Terms

Because this book seeks to reframe the way we think about the Social Gospel moment, a brief glossary of terms is necessary. As I have traced the evolution of the term "Social Gospel," I noticed that it transformed from a description of the conversation on Christian social justice (1880–1900) into a shorthand for the principles of the Federal Council's *Social Creed* (post-1908). Because this alliance among Protestant and Catholic ministers and trade union conservatives became recognized by journalists, theologians, labor leaders, and other public intellectuals as the *Social Gospel*, I use this term to describe minister-led social and legal reform.[11]

I define the *labor movement* as the strategic alliances forged to put working people in the position to win their demands.[12] In the United States, especially after around 1905, the AFL was the biggest federation of trade unions and thus dominated the American labor movement in both resources and access to legislative power. Trades unions, however, were only one particular type of union, and they were quickly becoming reactionary in their vision of how workers could transform society.

Trades unionists saw their leverage with business leaders primarily in their skills. They called themselves *skilled workers*, and over those skills they exercised extreme protection. They saw the primary goals of their unions in demanding a larger share of the wealth that their skills helped produce. When acolytes of Frederick Winslow Taylor began to simplify work processes through the division of labor and automation, trades unionists fought hard to keep their jobs from being subdivided and turned into work fit for "unskilled" laborers.[13] They federated nationally according to their unique trade and made it difficult for women, new immigrants, and African Americans to gain entry into historically white male professions. Yet this organizing only stirred tension with the increasing numbers of foreign-born, African American, and women workers who looked for work in cities and mining towns after 1900. These workers, sometimes called *proletarians*, found themselves increasingly shut out from training in some of the skilled trades and unable to find any work except that which was "unskilled," or perhaps better described as deskilled. Not until the Great War did the AFL dedicate significant resources to organizing large numbers of deskilled wage earners.

When historians refer to the *radical labor movement*, they usually point to all organizing that took place outside the trade union movement and that proposed a different organizational structure to lead the labor movement and forward the demands of working people. *Socialism*, like Protestantism, was a broad, decentralized movement in the period before World War I. Within a variety of spaces including churches, unions, and the Socialist Party, socialists demanded the equality of all people under the law despite social and economic status. *Social Democrats* supported universal suffrage, electoral reforms, legal collective bargaining, and "social insurance" programs like disability, old-age pensions, and unemployment. The movement, akin to sister movements in Europe, welcomed people of every religious background. Socialist Democrats, including the Socialist Party of America, supported the dual strategy of using the labor movement strategically alongside the ballot to drive social and political change.

Syndicalists, or *industrial unionists*, were radical socialists who emphasized direct action through local unions rather than slow change through the political process. Both the United Mine Workers and the Industrial Workers of the World, among others, harbored syndicalist ideals. These "radicals" had a point; before 1920, a large fraction of American wage earners were legally disfranchised due to voting restrictions. The poorest workers, especially new European immigrants, African Americans, and Asian Americans, consistently occupied the worst-paying, least stable, and most dangerous jobs and had the hardest time forming unions. This changed only slightly after 1905, when the AFL adopted the principles of what it called "new unionism," an approach to organizing across industries.

As an organization, the AFL offered no statement on the morality, or immorality, of the capitalist system. It sponsored legislation, including demands for the eight-hour day, the rights to bargain collectively, protective legislation for women, equal pay for equal work, and a weekly day of rest. Not coincidentally, these were also the goals Pope Leo XIII marked as legitimate demands for labor action within his 1892 encyclical *Rerum Novarum*.[14] Executive leaders of the AFL claimed that, as a trade union federation, they never officially endorsed candidates or political parties; they simply made their members aware of how candidates stood on these issues and did their best to advocate for labor as such. In part to maintain the fidelity of Catholic workers (whose churches opposed socialism) and in part to dispel radical organizers and the changes they wanted to make to the organizational leadership of the labor movement, the executive leaders of AFL held that the organization was officially against socialism. From the perspective of radicals, many of whom were swelling the rank and file of the union, this cooperation with the status quo earned leadership the title of *trade union conservatives*, or the even more disparaging title of *trade union aristocrats*.

I use the terms "Christian Socialists" or "socialist Christians" to refer to those Christians who offered critiques of capitalism and the *Churchianity*, or worship of churches, that socialists claimed sustained the economic system. I follow the historian Jacob Dorn in defining Christian Socialists as those who believed socialism played a role in their Christian faith.[15] I define this movement through membership in organizations such as the CSF, attendance within Debs' evangelistic campaigns within churches, and in readership of books and periodicals. Christian Socialists celebrated the possibility of new Christian orthodoxies, centered in churches and Christian economic cooperatives, to transform the social and economic system in the United States. I use the term *socialist Christians* to describe those who saw themselves as both socialists and Christians, but who demanded neither that socialism should change the practice of Christianity in the United States nor that churches should take an important role in the construction of a social democratic republic. Because the American socialist movement represented a big tent of free thinkers, atheists, Jews, Catholics, Protestants, and others, the dividing line among socialist Christians, Christian Socialists and *socialist secularists* was always in flux.

Socialist secularists expected to see all religious authority, including most traditional worship practices, eventually replaced by the authority of science.[16] They may have underestimated the power of a state-funded religious establishment operating under the myth of disestablishment, or maybe they simply banked on modern people giving up on believing in miracles. They won most intra-party debates with Christian Socialists.

Finally, the book focuses on Protestants to highlight their outsized role in defining American Christianity for the twentieth century. In fact, the Social Gospel was an ecumenical movement of Catholic, Protestant, and Jewish clergy who participated in parallel and sometimes united movements for social reform in the name of natural law and human decency.[17] AFL president Samuel Gompers knew that building relationships with religious leaders would be key to the success of the labor movement, and he cultivated these allies carefully. To Gompers's credit, both the US Council of Catholic Bishops and the Central Conference of American Rabbis supported the rights of collective bargaining and the principles inscribed in the Federal Council's *Social Creed*.[18]

But, because of Protestants' long history in the halls of American power, neither Jewish rabbis nor Catholic priests, nor even Gompers himself, were recognizable to Wilson and the Democratic Party as national authorities on Christian social justice. Among clergy, Protestants were most responsible for defining the terms of Christian justice for the twentieth century. In fact, after the Great War, ministers of the Federal Council used their credibility as allies of Gompers to represent organized workers before the president of the United States. They used this special relationship to convince lawmakers to move away from their support for the AFL and instead endorse the principles of welfare capitalism. Because of their outsized power over public policy, this book focuses on those white American Protestant social reformers and their relationships with wage earners. My hope is that it forms a foundation for further research into unions' long and complicated efforts to build alliances with a full variety of religious leaders.

Chapter Organization

Nine chapters trace the tension between a network of working-class Christianities, thriving outside of the well-resourced denominations, and a set of well-trained Protestant ministers who united to oppose their challenge. They highlight a national conversation on the meaning of Christian nationhood, the steps it would take to get there, and the extent to which it is a worthy cause.

The first chapter introduces readers to the vacuum of religious authority in the Gilded Age. Neither Protestant nor Catholic institutions were able to keep up with population growth, and nominal Catholics outnumbered nominal Protestants almost two to one. It was largely the wealthy who attended church, and their theologies reflected the ideals of capitalism. This vacuum of denominational authority opened space for the growth of working-class communities of faith, including the Holiness-Pentecostal movement, freethinkers, and Christian Socialists. Yet the rapid growth of independent churches outside any denominational authority deeply worried missionaries like Josiah Strong. These independent churches also inspired Protestants and Catholics to unite in declaring a common enemy in "socialism."

Meanwhile, as I show in the second chapter, a groundswell of working-class Americans celebrated a different kind of Jesus who was not comfortable in churches of the wealthy. Within socialist print culture and labor churches, working-class Americans rebelled against what they called "Churchianity." They created joint-stock cooperatives and labor churches and suggested that these were a better expression of the Christian faith than any denominational church body. Socialists' unorthodox biblical exegesis on the purpose and scope of the Church, the possibility of overcoming selfishness, and the ideal role of the state constituted a significant challenge to the major Protestant denominations.

Chapter 3 argues that Socialist Party leaders used this working-class rebellion against "Churchianity" to form the foundation of the Socialist Party of America. Eugene Debs, the party's first president and presidential candidate for the next two decades, hired socialist ministers as party organizers and authorized a national crusade to recruit more socialist ministers to the party. While he was not himself religious, Debs encouraged Christians disaffected by churches' complicity with the corporate world, especially women and people of color, to adopt the Socialist Party as a Christian crusade. The possibility of establishing a "Kingdom of God" on earth formed the foundation of the first and most important social democratic movement of the twentieth century.

Chapter 4 argues that, in their efforts to build a diverse and inclusive alliance against anti-Semitism and Christian nationalism, the party also muzzled its most popular arguments in defense of a cooperative commonwealth. The Socialist Party drew a large number of supporters among middling-class Christians who believed in the party's principle of "municipal socialism," or cooperatively owned and managed utilities that could serve as public works projects. It also had a large following among legally disfranchised wage earners, including African Americans, Mexican Americans, women, and recent European immigrants. Perennial arguments broke out over the party's position on "social questions" including race, gender, sexuality, and the party's relationship to church leaders. A vocal minority of secularists wanted to define American socialism as pluralistic and "scientific," with no official response to the perennial claims that socialists attacked "the family and religion." After tough deliberations, the party decided to remain silent on the "religion question" and most other social questions. They embraced the modern promise of secularism and religious pluralism. Yet this silence opened even more space for Catholic and Protestant ministers to claim that socialism was anti-Christian.

Starting at the turn of the century, Protestant denominational leaders came together to design a federation that could imitate the size and organizational momentum of the Roman Catholic Church, while also borrowing the appeal of the early Debsian coalition. Chapter 5 argues that the Federal Council of Churches of Christ in America formed in 1908 for the purposes of "churching" the United States and making ministers into authorities on social and industrial justice. They issued a mission statement in the *Social Creed* and planned a number of successive evangelistic campaigns to win workers "back" to their orthodox religious institutions. Through their first major evangelistic campaign, the Men and Religion Forward movement, ministers sought to dispel socialist theologies, draw workers into Protestant churches, and defend capitalism as a legitimate economic practice. In the process, they sought to plant new churches and to connect wage earners to local congregations.

The next three chapters overlap a bit in chronology. They examine three sites of Federal Council efforts—national, local, and international—between 1908 and 1919. Within each of these spheres of influence, ministers worked to elevate the claims of ministers over those of the labor movement and wrest the meaning of Christian nationhood from the socialist movement. Chapter 6, which focuses on major national strikes, illustrates how wage earners made use of the Federal Council's 1908 manifesto, the *Social Creed of the Churches*, for their own ends. The statement called for modest reform in comparison to the demands of the radical labor movement, but it was sometimes useful to workers for garnering positive publicity. Ministers, meanwhile, used the document to show off their bona fides to public policymakers and AFL executives. The popularity of Arturo Giovannitti, Wobbly leader of the 1912 Lawrence strike, reveals that the ideas of Christian Socialism were still quite powerful in both working-class and middle-class communities. The ministers of the Federal Council spent the period between 1908 and 1912 chasing and attempting to limit the allure of Christian Socialism that the labor movement had built.

Chapter 7, which takes as its focus a single church led by Charles Stelzle, shows how these ministers continually sought to recenter their white Protestant religious authority in urban space. In New York City, wage earners made use of the Presbyterian "Labor Temple" as an indispensable community center for English-language instruction, history and philosophy courses, and union meetings. It even functioned as a strike center for the major textile strikes of 1913 and 1914. Yet, while ministers claimed that the building belonged to the people of New York, they also censored its activities and monitored how workers could use the space, especially during the Great War. After President Wilson signed the Sedition Act, New York Presbyterian, and the Federal Council more broadly, defended the rights of ministers, but not wage earners, to speak prophetically on Christian justice. In cooperating with the Red Scare and Protestant efforts to shut down taverns, ministers used the power of the state to make their churches the primary, and perhaps even the only, legal space for working-class community building.

Chapter 8, which focuses on the international sphere, shows that the Great War represented a victory for white Protestant clergy of the Federal Council of Churches and their quest to turn the federation into something akin to a national church. These officers aspired to a status in the federal government akin to the office of the Archbishop of Canterbury in England. Ministers of the Federal Council wanted to continually advise the branches of the federal government on domestic and international policy matters as representatives of all Christians. Not only did these ministers play a major role in pressuring Congress to enter the European war in 1917, but US churches also became a major conduit for distributing prowar propaganda, and their statements in support of the war and of white supremacy had international repercussions. The Federal Council reimagined the nation as a union of white Protestants committed to racial paternalism, big business, and the open shop. Enchanted with the authority invested in them by the president of the United States, these ministers moved away from the alliances they had built with the AFL and encouraged the Wilson administration to do the same.

The last chapter, which focuses on the postwar moment (1919–1920), explains how the Federal Council came to completely reject unions' rights to collective bargaining and become a cheerleader for welfare capitalism. In 1919, when 350,000 steelworkers went on strike across the nation, the Federal Council briefly came under the leadership of John D. Rockefeller Jr. He used the council's newest church-planting campaign, the Interchurch World Movement, to distract media attention and moral gravity from the strikers and celebrate the new virtues of "stewardship" and "spirituality." This evangelistic crusade, like the Men and Religion Forward movement of seven years earlier, reminded white parishioners that churches cared more than any other group for working "families." Yet Rockefeller was also against unionization. The Rockefeller-funded evangelical crusade sent the message that Protestant ministers, working closely with employers, could erect plans for "industrial democracy" that would address the needs of workers better than unions. They thus used the Federal Council's rhetoric of white patriarchy to break the labor movement and institutionalize welfare capitalism.

Protestant clergy hoped and claimed that their authority within social work and in industrial relations, born of the Great War, might bring about social and industrial justice in the next generation. However, their influence over public policy was short-lived. While some of these clergy members were called upon during the New Deal, most saw their moral and political influence within municipalities and industries eclipsed by both evangelical fundamentalism and industrial leaders themselves. Overwhelmingly, the poorest working-class Christians remained outside the mainline Protestant churches before, during, and after the Social Gospel movement.

The book shows how the Federal Council of Churches created a concept of American Christianity that was hermetically sealed from political and economic critique of the present order. Many Americans had sought to build a Christian commonwealth based in a welfare state, public utilities, collective bargaining, democratic electoral reforms, and a commitment to the freedoms of speech and religion. The Federal Council's project to relocate the work of building a Christian commonwealth to its own brick-and-mortar buildings was inseparable from its efforts to thwart trade unionism, the Roman Catholic Church, the Black Baptist Church, and the promise of racial social equality idealized by the radical labor movement. Protestant ministers hoarded the concept of Christian justice. Indeed, the Federal Council's theological "liberalism" was built in an effort to co-opt, redirect, and ultimately hobble the coalition that organized labor had built.

After all, by the 1920s, Bellamy's vision of a socialist republic without opulent, powerful churches proved nothing less than a fantasy. Churches bought up larger sections of urban space to build teeming private schools with gymnasia, auditoriums, gardens, and athletic fields. Groups like the Salvation Army and church-related missions sometimes built directly on the remains of "vice districts."[19] In many cities, church groups raised more funds than their cities to run orphanages and functioned as the city's primary dispensaries of education, medical care, and public charity.[20] Though socialists had dominated religious spaces just a decade earlier, the Red Scare drove socialists out of many churches and underground within the labor movement. With the loss of allies in the ministry and state or local government, trade unions often had no choice but to succumb to open-shop schemes based in the generosity of good employers to offer "profit sharing."

In a 1923 article for *Collier's*, the journalist Charles Wood observed this trend as the modernity nobody had quite predicted. "Church attendance may soon be compulsory in America," he wrote with an air of sarcasm.[21] Of course, the passage of prohibition laws, state-sponsored censorship of theater and films, and the revival of the Ku Klux Klan had not made Americans more pious. But in the absence of powerful unions or an expansive welfare state, churches once again became indispensable as community centers and suppliers of education, health, and social services. As another journalist joked, "religion" was becoming "cheaper than candy."[22] Why have American church leaders so long sought the responsibility of defining and managing social services on behalf of the republic? As it turns out, we cannot understand the rise or fall of socialism in the United States without grappling with the heroic narrative of Christian social reform.

1

Gilded Age Churches and the Vacuum of Denominational Authority

From the end of the Civil War until the early twentieth century, Anglo, immigrant, and African American settlers were moving north and west faster than ministers within the major denominations could follow them with churches. In 1890, Northern Methodists, the largest Protestant denomination, only claimed 3.5 percent of the American population. Roman Catholics claimed 9.9 percent, and African American Baptists, the largest Black denomination, claimed only 18 percent of the African American population. In total, under 30 percent of Americans went to church on a weekly basis. While African American churches served a relatively larger role within their communities, the major white denominations played a minor role in the lives of the working poor. Clergymen like Dwight Moody reflected, "The gulf between the churches and the masses is growing deeper, wider and darker every hour." Home missionaries like Josiah Strong warned, "Few appreciate how we have become a non-churchgoing-people."[1]

Strong was right. In large fractions of the country, especially mining and industrial centers in the West, a simple lack of church edifices and long-term ministers to fund-raise for them gave way to a vacuum of Protestant, denominational authority. In part, this disconnect between the number of churches and the size of the population was a result of culturally dislocated migrants. In 1890, more than nine million Americans were foreign born, and only a small fraction of those Americans had any familiarity with Anglo-Protestant traditions. They were joined by another one million African Americans migrants from the South to northern industrial centers.[2]

But this was only one of many reasons the poor did not go to church with the wealthy. While middle-class families paid lip service to the importance of building capacious churches, their own policies and practices reinforced the class system. As one minister reflected in 1887, "The working men are largely estranged from the Protestant religion. Old churches standing in the midst of crowded districts are continually abandoned because they do not reach

The Gospel of Church. Janine Giordano Drake, Oxford University Press. © Oxford University Press 2024.
DOI: 10.1093/oso/9780197614303.003.0002

the workingmen." Meanwhile, he continued, "Go into an ordinary church on Sunday morning and you see lawyers, physicians, merchants and business men with their families[—]you see teachers, salesmen, and clerks, and a certain proportion of educated mechanics, but the workingman and his household are not there."[3] As the working classes swelled with the expansion of American factories, ordained Protestant ministers served an ever-dwindling proportion of the country.

To the extent the working-class majority encountered Christianity in their daily lives, it was primarily through Catholic missions, diocesan schools and hospitals, occasional street preachers, summer encampments, and the Salvation Army. This sprawling variety of working-class Christianities, in combination with the rise of skeptics, deeply worried Protestant ministers. Despite the millions of dollars that middle-class Protestants donated to home missions boards, very few among the poor had much contact with an ordained member of the Protestant clergy. By and large, white Protestant churches were small social clubs that ministered primarily to the wealthy and aspirant classes.

Catholicism Dominant

In the Gilded Age, there were almost three times more Roman Catholics than there were members of any Protestant denomination. With the exception of Indian boarding schools, federal and state funding for public schools was scarce. One diocese and religious order at a time, Roman Catholic churches footed the bill for 3,024 grade schools across the nation and a similar number of hospitals.[4] While the working poor often demanded more public schools, neither state legislators nor county legislators wanted to raise taxes and invest in alternatives.[5] Lobbyists like the strangely named National Reform Association wanted the United States to defend its status as a "Christian nation" by continuing to partner with the Catholic church in providing social services for the poor.[6] Protestants, realizing they were outnumbered, had begun to imagine a broader category of "Christianity" that was in peril.[7]

In 1890, Congress appointed Henry Carroll, scholar of religion and secretary to the Methodist Episcopal Church (North), to collect and interpret the Census of Religious Bodies. The religion census was a regular occurrence about every ten years, but the results of a religion census were never before published for the general public. Carroll framed the project as a measurement of the "character and strength of religious forces in the United States" and planned from the start to analyze the data for the public, with missionaries and ministers in mind.[8] As Carroll understood it, his charge by Congress was to capture the exact size of each church's membership, its beliefs and behavior, and the number of filled and unfilled seats in every congregation in every county in the states and territories. Indeed, Carroll counted all the small traditions he could find, including Theosophists, Ethical Culturists, communists, Spiritualists, and Baha'i. He also counted communities without any permanent edifices, including revivals and buildings owned cooperatively among a number of congregations.[9] The report boldly concluded that because less than 2 percent of Americans adhered to traditions outside of Christianity, "Evangelical Christianity is the dominant religious force the United States."[10] He used his 477-plus-page report, *The Religious Forces of the United States*, to offer an explanation for why census numbers appeared so low (Table 1.1).[11]

As it turned out, Carroll would have to significantly distort his numbers to suggest that Methodism was on the rise. It was not just that Roman Catholics were by far the predominant religious group in the United States but that Catholics had a much larger number of missionaries and schools. Among Protestants, all the liturgical churches that required well-trained ministers to interpret Scripture, including Presbyterian, Episcopalians, and Congregationalists, struggled to keep up with population shifts. Meanwhile Baptists, those who hosted weekly Bible studies, summer revivals, adult and children's Sunday school within relative congregational independence, were growing quickly. Known to church historians as "low

Table 1.1 Reported Membership of Largest Denominations in 1890

Denomination	Reported Members, 1890
Roman Catholic Church	6,231,000
Methodist Episcopal (North)	2,240,000
Regular Baptists, Colored	1,349,000
Regular Baptists, South	1,280,000
Methodist Episcopal, South	1,210,000

church," their hierarchies offered the pulpit to any man, broke with the liturgical calendar and lectionary, and exercised wide latitude regarding individual Scriptural interpretation. These churches had been growing after the Second Great Awakening of the mid-nineteenth century and multiplied since Reconstruction.[12] It appeared that independent congregations were the future.

But Carroll used his expertise as a scholar of religion to claim that the raw numbers, collected directly from ministers, were unreliable (Table 1.2). Catholic priests, he said, "count as communicants all who have been confirmed and admitted to the communion, and these virtually constitute the Catholic population." Most Protestants, he said, exercise church discipline and expect new members to make their own decisions about entering their communities. In truth, most Protestants counted their baptized communicants as members, even if they failed to attend regular services.[13] Moreover, both Protestants and Catholics dismissed members who did not uphold their community covenants. Yet, once again putting on his ministerial hat, Carroll explained, "The Protestant basis of membership is belief and

Table 1.2 Church Membership as Fraction of the US Population

Denomination	Reported Members, 1890	Fraction of US Population in 1890
Roman Catholic Church	6,257,871	9.9%
Methodist Episcopal (North)	2,240,000	3.5%
Regular Baptists, Colored	1,349,000	2.1%
Regular Baptists, South	1,280,000	2.0%
Methodist Episcopal, South	1,210,000	1.9%
Presbyterian	788,224	1.25%
Protestant Episcopal	532,054	.84%
Small Protestant Denominations	522,851	.83%
Jews (Orthodox and Reformed)	130, 496	.26%
Latter Day Saints (Mormons)[a]	166,125	.21%
Carroll's Estimate of active atheists, skeptics, secularists, infidels	5,000,000	7.94%
Total registered church members (all denominations except Jews and secularists)	14,180,000	22.5%

[a] This is a composite of the two sects of LDS in 1890: The LDS and the Reorganized Church of the Latter Day Saints.

conduct; the Catholic, belief and obedience." Catholics, he implied, counted members among those who were not truly faithful, and that made the comparison inequivalent. Carroll thought that the best way to measure religious character was by the Methodist standard of righteous conduct.

Carroll argued that one must apply "multipliers" to create what he thought was a fairer comparison between Catholics and Protestants. Unsurprisingly, after applying the multipliers, it suddenly appeared that Methodists had a greater presence in the religious landscape than Catholics (Table 1.3). Carroll's logic rested on a distinction between "communicants," or people in the pews, and "adherents," people who lived their lives in accordance with the professed principles of their church. He argued that in Protestant churches, unlike in Catholic churches, the members were the "adherents." He explained: "In any given thousand of Catholic population there are 850 communicants and 150 adherents; while a thousand of Protestant population yields only about 300 communicants, the rest, 700, being adherents. Thus, while the 6,231,000 Catholic communicants represent a Catholic population of about 7,330,000, the 2,240,000 communicants of the Methodist Episcopal Church, alone, indicate a Methodist population of 7,840,000."[14] He used Canadian census data to propose that if you multiply any given religious congregation by his assigned multiplier, you would arrive at a figure representing the larger "religious population" that orbited that church.[15] In Canada, for every adherent (or church member), there were probably about 2.5 additional Methodists, 3.5 Presbyterian, 4.6 Episcopalians, and 2.9 additional Baptists within that church's orbit.[16] He offered no multiplier for Jews, Mormons, or others within small denominations. He simply claimed that through word of mouth and publishing, communicants were still only a "conservative estimate" of rural religiosity.[17]

This proposed distortion of numerical survey data is not very persuasive. First, the report used ministers' own data. If ministers failed to count as members those who effectively functioned as such, it tells us something about their unwillingness to relax their rules for formally accepting new members. Second, Carroll already counted the body of occasional communicants through other methods that were designed to capture irregular meetings outside of church edifices. He counted more than twenty-three thousand Christian groups who "own no edifices, but meet in halls, schoolhouses or private houses" as equivalent to churches. This figure allowed for double counting of those who attended both religious revivals and churches. And he counted as "churches" groups that only met for "bi-monthly or monthly

Table 1.3 US Denominations as Fraction of the US Population

	Reported Members, 1890	Fraction of US Population in 1890	Imagined Additional Communicants	Total Imagined Orbit of Religious Adherents	Imagined, Inflated, Body of Contacts, Relative to US Population
Roman Catholic Church	6,257,871	9.9%	1,104,129	7,362,000	11.6%
Methodist Episcopal (North)	2,240,000	3.5%	5,600,000	7,840,000	12.45%
Regular Baptists, Colored	1,349,000	2.1%	3,912,100	5,261,100	8.35%
Regular Baptists, South	1,280,000	2.0%	3,712,000	4,992,000	7.93%
Methodist Episcopal, South	1,210,000	1.9%	3,025,000	4,235,000	6.72%
Presbyterian	788,224	1.25%	2,758,784	3,547,008	5.63%
Protestant Episcopal	532,054	.84%	2,447,448	2,979,502	4.73%
Small Protestant Denominations	522,851	.83%		522,851	.83%
Jews (Orthodox and Reformed)	130,496			130,496	.21%
Latter Day Saints (Mormons)[b]	166,125			166,125	.26%
Carroll's Estimate of active atheists, skeptics, secularists, infidels	5,000,000			5,000,000	7.94%
Total registered church members (all denominations)	14,180,000	22.5%		49,630,000	46.79%

[b]This is a composite of the two sects of LDS in 1890: The LDS and the Reorganized Church of the Latter Day Saints.

services," a figure that allowed triple counting of those who went to church, Bible study, and summer revival. In Carroll's report, even these inflated numbers, if Methodists or Baptists, ought to be multiplied.

Carroll's multipliers also rest on the assumption that most churches actively welcomed newcomers. Yet church records tell a different story. In 1880, unless one came with a letter from another "orthodox" church, an interested Methodist could become a church member only after standing six months "on trial," and either taking a series of classes or garnering the sponsorship of a parishioner.[18] Those seeking membership in a Congregational church needed a letter from their previous church to accompany their written application, and then an interview with the "Prudential Committee" comprising the pastor and deacons. To become a Presbyterian, one had to make a public profession of faith, followed by baptism. Baptists, which often catered to the lowest social station among the major Protestant denominations, required a public profession of faith and immersion baptism. Only those baptized by immersion were allowed to partake of communion.[19] If one could garner sponsors, it was not difficult to switch among denominations; this happened frequently. But for all churchgoers, membership indicated acceptance into an intentionally limited community of people.[20] Nevertheless, Carroll's inflated statistics would become the foundation of church statistics, used by historians and sociologists for decades to come.[21] Americans like to imagine Gilded Age religious leaders like Josiah Strong as agents of a powerful religious establishment. After all, their cathedrals reached the sky, and their books appeared strikingly popular. But nineteenth-century Protestant ministers had an incredibly narrow band of influence, especially outside the South.[22]

Classed Religion

By and large, Gilded Age Americans took the classed and raced segmentation of religious experiences as standard across the world.[23] Throughout Europe and its colonies, churches and the schools and hospitals they controlled functioned as mechanisms to cultivate a loyal elite.[24] Europeans and colonial elites together benefited from cheap, imported, finished goods, while they jointly exploited the labor of Black, immigrant, and Indigenous peoples.[25] American ministers similarly cultivated a small class of aspirants who saw themselves as different from the larger body of American workers and convinced themselves that they catered to a cross section of the nation. The few Gilded Age churches that marked their presence in city squares and near rural county seats largely functioned as social clubs, run by the church elder boards who fund-raised ministers' salaries. Ministers had little choice but to confirm the presumptions of the wealthy.

Even though each church was part of a larger denomination with its own history and theological convictions, most denominations had become what one scholar called "classificatory devices and symbolic markers of class status." In his *Church and Estate*, Rzeznik found that churches served as Gilded Age tools for both social mobility and preservation of social status. As families advanced in wealth, they often switched into more elite denominations.[26] The historian George Marsden illustrated this pattern with the southern maxim, "A Methodist is a Baptist who wears shoes; a Presbyterian is a Methodist who has gone to college; an Episcopalian is a Presbyterian who lives off his investments."[27] The majority of people who held membership in Protestant churches were the "professional" and middling classes. Despite their commanding size and highly visible preachers, Protestant churches commanded cultural authority over only a small fraction of the population.

The theologian Richard Niebuhr, drawing heavily from the German theorist Max Weber, observed that wealthy and poor Christians practiced recognizably different versions of Christianity. The wealthiest members of society were usually conditioned to think "in terms of personal merit and demerit more than fortune and fate." They understood their blessings as their achievements. They conceived of God as a taskmaster and of their "faith [as] a task rather than a promise." Their religion emphasized "the problem of personal salvation" over and against any concern for social or structural redemption.[28] Indeed, the wealthy saw wealth as blessings earned for making prudent, godly decisions.[29] Niebuhr could have mentioned the popularity of British economist David Ricardo's "iron law of wages" among Gilded Age American businessmen. As the thinking went, wages were naturally regulated by market conditions. If anyone was willing to take a job at a given price point, that price was inherently just.[30] Many such Americans understood their accumulated wealth not as the product of exploitation but as the product of shrewd and prudent financial decisions.

This set of economic and spiritual ideals often combined with the doctrine of Social Darwinism to construct the belief that the "invisible hand" of the free market had divine sanction and would bless businesses with the right kind of capital accumulation to further civilization's progress.[31] Indeed, Andrew Carnegie, the magnate who ruthlessly undersold his competitors until they failed, argued that the "law of competition" was hastening the progress of civilization. In his popular 1889 essay, "The Gospel of Wealth," Carnegie convinced the upper classes that their wealth, and their rights to that wealth without taxation or other meddling by government, was the life-giving foundation of civil society. He quoted Micah 4:4, an Old Testament passage about justice, to argue that civilization depends "upon the sacred-ness of property" and upon the government's nonintervention in the process of wealth making.[32] Carnegie suggested that it was foundational to the Christian nation to resist any efforts to restrain private enterprise.

Carnegie popularized these ideas among a new class of ministers who depended on the patronage of the wealthy for the existence of their churches and missionary organizations. When Russell Conwell, pastor of Philadelphia's wealthiest Baptist congregation, famously stated, "Money printed your Bible, money builds your churches, money sends your missionaries, and money pays your preachers, and you would not have many of them, either, if you did not pay them," he was trying to underline Carnegie's argument that accumulated wealth, despite socialists' protestations, was not inherently im-moral but the very engine of the missionary enterprise.[33] Yet this statement also reveals the dependence of white church leaders upon the patronage of the wealthy. Conwell spent his career allaying the consciences of the minority of white Protestants who could acquire large estates in the suburbs, cultivate ornamental gardens on grand estates, and then commute to the city for work. He even claimed that wealth made people into better Christians. As he put it, homeowners "are made more honorable and honest and pure, true and eco-nomical and careful, by owning the home."[34]

This prosperity gospel traveled through both sermons and dime novels which seemed to always prove that God's blessings flow to the faithful. Dwight Moody and John Wanamaker each told stories about their lives to suggest that it was their Christian faith and industriousness rather than their capital accumulation that was at the foundation of their worldly suc-cess.[35] They invited the rising class of foremen and clerks to understand their advancing position on the shop floor as an outgrowth of their Christian faith, not their white Protestant privilege or the fact that scientific managers created positions just for them. In Conwell's Philadelphia, Wanamaker sold presized clothing that resembled tailor-made clothing. He catered to the swelling ranks of middling-class whites who strove for the respectability that

could land them jobs as clerks, foremen, and managers, distinguishing themselves from the masses of workers whose skills were quickly losing their value
to the advent of machines. Similarly, Moody sold shoes as he cultivated patrons among Chicago businessmen.

Wanamaker was a shrewd businessman who used his ministry investments
strategically, but he preferred to be known for his public service, philanthropy, and piety. Ten years into his first department store's success and while
still holding office as US postmaster, Wanamaker began investing in the
Philadelphia YMCA and the American Sunday School Union.[36] When John's
son Thomas purchased the Philadelphia newspaper the *North American*, the
family effectively captured a major portion of the retail, advertising, and religious markets in Russell Conwell's Philadelphia, but this was not the story he
told about himself. He had his stores decorated to the hilt for Christmas and
Easter and installed stained glass images of angels to make the store resemble
a house of worship. Wanamaker wanted to be known as a man of God.[37]

Moody, meanwhile, built his ministry in the 1870s by purchasing secondary schools in the Chicago area, pastoring the nondenominational
Illinois Street Church in Chicago, and cultivating investments from the business class to create his Moody Bible Institute in 1889. As Moody's biographer
explained, "Both the British and American press regularly depicted Moody
as having the special capacity to reach the working classes," but the minister
spent most of his time socializing with elite businessmen—the Dodges, the
Goulds, and the Rockefellers—and gaining their support for his evangelistic
missions. Both Moody and Wanamaker capitalized on the trend to use advertising and direct mail to communicate with their consumers and patrons.[38]
Both used their missions to the poor as window dressing for their brand.

This sanctified class system even operated within African American
and immigrant enclaves. African American Baptists cultivated an educated class of Black men to attend universities and nourish the doctors and
lawyers for the Black community. Respectively, the National Association of
Colored Women cultivated a female "talented tenth," guided by the motto
"Lifting as we climb." The Black Baptist Church commanded membership
over 18 percent of African Americans; the denomination was nearly six
times more popular among blacks than the Northern Methodist church was
among whites.[39] As one scholar explained the African American Baptist
tradition, "The educated elite increasingly perceived the church as a public
realm through which blacks as a people would counter social and political
forces arrayed against them."[40] Ministers and elders enforced the "politics of

respectability" among members, expecting anyone in good standing with the church to live a life of temperance and thrift.[41] Not only were church membership rates lower among the poor, but many among the poor found themselves socially shunned by community leaders.[42] Black Methodists, a group that included both the African Methodist Episcopal (AME) and the AME-Zion denominations, were heavily concentrated in urban centers (Figures 1.1 and 1.2).

Even though the Catholic church was still a church of immigrants, Catholic elites behaved like their white and Protestant counterparts.[43] Their cathedrals served as monuments to Catholic respectability and often outdid their Protestant counterparts in size, detail, marble, and gold.[44] Elites invested in universities like Georgetown University and the University of Notre Dame to provide their children initiation into the positions of power that Ivy League universities offered Protestants. While many Catholic churches were planted by European missionaries and answered only to those European national Catholic churches, Gilded Age Irish Americans begged for the pope to consolidate and authorize their church as the official American Catholic church.

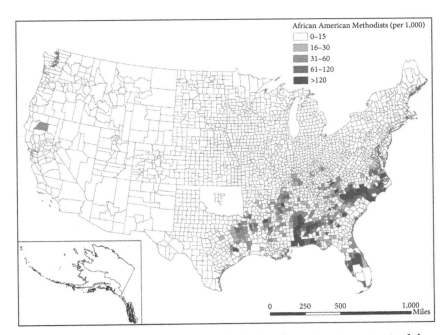

Figure 1.1 In 1890, African American Methodist denominations exercised the majority of their influence in particular pockets of the South.

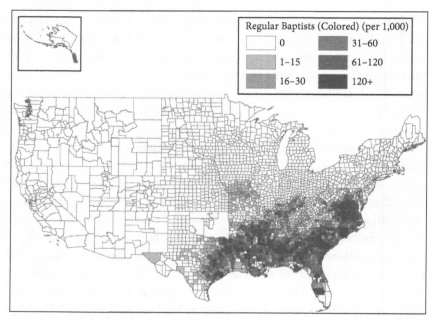

Figure 1.2 In 1890, African American Baptists counted members among more than 10 percent of their counties in many states across the South.

As Pope Leo XIII agreed to this transition over the next decade, Southern and Eastern European immigrants found themselves under the spiritual authority of the Irish, who already led their cities' unions and police forces.[45] Without further thought, "foreign language" masses were often confined to the "lower church," or the church basement, in the congregations which Irish Americans ran.[46] Many Southern and Eastern European Catholics stopped attending church altogether.

In communities where wealthy Catholic benefactors could not be found, it was not unusual for priests to expect payment from parishioners for the sacraments, even the sacrament of the weekly Eucharist. As one Italian worker testified before a special congressional commission in 1888, "I have tried to go to church here, but they want pay before I go in, so I don't go in."[47] Very often, especially after babies were baptized and officially counted as members, immigrants simply stopped going to church. Protestants did not usually command payment for the sacraments because they observed fewer of them, but many traditions charged for a seat in the pews. Pew rentals, common within a wide range of Protestant churches in the Gilded Age, had long functioned to invest the wealthy with the burden of building and maintaining churches. Seats were sold similarly to the way seats were sold in large theaters, with the most expensive in the front and the least expensive on the sides and in the back. This pattern functioned to put a church's wealthiest men on display front and center as emblems of Christian values, and literally sidelined the poor. Those who could not afford a pew were either discouraged from entering or ushered to the back or to the balcony.[48] Women too, especially if they were mothers to small children, were discouraged from seating themselves on Sunday morning. By design, most preachers directly faced the congregation's wealthiest men, a position that made it extremely difficult for a Gilded Age minister, who also depended on donations for his salary, to challenge the gospels of prosperity.[49]

Vacuum of Protestant Authority in Cities

Ultimately, while white Protestant, Black Protestant, and Roman Catholic church leaders exerted some influence over the aspiring middle classes within their orbit, the majority of Americans had little contact with well-resourced white Protestant denominations. It is worth returning to Carroll's statistic that the largest Protestant denomination, Northern Methodists, counted only 3.5 percent of the population as members (Figure 1.3). One might guess that this figure accounts for the average between a heavily churched urban population and a less churched rural population, but county-level data illustrates that Methodists had a presence in 79 percent of American counties. Nevertheless, there were only between thirty-one and sixty Methodists per one thousand Americans in any given county (Table 1.4). Methodist church growth seemed to directly track with wealth; these churches served the middle class and aspiring middle class (petit bourgeois) wherever they existed. Most Methodists lived in the major population centers and the revival-heavy regions of upstate New York, Ohio, Pennsylvania, and Indiana.

No wonder Charles Sheldon's *In His Steps: What Would Jesus Do* (1896), a story of a ragged Jesus finding himself rejected by church members for his look of impropriety, skyrocketed to popularity. The book suggested that most churchgoers were middling-class folks seeking respectability. "Real" Christians supported raising taxes to support public infrastructure for the poor. While churches "send money and missionaries to the foreign heathen," Sheldon wrote, "the fashionable, dissipated young men around town, the

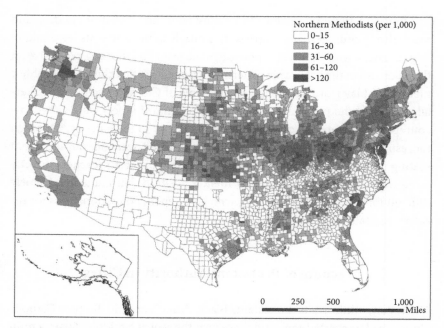

Figure 1.3 Northern Methodists were scattered across the northern part of the United States and even parts of the South, but only in a few counties did they approach 10 percent of the population.

club men," the working classes, "are left out of all plans for reaching and Christianizing."[50] No wonder the best-selling author Edward Bellamy forecast a future wherein Christianity would inspire a robust welfare state and celebrity preachers would lose their captive audience among lawmakers. As Bellamy's Dr. Leete explained the Gilded Age, "Religion, in a word, like industry and politics, was capitalized by greater or smaller corporations which exclusively controlled the plant and machinery, and conducted it for the prestige and power of the firms." Anyone who wanted to become a minister had to agree to the "conditions" set by the "great ecclesiastical corporations," which made it nearly impossible to preach the real principles of Christian love.[51]

Most church leaders, both Catholic and Protestant, were aware that their ministries were bankrolled, and hamstrung, by the wealthy. In fact, many expressed great frustration by this pattern and publicly recognized that their future depended on this pattern changing.[52] In his 1891 encyclical *Rerum Novarum* (1891), Pope Leo XIII shook the Christian world by encouraging

Table 1.4 Northern Methodist Church Membership by State

State	White, Non-Indian Population in 1890	Northern Methodist Church Membership, 1890	Percentage of Northern Methodists per Population	Imagined, Inflated, Body of Contacts, Percentage of US Population
New York	6,003,174	242,492	4.0	10%
Illinois	3,826,352	165,191	4.3	11%
Pennsylvania	5,258,113	222,886	4.3	11%
Kansas	1,428,108	83,288	5.8	15%
Ohio	3,672,329	240,540	6.5	16%
Indiana	2,192,404	162,989	7.4	19%
Maryland	1,042,390	82,069	7.9	20%
Kentucky	1,858,635	29,172	1.5	4%
Missouri	2,679,185	58,285	2.1	5%
North Carolina	1,617,949	16,433	1.0	3%
Oklahoma	258,657	1,224	.04	1%
South Carolina	1,151,149	43,200	3.8	9%
Tennessee	1,767,518	42,873	2.4	6%
Texas	2,235,527	27,453	1.2	3%

religious leaders to reach out to the poor and support organized workers in their demands for a living wage. Both Protestant and Catholic leaders built ministries designed to recruit the poor through urban missions (effectively homeless shelters), schools, hospitals, Sunday evening services, and programs for children. But, like the hypocrites of Sheldon's and Bellamy's novels, both Catholic and Protestant clerics rejected socialism as an assault on the true purposes of the church in America. Bishop James Quigley of Buffalo wrote that socialism denies the "independence of the Church as a society complete in itself and founded by God."[53] Another priest warned, "Socialism . . . is not a mere theory regarding the economic organization of society, but it is a theory regarding the nature of society and the end of man."[54] Catholic priests, like their Protestant brethren, worried that socialists wanted to build a world without the need for church.

A thin slice of the American wage-earning class did attend church, but this exception proves the rule. Aspirant-class clerks and foremen, members of the new white-collar middling classes, as well as some highly skilled artisans, did attend church with the wealthy.[55] Through their church membership, they extracted value from their racial privilege, what some have called their "whiteness," and distanced themselves from the largely unskilled and deskilled laborers who composed the majority of industrial working classes.[56] Dwight Moody, for example, claimed that his church included many among "the poor." But a historian who studied his Chicago Avenue Church in 1897 found his understanding of "the poor" were the "office clerks, employees of small businesses, day laborers and delivery boys who filled the down-town commercial district each day." These were not the racially "in between" Poles, Italians, Slavs, and African Americans who took the most dangerous and poorly paid jobs. Many of the nearly twelve hundred members of his congregation had German, Swedish, and Irish names.[57] His congregation admitted only two African Americans, both women, in 1896 and 1897. Within a few years, he segregated his worship services and evangelistic crusades and dialed back on most efforts to connect with the poor.[58]

Rev. Washington Gladden, a Congregational minister, also claimed that class was nearly absent in his Berkshire town of North Adams, Massachusetts. After all, he once attended a party that included "not only capitalists and merchants and professional people, but working mechanics and clerks and operatives of the mill of which the host was the owner."[59] Again, working mechanics were among the highest-paid trade unionists, and clerks were part of the emerging new management class.[60] The unskilled working classes, who worked for less than subsistence wages in most dangerous jobs within mines and factories, if not as domestics in private homes, were invisible to Gladden. Even after he moved to the industrial city of Columbus, he still made no real effort to welcome these poor within his congregations. As his biographer explained, "In the spirit of noblesse oblige, [Gladden] appealed to the native middle class to assimilate the immigrants to the American democratic tradition of thrift, industry and cleanliness—in short, to Christianize them." Gladden, known for his sympathy with the laboring classes, supported immigration restrictions to limit "paupers and criminals."[61] He opposed lynching but he maintained the color line and would go on to defend the doctrines of "separate but equal."[62] Immigrant women often found themselves invited to Bible studies and English classes sponsored through YMCAs and church missions in most major cities, but rarely did they have opportunities to become members of the churches from which these urban missionaries were sent.[63]

Chicago's Ada Street Methodist Church in Chicago was similar. As the historian Heath Carter observed, its composition indicated the fact that church leaders coveted the attention of "respectable working people."[64] Membership included a cross section of Chicago's Anglo-Protestants, but not a cross section of Chicago. George Drinkwater, a charter member of the Chicago Board of Trade, joined English-speaking immigrants from England, Canada, Scotland, and the Isle of Man, many of whom worked as clerks, bookkeepers, and foremen. About "half worked with their hands." Yet most of these members were skilled artisans and machinists, men who defined themselves in opposition to the "unskilled" refugees of Europe who poured into Chicago from Germany, Poland, Italy, Scandinavia, and the Balkans, to say nothing of African American migrants beginning to make their way from the South.

While church leaders reached out to ranking white trade union leaders in the 1870s, treating them as the professionals they claimed to be, they also reinforced a growing divide between white, skilled trade unionists and the growing masses of deskilled and low-skilled workers. For example, in 1877, Reverend McChesney of Chicago's Park Avenue Methodist church proclaimed, "The bible, as I read it, is the friend of the workingman. . . . This country cannot afford to fall out with its workingmen," and declared his support for both unionists and the work actions they took to secure working-class justice in Chicago. Yet the statement also revealed the fact that this outreach was necessary for the very sustenance of Chicago's Anglo-Protestant establishment. The union members who joined him were those who distanced themselves from those who truly struggled financially.[65]

Indeed, none of these ministers who claimed to minister to a "cross section" of their cities expected the Southern and Eastern European immigrants, Asian immigrants, and African Americans who occupied the lowest economic tiers and performed the most dangerous and deskilled jobs, to attend Sunday morning worship services with them.[66] By the turn of the century, many ministers began collecting demographic data on their churches and the districts within which they served. In 1904, the Methodist minister Worth Tippy, who studied the class and racial demographics of attendance at his church in Indianapolis, found that of the twenty-three churches in that city, members of labor unions were only 256 out of 7,725 people, or only about 3.3 percent of all members. Another 1.7 percent he counted were nonunion wage earners, and another 3.36 percent were families of wage earners. In total, that meant that only about 7–8 percent of Methodist parishioners stood among the "working class" ranks of union labor. According to Tippy, the other 93 percent of Methodists were not wealthy. But, 60–75 percent listed their occupations as "skilled" and earned wages in the white-collar sector as clerks, stenographers, and foremen. Many Protestants' perception of "working class" made little room for the very poor.[67]

Rather, when Gilded Age ministers spoke about their wide diversity of membership, they were often only celebrating their growing solidarity with aspirant-class white trades unionists and their families. In 1890, the four cities of New York, Chicago, Philadelphia, and Boston counted 1,589,898 total members within all religious communities, including those without buildings. That meant that even in cities with abundant opportunities for regular religious participation, 64.5 percent, a considerable majority of Americans, had no religious affiliation.[68]

Vacuum of Protestant Authority on the Frontier

This absence of the poor from most American churches was even more pronounced in rural areas. After pastoring a small church in Cheyenne, Wyoming, Josiah Strong grew anxious that Catholics had disproportionate cultural control over the new territories and states. He wrote about this in his 1885 *Our Country: Its Possible Future and Its Present Crisis*, a book meant to rally white Protestants behind efforts to build Protestant, "democratic" institutions to safeguard the future of the "Anglo Saxon race."[69] Less than a decade later, in his *New Era, or, The Coming Kingdom* (1893), Strong reiterated his previous concerns that there were not enough Protestant churches in the West to evangelize the nation. Yet he was now less upset about Catholicism and more concerned that the poor had so little connection to church. He celebrated the work of the Catholic Archbishop Ireland of St. Paul, Minnesota, and saw him as a partner in ministry to the 66 percent of the population did not attend any church on a regular basis. In Vermont, New York, and Maine, Strong reported, church attenders were no more than 25 percent of the population. Yet even in urban Ohio, which, he said, "has church accommodations for about one half of its inhabitants," less than one-fifth of the population attended church. While there were exceptions to the rule, he summarized, "It is the well-to-do classes which constitute the churchgoers and the poorer classes, the 'masses,' which constitute the nonchurchgoers."[70]

Strong observed that Catholic missionaries had a tremendous head start on evangelizing the poor. Long before the Civil War, French and Spanish Roman

Catholics had built missions to Native Americans along the Mississippi and Missouri Rivers and laid the groundwork of schools and hospitals that the federal government came to fund and endorse. Between 1860 and 1880, the US government signed more than 250 treaties with Indigenous nations, granting federal authorities millions of acres of land which they opened to white settlement. The Homestead Act, passed during the Civil War, granted about 160 acres to any American willing to live on and "improve" their homestead for at least five years.

Many first-generation homesteading families found themselves entering a world where the only "public" social services they could find, including schools and hospitals, were run by Catholics or, to a lesser extent, Mormons. Starting in 1875, Mormons had built thirty-four secondary school academies in North America, centering around the Salt Lake Basin in Utah but also including settlements in Idaho, Arizona, and Wyoming. In 1892, they established Latter-Day Saints University in Salt Lake City, the crown jewel of an educational system that enrolled around forty-eight hundred students eight years later.[71] Their well-developed, centralized Sunday School system and organized systems of wards provided the infrastructure to expand their kingdom well beyond Utah.

Meanwhile, the Catholic orders of Jesuits, Sisters of Charity, Sisters of Providence, Ursulines, and many others built missions, schools, and hospitals that both Catholics and non-Catholics depended upon throughout the West. For example, the French-speaking Sisters of Providence began establishing ministries to serve the poor and sick in the Pacific Northwest in 1856. By 1877, they had fifty-three sisters working in Washington State. The sisters built Spokane's first hospital, Sacred Heart, in 1886, a charitable effort but one that made the city dependent on their continued service. By 1902, the Sisters of Providence were running seventeen hospitals and eight schools in Washington, Oregon, Montana, Idaho, California, and Alaska, many of which operated near mines and missions to Native Americans.[72] The Ursulines, with a convent in Miles City, Montana, operated another dozen boarding schools for both children of whites and Native Americans throughout Montana, Wyoming, and Idaho.[73] In 1889, the year Montana became a state, Catholic orders were already serving more than one thousand students in twelve day schools and boarding schools, including four Indian boarding schools and five hospitals. Sisters were also the primary providers for medical care for the poor throughout the state. Catholics had the infrastructure in the West to serve well beyond the Catholic population.[74]

In emerging western and midwestern cities too, Catholic orders built the hospitals, schools, orphanages, and other social services that provided the essential infrastructure for the poor. Nuns, especially the Sisters of Charity, built New York City's first foster care system. Catholic bishops agreed in 1884 that their parochial schools were central to the faith and required all Catholic parents to do their best to send their children to Catholic school. The bishops similarly directed every American diocese in the United States to do its best to sponsor-build their own parochial schools.[75] Long before there were public grade schools within unincorporated regions of the territories and the new states, Catholic parishes were building the nation's foundational infrastructure.

In part because of this extraordinary Catholic presence in the West, white Protestants of every denomination donated money to grow denominational colleges in the Midwest to serve as training grounds for ministers in more rural and remote places. Congregationalists established Doane College (Crete, Nebraska, est. 1872), Washburn College (Topeka, est. 1865), Colorado College (Colorado Springs, est. 1874), Yankton College (South Dakota, est. 1881), and Whitman College (Walla Walla, Washington, est. 1859). Presbyterian founded Hastings College (Nebraska, est. 1882), Huron College (South Dakota, est. 1883), the College of Idaho (Caldwell, est. 1891), the College of Emporia (Kansas, est. 1882), and Westminster College (Salt Lake City, est. 1875). Methodists founded Nebraska-Wesleyan (Lincoln, est. 1887), Baker University (Baldwin, Kansas, est. 1858), and Rocky Mountain College (Billings, Montana, est. 1878). The composite Colorado Seminary, established in 1864, built an ecumenical school of theology to train ministers in 1889.[76] Religious schools offered training in denominational heritage and culture that land-grant universities could not usually provide. Yet, because of the cultural opportunities available at religious colleges, most mainline clergy stationed permanently in the West were involved in the administration of these religious colleges or preparatory schools and did not interact with laity within a parish setting.

Yet even among nominal Catholics, few among the poor had the opportunity to develop personal relationships with the priests who administered their sacraments.[77] In the 1880s, the Roman Catholic church hierarchy considered the entire region encompassing Oregon, Washington, Idaho, Montana, parts of Canada, and Alaska as the "Province of Oregon," overseen by the single bishop of Vancouver, Alexander Christie. By 1909, still only five dioceses operated in this entire region.[78] Diocesan priests drove wagons to visit parishes on a rotating basis of once or twice a month. Occasionally, missionaries like the Jesuits invited homesteaders into their chapels.[79] But the handful of brick-and-mortar churches that existed in emerging cities largely catered to those in managerial positions, often Irish and French Canadian, within the emerging railroad, mining, and ranching industries.

The primary contact most Anglo settlers had with major Protestant denominations was through itinerant preachers. These men, assigned to a large geographic area by a denomination, spent most of their time on the road. William Wesley Van Orsdel, for example, worked from 1872 until his death planting and overseeing churches in every city in Montana and many small towns in between. He built relationships with city officials and prominent community members everywhere and supervised the construction of churches, schools, and hospitals.[80] Daniel Tuttle had a similar responsibility to the Episcopalian Church, but he had to oversee all of Montana, Utah, and Idaho. Thomas Haskins, who worked under him, established the first non-Mormon schools in the state of Utah and the only schools in the state until public schools emerged around 1890. By the time Tuttle left the territories to become bishop of Missouri in 1886, he had overseen over three thousand baptisms, one thousand confirmations, 146 marriages, and 117 burials.[81] It was a rare privilege for white settlers to hear an ordained minister preach on Sunday.

To successfully lobby politicians and philanthropists for the funds to erect churches and public utilities, most of these ministers spent their time cultivating patrons among the wealthy and aspirant classes. Tenant farmers and migratory miners, ranch hands, farmhands, cowboys, and domestics, the majority of nonnatives in the West, were not welcomed into the churches of their managers. Church membership overall hovered around 5 percent to 15 percent of the population, a number that mirrored the numbers of aspirant-class members who could afford pew rent.[82] During the recession of 1893, unemployed rural men rode the railroads like "birds of passage" in search of low-wage jobs.[83] Few churches existed to serve the migratory population.

Wayland Hoyt, pastor of the First Baptist Church in Minneapolis, tried to remedy this problem by enlisting his brother, a railroad financier, to raise funds for railroads cars that could serve as mobile Baptist churches. There were already a few Episcopal chapel cars, but they seemed to reach only Episcopalians. Colgate Hoyt invited other Baptist businessmen, including John D. Rockefeller, Eugene Barney, Charles Colby, James Colby, and John Trevor, to finance the construction of Evangel, the first Baptist Pullman car, which they ceremoniously donated to the American Baptist Publication Society. Sixty feet long and ten feet wide, the Evangel had an organ, a brass lectern, and seats for one hundred worshipers. By 1900, the Baptists had commissioned five more mobile churches for the railroad, in addition to eleven chapel wagons.[84] The railroads allowed them to ride the rails for free, and Hoyt rejoiced that "as the Roman roads were pathways for the feet of the apostles, so the railroads have made themselves free avenues for the swift goings of the chapel cars."[85] Baptists boasted in 1894 that their cars had traveled 17,834 miles, distributing 681 Bibles and 74,945 pages of tracts. Stopping in each railroad town for two or three days, "Missionaries delivered 1313 sermons, held 207 prayer meetings, visited 589 families, celebrated 18 baptisms, constituted seven churches, and organized eleven Sunday Schools."[86]

These numbers illustrated the kind of "impact" that wealthy philanthropists wanted to hear, but they suggest that most of those who attended prayer meetings did not get baptized, and most railroad towns did not have their own Baptist minister to establish their own church. One historian has suggested that, considering the fact that the cars' popularity declined after they were regulated and charged in 1915, they may have existed largely as a public relations stunt for railroad financiers. After all, Charles Rust explained the chapel cars in 1905 as a way to meet the "demand and need for moral character among their employees."[87]

In 1890, the total fraction of Southern Methodists and Southern Baptists, denominations founded in defense of slavery, was higher than the total of churchgoers who memorialized the Union victory (Table 1.5). Southern churches preserved and transported theologies of racial paternalism by sponsoring circuit riders and church plants throughout the newly acquired territory. There were "Southern" denominations throughout the distant territories of California, Washington, Oregon, and Colorado. But only a small number of counties had more than 120 Southern Methodists per 1,000 residents (Figure 1.4). When we consider that both Methodists and Baptist ministers answered primarily to their congregation's elder board, not their denominational leadership, we again confront the reality that most of these congregations had little choice but to uphold the class system. Even after applying Carroll's multipliers, they reached only a small fraction of the South.

Table 1.5 Southern Methodist Church Membership by State

State	White, Non-Indian Population in 1890	Southern Methodist Church Membership, 1890	Percentage of Southern Methodists per Population	Imagined, Inflated, Body of Contacts, Percentage of US Population
Illinois	3,826,352	7,109	0.19	.46%
Kansas	1,428,108	3,346	0.23	.59%
Maryland	1,042,390	10,604	1.00	2.54%
Kentucky	1,858,635	82,430	4.43	11.09%
Missouri	2,679,185	86,466	3.23	8.07%
North Carolina	1,617,949	114,385	7.07	17.67%
Oklahoma	258,657	805	0.31	.78%
South Carolina	1,151,149	68,092	5.92	14.79%
Tennessee	1,767,518	121,398	6.87	17.17%
Texas	2,235,527	139,347	6.23	15.58%

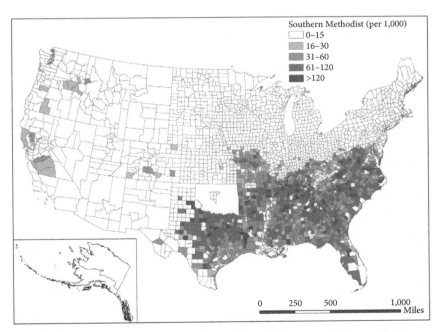

Figure 1.4 Southern Methodists had significant influence within population centers of the Southeast, but at their strongest they approached 10 percent of the population.

Whither Working-Class Christianity?

To a certain extent, historians have long known that working-class Christians of the Gilded Age were absent from most churches.[88] The poor were more likely to congregate in outdoor revivals, often consisting of either of an outdoor event celebrating a traveling evangelist or a festival held in a large field for a week in the summer, where evangelists, musicians, politicians, and artists would unite for worship, fellowship, and entertainment.[89] However, both Henry Carroll's painstaking census data and private church records confirm that attendance at these episodic events was relatively small before 1900. In 1887, the National Camp Meeting Association for the Promotion of Holiness, an offshoot of the Methodist church, reported organizing sixty-seven camp meetings nationally. By 1892, it maintained a speakers' list of 304 preachers and a network of publications.[90] The rise of Holiness-Pentecostalism ushered in a distinctly new set of theologies of sanctification. Pentecostals believed that baptism in the Holy Spirit saved them "from all unholy tempers" and "moral defilement."[91] They also elevated a set of spiritual gifts, including healing, prophecy, and speaking in tongues, that empowered believers to speak prophecy and heal others as agents of God.[92]

By 1906, such revivals had birthed an assortment of new Holiness denominations, including the Disciples of Christ, the Church of the Nazarene, the Salvation Army, the Christian and Missionary Alliance, the Free Methodist Church, and several Pentecostal denominations, including the Apostolic Faith Mission and the Church of the Living God. Historians estimate that between 1880 and 1905, a total of one hundred thousand Americans joined these new charismatic denominations. Meanwhile Baptists, essentially independent evangelical churches built in "common sense" personal Bible interpretation, were on their way to becoming the largest category of Protestants by 1906. Yet in the Gilded Age, these churches were slow to incorporate, quick to dissemble, and decentralized. Most held unorthodox interpretations of the doctrines of sanctification, elevated women to equality with men, and were beginning to form their own schools for training ministers.[93] Commentators were right to worry that over the next generation, they could pose a threat to the future of well-resourced, denominational churches, but in 1890 this eventuality was far from definite.

In the end, Josiah Strong's observation that working people had only thin affiliations with churches and were always on the verge of "leave[ing] the church and with it all faith in religion of any sort," pointed to something very real. Strong was not exaggerating when he continued, "Skeptical, soured, cranky, they are excellent socialistic material."[94] American business was thriving with the backing of the gospel of wealth, but working-class resentment against churches, and particularly church leaders, was building. Complaints about changing demographics made the most impact as fund-raising tools for Home Missions boards, but they could not move congressmen to invest in public services for the poor.[95]

Henry Carroll estimated that about *five million* Americans, about the same number of all Methodists and Baptists combined, a population about the size of Pennsylvania, belonged to the "non-religious and anti-religious classes, including free-thinkers, secularists and infidels." He framed the statistic as an evangelistic opportunity, arguing that these people were "probably opposed to the church for various reasons" and that many could be taught correct doctrine and invited into church membership with goodwill. He sanguinely made attempts to disaggregate those who opposed Christianity and those who kept their distance, summarizing, "One out of every twelve persons is either an active or passive opponent of religion; two out of every three are not members of any church."[96] But this statement included no evidentiary support.

As the historian Dave Burns has documented, a large fraction of these five million others were "skeptics" who believed in an alternate historical Jesus, preserved through the historical record recently uncovered in Europe, but rejected by the well-resourced churches. This imagined historical Jesus, brought to life by writers like Ernest Renan and Robert Ingersoll, was a poor carpenter, a labor organizer, and advocate of anti-imperial working-class revolution. Many socialists even preached on this Jesus on Sunday morning, discussed him in regular fellowship meetings, and sang about him in popular hymns."[97] Carroll did not identify socialist fellowships as churches, but maybe he should have.

Conclusion

Most brick-and-mortar churches of the Gilded Age functioned as meeting places for the wealthy and petit bourgeois to exercise their distance from the nation's poor. Those who occupied the lowest ranks of jobs in the cities and in the country likely encountered Christian missionaries within schools and hospitals, but most had little contact with ordained ministers. When the poor did run into preachers, in revivals and city streets, or within schools or missions, these religious leaders were most likely to be detached from the authority structures of the major denominations. Members of the Catholic religious orders who operated schools, hospitals, and orphanages provided the nation's primary social services for the working classes in many locales and often cultivated a sense of respect. However, a small fraction of the nation's poorest wage earners attended church services regularly, especially within the nation's northern and white Protestant denominations.

All this helps explain why Gilded Age Protestants, long suspicious of Roman Catholicism as a faith tradition, came to recognize Catholics as allies in a joint mission to grow the size and scope of their churches. Since the Roman Catholic Church hierarchy identified socialism as "materialistic" and a rival to the mission of the church, American Protestants adopted the same critique. In fact, socialism was nothing new to the United States, or the world, in the Gilded Age. German American Marxists swelled the ranks of the antebellum labor movement and helped form the First International in 1867. Many American Christians, including Josiah Strong himself, supported these early American socialists in their defense of the labor movement. However, as Gilded Age Protestants surveyed the causes of low church attendance, they elected to join Catholics in blaming the appeal of "socialism" as the greatest danger to Christianity.

In the late nineteenth and early twentieth centuries, a flurry of street preachers and labor organizers, professing hope in a cooperative commonwealth, offered bold critiques of churches' impotence to carry out their stated mission to the poor.[98] As one minister publicly reflected, "The zeal and devotion with which multitudes strive for those ideals compel observant people to ask whether there may be more of Christianity outside of ecclesiastical boundaries than within. . . . The best Socialists are inspired by an enthusiasm for humanity which, tho it does not speak of Christ, reminds of Christ."[99] Socialists pledged not only to revere the historical Jesus, the carpenter who preached the Beatitudes, but also to recognize collective bargaining rights, invest in social services for the poor, limit work hours, and allow everyone to observe the Sabbath. They intended dramatic social change that might actually displace the need for private Christian ministries in the spheres of education, social work, and healthcare. Indeed, the more socialism grew in popularity among working-class Christians, the more ordained ministers— Catholic and Protestant—worried that church leaders were losing the moral gravity they used to have, and that churches might lose their relevance as chief purveyors of charity.

At the dawn of the twentieth century, Americans deeply disagreed over what it meant to build a more Christian nation. In the books and magazines that Americans carried into the new territories, socialists critiqued the version of Christianity that rationalized the class system. They built an alternative national infrastructure of Christian organizations, including "labor churches," unions, cooperatives, publishing companies and political parties, which both mimicked and mocked those of aspirant-class churches. They demanded that their working-class institutions form an alternative Christian infrastructure for the nation. A just state, socialists claimed, supported businesses that paid their workers proportionately to their profits and truly benefited the general welfare. It is to that alternate vision of a Christian commonwealth that we next turn.

2

Christianity and
the American Commonwealth

Charles S. Coe, raised a Congregationalist in Madison, Connecticut, was not shocked to learn in September 1897 that both he and his former pastor had both independently converted to socialism since the end of the Civil War. As Coe understood it, becoming a socialist represented not a rejection of the Christian faith but a richer understanding of it. "At last I found that Christ, the 'light of the world,' had been hidden under a theological bushel," he testified to fellow socialists. He now believed that "the Christ idea and principles were buried under the accumulations of ages of musty, cob-webbed ignorance and superstition." In socialism, Coe found a spiritual motivation for selflessness, disciplined cooperation, and the eradication of competition. From the frontier mining town of Pueblo, Colorado, he wrote a letter to the editor of the *Coming Nation* applauding not only his childhood minister but his "former schoolmates and townspeople" for their courage in supporting a controversial minister's public stand. The newspaper editor commented, "Socialism has been working in the church, where it belongs and has long been needed."[1]

In the late nineteenth century, the nation was filled visionaries intent on creating a more Christian commonwealth, but most of those people mistrusted the most well-resourced denominations as vehicles for social change. The Knights of Labor, a large union that insisted that workers were entitled to the value they produced, sang spiritual songs and incorporated prayer into their meetings.[2] Hundreds of socialist "colonies" set up in the Old Northwest Territories broke with the major denominations to restore the type of Christian community they believed the apostles had originally intended.[3] Women temperance advocates lobbied to restore Christian justice to the domestic sphere by eliminating drinking, prostitution, gambling, promiscuity, and the violence that accompanied what they called "vice."[4]

The Gospel of Church. Janine Giordano Drake, Oxford University Press. © Oxford University Press 2024.
DOI: 10.1093/oso/9780197614303.003.0003

Farmers, forming the People's Party, defended social, economic, and monetary policies that they said would effect a more Christian and "Cooperative Commonwealth." As the economist Richard Ely reflected in 1885, the country was full of Christians. They were not "atheists, not unbelievers in Christianity, but unbelievers in the Church."[5] These Americans imagined a different kind of Christian nation.

If religion is, according to Émile Durkheim, "a unified system of beliefs and practices relative to sacred things," then, as several scholars have observed, the social democratic movement was a religious movement that sacralized a social order based in the principle of social equality.[6] More and less explicitly Christian critics of capitalism spent time together in a number of types of community, including print culture, labor churches, and socialist fellowships, and they tolerated a diversity of beliefs on a number of topics, including Jesus's divinity and the importance of sin sacrifice. But the group cohered around a common opposition to the profit system and a rebellion against the denominational churches for their distortion of what they believed to be the true mission of Christianity.

These socialist communities rivaled their church-based counterparts in print culture, community building, theology, ecclesiology, and missions. They referred to their proposed social services as state "ministries," their classes as "Sunday school," and their organizing work as "missions." Organizing relied on testimonials, often called "How I Became a Socialist," that directly mimicked those of evangelicals. They planted dozens of "labor churches" or "people's churches" in working-class communities and circulated both their own catechisms and their own hymnals. Socialists imagined Jesus of Nazareth as a carpenter and refugee of a poor ethnic group whom God created to comfort the poor and afflict the rich and comfortable with the gospel of social equality. Christian Socialists, even those who did not call themselves spiritual, believed that Jesus's Sermon on the Mount, his speech about sacrificial love and the mystique of material satisfaction in the world, ought to become the foundation for social and political renewal in the United States. Socialist print culture, especially on the purpose and scope of the Church, the possibility of overcoming selfishness, and the ideal role of the state, soon posed a significant challenge to the "Churchianity" of the major Protestant denominations.

Radical Christianity and Print Culture

In the two decades after the Civil War, Americans widely participated in a print culture that questioned both laissez faire economists and church leaders as authority figures on human nature.[7] On average, Gilded Age wage earners spent \$4.23 per year on books, newspapers, and magazines, just below 1 percent of family income.[8] Popular books like Henry George's *Progress and Poverty* (1879), Laurence Gronlund's *Cooperative Commonwealth* (1884), Edward Bellamy's *Looking Backward* (1887), and Robert Blatchford's *Merrie England* (1893) railed against the churches for presuming the worst about human nature and reinforcing those expectations through what they called a "profit system" that rewarded selfishness and exploitation. Gronlund, building on George, traced the problem with capitalism back to the Christian dogma of American and European elites. As he put it, "It is not our morality or want of morality that makes our economic relations what they are, but our economic system that makes our morality what it is." He encouraged wage-earning Christians to reimagine incentives to inspire good in one another outside of the church's declarations.[9] Blatchford, a British writer, agreed that "man is a great deal better than the church and the economist suppose him to be."[10]

Bellamy's *Looking Backward* (1887) brought all these ideas to the ordinary American who did not want to read economic and social theory. The book was a work of speculative political fiction that imagined a future American commonwealth built in government ownership of all industry, a change that Bellamy believed would positively incentivize people to care for their neighbors. It sold more than a million copies in its first printing, and inspired a cult following and an 1897 sequel, *Equality*, which discussed the problem with "ecclesiastical corporations" at greater length.[11] Bellamy also founded and ran a weekly magazine, *The Nationalist*, with a mailing list of 690,000, and four thousand Bellamyite clubs nationwide.[12] Henry George's treatise on the importance of property taxes to create a revenue source for public infra-structure inspired a similar wave of "Single Tax" societies and publications across the country. It also sparked Charles Sheldon's 1897 *In His Steps: What Would Jesus Do?*, which sold eight million copies in the United States in its first several printings.[13] Also in plain vernacular, Sheldon encouraged Christians to distinguish between the mission of Jesus, the poor carpenter, and those of the churches.[14] The book struck a nerve in its encouragement to believers to salvage Christianity by rejecting the "Churchianity." Before long, the Reverend George Allen White popularized the term "churchians" to distinguish churchgoers from Christians.[15]

The entrepreneurial J. A. Wayland capitalized on this print culture of socialism by making critiques of capitalism and the churches available weekly through the subsidized rural mail. He published the *Coming Nation*, which began as a newspaper for the Ruskin Cooperative Colony, a socialist communal settlement in Tennessee. When that dissolved, he moved the paper to Girard, Kansas, and renamed it *Appeal to Reason* (1895). Early articles imagined a white Protestant socialist republic without Catholics, Jews, or African Americans, but the newspaper evolved with the Socialist Party throughout the late 1890s.[16] By 1899, the *Appeal* reached sixty-one thousand weekly subscribers, a figure that suggests this rural and Christian Socialist tradition was far more popular than its more "Marxist" alternatives in the Second International. A weekly column on matters of religion reminded readers that the churches maintained prohibitions on usury—and by extension, the capitalist system—for centuries until corrupt popes relented. Jesus, meanwhile, supported social democracy.[17]

The "Appeal Army," as *Appeal to Reason* salespeople became known, carried the message of Christian social justice door to door throughout the poorest agricultural and mining regions of the United States, especially Arkansas, Oklahoma, Indiana, Illinois, and Ohio. They asked new members to affirm their faith in the cause by signing "cards," a ritual designed to parallel those cards signed in church by those who newly professed faith. By 1906, the *Appeal* reached 342,609 weekly subscribers.[18] By 1915, that number had climbed to 500,000 weekly subscribers.[19]

The growing number of Irish, Jewish, German, and Polish American wage earners of the Gilded Age were more likely to get their weekly helping of socialist print culture from other sources. In 1899, thirty-five thousand people subscribed to the *Journal of the Knights of Labor*. The Knights had a long a history of elaborate ritual culture, Christian imagery, weekly meetings, and public prayer and cited Scripture in their masthead.[20] For the more erudite, the *International Socialist Review*, a monthly magazine describing socialist movements in Europe and their potential in the United States, counted 7,415 subscribers in 1901.[21] American cities hosted several socialist publications in European languages, including the German-language daily *Volkszeitung* (eighteen thousand subscribers) and the daily *Albeiter-Zeitung* (ten thousand subscribers). The Polish Socialist Alliance's *Robotnik*, established in 1895, counted four thousand in 1904.[22] Most papers in the United States and

Canada did their best to hold together the full spectrum of Christians and skeptics.[23] They ran a few articles on local labor conflicts, a few pieces on national events, a handful of political cartoons, critiques of the one-sided "capitalist press," and commentary on the doublespeak about the virtue of American farmers and their abuse at the hands of eastern bankers. In the absence of any common socialist nationality or culture, what most held together the Gilded Age community of socialists was the heroic figure of Jesus and the running expose on the Jewish carpenter's real aims.

Rethinking the Church

Indeed, working-class Christians of the Gilded Age loved to reimagine Jesus as a Jewish carpenter who felt deeply out of place in a stained-glass cathedral but at ease among the poor and in communities of reformers. A large group of critics in the United States and Europe, including Charles Sheldon, Robert Blatchford, William Stead, Bouck White, George Herron, Cyrenus Osborne Ward, and Sir John Robert Seely, reimagined the concept of "church" as a cooperative community of believers who inspired one another to do good. In *real* churches, members worked cooperatively, shared in the bounty of their hard work and attended to one another's spiritual and emotional needs. These books established a print culture of Christian dissent from established churches in the United States.

In William T. Stead's 1894 *If Christ Came to Chicago*, Jesus returns to earth looking for churches and cannot find them. Jesus observes, "If the churches are the divinely appointed instrument for carrying out the divine will in this world in Chicago, it would seem as if either God had forsaken His Church or his Church had forsaken him." Eventually, Stead's Jesus identifies Chicago's city hall as the institution that most approximates a church. Jesus declares that "the dedication of the citizen to municipal work" is "one of the most important and sacred means of helping bring in the kingdom of Christ on earth."[24] The book sold seventy thousand copies on its publication day alone.[25] Similarly, in Bouck White's *Call of the Carpenter* (1911), Jesus is a movement organizer but the foe of all organized religion. He aims to unite Jews and Gentiles by redirecting them both back to the principles of the Beatitudes. "The Jews are the foremost among the agitators for a new social order," White wrote.[26] At the pulpit and in his books, White aimed to unite Christians and Jews in accepting the "Revolutionist of Galilee" as the leader of their faith.[27] White's work was frequently advertised in the *International Socialist Review*. One advertisement summarized, "Jesus of Nazareth TAUGHT the very things the Churches and so-called Christians today CONDEMN in the name of Christ." Not only did Jesus "love the poor" and "despise ALL the rich," but, "when a rich man asked permission to follow Jesus and became one of his band of OUTLAWS, Jesus said to him: Sell ALL you have and GIVE to the POOR and take up your cross and follow me." The real Jesus was a "FIGHTING CARPENTER."[28]

In reimagining Jesus's central aims, writers reimagined the purpose of the church. The British writer Sir John Robert Seeley's *Ecce Homo* (1893) claimed that "Christ's object in founding the Society which is called by his name" was to provide a higher "law" through which humans could treat one another with respect and dignity.[29] He implied that to see Jesus simply as a martyred sin sacrifice distracted from the calling to radical ethics. In response to his concluding question to his parody catechism, "What is the Christian Church?" he said that it is a "commonwealth" of self-sacrificing members for the greater good.[30]

Cyrenus Osborne Ward, an American writer from central Illinois, argued that the purpose of the church was to inspire cooperative enterprise.[31] His *Labor Catechism of Political Economy* (1877) critiqued churches for offering material aide to the poor without solving the problems that cause poverty. He said that the people of God should build cooperatively owned industries, "groceries, dry goods, fuel and medicines" to incentivize the best in human nature, and to "provisio[n] the people": "How can a man learn to love his neighbor as himself when his means of existence set him in ghastly antagonism with his neighbor?"[32] Similarly, Ward's *Ancient Lowly* (1889), a historical examination of the ancient world, explained how godly communities are always inherently at odds with profit-driven enterprise.[33] As a Marxist who had spent time in the First International and cared a great deal about bridging the cultural distance among the working classes, Ward suggested Jews and Christians recognize their commonalities in the Mosaic covenant and unite as a moral community in demanding honest wages and a new social infrastructure within a moral, cooperative economy. Ward persuaded his many readers that Christianity was not just a tradition to espouse through musical worship and prayer, but a new spiritual praxis for social and economic relationships.

This new meaning given to the practice of Christianity inspired the emerging field of "Christian Sociology." In Christian colleges and divinity schools, a growing body sociologists queried what they called the "social teachings of Jesus" and asked which types of social structures encouraged social cohesion, human kindness, and forgiveness, and which types of structures encouraged social stratification and anarchy. By 1900, 227 colleges and universities out of the total 683 had courses on the books that addressed these questions.[34] Middling-class Americans who could attend religious colleges and sought a future in ministry, social work, law, or politics likely read some of these books as a framework for debating the meaning of a "Christian commonwealth." George Herron, a Christian Sociologist at Iowa College, argued in a succession of books between 1891 and 1899 that it was impossible to practice one's faith as a Christian inside a society that encouraged the exploitation of labor. He not only argued that the United States should strive to become a "Christian State," which evangelized the message of radical mercy, and built cooperative enterprises to make that possible. He also argued that the American churches needed to relinquish their unfounded worldly authority and teach the virtues of "cooperation" until they dissolved.[35] For, as Herron put it in 1894, "To establish the authority of a religious institution is to usurp the throne of God."[36]

Herron did not want to see churches vanish all at once, but he wanted ministers to focus their attention on building a better society rather than a better church. In his book *The Larger Christ* (1891), Herron argued that the group he called the "church of the Messiah," the body of Christians who wanted to build a truly better world, would soon overcome the worldly "church of Mammon" that prevailed in Gilded Age America.[37] As Jackson Stitt Wilson echoed in his socialist conversion narrative, "No church member who is not willing to lay down his life, if need be, for the cause of the people that need[s] assistance," should call themselves "spiritualized, regenerated, or Christian." The Indiana minister was referring, of course, to the emerging socialist and labor movements.[38]

Reimagining Business

For many Christian Socialists, the "labor movement" was a broad term for all efforts to rethink the system of private enterprise with incentives that encouraged Christians to be more Christlike. After all, this is how the Knights of Labor framed their mission. The Knights grew out of an antebellum labor movement that had nominated joint-stock "cooperatives" as the only truly

"Christian enterprise."[39] They also lived in a world where "experiments" in joint-stock cooperative societies, including New Harmony, Nashoba, Brook Farm, and Oneida, seemed ubiquitous. Within each of these experiments in American socialism, families collectively owned property, worked together in a business, and saw themselves living out the Christian calling to share "everything in common."[40]

For many Gilded Age Christians looking for examples of genuinely Christian fellowship, these cooperative communities appeared to set the best example. As one socialist minister argued, "Christian Socialism will conform men to Christianness; whereas churchianity can never do so, were it to last until the end of time."[41] Believers in the cooperative movement, which included Knights and a rising contingent of Christian economists, theologians, and ministers, expected that they could consign the "the profit motive," like chattel slavery, to the dustbin of antiquated economic principles. It would be replaced with the "service motive." As the argument went, once one's investments in time and treasure were tied to those of friends, relatives, and coworkers, people would have fewer incentives to exploit one another and more incentives to treat others as they would treat themselves.[42] As the socialist economist Cyrus Camp framed it in 1887, cooperatives were the only real tool to move the nation in the direction of democratic socialism without discounting what we know about human nature.[43]

Voluntary cooperative associations fell into several categories, including "distributive cooperation," such as joint-stock groceries; "productive cooperation," such as jointly owned factories and farms; and cooperatively owned banks and insurance companies. In 1885, Richard Ely founded the American Economic Association with the mission of supporting the labor movement and galvanizing an effort to change the way Americans did business. He estimated the value of joint-stock companies in New England alone at around two million dollars and rising, and believed that cooperatives would help save American Christianity.[44] Founding members of his society included Lyman Abbott, the former abolitionist preacher, Christian Socialists Henry Carter Adams and John Bates Clark, Congregationalist pastor Washington Gladden, and members of the Knights of Labor.[45] Already, through the infrastructure provided by the Knights, Americans were establishing cooperatives throughout cities and small towns. Minneapolis boasted dozens of cooperative grocery stores, laundries, painters' associations, a "house-building enterprise," cooperative shoe retailers, and a network of building-and-loan associations.[46] As Walter Rauschenbusch later affirmed their mission, "If our social order is to be christianized, wealth by extortion must cease; work and service must become the sole title to income."[47]

This confidence about the possibility of shifting human nature away from selfishness directly challenged church leaders' endorsement of a dismal view of human nature. Roman Catholic authorities officially held their ground, believing that human nature would never change substantially enough to support a socialist society. As one priest commented on cooperatives in the pages of the *Catholic World*, "These proposals . . . involve a complete transformation in human motives." Around the world, Roman Catholic ministers defended capitalism with this understanding of human nature.[48] But, on the other end of the spectrum, the rising number of Holiness-Pentecostals and Christian Socialists demanded that these paradigm shifts in human nature were not only possible but necessary to the formation of genuinely Christian communities.

Labor Churches

All over Gilded Age America, Christians were founding and joining independent Christian congregations dedicated to the common agreement to build a more "cooperative," just society. In Britain, "Labour Churches" were major vehicles of socialist organizing. According to John Trevor, the Calvinist-turned-Unitarian "father" of the British labor church movement, these independent communities served as both political and spiritual havens for inquiry into the potential of human nature.[49] American "labor churches" of the Gilded Age took on a similar mission. They had no required pew rent, very loose terms of membership and rejected the stratification of space according to wealth.

W. D. P. Bliss, an Episcopalian minister in Boston, founded the "Brotherhood and Mission of the Carpenter," one of the first American labor churches, in 1890. Bliss imagined an ideal church as a community of believers who lived together in "an inclosure," working together in a joint cooperative business in children's clothing for eight hours per day and sharing all costs and responsibilities in common. Congregants would meet on Sundays for communion supper and services, but their faith would be most deeply expressed in the way they lived their lives. Many members of the "mission" lived in one of three Boston-area cooperative houses, including the Wendell Phillips Union, the Andover House, and an older mission/church, the

Berkeley Temple.[50] Bible classes occurred weekly to study the Sermon on the Mount. He reported to the Episcopal diocese that year that seventeen of the ninety members who attended weekly study sessions were Christian church members. During the evenings, meals honored different organizations that the church supported, including the Knights of Labor, the (American) Federation of Labor, and the Nationalist Party. All profits went right back to the operatives who worked machines, and Bliss reported that the high wages inspired many who had worked in department stores to leave to join their cooperative shop or demand higher wages at their present jobs. As the Homestead massacre made the news in 1892, a reporter on Bliss's church said that "very little else was talked of." Though members were a mixture of middling and working class, Bliss hoped that such reimagined churches could set the model for a new concept of Christian, cooperative enterprise.[51]

Bliss also hoped his church's self-sustaining, cooperative commercial mission might set a trend for how churches could reimagine their goals.[52] "Whosoever would be chief among you, he should be the servant of all," he declared, for "This is the only Christian competition, a rivalry of self-sacrifice."[53] In his *Encyclopedia of Social Reform,* Bliss recorded the religious principles common to members the labor church movement internationally. His first principle was that "the labor movement is a religious movement." He believed that middling-class Christians needed to support organized labor in their struggles for the eight-hour day and improved wages and working conditions. Like Trevor, though, Bliss did not outline a particular orthodoxy. If the purpose of Christ's ministry was a transformation in social and economic relationships, Christology seemed irrelevant. Rather, Bliss held that each man was "free to develop his own relations with the power that brought him into being." For Bliss, religion did not signal dogma but a higher commitment to morality and ethical behavior. The fourth principle of the church's mission read, "That the emancipation of labor can only be realized so far as men learn both the economic and moral laws of God, and heartily endeavor to obey them."[54] In this respect, Bliss affirmed the work of the American Economic Association, a growing community of economists who agreed that discussions on economic principles needed to be connected to discussions on Christian morality.[55]

Bliss, Rauschenbusch, and Herron stood together in inviting criticism from "Lasallean" Marxists like Daniel DeLeon for perceived naiveté, but they believed that the socialist movement should be driven in and through the church networks. In 1896, the Socialist Party leader Eugene Debs would join Herron, Rauschenbusch, and Bliss in founding the Brotherhood of the Cooperative Commonwealth, a socialist missionary operation founded on the possibility of cooperative enterprise.[56]

Bliss also inspired Herbert Casson, former Methodist minister who "converted to socialism," to found a labor church in the labor stronghold of Lynn, Massachusetts, in 1893.[57] As he explained it, his church was a sincere attempt to mimic the first-century church in Jerusalem, which was "a Christian commune" and "the first unorganized form of the cooperative order." Casson's church was quite a change from the Methodist church wherein his father preached and still different from that which he was trained to lead in Methodist seminary. Membership was not limited to those who tithed or paid expensive pew rents as it was in many urban churches at the time. In fact, the sixth of his church's ten cardinal principles was "Thou shalt treat private luxury as immoral as long as poverty exists." In this respect, his congregation, which he described as "either middle class or poor," carried on old conservative Protestant values of austerity.

Casson experimented with many popular suggestions about what a "church" should do. In 1895, he organized weekly labor conferences with local labor leaders, businessmen, and others, and in 1896, his church established a joint-stock cooperative grocery.[58] According to his interview with the *Coming Nation*, belief in Jesus as Savior was less important to him than participation in contemporary reform movements. He did not reject those members who did believe, and, in fact, he scheduled his services to start at noon on Sundays to "allow some members time to attend regular church services elsewhere." After the congregational meeting, members would frequently gather for dinner in the sanctuary and follow the Sabbath afternoon with music, recitations of literature, and discussions of politics, as well as invited speakers. These at times included a range of progressive reform advocates such as the labor agitators Frank Parsons and Eugene Debs.[59] One might argue that Casson's church was no more "church" than a community center, but Casson contended that "church" was the best label for a community eager to transform the expectations of human community.[60]

Casson was both a Christian millennialist and a Marxist. He believed that a "Coming Nation," a future Christian commonwealth, the Kingdom of God, was inevitable, but he also believed it was the responsibility of all believers to raise "consciousness" about the problems with the present society.[61] As a Christian, he also had strong convictions about the misdirected priorities of the orthodox churches in Boston. Casson blamed the apostle Paul for emphasizing the crucifixion and atoning sacrifice, matters most important to observant Jews, over what Casson understood as Jesus's deliberate breaking with Jewish laws for the inauguration of the Kingdom of God.[62] "It is utter nonsense the preach the gospel of individual conversion," he wrote, "without adding the gospel of social regeneration." He believed that the denominational churches were defenders of "special privileges." They failed to "denounce the criminal and sinful monopolies which are sapping the land of its vitality and manhood." Members of his two-hundred-person church joined him in publishing essays for the *Coming Nation*, and some joined him in the Ruskin Cooperative Colony in Tennessee.[63] There Casson would serve as a spiritual director within a commune that would serve as an incubator for the emerging socialist movement of the early twentieth century.

Bliss and Casson helped inspire dozens more radical churches.[64] Among these was John Rusk's "Church Militant," which critiqued "Churchianity" and its profession of dogma to such an extent that his freethinking congregation in Chicago lost its opportunity to rent space in the Woman's Christian Temperance Union's Willard Hall. Rusk's stated goal was to give Christianity "a secular character . . . making it influence the affairs of this life."[65] He would "attack some of the social problems of the day, applying wholesome Christian remedies."[66] "Man should cease to expect aid from any supernatural source," argued Ingersoll to an eager and packed auditorium rented by the Church Militant on a nationally highlighted evening in April 1895. "He should know that the supernatural has not succored the oppressed, clothed the naked, fed the hungry, shielded the innocent, stayed the pestilence, or freed the slave." To radicals like Ingersoll, the new "religion of science," also known as socialist secularism, was as an updated reinterpretation of the primary purposes of Jesus's ministry.[67]

While both Protestants and Catholics in Chicago voiced outrage that such an atheist could preach from a Christian pulpit, newspapers throughout the increasingly socialist Midwest reprinted Ingersoll's controversial sermon with commentary that perhaps this was a healthy turn of events for the future of Christianity.[68] The *Cleveland Plain Dealer* reported, "The appearance in the pulpit of a Christian church of a man who for a score of years has been pouring his invectives upon the church is indeed a notable event, giving hope for the dawn of that day in which intolerance of honest differences of opinion will be only a memory among intelligent men." The writer backed up his sentiments with those of Dr. Thomas of the People's Church in Chicago, who argued that Ingersoll was unnecessarily abrasive to those who still believed in the supernatural, but his point was ultimately correct.[69] The *Kansas City Times* reported that Ingersoll "obviously strives for the object of the church— the purification of the world and the elevation of man."[70] The *Omaha World Herald* reported that Ingersoll's views on "the treatment of his brother are in accord with the Decalogue, the Golden Rule, the Beatitudes, as well as the whole Sermon on the Mount,... Whether Col. Ingersoll admits it or not, the greater portion of his remarks are based on what is generally conceded are to be the true Christianity."[71]

Members of labor churches effectively carried out the calls of Christian economists and sociologists to relocate Christianity from ornate buildings to the fabric of Christian community, the original calling of the first-century church. Explained one member of a labor church in the Southwest, "Those who think more of their churches, their sects, and creeds than they do of orig- inal, genuine Christianity should not claim to be Christians. If they like the counterfeit more than the genuine they should not murmur and lament over the hardships, the injustice, the poverty and wrongs they are suffering for thus being cheated and cheating themselves."[72] The working-class Americans who attended growing numbers of radical churches saw their participation as defiance of the faith traditions that supported the class system.

Further Decentralization of Christian Authority

By 1906, this working-class rebellion against Churchianity had substan- tially changed the cultural authority structure in United States. Independent churches and public forums on political questions had displaced ordained clergy as authorities on matters of public morality. The churches that now thrived were those that were easy to plant, permitted women preachers, and offered little denominational oversight.[73] These included Baptist churches, Disciples of Christ, and Christian Scientists, all of which bucked liturgical traditions. The Roman Catholic Church grew too, but only in proportion to population increases from Europe.

The most rapidly growing congregational units were independent churches, which skyrocketed from 155 in 1890 to 1,079 in 1906 (Table 2.1), a notably "phenomenal" 596 percent increase over sixteen years. This classifi- cation included any congregation that felt stifled by denominational unions, including the many new church-plants established through Holiness revivals and those affiliated with the nascent Christian Socialist Fellowship. These congregations may have practiced speaking in tongues and given special

Table 2.1 Shifts in Denominational Affiliation 1890 and 1906.

Denomination	Number of Communicants, 1890	Number of Communicants, 1906	Percentage Increase from 1890
Baptist bodies	3,712,468	5,552,234	52.5
"Disciples of Christ" or "Christians"	641,051	1,142,359	78.2
Methodist bodies	4,859,284	5,749,853	25.3
Presbyterian bodies	1,277,851	1,830,555	43.3
Independent churches	13,360	73,673	451.4
Roman Catholic churches	6,241,708	12,079,142	93.5

attention to healing, but many also included elements of other traditions, including weekly Scripture readings, the sacraments, principles of church discipline, and spiritual songs. Denominational leaders in the Northeast lamented these changes as a lapse in organization and orthodoxy, but the religious landscape reflected how successfully working-class Christians resisted the moral and spiritual authority of Protestant elites.

Compounding this splintering of denominational power was the fact that European migrants comprised a growing fraction of the United States, and only a small fraction of those migrants joined the major Anglo-Protestant denominations. In 1890, the nation counted 9.2 million immigrants, a full 14.8 percent of the population.[74] The nation gained 10.5 million immigrants between 1890 and 1900, including 2.6 million immigrants from Germany, 1.6 million immigrants from Ireland, and just under 500,000 immigrants from both Italy and Russia. The Deep South received the smallest fraction of these newcomers, and Baptists predominated in most southern states. But in all other regions of the country, European immigrants comprised between 15 and 35 percent of their states' total population. As the Roman Catholic Church consolidated ethnic parishes into an American denomination, most churchgoers surveyed by the census were either Roman Catholic or Baptist.

Churchgoing Protestants were a distinct minority in most of the nation. Protestants comprised less than a fifth of the population in Maine (13.5 percent), New Hampshire (14.9 percent), Massachusetts (14.8 percent), Rhode Island (13.1 percent), New York (15.0 percent), New Jersey (18.6 percent), Louisiana (19.4 percent), Oklahoma (15.5 percent), Montana (8.0 percent), Idaho (11.1 percent), Wyoming (7.2 percent), New Mexico (6.7 percent), Arizona (6.3 percent), Utah (2.6 percent), Nevada (7.6 percent), Washington (18.6 percent), Oregon (17.2 percent), and California (14.3 percent). Meanwhile, overall church attendance was less than 30 percent in many states, including Maine (29.8 percent), West Virginia (28.0 percent), Kansas (28.4 percent), Oklahoma (18.2 percent), and Oregon (25.3 percent) (Figure 2.1).[75]

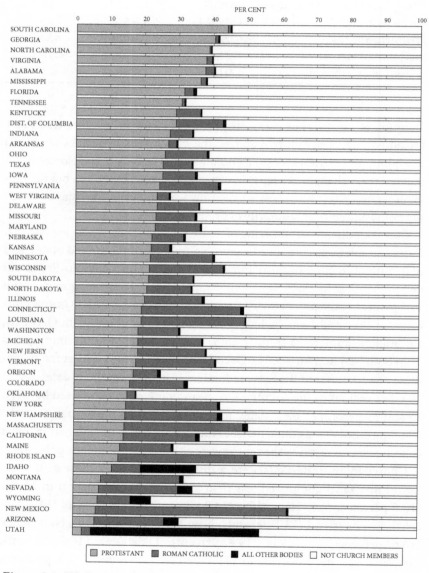

Figure 2.1   US Census of Religious Bodies, 1906.

Meanwhile, the largest category of Americans in the 1906 census were, as was true a decade earlier, those with no religious affiliation. Methodist minister Henry Carroll, who supervised both the 1890 and 1906 censuses, did his best to distract attention from the size and significance of this category. He urged readers not to place "too much importance" on membership figures, for he still believed that raw data underreported Protestants and overreported Catholics. In fact, in commenting on changes since 1890, he changed the reporting category from "members," those officially counted by ministers, to "communicants," those who might have participated in services somewhat regularly. Using these inflated numbers, he retrospectively projected only 67.3 percent of Americans in 1890 as unaffiliated with the churches. Applying the same multipliers to 1906 raw data, Carroll reported a seven-percentage-point decrease, to 60.9 percent, in the fraction of Americans unaffiliated with churches. It is difficult to find these inflated estimates persuasive, especially considering that Carroll estimated an additional three Baptists for every reported Baptist, and this group comprised the largest fraction of American Protestants. Yet even if Carroll was correct and his inflated estimates more accurately reflected church affiliation than raw figures, that growth came primarily from the informal orbit around independent and Baptist churches, or Roman Catholic efforts to place more priests in cities and towns. It remained true that in most states, less than half of Americans had any church affiliation.[76]

This international trend toward disaffiliation from the major denominations was correlated with the rise of social democracies in Europe. As a replacement for conventional church services, both socialist Sunday Schools and labor temples had become regular fixtures of most major cities, especially London, Berlin, and New York. Within these spaces, working-class children and adults learned history, sociology, economics, philosophy, and religion. In England, most socialist Sunday Schools were led by ministers officially connected to the national Labour Church Union and ultimately the Labour Party.[77] In the United States, some ministers rejected such schools completely, but others recognized their ministries as God's work among the poor. The Sunday School Council of US evangelical denominations recognized the Socialist Sunday School Union and the three thousand programs it operated nationally.[78] As one evangelical minister reported, "With minor exceptions, the capitalists dominate [the church] and use it for their own purposes. They hold the purse strings of the church." Socialist schools offered a "valuable side light upon the problem of religious instruction," an examination of religion from a more "modern," scientific perspective, and therefore served the greater evangelical mission for public education.[79] In New York City alone, socialists counted between eighteen hundred and two thousand students per year, spread across thirteen schools. Socialists maintained Sunday School classes in every major industrial city, including Rochester, Buffalo, Hartford, Boston, Lynn (Massachusetts), and Baltimore, as well as several overseas.[80]

In his 1898 essay "The Waning of Evangelicalism," the British minister Richard Heath observed this crumbling of denominational power as a working-class effort to reimagine the meaning of "Church" in industrializing nations around the world, especially England, France, and Germany. He expanded the essay into his 1904 international bestseller, *The Captive City of God*, which argued that most state churches had so bowed to capitalists and turned their backs on wage earners that they were allowing socialism to "eclipse" the place of church in modern society.[81] This trend, Heath noted, was especially apparent in the United States. Heath used Carroll's census data from 1890 to remark that only 17.60 percent of the residents of Manhattan Island had church affiliations, and of those only 7.22 percent were Protestants. He quoted a variety of American commentators speaking to this phenomenon, emphasizing the words of H. M. Brooks, published in his 1898 single-tax pamphlet, *The Church Impeached*. Brooks wrote,

> According to the best information I can gather there are at least twenty-five millions of people in America who never go to church at all, and they have no use for the Church, but still they believe in the teachings of Christ, and there are twenty-five millions, who go to church occasionally, but are disgusted with the church. The truth of the matter is, there never was a time when the people had as little confidence in the Church as they have at the present time.

Connecting this trend in the United States to the parallel rise in Europe of what he called "Nonconformist Denominations," including Baptists other independent congregations, Heath concluded, "Today, not only in the great industrial and commercial centres, but throughout the north and northeast of Germany, the People as a whole are so completely estranged from the Church that for them it may be said to be almost totally eclipsed by Social Democracy."[82] As the historian Hugh McCleod observed, Heath was not wrong. In both Great Britain and Germany, social democrats were

successfully organizing through churches and creating a new public consensus on the meaning of Christian social democracy.[83] Many Americans expected the same would soon take place in the United States.

Socialism as American Religion

Hence, in creating a massive Christian Socialist print culture, erecting labor
churches and socialist Sunday schools, and using these spaces to reimagine
structures to bend human nature toward cooperation, socialists offered a
new vision for both the churches and the economic system. Many among the
five million "socialists, atheists and unbelievers in the church" whom Carroll
observed in 1892 believed that some version of socialism or social democracy was the most sincere way to carry out the mission of the Church. They
wanted to build a new kind of Christian commonwealth, shepherded not by
ordained ministers of the church, but by elected officials, ministers of the
public good.

Yet the breadth of vision among Christian Socialists made it difficult to
prioritize goals. Some wanted socialist churches to lead the nation in a new
social democracy, while others wanted churches to disappear much more
quickly. It was relatively easy to call the problem "Mammon," to host regular
newspaper columns critiquing Churchianity, and even to organize Christian
Socialist fellowships, Sunday Schools, and professional associations on the
possibility of a "Cooperative Commonwealth." It was much harder to agree
on a national strategy for granting the poor political and economic power in
a nation that only enfranchised a small fraction of its citizens. That project,
the task of building a socialist movement in the United States, would rely
heavily on the infrastructure built through this late nineteenth-century rebellion against the churches.

3

Planting the Church of Social Democracy

Socialism and Christian Socialism in the Socialist Party of America

Eugene Debs declared in an 1897 circular to the American Railway Union members, "I am for Socialism because I am for humanity. The time has come to regenerate society—we are on the eve of a universal change."[1] Over the past ten years, he had witnessed the crushing of the Knights of Labor, the public execution of labor leaders and newspaper editors after the Haymarket Affair in Chicago, and a flooded labor market. The labor movement was plagued by court injunctions, industrial spies, hired strikebreakers, and the two-party political system. The nineteenth-century presumption that workers could build a labor movement around the value of their labor was appearing increasingly naive. Not only did the growing bulk of American wage workers hold jobs that did not require substantial training—a condition that made strikes ineffective tools because of the easy replacement of workers—but the largest fraction of Americans, including women, sharecroppers, and tenant farmers, did not work for cash wages.

If the election returns from 1896 revealed anything, it showed that the labor theory of value, the concept that "wealth belongs to him who creates it," had failed to mobilize a successful social democratic movement.[2] William Jennings Bryan championed this vision in his efforts to build a farmer-labor alliance, but he lost in the presidential election. The biggest problem was voter suppression. Bryan theoretically supported the voting rights of tenant farmers, women, and people of color, but most of those people could not vote for him. He won majorities in twenty-two states, including 176 electoral votes and 46.7 percent of the popular vote.[3] But many branches of the Democratic Party were deeply embedded in the systems of racial patriarchy. Party leaders resisted efforts to extend voting rights to women, Mexican Americans, and African Americans and thus crippled the party's efforts to represent the American working classes.[4]

The Gospel of Church. Janine Giordano Drake, Oxford University Press. © Oxford University Press 2024.
DOI: 10.1093/oso/9780197614303.003.0004

In the years following Bryan's defeat, the Populist union leader Eugene Debs tried a different strategy for building a more successful farmer-labor alliance. Debs embraced a vision of the Cooperative Commonwealth grounded in Christian theologies of land, cooperation, and the possibility of human perfection. In his efforts to mount a third-party movement, Debs joined hands with competing initiatives for social redemption, including Marxist materialists, but also Christian Socialists, women suffragettes, and the temperance movement. Debs redefined American socialism not as a class struggle but as an effort to create a new kind of Christian nation. He offered a new vision of Christian citizenship that valorized the poor and politically marginalized, including women and people of color, and endeavored to build a welfare state on the model of a community church. In recruiting ministers as organizers in both small towns and cities, Debsian socialists soon rivaled the Catholic and Protestant churches for the prized place in society as the moral compass of the nation. Socialist leadership on the meaning of a Christian commonwealth soon offered a powerful counterweight to the teachings on social justice offered by either Catholic or Protestant churches.

Imagining a Christian Commonwealth

If Bryan's presidential runs had naturalized the role of a politician who preached on economic morality, Debs knew there was room for elaboration. As early as 1894, when Debs was thrown in jail for disobeying a court injunction in the Pullman strike, Debs spoke of his socialist "conversion." In his 1895 Labor Day address, which he wrote from jail, Debs claimed that he had obeyed a "higher law." He compared himself to the biblical prophet Daniel, who was forced to worship the "Persian religion," with their "gods of gold, brass, stone, clay, wood, anything from a mouse to a mountain." This idol worship was, he added, "in modern parlance, an 'established church.'" He identified himself among the *real* Christians who were "pleading for sympathy for the poor and the oppressed."[5] In using such language, Debs was turning the working-class rebellion against the churches, popularized by writers like Cyrenus Osborne Ward and George Herron, into a political movement.[6]

Debs's homegrown socialist party, the "Social Democracy," would reimagine a future for the American labor movement outside the Socialist Labor Party's confines of secular, "scientific socialism." As George Herron explained on a tour through California, true democracy had never been tried in the United States. For "The ideal democracy can be realized only in an economic commonwealth and connected thorough industrial reform."[7] Soon after his release from prison, Debs addressed a crowded park with his version of testimony of conversion. As he lay awake in bed, he said, "The reverend stones of the prison walls preached sermons, sometimes rising in grandeur to the Sermon on the Mount." Recognizing the potential awkwardness of discussing a spiritual experience before a mixed audience, some of whom were likely agnostics and practitioners of other traditions, Debs added, "It might be a question in the minds of some if this occasion warrants the indulgence of the fancy." He told his audience that they could choose to take his story as that of a fable, parable, or epigram. The day following his release from prison, the *Coming Nation* published a letter from Debs arguing that workers are not slaves but freeborn citizens and ought to use the ballot to change the structure of the country. The ballot, he said, "can give our civilization its crowning glory—the Cooperative Commonwealth."[8]

Debs did not argue publicly, as his friend George Herron did, that the Social Democracy should usher in a new era of Christian social democracy. Yet it is very likely that Herron's *The Christian State* (1895) was timed to make this point for him. Herron asked Christians to imagine a truly Christian government offering "the visible manifestation of the invisible government of God." This was, mostly, a thought experiment. Herron offered that in such a state, the market would be regulated by the Church and "set the people free" from the oppression of exploitative work.[9] Debs would never speak explicitly in these terms, but he borrowed a similar framework of dispensationalism to suggest that a new era was dawning wherein the state harnessed capital, and shared essential resources, for the common good. "There is to come a day," he said, "when from the center to the circumference of our mighty Republic . . . , the people shall be free, and it will come by the unified voice and vote of the farmer, the mechanic, and the laborer in every department of the country's industries.[10] Vast crowds, representing over fifty labor unions, followed Debs from his prison cell to his hearing in a statement of solidarity.[11]

When Herron and Debs founded the Social Democracy in 1897, it was to turn the working-class Christian rebellion against the churches into a real political party. The party's "Declaration of Principles" offered an argument on the limitations of democracy within the confines of capitalism. Social Democrats called for immediate public ownership of trusts, mines, and systems of public transportation, for public works projects to meet the needs of the unemployed, and for myriad electoral reforms. But perhaps most of all, the party offered a new vision of citizenship that mandated the sharing of essential resources to "inaugurate the universal brotherhood of man." The party's preamble echoed the sentiments of Jean-Jacques Rousseau's *Discourse on Inequality*. After all, Debs was born of French immigrants who celebrated the French revolutionary tradition. It stated, "We hold that all men are born free, and are endowed with certain natural rights, among which are life, liberty, and happiness." Because citizens are not in fact equal due to differing economic circumstances, "political equality is useless" and "destructive of life, liberty and happiness." Hearkening to the Knights' vision of cooperation, the party proclaimed, "In spite of our political equality, labor is robbed of the wealth it produces. By the development of this system it is denied the means of self-employment, and by enforced idleness, through lack of employment, is even deprived of the necessities of life.[12]

For these founders, social democracy was a commitment to building a democratic community based on the goal of closing the wealth gap.[13] But it was also a commitment to a kind of Christian state. Debs called the party a "holy alliance" that "liberates the enslaved, gives a new birth to hope, aspiration, and ambition, and makes the desert blossom and the waste places glad."[14] As a socialist minister echoed, a redeemed, Christian "brotherhood" encourages equity, not equality. It encourages the "strong to advance the interests of the weak and to recognize the debt which advantage owes to disadvantage."[15] The socialist Episcopal minister William Bayard Hale called the principle of cooperative agriculture "the new obedience" to the cause of worldly self-sacrifice.[16]

From the day of its inception, leaders of the Social Democracy invested heavily in their relationships with Christian Socialist organizations, especially the Society of Christian Socialists (founded 1889), the American Institute of Christian Sociology (founded 1894), and the Brotherhood of the Cooperative Commonwealth (founded early 1897).[17] Each of these organizations had regular contact with leaders and members of labor churches, people's churches, and Christian Socialist fellowships. Party leaders hoped that by speaking the language of Christians unaffiliated with the major denominations, Christians outside the churches would come to adopt socialism as the heart of their faith.

The Society of Christian Socialists, founded by W. D. P. Bliss and Francis Bellamy, committed itself to two simple goals. First, it would spread the gospel of salvation through Jesus Christ to class-conscious socialists, largely in the trade unions and the Socialist Labor Party. It would "show that the aim of socialism is embraced in the aim of Christianity" and encourage its friends, also disenchanted with churches, to join labor churches, people's churches, and other socialist fellowships. Second, it committed to teaching Christians, especially budding ministers in college and seminary, that "the teachings of Jesus Christ lead directly to some form of socialism; that, there-fore, the Church has a definite duty upon this matter, and must, in simple obedience to Christ, apply itself to the realization of the social principles of Christianity."[18] As Bliss regularly explained it, "Christ's yoke means vol-untary self-sacrifice, the application of the golden rule," and that sacrifice should dictate Christians' mode of operating in all economic relationships, too.[19] The fellowship connected a national network of chapters, especially ministers, of all denominations.[20]

Christian Sociologists, who worked in both colleges and settlement houses, believed they were applying the principles of Christian Socialism to the world. The American Institute of Christian Sociology, founded by Richard Ely and George Herron, sought to encourage both sociologists and ministers-in-training to "endeavor to ascertain the truth in regard to the social questions," to "apply the truth practically," and to "present Christ as the living Master and King of men, and his kingdom as the complete ideal of human society, to be realized on earth."[21] Edwin Wheelock's Christian Socialist League in Chicago, for example, carried out this mission through the Chicago School of Social Economy.[22] The Brotherhood of the Cooperative Commonwealth had a mission and constituency that overlapped with these kindred organizations, but its members committed themselves both to uni-versal suffrage and the socialist project of "colonization."[23] Colonization was an old strategy into which late nineteenth century socialists breathed new life. In small, cooperatively owned communities throughout the former Northwest territories and even in the South and the West, members made a statement about the possibility of establishing socialism in the United States. These "colonies" jointly purchased land, produced something profitable, and shared cooperatively in the profits of their work.[24]

At that founding convention, the Social Democracy agreed to two basic organizing methods. It would recruit party members and candidates for public office. And it would build a socialist colony in a western state with the goal of immediate relief for the unemployed. Debs was silent during the debates between what one scholar called the "political-action-only socialists," like Victor Berger, Jesse Cox, and Frederic Heath, and the group of direct-action socialists in the Western Federation of Miners—men who had recently executed strikes in Cripple Creek and Leadville, Colorado. Debs probably saw Christian Socialists, represented at the party level by George Herron, as a third strand of socialist believers who could help ground the party in imagery and ideals. Speaking the language of both the Holiness-Pentecostal movement and the Christian Socialist movement, Debs said that the cooperative settlement would allow workers to "work out their salvation, their redemption and independence . . . break every fetter, rise superior to present environments, and produce a change such as shall challenge the admiration of the world."[25]

Debs affirmed the fundamental Christian Socialist claim that human nature was fundamentally good and could overcome its tendencies toward greed and instead value cooperation. "It is no utopian vision," Debs said of the project for colonization and suffrage in 1897, "but a theory of life and labor in which the humblest individual owns himself and by his labor secures life, liberty and happiness." He was hopeful that unemployed workers seeking justice and a living wage would find peace in cooperative work. The mass of unemployed, he argued, "is enough to make the 'dry bones' Ezekiel saw in his vision stand up and swing their skeleton arms in approval of the crusade" and to apprehend "from the grasp of a soulless plutocracy the sacred shrines of homes despoiled by pirates who build palaces of poor men's skulls and cement them with workingmen's life blood." He compared the Social Democracy party to the star in the East that "the wise men saw when Christ was born," proclaiming, "Peace on earth, goodwill toward men."[26] Debs also appropriated the evangelical strategy of "witnessing," or proving by example, the truth of fundamentally good human nature through the example of successful socialist colonies. Immediately after the convention, newspapers around the country, and especially in mining towns in the West, announced the creation of the Social Democracy party by emphasizing Debs's recruitment of the unemployed. Several newspapers reported that the party received "more than 500 applications for charters" for independent colonies, including a serious consideration of land in Tennessee, Colorado, New York, Washington, and Idaho.[27]

Debs spent much of 1897 in a tour of the West and the South, entreating working-class people to consider the party as their church. By fall, Mary Harris "Mother" Jones became a party organizer among mineworkers. Anarchists Lucy Parsons and Emma Goldman also joined the party.[28] He even sent a letter to John D. Rockefeller in search of financial seed money for this venture in putting the poor to work. "The Social Democracy of America," he told news reporters, "proposes to lead the unemployed away from the unequal, squalid, and crime inciting surroundings of the cities and establish them in a commonwealth where no man will be rich enough to oppress his fellows and no man or woman or child need go hungry, houseless or naked." Rockefeller was investing in many religious charities in the name of poverty relief at the time, and Debs reminded him that eight thousand families were homeless and forty thousand workingmen were starving in Chicago. "The picture is well calculated to appeal to men and angels, and . . . you are a Christian gentleman and widely known for your benefactions," he continued, asking for an investment of money on behalf of the poor.[29]

We have no evidence that Rockefeller sent money, but Debs's description of the project illustrates that he imagined colonization as an effort to build Christian Socialist missions for the poor. As Debs preached on this strategy, he said that his socialist colonies, like the socialist communes of the antebellum era, would have "factories, creameries and flour mills." They would use "labor saving machinery producing enough for the wants of the people and a slight surplus to provide for unfavorable seasons." Thus, he said, "People would not have to work so long" and would still have their basic needs met.[30]

Evangelism and Other Organizing Strategies

In building a party in the union of Christian Socialist ideals and direct action, Debs was rejecting Friedrich Engels's 1880 distinction between "utopian" and "scientific" socialism. Engels characterized "utopian" socialism as "the expression of absolute truth, reason, and justice [that] has only to be discovered to conquer all the world by virtue of its own power." He was referring, of course, to Christian Socialism, particularly as it was expressed in the communalist experiments of the early and mid-nineteenth century.[31] Daniel DeLeon, the "American [Vladimir] Lenin" who saw himself as interlocutor of Marx, stood with Engels and other "scientific" socialists when he said that the Socialist Labor Party (SLP) stood for "the class interests of the proletariat, of the wage slave" and that alone.[32] On the last day of the Social Democracy convention, the SLP, convening in parallel, protested the founding of the Social Democracy by endorsing the *Communist Manifesto* as its set of party principles. DeLeon lampooned the Social Democracy's endorsement of colonization as the "Duodecimo Edition of the New Jerusalem

Known as the Debs Plan," a reference to the Christian Socialist energy behind the movement.[33] Yet many of the most prominent American socialists
aligned themselves with Debs. Neither Frederic Heath nor Victor Berger
loved the idea of colonization, but they affirmed a "gradualist" strategy,
akin to that of the Social Democratic Party in Germany, that focused on
universal suffrage and the winning of elections within the existing parliamentary system. German Social Democrats were gaining in power, and this
strategy appeared promising.[34] Still others, like Laurence Gronlund, author
of *The Cooperative Commonwealth*, were attracted to the party's vision precisely because it rejected Marxist dogmatism. As Gronlund put it, "Class
consciousness' is a fatal German theory . . . unfortunately our brothers of
German origin will never condescend to give way to American characteristics and conditions."[35]

Unfortunately, the majority of publicity that the Social Democracy was
able to generate concerned the establishment of a cooperative settlement for
the unemployed. It is unclear to what extent this enthusiasm represented the
sentiments of the rank and file, but those who made up the self-described
"political action" wing of the party saw themselves as a minority among the
many Christian Socialist delegates to the second annual convention. They
knew that the "masses" who supported Debs were excited by his language of
a new kind of commonwealth. Worried about a populist takeover, the night
before the official convention reconvened, a group of party delegates led by
Victor Berger and Frederic Heath caucused in a nearby hotel and decided
to rename themselves the Social Democratic Party. Berger contended that
many Americans had been duped into the hope of a utopian community
without full knowledge of what a socialist republic entailed. He argued that
despite what other delegates claimed, the party's primary aims were universal
suffrage and the political empowerment of trade unions. Berger was a Jewish
émigré from the Austro-Hungarian Empire with little tolerance for symbolic rhetoric. He held that it was "nonsensical to talk about the 'Socialism'
of Christ and the early Christians." He admitted that the early church may
have practiced primitive communism, but socialism "means a higher civilization by multiplying and making use of all the means of culture of capitalist society."[36] Frederic Heath, a much younger, American-born socialist
in Milwaukee, agreed. He described colonization as "utopian and fantastic,"
an idea that "drew support from gullible people of all classes." This group of
dissidents knew that Debs would forgive them for organizing a competing
party based on a political action strategy. There were not only right, but Debs

soon agreed to join the executive committee of the new Social Democratic Party.[37]

Yet, while Debs was willing to let go of colonization as a primary organizing strategy, he was not willing to sever his ties to the many Christian Socialist ministers and working-class believers he had recruited over the previous several years. In efforts to reconcile this splintering, Debs accepted election to the executive committee of the officially renamed Social Democratic Party of America and agreed that the new party organ would be Berger's Milwaukee paper, the *Social Democratic Herald*. The new party's founding principles were largely the same as those of the Social Democracy, with emphasis on the need for electoral reforms, the "abolition of war" (a reference to US entrance into civil wars in Cuba and the Philippines), and "equal civil and political rights for women and the abolition of all laws discriminating against women." Instead of colonization, the new party would emphasize registering working-class people to vote and securing social democrats in public office.[38]

Debs also continued the Social Democracy's mission to win ministers and other church leaders to the socialist cause. In the fall of 1898, George Herron, Jackson Stitt Wilson, and two Methodist ministers (J. H. Hollingsworth of Frankfort, Indiana, and W. H. Wise of Greencastle, Indiana) launched the Social Crusade, and the magazine the *Social Crusader*, to enlighten clergy with the image of Jesus as a social revolutionary seeking a Kingdom of Heaven on earth.[39] The ministers helped organize a set of cooperatives in Chicago and emphasized the importance of voting, but they connected this socialist vision of citizenship to the "social teachings of Jesus Christ." As Wilson put it, "I have had impressed on my mind that what we need socially and politically is an extension of real socialism among the working classes."[40] Indeed, Debs redefined "real" socialism in the United States. He won almost ninety-five thousand votes for president in 1900 despite tremendous working-class voter suppression, especially in the South. He had created an American coalition for social democracy based in a new concept of American citizenship, and he had done so through explicit efforts to connect with Christian Socialists.

The one group he had not won over were the socialist secularists, especially the large number within the SLP. As the conflict over the founding of the SDP illustrated, an important minority of American socialists saw Debs' unorthodox strategies as destructive to the prospect of socialism in the United States. James Connolly, for example, an Irish American socialist SLP member, warned comrades from his experience in Ireland that religion must remain secondary to cause of socialism.[41] He contended that when the SLP endorsed the principle that religion was "a private matter, and outside the scope of Socialist action," it was not just because this was consistent with the principles of the Second International. Connolly also believed it was a superior strategy, for it left room for freethinkers, agnostics, and Christians to healthily disagree. A "universal, non-sectarian character" was, to Connolly, "indispensable to working-class unity." He believed that religion would "inevitably entangle us in the disputes of the warring sects of the world, and thus lead to the disintegration of the Socialist Party."[42] Connolly argued that socialists should never succumb to the temptation to critique another's national or religious affiliations. Rather, socialists as a group should respond only to political statements. Defending this SLP policy on religion, he said, "We do not mean that its supporters are necessarily materialists in the vulgar, and merely anti-theological, sense of the term, but that they do not base their Socialism upon any interpretation of the language or meaning of Scripture, nor upon the real or beneficent Deity. They as a party neither affirm or deny those things, but leave it to the individual conscience of each member to determine what beliefs on such questions they shall hold." Connolly rejected Debs' vision of a Christian social democratic republic, calling it utopian and premodern. He said that socialism was not "stronger, or its position more impregnable, because of its theological ally," the churches.[43] Debs was not sure about that, but he did know that socialists needed to stop fighting among themselves if they wanted to build a successful social movement.

A "Spiritual Appeal" to an Expanded Voting Base

Over the next few years, the right wing of the SLP ("Kangaroos") began talks with both the Springfield (Massachusetts) and Chicago branches of the Social Democratic Party to consider unification. In 1901, regional delegates met in Indianapolis for a "Unity Convention," renaming the Social Democratic Party the Socialist Party of America, and appointing Eugene Debs as president.[44] George Herron helped instigate the event through his relationships, a detail that indicates the popularity of Christian Socialism among the rank and file, and his hope that the unified party would foreground socialism as a holy mission. Indeed, when Herron took the podium at the unity convention, he spoke like a preacher at the start of a revival. "If we strive with each other upon questions of detail," he entreated, then the Democrats and the two-party system will win. Even worse, he said, "Socialism as a distinct issue will be postponed for a generation." Rather, he continued, "Socialism must pass out of the sectarian stage . . . , into lines that shall win American sympathy, and nobly awaken American labor to that class-consciousness without which we are helpless." For socialism to take root in the United States, he entreated, "The Socialist can no longer neglect what we might call the ethical or spiritual appeal."[45]

Just what that vision looked like would involve long debates over party dogma and strategy. Despite the accusations of their critics, socialists did not discuss marriage, religion, or the abolition of private property at the 1901 convention. Rather, delegates debated the role of trade unions in the movement, the importance of elections, and the extent to which farmers could play a key role in the foundation of a new socialist state. If the "gradualists" favored local strategies of electing socialists to public office and empowering unions, and "radicals" wanted nothing short of the people's ownership of factors of production, the gradualists dominated the party convention by a vote of 5,358 to 1,325.[46] Yet, in a nod to unity, platform language emphasized that the party's list of demands were merely "steps in the overthrow of capital and in the establishment of the Cooperative Commonwealth." Most platform demands carried over from the Social Democracy and the Social Democratic Party.[47] While discussion of colonization waned, the *International Socialist Review*, one unofficial mouthpiece of the party, reminded readers of the compatibility between Christian and socialist beliefs.[48] The party also endorsed a second, unofficial mouthpiece of the party. In 1906, the two weekly newspapers of the Christian Socialist Fellowship combined and moved their offices to the Socialist Democratic Party headquarters in Chicago.[49]

By 1906, the party stood for an expansive welfare state with generous protections for wages and working conditions, and it endorsed the list of progressive electoral reforms that would make it easier to elect socialists to federal offices. Enumerated goals included an increase in share of profits to workers, national and state accident insurance, public grade school education, and equal civil and political rights for men and women. The party encouraged membership in trade unions and considered them essential to the class struggle but also maintained that only "the possession of all the means of production for the benefit of all the people" would truly establish labor justice.[50] Most important, delegates agreed to continue the principle of subsidiarity; state parties would retain the latitude to direct their own affairs. They would pay dues to the National Executive Committee, but elected leaders could set their own agendas and even their own names. Across the country, the Social Democratic Party was known locally as Public Ownership, Union Labor Party, and Socialist Party, with "policies as varied as its names." In the Midwest, socialists would emphasize "municipalization for the benefit of the taxpayer." In the West, they worked closely with farmers, and in California, they worked with trade unions. They agreed that private capital was always the problem, but class consciousness was only one of many strategies for social change.[51]

Above all, party leaders agreed to expand the legal voting base to topple the two-party system and elect socialists to public office. Three African American delegates stood in attendance at the Unity convention: William Costley, a party leader from San Francisco, and coal miners John H. Adams (Brazil, Indiana) and Edward McClay (Richmond, Indiana). Costley led the group in passing the "Negro Resolution," a statement demanding that African American "social and political equality are the effects of the long exploitation of labor power." The party affirmed that African American oppression was a result of capitalism, and therefore they should "invite the negro to membership and fellowship with us in the world movement for economic emancipation by which equal liberty and opportunity shall be secured to every man and fraternity become the order of the world."[52] The "Resolution on Puerto Rico" offered similar support for the political power of people of color. Socialists officially condemned the role of US business leaders in undermining the trade union movement. They resolved to "appeal to the organized workers of Puerto Rico to continue their struggle for the right of organization and the emancipation of labor." Both statements led to broader resolution to "call upon the working classes to use the ballot in defense of their own interests by voting the Socialist ticket."[53]

In championing the voting rights of African Americans and demanding that they deserve public works projects and public infrastructure on par with whites, Debs sought to empower African Americans, even within the limitations of the Jim Crow system. Some white socialists, building upon precedents set by the Knights and the People's Party, imagined building a coalition around the "separation of the black and white races into separate communities, each race to have charge of its own affairs."[54] Debs respected Black separatism, like the separatism of separate socialist federations by nationality, as a vital political strategy that allowed minority groups the space to set their own agenda.[55] But he also recognized that white socialists benefited from the system of white supremacy and were unwilling to recognize African

Americans as equals in the class struggle. For example, in his 1903 essay, "The Negro in the Class Struggle," Debs chastised white supremacists, arguing, "As a socialist party we receive the negro and all other races upon absolutely equal terms. We are the party of the working class, the whole working class, and we will not suffer ourselves to be divided by any specious appeal to race prejudice."[56]

More difficult were the debates about how to organize for this new vision of citizenship. Critics like Karl Kautsky maintained that smallholding farmers were part of a preindustrial economy that would always offer a conservative counterweight to industrial wage slaves. As he put it, "In this country the love of title deeds to homes is inbred among the people." Landowners, no matter how poor, could not grasp "class consciousness" on par with those whose labor power was systematically stolen.[57] Yet agrarian socialists like Algie Simons argued it was foolish to presume that America's foremost producers would not make good socialists. In *The American Farmer* (1902), Simons argued that tenant farmers were already in the process of leaving cash-crop agriculture for cooperative agriculture. Moreover, the bulk of American land, including "millions of acres of the most fertile land in America [that] still lie untouched by the plow," was under public ownership and "awaiting the time when adequate irrigation works can be constructed" to make it profitable to homesteaders. As states invested in public works for irrigation, tenant farmers would continue to leave agribusiness and make cooperative agriculture the future.[58] While Simons did not convince all his comrades, the party agreed on a plan to send Christian Socialist ministers and organizers to the South.

Throughout Debs's tour of the South in 1903, he reinforced the platform argument that both white and Black sharecroppers were "farmers" and deserved access to a robust public infrastructure.[59] As the California Christian Socialist Clarence Meily explained, the Socialist Party stood for "absolute economic equality for white and black, covering perfect uniformity not only in opportunities for labor, but also in all those public services, such as education, transportation (including, let it be added, hotel accommodations), entertainment, etc., which may be collectively rendered, together with complete recognition of political rights." He said these demands "must be insisted on more strenuously by the socialist than ever they could have been by any abolitionist agitator."[60] Meily described socialists' goal as a "reconstructed society" wherein "the practice of brotherhood" is no longer "limited by race or nationality or sex or faith."[61]

William Noyes and Oscar Edgar pushed the party to take a stand on public education for African Americans and antiracist education for whites.[62] While the *International Socialist Review* published an article or two by people who defended the color line because they feared "miscegenation," it followed these articles with critical responses.[63] Debs joined African American comrades in reminding his audiences that miscegenation was not a terrible outcome and was also not a foregone conclusion.[64] In 1904, the *International Socialist Review* offered a glowing endorsement of W. E. B. Du Bois's *The Souls of Black Folk* (1903), a book of essays on the function of racism within American Christianity. The reviewer gushed that "when the history of the black race is written, [Du Bois] will rank infinitely above [Booker T. Washington,] the instrument of capitalism who is perfecting black wage slaves at Tuskegee."[65]

Several historians have correctly observed that the party's efforts to court Black voters were minimal in comparison to the work that was necessary to build a viable interracial agrarian socialist movement in the South.[66] Early twentieth-century white socialists largely joined their white European comrades in believing the Marxist dictum that the race problem would be addressed in the "labor problem." Debs' statement in 1903 that the Socialist Party was "absolutely free from color prejudice" and that "not a trace of it will remain in the so-called black belt of the Southern states" was, at best, aspirational. Debs was naive in his presumption that the color line would fade away through the socialist movement. Debs's efforts to silence arguments about race with broad statements ("The Negro is not one whit worse off than thousands of white slaves who throng the same labor market to sell their labor power to the same industrial masters") stemmed from a combination of ignorance and dogmatism on matters of race. These statements often only served to exacerbate class segmentation based in race.[67] African Americans were much more heavily targeted by white elites for talk about both labor organizing and voting. But, in many parts of the country, the party did continually seek partnerships with African American groups, like ethnic societies, in defining the shape of the movement.[68]

Several socialist parties, including those in Georgia, Alabama, and Tennessee, stated their opposition to poll taxes and Black disfranchisement in their platforms. The party won wide support within working-class Black communities, including endorsements from *The Broad Ax* (Chicago), *The Bee* (Washington, DC), and the *Voice of the Negro* (Atlanta).[69] In New Mexico, a Mexican, Mexican American, and Indigenous socialist rank and file not only opposed Jim Crow laws but also officially condemned "native domination and control," a reference to white oppression of Native Americans through the reservation system and the system of federally required boarding schools.[70] In Southwestern cities and mining towns, these socialists started their own federations that became official partners with the Socialist Party in 1910. Within this Debsian Christian Socialist, orbit W. E. B. Du Bois, Charles Edward Russell, Mary White Ovington, William English Walling, and Anna Strunsky came together to extend class analysis, name the system of white supremacy, and create the National Negro Committee, a group that soon renamed itself the National Association for the Advancement of Colored People in 1909.[71]

The Socialist Party invested in similar efforts to court women voters, a group that was only enfranchised in a handful of western states in 1901. Frances Willard, founder of the Woman's Christian Temperance Union (WCTU) in 1874, spent her lifetime imagining a new kind of polity wherein women could participate as equals in the home, in churches, and in the public sphere. Under her leadership, the WCTU helped Christian women find their voice politically and spiritually.[72] Yet after Willard's death, when the WCTU refocused on human trafficking and the rehabilitation of sex workers, Debs reached out to the first generation of temperance activists and claimed Willard's work for socialism. In one pamphlet, the party reprinted Willard's support for the ideas "that the corporation of humanity should control all production," and that this approach to life "eliminates the motives for a selfish life" and "enacts into our every-day life the ethics of Christ's gospel . . . nothing else will bring the glad day of universal brotherhood."[73] Several state socialist parties, including that in New Mexico, aligned themselves with Christian temperance work, urging socialists to "refrain from the use of alcoholic and narcotic drinks and drugs, that we may retain our intellectual, physical, and moral manhood and womanhood, to the end that we may more successfully cope with the capitalist class and a more just and sane system of government and industry."[74]

These efforts to cultivate a membership among those who could not legally vote would play a significant role in shifting cultural attitudes about both race and gender. May Wood Simons, wife of Socialist Party leader Algie Simons, emphasized the parallels between the oppression of women and other disempowered groups in her classic pamphlet, *Woman and the Social Problem* (1899). She acknowledged that other parties rarely spent their time or money on women voters, presuming that "woman has no power in politics." Yet, she maintained, women's unpaid domestic work had long served as the foundation for capital accumulation. Socialism, as a political philosophy, "recognizes the full significance of equal suffrage for men and women. It sees that a large body in society, politically powerless and politically ignorant, who yet exercise a wide influence, will in time become a dangerous factor." While the "capitalist class would restrict the right of the ballot as far as possible," including the suppression of white and Black tenant farmers through "property and educational qualifications," socialists dignified the value of these vital contributions to the economy.[75]

Socialists' partnership with advocates of both universal suffrage and temperance gained the Socialist Party a substantial following in both the Midwest and the South. The party sponsored dozens of aspiring women preachers as organizers. Mary Kules left five years of ministry as a settlement worker in Pittsburgh to become a traveling speaker for social democracy, temperance, women's rights, and the end to child labor.[76] In her book, *The Religion of a Socialist*, she grieved for the fact that churches were receding from the center of society because of their failure to address the needs of the poor. She also lamented the patriotic nationalism that ministers placed ahead of Christian community. When party leader Oscar Ameringer quipped, "If a modern preacher repeated the utterances of the Lord on the land question before a congregation of Christian landlords, he would most likely lose his job," he was hardly exaggerating. Many ministers faced discipline for preaching on the compatibility of Christianity and socialism.[77]

Kules saw her organizing work for the Socialist Party as an extension of her Christian ministry. As she reflected, "In each of our cities are great, fine churches, representing millions invested, but empty and dark most of the week and not any too well filled on Sunday." Poor people were cheated when they were told to be satisfied with "coarsest food, with unhealthy tenements, with shabby clothes . . . cheap furniture and bare walls." Socialism offered God's promise of the abundant life.[78] Kules joined Kate Richards O'Hare, Caroline Lowe, Winnie Sherley Branstetter, Mary Wood Simons, and dozens more as stump speakers for the rights of women, sharecroppers, and tenant farmers to collectively benefit from the privileges of citizenship and make a more Christian nation.[79]

Planting a New Kind of Church

While the National Executive Committee, the small group of officers that steered the national party, never included a majority of Christian Socialists, it appears likely that Christian Socialists swelled the rank and file. The

Socialist Party recruited dozens of ministers and former ministers to serve as organizers and shepherds to the party's rank and file. Socialists not only helped incite the working-class rebellion against "Churchianity" but hoped their local, elected officials would take the place of formal church leaders to become the moral compass of the nation's political economy. By 1908, most Christian Socialists had moved beyond George Herron's early vision Christian theocracy and embraced a version of cultural and religious pluralism.

The popularity of the Christian Socialist Fellowship (CSF) grew precipitously after its relocation to party headquarters in 1906. By 1908, it had more than twenty-five chapters, three hundred ministers, and more than five hundred thousand subscribers to the *Christian Socialist*. Ostensibly still independent of the party—a strategy to keep from alienating non-Christians—the fellowship officially endorsed the Socialist Party of America as the engine that would "end the class struggles by establishing industrial democracy and . . . hasten the reign of justice and brotherhood upon earth."[80] Fellowship members stood for changes to the polity "in order that men may live the Christian life," equal with others in "privileges, opportunities" and the governing of their affairs.[81] They also enumerated the importance of "the operation and distribution of production by the people and for the people." As the historian Jacob Dorn emphasized, the CSF was not entirely committed to socialist ecclesiology. Some members of the fellowship believed that the only way one could be a Christian was through the practice of socialism, but others were agnostic on that point. These people, whom Dorn called "socialist Christians," simply sought to illuminate that one could be a socialist and Christian simultaneously.[82] What is important is that the CSF saw itself as a big tent which welcomed both socialist Christians and Christian Socialists. Publications reveal that members imagined the socialist movement as a moral community, knit together by the principles of universal suffrage, collective bargaining, economic cooperatives, and a social safety net. Debs's fleet of stump speakers, including ministers like Rev. George Washington Woodbey, Fr. Tom Hagerty, Fr. Tom McGrady, and Rev. Mila Tupper Maynard, illustrate the reach of socialist organizing within the nascent moral and spiritual communities of the working classes.

George Washington Woodbey, born enslaved in Tennessee, was ordained a Baptist minister in Kansas in 1874 and became an early member of Bliss's CSF. Woodbey regularly discussed the tenets of socialism within his church, in the columns of the *Christian Recorder* and *AME Church Review* (organs of the African Methodist Episcopal Church), and on a broad lecture circuit for the Socialist Party in the South. In Woodbey's 1903 pamphlet, *The Bible and Socialism: A Conversation between Two Preachers,* he argued that the Bible "opposes both rent, interest and profits, and exploiting the poor," and thus "stands just where the Socialists do."[83] In his *Why the Negro Should Vote the Socialist Ticket,* he emphasized the fact that "socialism means the collective ownership of the mines, factories, shops, railroads" and that the party fought harder than any other against Black disfranchisement.[84] While many Black Social Gospelers, including Booker T. Washington, internalized the classism of white church and condescended to Black socialists as undereducated theologically, Woodbey trained a network of Black socialist preachers within the AME tradition.[85]

Father Thomas McGrady, a Catholic priest assigned to Bellevue, Kentucky, affiliated himself with George Herron and his societies from the early days of the Social Democracy, and preached on how socialism provided the conditions to engage in true Christian worship. Like his fellow Protestants, he frequently invoked medieval church fathers to rebuff claims that Christianity and socialism were incompatible.[86] He lectured for the Boston School of Political Economy as a socialist and spoke widely about socialism and Catholicism among Irish, German, Italian, and Polish Catholic workers along the East Coast. McGrady's pamphlet *Socialism and the Labor Question* offered a critical engagement with *Rerum Novarum,* holding that the pope neither understood the aims of socialism nor fully grasped the dangers of an open shop. Catholics in the hierarchy condemned this critique as insubordination, and McGrady resigned from the priesthood in 1902 to dedicate himself to Socialist Party work. But he maintained that he could practice his faith better as a socialist organizer than as a priest and would defend Catholic beliefs and rituals within both the Socialist Party and the IWW.[87] When McGrady died prematurely at the age of forty-four, Eugene Debs praised McGrady's "conviction that the orthodox pulpit and the forum of freedom were irreconcilable."[88] In his honor, sympathetic Catholic priests formed the secret Catholic Socialist Fellowship, an underground group that is likely to have influenced the Catholic leadership of the next generation, including Edward Gibbons, Edward McGlynn, John O'Grady, and John Ryan. Of course, it was secret because the Roman Catholic Church still officially condemned socialism, but it was growing because many Catholics disagreed.[89]

Thomas Hagerty, a Catholic priest assigned to work in New Mexico, often dedicated his books to the memory of McGrady. He toured the mining camps throughout the West and Southwest, preaching in English and Spanish on workers' rights to collective bargaining and to free speech. He formally withdrew from the priesthood after 1903 to become a full-time organizer, settling in Van Buren, Arkansas, and working with Ameringer on the vision of agrarian socialism. Yet Hagerty, as a Catholic, differed with Herron on the meaning of "religion." While Herron saw politics as an expression of faith, Hagerty saw the two as independent of one another. Hence, when church leaders claimed that the pope had rejected socialism, Hagerty claimed that "socialism has no more to do with religion than astronomy or biology." That said, Hagerty hoped that an American social democracy would "abolish profit, usury, interest and rent, . . . and it would throw open the earth and the fullness thereof to every son of Adam who is willing to work for the comforts and joys of life in unison with the cosmic efforts of humanity."[90] He authored the preamble to the *Constitution of the Industrial Workers of the World* (1905), the famous Wobbly founding document. The strength of socialist unions in New Mexico, Arizona and West Texas were probably related to his mentoring.[91]

Finally, Mila Tupper Maynard was a socialist, feminist, Unitarian minister who ran the First Unitarian Church in La Porte, Indiana, before marrying and moving West to preach the socialist gospel. After a brief stint as copastors with her husband in a Unitarian Church in Salt Lake City, the Maynards moved to Denver, where they became members of Myron Reed's Broadway Temple, also known as Denver People's Church. Mila served as associate editor of the socialist *Rocky Mountain News*, worked as a freelance writer and speaker, and was an active member of Denver's Socialist Party. Her soapbox speech, "Socialism the Hope of Religion" celebrated socialism as the fulfillment of Christian thought and helped stump for Eugene Debs. She also spoke widely about women's suffrage.[92]

Debs reappropriated the evangelistic crusade, a classic tool of both church planting and nation-building, to spread the message of collective bargaining, public utilities, public works, social insurance, and racial equality. He also reimagined the public sphere. While Dwight Moody was segregating his revivals, Debs refused to speak to segregated audiences. Many of his organizers who were ministers spoke in revival meetings or open forums that ran adjacent to meetings of local trade unions. Broadsides advertised public forums on topics like "Prisoners, Paupers, Prostitutes and Parasites,"

"Women under Socialism," and "Is Socialism Opposed to the Teachings of Christ?"[93] For those interested in further reading, the party distributed pamphlets by these speakers and others, including *Socialism: What It Is and How to Get It* (Ameringer), *What the Socialists Want* (Woodbey), *Why the Negro Should Vote the Socialist Ticket* (Woodbey), and *The Spiritual Significance of Socialism* (John Spargo).[94]

Building on the strength of his organizers, between September 1909 and the summer of 1910, Debs worked with E. E. Carr from the CSF on a national crusade to create a secret "Ministers Socialist Fellowship" in each state. After all, most denominational leaders still held socialism as a heresy. It was important to Debs to protect these ministers from losing their jobs so they could continue to plant socialist ideas within church networks. As Debs explained the investment to secular comrades, "I believe in being tolerant of other people's beliefs." That was a strong statement in an organization whose leadership was dominated by secular Jewish and free-thinking socialists, including Morris Hillquit and Victor Berger. But Debs knew that many ministers genuinely supported a cooperative commonwealth and felt constrained by the antisocialist positions of their denominations. He also knew that churches were natural spaces to discuss the problems of the profit system, the value of direct action, and the importance of municipal socialism. As he framed this to his secular colleagues, Debs emphasized that churches offered "new channels which the regular socialist propagandists do not reach."[95]

Around the country, newspapers reported on John Long's "secret" crusade to inculcate socialist ideas among ministers. Charles Kerr published *Socialist Songs with Music* (1901), including many socialist hymns.[96] Long was a Presbyterian minister in New York City, member of the CSF, and believer that "Christianity will not work under a competitive system."[97] He collected more than 120 signatures in the New York area, and planned to launch an International Socialist Educational Alliance, presumably in concert with the socialist Sunday School movement, within the coming years.[98] In Texas, "160 ministers of practically every denomination" signed on to the agreement to "show that socialism is the economic expression of the religious life; to end the class struggle by establishing industrial democracy, and to hasten the reign of justice and brotherhood on earth." These men and women agreed to emphasize the "economic teachings of the Scriptures" and affirmed that the "covetousness" that characterizes the "profit system" "makes the ethical life as inculcated by religion impracticable."[99] Debs knew that the success of the socialist movement would depend on the relaxation of tensions with American clergy, and he was right.

The Church of Social Democracy

Hence, the coalition that became the Socialist Party built directly on the infrastructure laid by the groundswell of Christian Socialists in the Gilded Age. Working-class Christians had rebelled against the procapitalist churches of the Gilded Age and reimagined Jesus's ministry, the meaning of "church," and the possibilities of human cooperation within a Christian commonwealth. Though Debs was not himself a churchgoer and the party welcomed members of a variety of cultural and religious backgrounds, he made constant efforts to connect with Christian Socialist ministers in building the Socialist Party of America. Though he did not advocate for any singular definition of Christian citizenship or Christian nationhood, he endeavored to reimagine socialism in the United States around a moral community that practiced the principles of equality, cooperation, and seeking the common good.

By 1908, with the help of the CSF, the Socialist Party had come to rely heavily on ministers and former ministers as organizers. This was not only because ministers could extend the reach of socialism farther than the tools of trade unions alone, or because ministers had often proven socialists' most eloquent spokespeople. All this was true, but Debs saw ministers as allies who could inspire Americans to think about socialism as a set of moral ideals. In funding the expansion of the CSF with national party funds, Debs urged Americans to rethink the applications of Christian doctrine to the realms of politics and economics. In contrast to the SLP, Debs imagined the Socialist Party of America as a different kind of socialist coalition, one that celebrated farmers, women, African Americans, and ministers in the rural locations where they worked and worshiped. The party invested heavily in using the voting power of disfranchised people to establish a cooperative commonwealth.

These efforts came with considerable risk. The SLP rivaled the Socialist Party in local and national elections and vehemently opposed Christian Socialism. Daniel DeLeon literally announced in 1908 that "Christian Socialists, who deny the class struggle," should be prohibited from participating in the Second International, the international convention of the working classes. DeLeon believed that in their "special" appeals to religion and race, Debsian socialists refused to acknowledge the class struggle as the only meaningful social movement worth fighting.[100] As it turned out, conflicts with the SLP would last throughout the twentieth century. But Debs wanted to create a different kind of socialist movement, one that developed alliances between the disenfranchised and the enfranchised middling classes to build public infrastructure within cities and towns, one locality at a time. By 1912, Debs' Socialist Party had elected twenty-one state legislators, mayors in thirty-four cities, and alderman in ninety-eight cities.[101] Christian Socialists' vision of a Cooperative Commonwealth, built in collectively owned utilities, was already coming to fruition.

That said, the nation was also experiencing significant demographic change. The proportion of European immigrants to native-born industrial workers was growing quickly. Some members worried that the CSF offered an old-fashioned, sectarian and exclusionary vision of socialism that resonated too much of white, rural, and evangelical America. They worried that the Socialist Party of America was overreliant on relationships with ministers. Several prominent socialists spoke out that wherever evangelical Christian ethics were officially endorsed, they would detract from potential partnerships with European immigrants, their range of religious traditions, and their competing sensibilities about the connections among faith, justice, and democracy. As party leaders caucused about how to capitalize on their expanding membership, some wondered if a Christian moral vision had a place in an international socialist movement. The rebellion against the churches had made the Socialist Party into a viable national party. But would organized Christianity survive the industrial era? The party had to decide whether it was worth going to battle for a new Christian praxis, or whether the Christian faith as Americans had known it was already on its way out.

4

Christian Socialists and the Socialist Party

In the summer of 1912, as the presidential election season was coming into full swing, Frederick Guy Strickland, editor the *Miami Valley Socialist* in Dayton, Ohio, challenged the Presbyterian minister and principal of the local high school for the Congressional seat in his Ohio district. The socialist editor asked his opponent, the Reverend Dr. Maysilles, to a public debate on whether socialism was "practicable," or possible, within the strictures and traditions of the American republic. Overflowing crowds gathered in a school auditorium on a hot August night to hear the two spar. Strickland opened the debate with the argument that socialism represented the "New Spiritual Awakening." Society, he said, was moving past the epoch of submissiveness to the "spiritual police force of the reigning order." "Real salvation," he argued, does not require a church. Rather, it asks followers "to lose one's life" in pursuit of the good of others. Strickland maintained that the mark of a Christian society was an economic arrangement in which the "machinery of production and distribution [is] socially owned so that all may be employed and each worker paid according to the labor performed." The crowd, presumably including a sizeable number of Christians, roared in approval.

And yet, when Strickland returned to his seat and the Presbyterian minister took the podium, the mood quickly changed. Maysilles dramatically raised the red flag (of International Workers) alongside the Stars and Stripes and stood for a moment in silence. Then he somberly argued, both as a minister and a public servant, that Christianity could not exist without a well-ordered accountability structure. Socialists, despite claims to the contrary, answered not to God but to international authorities who opposed "the home, public school, and religion."[1]

Between 1908 and 1916, it seemed inevitable to many American Christians that the future would behold some version of a cooperative commonwealth. The only question was the proper role of churches, and the rank and file, within this coming social revolution. More than a million voters elected socialists to public office, establishing municipal governments with public utilities and public works programs that paid overmarket wages. Meanwhile,

The Gospel of Church. Janine Giordano Drake, Oxford University Press. © Oxford University Press 2024.
DOI: 10.1093/oso/9780197614303.003.0005

the bulk of the party's rank and file, including women, African Americans, and immigrants, often did not have the right to vote. Party members read socialist publications, paid dues, and participated in religious and socialist revivals. They were represented at the national level by regional delegates. However, while the party thrived because of its decentralized network of churches, locals, revivals, and print culture, these multiple socialist networks continually bumped up against the elected leadership of the party's National Executive Committee. Party leaders had to decide to what extent they would directly address the demands of the rank and file, especially the power structures underlying race, gender, nationality, sexuality, and religion, within their national platform. The Socialist Labor Party maintained its position that disciplined silence on these questions would neutralize battles with religious authorities. By 1912, Socialist Party officials at the national level agreed; they supported the strict separation of church and state. However, in conceding to this strategy, overruling the rank and file, and imagining socialist politics as a category distinct from social questions, socialists hobbled their own efforts to build a social democratic alternative to the reign of Churchianity.

The Future of American Christianity

By 1908, there was no question that socialism was threatening world-wide Christianity as the dominant expression of justice and morality. The Reformed German minister Herman Kutter spelled it out most succinctly in *They Must; or God and the Social Democracy: A Frank Word to Christian Men and Women*, which Rufus Weeks of the Christian Socialist Fellowship translated into English in 1908. Kutter argued, "The Kingdom of God proclaimed by Jesus, and the Co-operative Commonwealth foreseen and willed by the Socialists, are one and the same. . . . God knows no distinction between internal and external questions—questions of piety and questions of economics."[2] Christians, he said, should carry out the gospel message by creating a political economy built on justice and equality. Richard Heath, the British socialist cleric, echoed these sentiments. He said that socialism was "the modern version of Christ's Christianity, separated from all theology, all clericalism, all public worship, and from the very idea of a Church." It was serving as a "new universal religion which has sprung up in moribund Christendom."[3] By 1910, Heath brought Kutter's essays to a British audience with his own preface. Heath wrote, "Social Democracy . . . is as essentially as religious as Christianity itself."[4]

It did not take long for American Protestant ministers to observe this conversation and express their concern. "Socialism," the Black Unitarian minister Bertrand Thompson wrote in 1908, "has become a distinct substitute" for the church. After all, he said, "Its organizations usually meet on Sunday, that being the only day of leisure its adherents usually have. It has regularly organized Sunday-schools, in which the children are instructed, by the most approved methods of lesson leaves and catechism, in the fundamental principles of the economic creed. Evenings at the socialist clubs have taken the place of the old church meetings." In Thompson's view, there were several types of socialists, including "atheistic" folks who only saw the world in material terms, and "Christian Socialists," who believed in voluntary cooperation within economics and politics, but all of them threatened Christian institutions through their claims to moral leadership of the working classes.[5]

Thompson correctly observed that many Christian Socialists sat on the boundary between the church and the movement, regularly discussing the proper relationship between faith and social democracy and debating who was more trustworthy to carry out the mission of Christ in the world. The socialist theologian Walter Rauschenbusch, who moved in both socialist and ecclesiastical circles, was conflicted himself. His *Christianity and the Social Crisis* (1907) continued the Gilded Age conversation on the problems of "economic individualism." He pushed further, declaring this individualism a "social sin" and holding that it was the responsibility of churches to "redeem" or rectify this structural oppression. Rauschenbusch's book sold more than fifty thousand copies between 1907 and 1909 and had a deep impact on pastoral training across the Protestant denominations.[6]

However, Rauschenbusch equivocated on whether churches or the labor movement should lead in the efforts to rectify the problems with capitalism. On one hand, he encouraged church members to support the "social movement," a vague term for the labor, reform, and socialist movements. He was a Socialist Party member and friend to Eugene Debs. Rufus Weeks, head of the Christian Socialist Fellowship, saw him as an ally and distributed his books as testaments to the value of socialism. Rauschenbusch warned readers that church leaders "must not attempt to control and monopolize [social movements] for [their] own organization." For "If a man wants to give honest help, he must fill himself with the spirit of Jesus and divest himself of the ecclesiastical point of view." His book can be read as an explicit encouragement for socialist goals.[7] On the other hand, Rauschenbusch emphasized that the primary reason Christians should support the "social movement" was to ensure the posterity of their own churches. Just like his colleague Josiah Strong, he warned that "working people will pass from indifference [to the churches] to hostility, from religious enthusiasm to anti-religious bitterness," and churches would lose all relevance in modern society if they could not cultivate good relationships with the wage-earning population. His book equally argued that the sharp European declines in church attendance should be taken as a "warning" to American churches to "avert the desolation that threatens us."[8]

Rauschenbusch was part of the large group of church leaders who had been developing relationships with the Socialist Party for the previous decade and wondered whether they should simply throw their support behind the leadership of the Socialist Party or galvanize a parallel movement with its own spiritual and political goals. In his 1912 theology dissertation, Clarence Andrew Young, Presbyterian pastor in Philadelphia, openly questioned whether churches were vestigial organs of primitive Christian societies or institutions worth rehabilitating.[9] It almost seems wild for a minister of a prominent, wealthy urban church to question whether that church has a purpose, and then to have their dissertation on the topic published. But the socialist challenge to "Churchianity" was really that effective in changing the national conversation on the future of churches. In 1908, Debs himself addressed a group of ministers with the reflection, "I'm glad I can call you ministers of the man of Galilee my comrades, for it isn't long ago that I felt a great prejudice against you as a class."[10]

This national conversation that made Rauschenbusch's book into a bestseller preoccupied a whole generation of young Christian social reformers, including Kate Richards O'Hare, A. J. Muste, Arturo Giovannitti, Harry Ward, Charles Stelzle, Mary Kules, and Worth Tippy. W. D. P. Bliss found that 753 out of a surveyed 1,012 of the nation's social reformers identified as churchgoers.[11] Even though many would find themselves taking sides against one another over the next decade, all their memoirs point to this moment around 1912 as a time of personal trial. All had studied theology, Christian Sociology, and economics in college or divinity school, but during these years felt conflicted between working in ministry as ministers—especially within settlement houses or working-class churches—and working toward political action in concert with the labor movement. Rufus Weeks, editor of the *Christian Socialist* and head of the Christian Socialist Fellowship within the Socialist Party, catered to this national conversation with a large catalog of books. He printed an array of tracts for Christian Socialism, including George Haw's *Christianity and the Working Classes*, George Strobell's *A Christian View of Socialism*, and his own *The Socialism of Jesus*, but also classics by orthodox Protestant theologians like Rauschenbusch. The eclectic list suggests that he believed churches might be preserved in the coming social democracy, but they would have to allow themselves to be reimagined, refocused, and transformed by the needs of the working classes.

Some socialists found it easy to take a position in this national conversation; they would project all their energy into Christian social reform. Ministers and aspiring ministers were running for public office, and winning, on the platform that they were doing better ministry as public officials than they would as church leaders. Jackson Stitt Wilson (Berkeley, California), George Lunn (Schenectady) and Myron Reed (Denver) all began their careers as ministers within Christian Socialist churches before they became mayors of their cities.[12] As Frederick Strickland of Dayton, Ohio, explained the goals of socialists, "We do not deny the Gospel; we proclaim it. We do not abolish the church; we will capture the church, the called-out. We do not deny the Christ. . . . The morally satisfied are the greatest obstacle to the prophet who comes to establish a new world order."[13]

The national socialist papers, including the *National Rip-Saw, Miami Valley Socialist, Appeal to Reason, Chicago Daybook, Christian Socialist*, and *International Socialist Review* underlined this argument that socialists were more trustworthy Christian leaders than many religious officials.[14] Kate Richards O'Hare wrote *Church and the Social Problem* (1911) to explain why she felt comfortable, as a Christian, leaving the church behind to build a Christian community through the socialist movement. Everywhere, she said, church folks asked the question: "Why is the church, as an institution, losing its hold and influence on the lives of the people?" Her answer was simple: socialists did a better job practicing the principles of the faith than churchgoing Christians. She said she yearned for the day when, through the vehicle of the socialist movement, land would be more equitably shared, "race prejudice and hatred [would] melt away," usury and the abuse of women were abolished, and the socialist republic could grow on a Christian foundation. She believed that the church's "blindness to the economic need, its subservience to wealth . . . signed its own death warrant and struck its own death-knell."[15] The fact that these conversations took place within Socialist Party publications indicates that many participants in this conversation considered spiritual guidance from an alternative set of Christian authorities and hoped to reimagine Christianity within the framework of social democracy.

Churches Respond

Vincenzo Pecci, the eighty-one-year-old Pope Leo XIII, had witnessed tremendous social and political change in his lifetime, but he was not crazy to argue that socialism posed the greatest threat to the church in the history of Christianity. His *Rerum Novarum* (1892) drew upon the earlier work of Heinrich Pesch, the German Catholic ethicist and economist, who argued that it was a Christian value to support "solidarity" with the poor, even if that solidarity did not come through radical socialist parties. Leo said the church stood for all efforts to protect collective bargaining, end child labor, establish a living wage, and ensure Sabbath rest. Responding to the Gilded Age rebellion against Churchianity, he chastised "men of greed who use human beings as mere instruments for money-making." Yet Leo explained that his main problem with socialism was that it projected the mirage of satiation while endangering the "soul for lack of spiritual food."[16] In simple terms, the reasons Leo did not support socialism had as much to do with theology as with his fears that socialists would find so much satiation in the material world—especially through a robust welfare state—that it would foreclose the need for churches.

Since there was no such thing as an American Catholic church "hierarchy" to convey the pope's message, it took many years for this encyclical to make its way to ordinary Catholics in North America. The continent hosted more than a dozen "national parishes" in North America, largely offshoots of European national churches, which had long supported parishioners' work in building voluntary associations that supported mutual aide. As the pope moved to consolidate these national parishes under an American, effectively an Irish American, hierarchy, regional archbishops hoped to use this new authority structure to make bolder statements on the "heresy" of socialism. They hoped that a new, more centralized structure for Roman Catholicism in the US would "Americanize" Catholics and illustrate their civic and social respectability to white Protestants.[17] During the process known as Americanization, a few bishops dramatically removed socialist-leaning priests to show off their power.[18] But these public acts of church discipline also lost the hierarchy credibility, especially among the many immigrant

Italians, Poles, Mexicans, Germans, and Eastern European Catholics whose national churches allowed for harmony between the principles of municipal socialism and the dictates of the encyclical *Rerum Novarum*.[19] The Western Federation of Miners, Industrial Workers of the World, and United Federation of Miners counted a large fraction of Catholic immigrants and all supported some form of social democracy. In fact, IWW locals, founded after 1905, soon functioned as yet another set of cultural centers for discussion and debate on the principles of Christian justice.[20]

Josiah Strong and Shailer Matthews, emerging leaders of the "Social Gospel" in the United States, refrained from attributing their ideas to Pope Leo but held a very similar position on the heresy of socialism. While they admitted that many labor organizations only wanted to improve working conditions and supported these goals, they critiqued Christian Socialists for wanting to glorify the present world instead of the world to come.[21] Matthews went so far as to claim that Jesus was primarily a spiritual leader and endorsed no political or economic theories. He took a strong side against the Socialist Party in *Church and the Changing Order* (1907), which claimed that "Christianity seems more capable of producing permanent social betterment than does socialism." But the fact that this wealthy divinity school professor considered the question reminds us who had control of the national conversation.[22]

Municipal Socialism in American Cities

In 1908, when the Socialist Party inaugurated what the Wisconsin socialist legislator Carl Thompson called "municipal socialism," Walter Rauschenbusch cheered the trend as a constructive effort to establish the "Kingdom of God" on earth.[23] This plan, akin to Liebknecht's vision for the German Social Democratic Party and the Fabians' vision of the British Labour Party, sought to use state and local offices to create publicly owned corporations and public works projects through the power of state and local governments (Table 4.1).[24] A cover story of the *International Socialist Review* contrasted it with the work of syndicalists as "The New Socialism."[25] Socialists called for publicly owned streetcar systems, waterworks, elevated and subway systems, gas and electric lines, bridges, hospitals, schools, parks, parkways, bathhouses, railways, ferries, and telegraph lines. They argued for these measures in terms that made sense to Christian capitalists who cared

Table 4.1 Minimum Wages and Hours for Common Laborers in American Cities [1907] Public and Private Enterprises

City	Municipal		Private	
	Wage	Hours	Wage	Hours
Syracuse	$1.50	8	$1.50	10
Detroit	1.75	8	1.80	9
Allegheny	2.75	8	1.75	10
Wheeling	1.85	8–9	1.85	10
Cleveland	1.76	8	1.75	10
Indianapolis	1.60	8	1.75	10
New Haven	1.50	8	1.50	9
Richmond	2.00	9	1.20	9
Atlanta	1.00	10	1.00	10
Average	$1.77	8½	$1.56	9¾

Source: Carl Thompson, *The Constructive Plan of Socialism* (Milwaukee: Social-Democratic Publishing Company, 1908), 23.

about the poor. As the argument went, "public enterprises" delivered more value to the community at a lower cost, for the public servants who worked in the municipalities could earn old-age pensions and qualify for sick benefits and accident insurance through a large, public investment in mutual aid. Cutting out the "middleman" of private ownership also allowed workers to take home more salary and work shorter days.[26] Christian Socialist minister Edward Devine described municipal socialism as "The New View of Charity." A social safety net, he explained, served the poor who rarely had the "surplus savings, or energy" to invest in vital infrastructure.[27]

This emphasis on local infrastructure was wildly popular in working-class cities like Butte (Montana), Flint (Michigan), Schenectady (New York), Berkeley (California), and Milwaukee, most of which lacked substantial charitable investments in private entities to enable working-class social mobility.[28] The socialist focus on local elections dodged some of the notorious machine politics that crushed third-party candidates at the state and national levels, and enabled candidates opportunities to address antisocialist critiques by naming specific ways they could enact the dictates of the "brotherhood of man." As one socialist explained it in the pages of the *National Rip-Saw*, an agrarian socialist newspaper that year, "I am a Socialist because I believe in the rational doctrines of Jesus Christ, and believe that all men were created equal, and believing such I refuse to permit any man to consign me to an everlasting damnation simply because I will not permit him to make of me a SLAVE for the benefit of one who wants to pray upon my energies."[29] Socialists maintained that their faith in municipal socialism did not constitute a rejection of churches or of Christianity, but an affirmation of their belief in the possibility of Christian cooperation.

Municipal socialism built upon the moral communities which the Socialist Party had built over the previous decade and became the expression of Christianity that rose above "Churchianity." One political scientist, surveying political shifts between 1908 and 1910, totaled 16 socialist state representatives, three city commissioners, twenty-eight mayors, and 167 city trustees (Figure 4.1). He also noted sixty-two socialist school officials, sixty-five elected leaders in law enforcement, and thirteen county assessors.[30] In the same years, an estimated 300 socialists were elected to municipal offices in England, 400 in Denmark, 1,268 in Italy, 100 in France, and 39 to the cantonal council of Zurich, Switzerland.[31] Socialist voters, of course, were only a small fraction of the party membership, as a large fraction were disfranchised due to voting restrictions. Nevertheless, the elections reveal that large numbers of middle-class Protestants were reading Walter Rauschenbusch's *Christianity and the Social Crisis* and taking a stand against "monopolies" and "starvation wages" as Christians.[32] Whether they called themselves socialists or not, these voters supported the expansion of publicly owned utilities, labor reforms, and public works projects. Even in the towns and cities where socialists did not declare victory, such as the coal and oil fields of Pennsylvania, Kansas, Illinois, Louisiana, and Oklahoma, socialists won at least 20 percent of the vote for congressional seats.[33] However, because socialism was gaining so much popularity among the middling classes with power, money, and influence, party executives sometimes lost track of the priorities among their base.

The Swelling Rank and File

The truth was that the immigrant and landless working classes—those who often lacked the right to vote because of their race, class, or immigration status—were the party's most faithful contributors and party loyalists. Whether or not this was explicitly stated, racial and gender egalitarianism

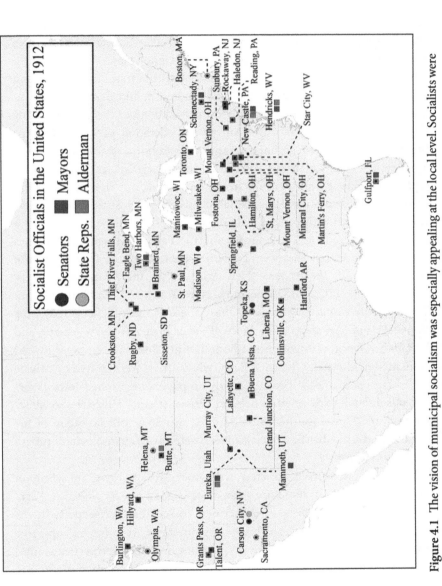

Figure 4.1 The vision of municipal socialism was especially appealing at the local level. Socialists were elected to city, county and state offices across the country.

was becoming the implicit foundation of organizing campaigns, and the very promise of "social democracy" was shifting the conversation in American politics. It was not simply that party locals, trade unions, and ethnic mutual aid societies were moving in to fill the void left by churches. Socialists, with the support of socialist theologians like Walter Rauschenbusch, were redefining the moral authority structure of the United States.

In the mining and factory towns that dotted the mountain ranges and major river systems, German, Irish, Italian, Polish, and Eastern European immigrants and their children formed the backbone of the growing trade union movement. By 1906, the American Federation of Labor counted fifty full-time, salaried organizers, and an additional thirteen volunteer organizers.[34] Many of these volunteers were socialists and syndicalists, hoping to organize a strong trade union movement, but also to "bore from within" to produce a more radical labor movement.[35] Socialist organizers worked in concert with a continually expanding print culture. By 1916, there were three hundred English-language Socialist Party newspaper affiliates nationwide (Figure 4.2). They went by names like *Cooperative Commonwealth* (South Dakota), *The Masses* (New York City), the *Christian Socialist* (Chicago), *The Citizen* (Schenectady, New York), the *California Social-Democrat*, the *Hamilton Socialist* (Ohio), the *Iconoclast* (Schenectady), the *People's Friend* (Arkansas), *The Voice of Labor* (Camden, New Jersey), and the *Labor Advocate* (Providence, Rhode Island). Some papers were owned and edited by the state's Socialist Party, while others were owned by private publishing companies.[36] Because nearly all papers mentioned Jesus favorably, it is difficult to distinguish between "socialist" and "Christian Socialist" publications. Again, the *Christian Socialist* was an unofficial organ of the Socialist Party, so Christian Socialist ideas were always, if unofficially, part of the party platform.

The more workers interacted with socialist and syndicalist union organizers and their literature, the more signed up as Socialist Party members, IWW members, or subscribers to socialist newspapers. In the rural West, farming and ranching conglomerates were buying up large parcels of land and its accompanying livestock in attempts to vertically integrate the meat production industry. With the help of Mexican migrants and mechanization, large-scale cotton production was shifting westward.[37] As an increasing number of western whites failed at the mythical homesteading ideal and found themselves working for wages as cowboys and farmhands, they, too, came to believe in the goals of social democracy.[38] Socialism had

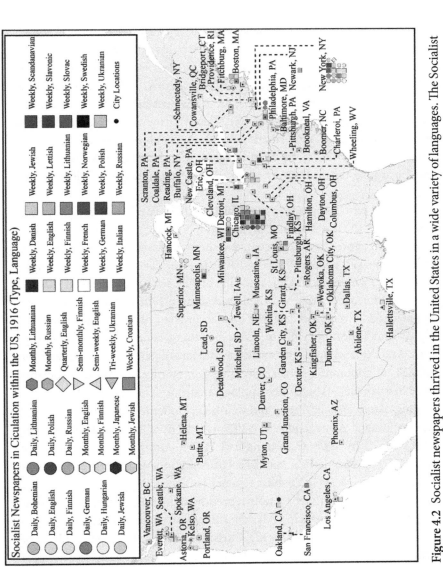

Figure 4.2 Socialist newspapers thrived in the United States in a wide variety of languages. The Socialist Party of America exerted no editorial privileges over these many other papers, but they did keep track of their circulation rates and count them as part of the larger socialist movement in the United States.

clearly taken off as a social movement, and it owed a great deal to the pre-vious decade's work in organizing within the churches.

Oscar Ameringer, a socialist organizer stationed in Pennsylvania, Arkansas, and Oklahoma, preached a message of Christianity and agrarian socialism that gained the party more than twice as many dues-paying members in Oklahoma as any other state.[39] In this former Indian territory, recently opened for white tenantry, many farmers were taking mortgages and supplemental wage jobs to keep their farms. When they rebuffed Ameringer's social democratic pitch about the possibility of collective agri-culture, Ameringer famously quipped, "Many farmers have landlord heads on farmhand bodies." Yet farmers' woes went from bad to worse, and many families who aspired to be homesteaders found themselves losing their land, becoming tenant farmers, and losing voting rights to prohibitive poll taxes.[40]

Socialism had tremendous popularity within rural America. Between 1890 and 1910, the number of farms operated by tenants grew from 26 percent to more than 38 percent, and the average mortgage debt per farm increased by 111 percent.[41] Using Christian Socialist imagery, Ameringer argued that farmers should reject the life of debt service and instead join the movement for cooperatively owned land, also known as agrarian socialism. He preached, "Even God declared himself in favor of the common owner-ship of land," quoting Leviticus, "You are strangers and sojourners on this earth. And the land shall not be sold forever, for the land is mine." Ameringer shepherded a vibrant Christian Socialist community that melded socialist and Christian beliefs into a cosmology that one scholar described as the "coming of universal harmony and well-being under the reign of Christ only after standing at Armageddon to battle with an oppressive and wicked cap-italist class."[42] By 1908, Oklahoma had 21,779 dues-paying Socialist Party members, and they led the nation in contributions to the national party's treasury (Figure 4.3).[43] Oklahoma voters sent several socialists to the state legislature, and Ameringer proudly represented this large contingent of what he called "200,000 renters in Oklahoma" at national party meetings.

Thanks to the early work of the Christian Socialist Fellowship, ideals of agrarian Christian Socialism were also popular in Texas and New Mexico. Ameringer and Hugh Moore founded the Tenant Farmer's Union in Texas and made *The Rebel* (Hallettsville, Texas) its official organ. The paper cele-brated the possibility of collective agriculture and maintained a weekly "Five

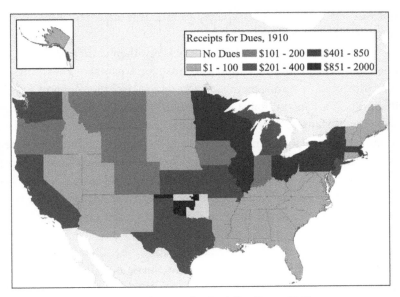

Figure 4.3 Dues-paying members to the Socialist Party, 1910

Minute Sermon" that offered biblical insights on land justice and the errors of "capitalist preachers" who misled their flock.[44] The paper also encouraged solidarity across the color line, demanding voting rights and equal pay for all farmers regardless of their color. As editors framed the political grid-lock in 1913, poll tax laws "disfranchise the white working man" in a pro-portion of "about five to one. . . . only one adult out of 17½ can vote."[45] At its height, the English-language paper commanded a weekly readership of twenty-two thousand subscribers and directly fed into Texas Socialist Party membership.[46]

In cities, labor churches served as both community centers and party vehicles. The United People's Church in Pittsburgh, Pennsylvania, founded by William Prosser in 1914 with the support of the local readers of the (Pittsburgh) *Christian Socialist*, started with 85 members and grew to 228 by the end of the first year. The church constitution declared agreement in the universal "Fatherhood of God" and "Brotherhood of Man," including the equality of the sexes. Church members also agreed to "the establishment of the Kingdom of God and His justice on earth by destroying the profit system, educating and organizing the people, preaching true catholicity and

righteousness and practicing charity to all." This statement was likely repeated aloud like other creeds.[47]

A growing body of labor church members saw their churches as tools, akin
to newspapers and socialist Sunday schools, for organizing a working-class
population of faith. As one member wrote on behalf of the People's Church in
Pittsburgh, "Our Institution stands out as *the one* truly socialist institution;
it is known locally as 'The Socialist Church,' and has gone far to silencing
the opposition to socialism because of [socialism's] reputation for being
atheistic." From the start, the Pittsburgh church made plans to be replicated
around the country. Even though it called itself an "undenominational" body
striving for the "democratization and socialization of society," other bodies
of socialist believers could apply to it for "recognition and affiliation" as a
"congregation."[48]

Bouck White's New York City congregation, the Church of the Social
Revolution, was also fundamentally a labor church, even as it leaned more in
the direction of freethinkers and secularism. White argued that the "ritual-
istic and priestly strain" of interpreting Jesus's life, death, and atonement was
"in great part a fictitious interpolation." He envisioned his modern version
of Christianity as the religion of the socialist movement, for both worked toward the establishment of an "ethical empire."[49] In his book about his church,
White argued, "Socialism is a religion or it is nothing." To Jews, he entreated
that dogma on the messiah was unnecessary; "spiritualized socialism" ful-
filled all ancient prophecies about the coming Messiah.[50] White declared,
"For the creeds, we give the Carpenter, cornerstone of romance and divine
adventure. For war, we give the pure, the gracious, the plentiful arts of peace.
And God, Friend of Freedom, shall be prince forever."[51]

In the Southwest, large numbers of Mexican American socialists signed
up with the party. The Texas state party officially stood for the abolition
of the poll tax and universal adult suffrage, but many Mexican Americans
expected more from a labor organization and worked to make that the
case with the Socialist Party.[52] El Partido Liberal Mexicano, the Western
Federation of Miners, and the IWW all maintained support for cooperative
enterprise. The French-born Catholic archbishop Peter Bourgade of Santa
Fe, who apparently bristled at the emergent Irish American authority structure of the Catholic hierarchy, also supported the labor movement. He said
that *Rerum Novarum* "authorized" the power of unions and the tool of strikes
as work actions. He said that the pope opposed socialist *governments*, but

not collective action.[53] Thomas Hagerty, the former Catholic priest, built on this foundation in his organizing work for the Socialist Party and later the IWW in the Southwest. He cooperated with the state party's goal of forming Spanish-speaking branches and mutual aid societies, including the Federal Labor Union in Laredo, Texas. One historian found that Mexican American socialists' newspapers often "served notice of an impending socialist millennium."[54]

Of course, Mexican American support for the Socialist Party was not only a product of Christian Socialist organizing.[55] Spanish-language newspapers in the Southwest frequently noted that the Socialist Party was a pragmatic choice for other reasons. Even though socialists could not win every election, voting with the party signaled opposition to both the Republican and Democratic Parties, neither of which took seriously Mexican American concerns. New Mexico's Socialist Party selected the well-respected Mexican American physician T. C. Rivera of Chamita, New Mexico, as its candidate for governor in 1912. As he defended his platform, Rivera connected socialism to the histories of unfree laborers in both the United States and Mexico. "The price of living keeps going up," he said in Spanish, while the margin of profit for tenant farmers keeps going down. "Nothing in our history, apart from the abolition of slavery, can compare to [the hope offered by the Socialist Party]." Rivera claimed that socialism offered freedom for "seventy million people," the whole of the United States.[56]

One party official in *The Rebel* estimated that in 1915, the Socialist Party had about one thousand Mexican American members in Texas alone. Both Texas and New Mexico had socialist parties controlled by whites, who sometimes dismissed Chicano unions' wage disputes.[57] In New Mexico, Fernando Baudox formally repudiated his connections with socialists when he said that their "fraternity . . . consists in the slavery of all those who are independent. . . . Fortunately for me, I have now realized that socialism is the most sectarian of all tyrannies."[58] It is likely this failure of stronger interracial solidarity that caused organizer Tom Hagerty to leave the Socialist Party for the IWW. Nevertheless, just as socialists hoped to "bore from within" the AFL, African Americans, Mexican Americans and other people of color similarly attempted to bore from within the Socialist Party. Unfortunately, their work would consistently face opposition from the white men in the leadership of the national party, who denied that race, gender, and nationality operated under their own structures of oppression.

The Race Question

By 1908, as the Great Migration made Black Americans a larger fraction of Northern urban life and the industrial workforce, every left-leaning organization had to address the "race question." Historically, the Socialist Party had supported full citizenship and bargaining rights for African Americans, and Black ministers around the country had celebrated the party as a vehicle of Christian change. Black socialists George Washington Woodbey, Charles Vail, Reverdy Ransom, George W. Slater, and George Frazier Miller enthusiastically participated in Debs' ministers crusade by emphasizing the principles of cooperative production, Black self-sufficiency, and Black nationalism.[59] Reverdy Ransom explained in 1908 that he backed the Socialist Party because of its support for public works and public utilities. He said, "The poor whites and blacks hate each other because they are fighting for each others' little morsel of bread instead of working together to produce more bread."[60] George Slater emphasized the party's support for Black "emancipation" and "self help," and presumed, like Ameringer, that socialist collective agriculture would include African Americans.[61] He suggested that the party create a permanent bureau, like the Women's Bureau and the many ethnic federations, to focus on organizing African Americans and represent their demands to the party.[62]

Yet many white socialists, especially in the South, not only maintained deep-seated contempt for social equality but patronized Southern Baptist churches that claimed segregation was God ordained.[63] Debs refused to speak before segregated crowds, but the party hosted segregated locals in a few states.[64] The *National Rip-Saw*, a socialist newspaper dedicated to the possibility of collective agriculture in the South edited by Kate Richards O'Hare, offered little challenge to Southern Baptist ideals on race and gender. She essentially supported the idea of outreach to African Americans but advocated for the Black colonization into "one section of the country where every condition is best fitted for them." She, not unlike some Black Social Gospel leaders, could not imagine integrated collective agriculture or industry. As O'Hare explained it in her ironically titled pamphlet *N****r Equality* (1912), she wanted to see the extension of racial apartheid within "the factory, workshop, mines, [and] cotton field" and believed that white occupation of "Black" jobs was the tragic result of the social leveling created by capitalism.[65] O'Hare won more than eleven thousand votes in her effort to become Debs's vice presidential running mate in 1916, a sign that while her intolerance for social equality and desegregation was never official policy, her positions were popular.[66] National party leadership left a great deal of latitude to state and local organizers, and decentralization papered over major internal fissures.

Nevertheless, by 1910, propertyless Americans, including immigrants, African Americans, tenant farmers, and farm laborers, comprised the bulk of the party's rank and file, and the white "municipal socialists" at the national office were only beginning to grapple with this reality.[67] When Morris Hillquit, Victor Berger, Ernest Unterman, and Robert Hunter proposed echoing the language of the AFL and advocating for immigration restriction and against collective agriculture, party delegates from the South and West opposed those measures. They contended that international economic migrants, like African Americans, were legitimate members of the international working classes. Joseph Cannon (Arizona) explained that socialists needed to offer more critique for national borders and recognize economic migrants from Mexico, China, Korea, and Japan as legitimate members of the international working classes. As he explained, "We have the Mexican peon escaping across the line. Am I going to send him back across the line? No; I am going to try to lift him as high as I am myself and perhaps higher. The Mexican peon is a convict. So was Jesus Christ; so was Eugene V. Debs."[68] W. P. Collins, delegate from Colorado, agreed: "I can go into an audience of 500 people, black and white, and I can get a bigger percentage of converts to Socialism among the black men than among the white men. I have been there and I know it's true." Collins observed that Japanese immigrants were not unlike Russian immigrants in their willingness to take whatever work they could get. He affirmed, "I do not see that it would help them any to land them back in their own country, where capitalism will use them and then dump their products on American soil, to compete with American labor." While an earlier vote on the possibility of collective agriculture failed, the resolution to restrict immigration also failed.[69] Debs affirmed his support for an "international, revolutionary Socialism" that did not fall prey to nationalist politics.[70]

Later in the same meeting, party delegates also addressed the question of their relationship to what they called "foreign language federations," the Finnish, French, German, Italian, Lettish, Lithuanian, South Slavic, Scandinavian, Polish, Slovak, Jewish (Yiddish), South Slavic, Hungarian, Bohemian, and other national socialist organizations whose immigrants in the United States operated their own newspapers, printing presses, mutual aid societies, and fund-raising projects for socialist movements and mutual aid in their home countries. The *Jewish Daily Forward* alone commanded two hundred thousand subscribers.[71] Many of these federations, like the Jewish Socialist Club, predated Debs' Socialist Party, and had for years met on equal terms with the SLP at meetings of the Second International. As each of these federations swelled with members, Debs' party came to recognize the need to establish official partnerships with each of these organizations.

Yet the more American socialists recognized themselves as part and parcel of an international movement that welcomed people of other races, cultures and creeds as equals, the more they confirmed the suspicions of conservative Protestant and Catholic clergy. Socialists were functioning as competing moral authorities over the poor and immigrant working classes, not only through their platform priorities, but also through their examples of social democracy in practice.

The Gender Question

Nowhere was their assault on traditional white Christian authority structures more evident than in party statements and policies that demanded that women and men were social and economic equals. By 1915, there were more women subscribers to the *Progressive Woman* than total subscribers to any other socialist newspaper, including the *International Socialist Review*.[72] White women had spent the previous decade attending college, preaching and teaching on Scripture, traveling independently, managing offices, and voting in state and local elections in the West. Recognizing the importance of gender equality from the start, the party had bankrolled the creation of the *Socialist Woman* in 1907 as a newspaper dedicated to the rights of workingwomen to equal pay, opportunities in the trades, education, and voting rights. The following year, it created a Woman's National Committee (WNC), comprising five woman delegates elected by the entire membership.[73] In 1910, the WNC established a Women's Bureau, designed to compete with wealthy women for workingwomen's attention in every state. As May Wood-Simons explained the decision, "We cannot speak of the class struggle from the platform of the suffrage association. You cannot wipe away the class struggle among women and say it is just a beautiful sisterhood."[74] As the number of workingwomen suffragettes rose dramatically, the *Progressive Woman* challenged suffragettes to consider how much they supported the thriving of women in waged and unwaged domestic work.[75]

State-level bureaus opened leadership and writing opportunities for young, socialist suffragettes in every state. Many were like Lilith Martin, born in rural Dublin, Indiana. At the age of twenty-six, she served as the head of the Women's Bureau for the Indiana Socialist Party and supervised the collection of between three thousand and five thousand signatures from residents of Indiana to support women's suffrage. Martin supervised organizers Rosa Lenhert, a mother of thirty-five with kids ages four and six, and Florence Wattles, daughter of Wallace Wattles, a Methodist minister and protégé of George Herron. Wallace was a Christian Socialist writer, and Florence carried on his work, traveling widely to register the wives and daughters of industrial workers with the Socialist Party. She was invited to speak at the state convention of the United Mine Workers in 1915 and there secured a "unanimous resolution favoring state and national woman suffrage from the 1,600 delegates," a sizable fraction of miners in the state.[76]

In part, party silence on matters of sexuality stemmed from socialists' quiet competition with syndicalists and anarchists. In radical communities like Greenwich Village, sexual libertinism was part and parcel of liberation from the straitjacket of capitalist culture. Emma Goldman, a socialist anarchist, spoke openly about the importance of birth control to building social equality.[77] As Lawrence Langner, New York theater impresario put it, "As you clutched your feminine partner and led her through the crowded dance floor, . . . you felt you were doing something for the progress of humanity, as well as for yourself, and, in some cases, for her."[78] Radical Floyd Dell suggested that love without marriage was superior to love within marriage, for "One's sexual impulses were indulged, not impulsively or at random, but in the light of some well-considered social theory."[79] As one historian explained, libertines "linked sexual repression to the spiritual barrenness of middle-class society, its conventions and artificialities. They hoped to destroy 'polite society' and thereby recapture a sensuality purportedly lost in a materialistic age."[80]

Most Socialist Party leaders, in large part catering to conservative Catholic and Protestant distaste for sexual libertinism, went out of their way to distance themselves from any suggestion that they supported sexual revolution.[81] The *Progressive Woman* ran articles that emphasized how socialism would redeem the oppression of housework and childcare but assured readers that the movement would not bring about the end of cherished maternal relationships with children. Kate Richards O'Hare, working in Southern Baptist country, said it was difficult to tease apart the "specific oppression of women and children from the general oppression of the working class," but "monogamic marriage has not been given a fair test." While she lamented men's ownership of both women's bodies and their labor, she hoped to fix the problem of "women's work" through household machinery. "The common ownership and cooperative management of the means of production will give to the future homemaker access to the scientific lore of the age," she explained, and "make labor a joy."[82] As "social consciousness" continued to develop, she hoped to establish women as equal partners with men and thus eliminate the poverty that forced women to suffer from domestic violence and oppression.[83] O'Hare was a lightning rod. For some white women, particularly in the South and West, she represented just the right amount of conservative Christian morality and women's liberation. For others, O'Hare was a racist zealot whose strong following indicated everything that was wrong with the rural socialist movement.

By 1908, "modernist" libertines and traditional socialist feminists went to battle over socialist feminism.[84] In the pages of *Progressive Woman* and *Appeal to Reason*, O'Hare, Josephine Conger, and Meta Stern Lilienthal tried to reassure readers that they were the real socialists. As Lilienthal explained, "The only home that Socialism will destroy is the home as a workshop. The only family that Socialism will break up is the family founded on the economic dependence of women."[85] Many stood on the sentiments of socialist feminist Charlotte Perkins Gilman, whose *Herland* celebrated the capacity of women to achieve what they set their minds on. O'Hare said, "A few generations of free women will produce a race free from sensuality, and that old falsehood of the male's greater need of sexual expression, and its natural weight, a double standard of morals, will cease to carry weight."[86] Lilienthal underlined the high value of motherhood in the cooperative commonwealth, explaining "socialism will set love free by removing the sex relation from all economic considerations and placing it upon the high pedestal of idealism where it properly belongs."[87] In their private lives, many of these socialist feminists enjoyed significant intellectual and financial independence from their partners, so it is difficult to determine why their organizing work so underemphasized the sexual revolution that would result from equal power-sharing within society and the home. The Woman's Christian Temperance Union had built a powerful movement around the idea of preserving women's dignity, and it appears that social democratic feminists found this the path of least resistance amid regular attacks on socialists' irreverence toward the sacred institutions of church and family.[88]

The Religion Question

Religion was always intertwined with discussions of race, gender, and internationalism. But to party leaders, taking a position on these cultural matters would only spark a culture war they did not think they could win. At the party's 1908 convention, Morris Hillquit asked delegates to consider following the many European examples and the example of the Socialist Labor Party and officially state in the party platform that religion was a "private matter." Hillquit hoped that the statement would neutralize antisocialist campaigns on socialist "heresies," "atheism," and sexual libertinism, redirecting attention to socialists' most popular talking points. He wanted to make it clear that socialists' vision for social change mainly comprised support for municipal socialism, universal suffrage, a social safety night, and collective bargaining rights. In Ireland and Germany, similar declarations had helped build class solidarity. Yet what Hillquit probably did not realize is how his suggested language also affirmed a separation of "religion" from class, gender, racial, and sexual ethics, a statement that many of his own party members would understand as an attack on the tenets of their socialist beliefs.

As the convention debate unraveled, most delegates agreed it was prudent to leave out the statement. Many of the party's most effective organizers, including Oscar Ameringer, George Washington Woodbey, and Kate Richards O'Hare, spoke the language of American evangelicalism. They relied on the freedom to declare that socialism was really a Christian movement for redemption of the cultural and political sphere. However, in agreeing to leave out the statement that religion was "private," the party also failed to formulate an alternative statement that articulated what socialists stood *for* in their simmering culture war with the churches. That is, while church leaders insisted on their authority to make moral claims regarding family and community, party leaders failed to formulate any cogent counterargument on the relationship between socialism and the promise of gender, sexual, and racial equality. Party leaders seriously misjudged the cultural transformation that the socialist rank and file were demanding.

Convention delegates were quick to recognize that socialists offered an alternative set of Christian moralities from those espoused in most churches.

Emil Herman, a German-born lumber worker, farmer, and baker who had lived in Arkansas, Kansas, and Washington, suggested that the party state publicly their opposition to Churchianity, or formal "Christianity."[89] He said, "Christianity is organized in the church, and that is the only kind that we have the right to recognize." The church, he said, does not stand with the working classes. He continued,

> Where does John Pierpont Morgan stand when he goes before the country and says that Socialism would destroy religion, that Socialism would destroy the home; I ask you, has he been excommunicated from the church? Is not the Catholic Church a Christian institution? The church is the organized expression of Christianity and they are opposed to us, the wage working class; they are lined up with the capitalist class and are fighting with the capitalist class, helping them to keep in slavery the proletariat of the United States and of the world.

Herman convinced many convention moderates, including Victor Berger, that this point was one socialists should agree upon. Berger was a charter member of the Socialist Party of America and a Jew who spent much of his political life in immigrant Milwaukee. "Now, the church is with the capitalist class," Berger agreed, "without doubt, especially the Roman Catholic Church. That church has always sided with the class in power. That church was with feudalism as long as feudalism was in power." Berger echoed Frederick Engels and thought he was merely stating the facts.

But, as most Christian Socialists defined "church," this statement was patently false. The next to take the podium was Mila Tupper Maynard, a forty-four-year-old female Unitarian minister who had pastored large churches in La Porte (Indiana), Grand Rapids (Michigan), Reno (Nevada), and Salt Lake City (Utah). Most recently, she pastored at the People's Temple in Denver, a Christian Socialist congregation. She wrote for several Denver newspapers and "lectured continuously," especially for women's suffrage. "Comrades," she declared at the 1908 convention, "are we really anxious to have working class solidarity by the revolutionary victory, or are we anxious to air our special theories of religion or intolerance?" She interpreted any declaration suggesting religion was irrelevant as an act of intolerance against the many socialist ministers, suffragists, and others who saw the Party leading a transformative cultural movement. She held that a statement against religion alienated her and her constituents and undermined the foundation for socialist organizing in many parts of the country. She believed the party needed to make it clear to potential new members that socialists were opposed to *organized, institutional* Christianities that condoned capitalism, but friendly to the growing majority of Christians outside of any major denominational umbrella.[90]

Delegates E. J. Brown and Algie Martin Simons struggled to find common ground so that potential Christian "converts" to socialism were not turned away. These overtures are suggestive of the number of Christian Socialists estimated to be part of the rank and file. Brown, a Seattle dentist, suggested a statement that clarified that socialism would not destroy the practice of true Christianity.[91] Simons, editor of the Chicago *Worker's Call*, suggested a line that would oppose institutional churches for the role they played in the capitalist superstructure, but not in their moral and spiritual sense. Simons, like Maynard, had the full-time occupation of advocating for socialism among a population of Christian workers. He suggested that socialists publicly recognize the extent to which Christianity had animated the lives of working people throughout history with the line, "A religion which has survived savagery and barbarism and feudalism and well through capitalism is not going to die tomorrow." He hoped the statement would affirm socialists' lack of interest in destroying Christianity, but even that statement was controversial.

A few delegates pushed the party to go in the other direction and declare that one cannot practice Christianity without accepting the tenets of socialism. After Maynard announced that she believed in the "cosmic significance of Socialism," another delegate echoed, "I have a right to believe in the existence of a heaven or a God. I am as good Socialist, so far as I am concerned, as I can be." Delegate Brown declared that "a person almost necessarily [must] be a Socialist in order to be a real Christian in spirit." He argued that the party took a great risk in refusing to address the religious authorities who attacked them. He warned, "I serve notice on you that whether you do take it up or not, you will have organized religion to meet. Please note that if we dodge this issue today, it will come up at another time."[92] Brown was not wrong.

Yet while most delegates could agree that the major religious institutions in the United States were crumbling and the movement for social democracy was taking its place, they disagreed about how to address this. Reverend Eliot White, a member of the Church Socialist League, the Episcopal alliance of clergy and laypeople dedicated to "social revolution" in both society and the churches, argued from the podium of the party convention that "Christianity is up against the biggest crisis it has ever faced . . . it is in [the greatest] danger of going to pieces as a formal institution, that it has ever been in. I am perfectly frank to say to you that Christianity as some Christians understand it today is bound to go under, has got to go down."[93] Edward Devine of Ohio, another delegate who was also a minister, agreed. He said that he wanted to "be in a position to harmonize things" for Catholics who wanted to be Christians and socialists at the same time. He explained, "I recognize that the church has taken a position against the Socialist Party. I know of a comrade in the factory who was refused absolution because he was a Socialist." Devine begged delegates not to declare religion either private or irrelevant, but to officially institute religious freedom in the party platform.[94]

This was a persuasive argument. Hillquit commanded great applause when he prodded his German comrades with a smile, "If you want a party of free thinkers only, I can tell you right now how many you are going to have. If you want to wait, with our cooperative commonwealth, until you have made a majority of the people into free thinkers, I am afraid you are going to have to wait a long time." His comment indicated a gentle resignation to the popularity of Catholic and Protestant religious beliefs within the party. But Hillquit did not recognize what the party had to do to accommodate religious socialists on their own terms. He went on, "I ask not my fellow workman whether he is an agnostic or a Catholic or a Protestant or a Presbyterian or a Jew. I am simply to ask him whether he is a Socialist." The minutes note applause again, but the applause and agreement to drop the discussion muted any further discussions on social questions.[95]

Conclusion

By the mid-1910s, the Socialist Party had built a substantial social movement with more than a million voting members and another several million working-class supporters who had no right to vote. Yet, in their hopes of consolidating their party strategy, national leaders marginalized many of the women, immigrants, and members of color at the party's base. Their disciplined silence on "social" questions was intended as an act of resistance against the Christian white supremacy, patriarchy, nationalism, and anti-Semitism that dominated political discourse. White men, Jews, and Christians alike, stood together to demand discussions on economic power independent from debates on what Jesus intended for the church or how God regarded questions of race and gender. They wanted, more than anything, to build public social services separate from those offered by any religious institutions. However, in the act of inventing a socialist politics independent from social and ecclesiastical questions, the white male socialists at the leadership of the party conceded to Protestant and Catholic clergy the right to define both Christian orthodoxy and the purpose of the church.

Essentially, by refusing to give language to the Christian Socialist principles that mattered to a large fraction of their rank and file, the executive committee of the Socialist Party added evidence to the public accusation that the socialist movement had no respect for Christian principles. This decision pushed the many Christian Socialists who sat on the boundary between support for the church and the movement in the direction of creating an independent, church-based social movement. Hillquit's statement, "The Socialist movement is primarily an economic and political movement. It is not concerned with the institutions of marriage or religion," even while it was not officially ratified, constructed a new, secular socialism that hobbled the party's efforts to build a robust social movement. Ironically, the secularist statement opened space for well-resourced ministers to claim that they were right all along. Socialists, they said, denied the existence of God, had no social conscience, and had no clear plan for instituting Christian justice, either at home or abroad. Threatened by the large number of Christians who appeared to mingle freely with Jews and freethinkers, aimlessly practicing their faith outside of church, both Protestant and Catholic clergy invented their own social gospel.

5

Socialism and the Limits
of American Protestantism

Charles Stelzle, a German immigrant and union machinist, shared with Josiah Strong a love for church statistics. He read Henry Carroll's books on the 1890 and 1906 religion censuses with great care and would spend decades turning Carroll's analysis into flashy infographics for preaching and church fund-raising.[1] But more importantly, he shared Strong's conviction that American churches were in danger of dissolving or being replaced within the coming socialist revolution.[2] Stelzle left his job on the shop floor in his early twenties to pursue ministry training at Moody Bible Institute in Chicago, and there met theologians and ministers like Strong and Moody who confirmed his suspicions. His first pastoral job was with a Presbyterian church in St. Louis that catered to the large, wage-earning German American population. A man after Strong's heart, Stelzle claimed to have the "biggest Sunday School west of the Mississippi River" and sponsored regular summer tent meetings. "It was a real people's church," he recalled, "and I was glad to be its pastor."[3]

The term "people's church" generally meant something else, of course. It referred to a socialist church in rebellion against the denominational churches of the wealthy. But Stelzle believed that his congregation incorporated all the best elements of a labor church, while it also had the virtue of orthodox Christian theologies on economics and ecclesiology. He grew his congregation so quickly that in 1901, Strong encouraged him to join the Presbyterian Board of Home Missions as the inaugural Director of Church and Labor, a post Stelzle held for the next nine years. As a nationally syndicated authority on what he called "social and religious conditions," Stelzle would both design and analyze social surveys within poor immigrant communities, as well as write regular columns for labor newspapers that encouraged those workers to join denominational, Protestant churches.

It was not simply that this emerging cohort of ordained ministers—men like Strong and Stelzle—considered socialism a Christian heresy. But Stelzle

The Gospel of Church. Janine Giordano Drake, Oxford University Press. © Oxford University Press 2024.
DOI: 10.1093/oso/9780197614303.003.0006

was fundamentally jealous that American socialists had appropriated the concept of Christian missions from the churches. As the young pastor observed, members of socialist locals got up at 5:00 a.m. every Sunday morning and placed socialist literature on the doorsteps of all the workingmen in their assigned district, including literature in a variety of European languages. In their meetings, everyone present shared "how they had been converted to Socialism," and "Practically every man present testified that he had been first attracted by something that he had read." He was especially fascinated with the fact that young people were graduating from Christian colleges to work as socialist "missionar[ies]" and "tell[ing] the working people in their [assigned] city that their economic salvation was in Socialism and Socialism alone."[4] Stelzle was determined to cultivate this kind of zeal for the orthodox churches, and over the next decade he would find himself tremendously successful.

Between 1908 and 1916, the very years that socialism was at its height in American politics and popular culture, Stelzle and Strong spearheaded the formation of the Federal Council of Churches, a union of thirty-three of the largest Protestant denominations, which they coaxed to come together as a single unit to collect data and speak on behalf of American Protestantism. Through this organization, formed for the ostensible purpose of "Social Service," or ministries for the poor, the team planned and executed a number of antisocialist, evangelistic, and direct mail campaigns aimed at workers. First and most famous among these was the Men and Religion Forward movement (MRFM, 1911–1912), cosponsored by the American Federation of Labor.

Through this combination of an evangelistic crusade, revival, social survey, and union-building campaign, Stelzle and the team he built accomplished several goals. They collected a massive amount of data on working people, including their names and addresses and their attitudes toward socialism and the churches, in the more than three hundred cities they visited across North America. They also built relationships with Protestant church leaders in every major city, forming the infrastructure for state-, city-, and county-level "federations" of orthodox Protestant church leaders. These state and city councils of churches would come to think of themselves as a single unit and follow up with wage-earning families within their own evangelistic campaigns long after Stelzle's revival was over.

But perhaps most importantly, through the data Stelzle's team collected and communities they built, Stelzle set up the Federal Council of Churches as the nation's public authority on orthodox Protestantism. With the backing of thirty-three denominations and several million members, the Federal Council of Churches' statements on the heresy of socialism, the proper mission of a church, and the need for modest labor reforms held gravitas that rivaled the that of the Christian Socialist Fellowship (CSF) within the Socialist Party. When Stelzle and his ministerial team claimed that the best way to support workers was through a modest improvement in wages and working conditions and more robust church-based ministries for working people—not socialist reforms—middling-class whites paid attention. Stelzle constructed a small group of white, male, Anglo-Saxon Protestants as the voice of orthodox American Christianity and effectively argued that socialist critiques of capitalism were outside the boundaries of the faith.

Imagining a Unified Protestantism

The idea of interchurch partnerships among Protestant denominations was nothing new to the twentieth century. The Businessmen's Revival of 1857–1858, an antebellum evangelistic revival, had invited white men of all denominations to leave their desks during the noon hour and pray with other men against the seduction of "Mammon." After the Civil War, Protestant denominations came together again in "Religious Reconstruction," work that included evangelistic campaigns by figures like Dwight Moody and Frances Willard, the distribution of aid, and the building churches, hospitals, and schools, especially in the South. In print culture, too, Protestants of various denominations began to think together about matters of Christian morality and justice. The interdenominational Christian magazine that began as the *Christian Union* in 1870 changed its name to *The Outlook* in 1893, reflecting the continuation of cross-regional, middle-class, white, Protestant discussions on matters of culture and politics.

The ordained clergy of the Protestant denominations were becoming increasingly aware of what Henry Carroll called the "phenomenal" growth of independent evangelical churches, the rising numbers of Christian Socialists, freethinkers, skeptics, and atheists, and the deluge of traveling evangelists unattached to any major denomination. As many clergy framed the problem, the nation needed visible Christian leadership. In 1894, the Methodists Frank Mason North and Elias Sanford joined Presbyterian Charles Thompson, Charles Stelzle, and Josiah Strong in the Open and

Institutional Church League, an organization that met regularly to discuss the "problems" of ministry in the Gilded Age. Sanford served as first executive secretary of the League and would go on to become the primary instigator for forming the Federal Council of Churches.[5] Within the League, each of these ministers shared their concerns about operating a Protestant church in an urban environment with high-density neighborhoods full of poor, European immigrants. North called his colleagues in the ministry to act as sociologists: to draw up social surveys of one's parish neighborhood and determine what those people needed and how the church could help meet those needs. Washington Gladden enthusiastically participated, encouraging colleagues to treat their cities as an "organism."[6] Across the Protestant denominations, ordained ministers were realizing that their future was bound up not only in the future of other neighborhood churches, but also in their ability to stop the growth of the socialism.

Stelzle was not wrong in his observation that the CSF had successfully organized networks of affiliated churches throughout the country and were electing socialists to public office at a rapid pace. Stelzle observed that there were nine million socialist voters in the world, and socialist voting in the United States had increased sevenfold since the last election. At this rate, he argued, "The Socialists will elect a President of the United States" within the next eight years. He went on, "Whatever one may think of the economic value of Socialism or the probability of its success as a political party, this fact remains . . . Socialism has become to thousands of men a substitute for the Church."[7] In a series of talks he gave to college students in 1907 and 1908, Stelzle drove home the same point. "The literature of Socialism far surpasses the literature of the Church," he said, with a clear implication that the socialist movement was inimical to that of the Church.

Stelzle challenged audiences to evangelize for the church as socialists did for their movement. With the voice of a preacher, he entreated candidates for the ministry,

> Imagine, if you can, if in Chicago, or New York, in Detroit, Philadelphia, or in any other American city, three hundred Christian men pledged to get up every Sunday morning at five o'clock to go the rounds of particular districts for the purpose of putting Christian literature into the Sunday morning newspaper or under the doorstep of working people in their community, because they felt that the message of Christianity was far more important than the message of socialism.[8]

He reiterated to an audience of workers a few years later, "Socialism has become to thousands of workingmen a religion, and they strive with the utmost sincerity to solve the social, economic and political problems by which they are confronted."[9] In 1910 he published a review for a British paper on the alienation of workers from churches worldwide, arguing that ministers around the world should worry about losing their place in society.[10] His alarm, once again, was not without grounds.

When Stelzle, Strong, Thompson, and their colleagues participated in the founding convention of the Federal Council of Churches in 1908 in Philadelphia, they had several goals, both stated and unstated. Officially, the thirty-three denominations agreed to collect data on all Protestant churches in the United States and Canada to create a "clearing house" for cross-denominational partnerships and a national nerve center for "Service," a category that included charitable relief, evangelism, and peacemaking, both domestically and abroad. According to its constitution, they sought to show the nation that the "Christian Churches of America," as they called themselves, spoke with a singular voice on matters of morality and public policy. Unstated was their goal to create a mirage of American, Christian authority to counteract the growing public authority of socialists and Roman Catholics in the urban North. Nobody stated directly that by "Christian," they meant only "Protestant." Not only were Catholics left off the invitation list, but members hoped that their presence as a united body would begin to resemble the Roman Catholic Church, which was in its own process of centralizing leadership.[11] After all, just one year earlier, in 1907, the pope had ruled that the "national churches" in the United States would all fall under the umbrella of a single, American, Roman Catholic Church.[12]

Ministers at the helm of the Federal Council saw the centralization of a united Roman Catholic Church in the United States as both a rival and a threat. Much more effectively than Protestants, the Irish had considerable traction in leading other immigrant groups in navigating urban centers. Through their leadership on the city streets as police officers and civil servants, through their domination of the city teachers' unions, their ubiquity as nurses within the system of Catholic hospitals, and their leadership of trade unions and charitable aide associations, Irish Americans were the ethnic group that taught all other European immigrants how to perform American identity.[13] To make matters even more frightening to men like Charles Stelzle, the Roman Catholic Church was developing official relationships with the AFL across multiple dioceses. The growing esteem for

Catholic clerics, and for *Rerum Novarum,* as an authority on Christian social teachings, frightened Protestant leaders and played a role in their desire to do similar work as Protestants.[14]

While this rivalry with Catholics and its broader commitment to white supremacy was not directly stated in the Federal Council of Churches' mission statement, it was implied. As one early historian of the Federal Council explained the reasons for its formation, the Roman Catholic Church membership was "rushing ahead by leaps and bounds." Protestants sought to "secure a larger combined influence for the churches of Christ in all matters affecting the moral and social conditions of the people," and thus to create a "common terminology and a common basis for a united kingdom."[15]

The council made claims to interracial unity that appeared to deny its commitment to white supremacy. After all, North invited the four largest Black denominations, including Black Baptists and the three African Methodist Episcopal denominations, into equal membership with white southern denominations, even though Southern Baptists and Southern Presbyterian notably declined the invitation. Southern white denominations had spent the previous two decades erecting monuments to the Confederacy and teaching their children that enslaved people were "treated with great kindness and care in nearly all cases, a cruel master being rare," but they were nonetheless invited to the federation as equal partners.[16]

The very idea of uniting these northern and southern white denominations with Black denominations was possible only by accepting the color line as an inflexible part of the future of American Christianity. Indeed, not one of the Federal Council's committees in 1908 would offer comment on legal segregation and Black disfranchisement, not to mention racial violence.[17] Not one of the eight special committees appointed in 1908 to address "social problems" was directed to problematize the color line. W. E. B. Du Bois excoriated white pretensions to interracial "unity" in his 1903 *Souls of Black Folk,* likely a direct comment on the groundwork that materialized into the Federal Council.[18]

In President Frank Mason North's keynote address that opened the meeting and gave purpose to the organization, he articulated what he saw as the central problem of the church in the modern age: the "class gospel." This term, of course, referred to the Christian Socialist claim that capitalism was inconsistent with the foundational principles of the Christian faith, and Christians should organize to unseat this alliance between businesses and the churches. North claimed that the idea of working-class consciousness was "abhorrent to the Christian conception of life," for "rich and poor, capitalist and laboring man, are not classifications and distinctions made by the Church of Christ: they are natural or artificial groups, existing in society."[19] He invited Protestants to unite in order to find "common ground" in the quest to bring "the Protestant Christianity of America into relations of closer sympathy and more effective helpfulness with the toiling millions of our land." He titled his talk "The Church and Modern Industry," a deliberate dismissal of recent work among Roman Catholics to accomplish the same goals.[20]

North's stated mission for the Federal Council was to apply "the law of Christ in every relation of human life"; in fact, his goal was to build a white Protestant lobby for all three branches of the federal government. He wanted his organization to do advocacy on topics including industrial affairs, marriage and divorce, temperance, "graft," education, urban poverty, rural poverty, and immigrant "assimilation." Elias Stanford went out of his way to emphasize that their "service" to the nation was not to be confused with efforts to "erect an established church for the state." Rather, members saw themselves supporting the nation's commitment to realizing a Christian civilization, built on natural law. As one minister framed it, "We are here to establish the State and make it strong."[21] The fact that this had to be stated publicly offers a window onto the many conversations ministers had about the potential of a unified Protestant "voice" in industrial America.

North appointed a number of "departments," or "commissions," that would carry out the work of study and reform. Among these were the Department of International Justice and Goodwill, which dealt with domestic and overseas peacemaking, and the Department of Evangelism, which organized national and international revivals. The largest and most prolific of these commissions was the Department of Church and Social Service (sometimes described as a commission or a committee), a unit that sought to disseminate information to member churches on the necessity of cooperative church action on the matters of industrial justice. This committee included the many ministers who had been worrying about the rise of socialism over the previous decade, including Stelzle, Strong, Worth Tippy, the socialist-leaning Methodist Harry Ward, and Frank Mason North himself.[22] It was not long before Stelzle suggested that the Federal Council undertake a nationwide revival, similar to exploratory work by the Catholic father Peter Dietz, to dispel socialism through a campaign coordinated with the AFL. Within three years, this idea would materialize in an international, Protestant revival against that "class gospel."

Capturing the Labor Movement

The Men and Religion Forward Movement began with a labor leader, Sam Gompers, and two ministers, Peter Dietz and Charles Stelzle, who would come to share a vision for working together to thwart socialist strength within both labor and political spheres. Gompers, president of the AFL and a secular Jew, had long held that the union movement would be more successful if it stood independent of partisan politics. However, a rising number of rank-and-file members in trade unions openly stated their intentions to infiltrate, or "bore from within," the AFL and change this apolitical posture. Socialist organizers, delegates, and local presidents were growing in number by the year. Gompers also knew that the most eloquent adversary of socialism, a vehicle already present in many immigrants' lives, was the Roman Catholic Church.

Gompers's partnerships with Catholic antisocialists went back more than a decade before he met Stelzle and contemplated a nationwide movement. Starting in 1901, Gompers had supported the work of Catholic antisocialism by citing and repeating the statements of antisocialist bishops and archbishops.[23] Many bishops, including Bishop Ignatius Horstman of Cleveland, Archbishop James Quigley of Buffalo, Bishop John Spalding of Peoria, and Archbishop Michael Corrigan of New York City, insisted that their parish priests preach against socialism on a regular basis. Quigley, for example, issued a pastoral letter in 1902 that held that no Catholic could either become a "member of a Social Democratic organization" nor subscribe to any such newspaper because of the vileness of class warfare. The *American Federationist* repeated many of these Catholic arguments in its pages that year.[24] Gompers endorsed the classic Catholic argument that socialism tore apart families by encouraging women's independence. He praised David Goldstein's 1903 *Socialism: The Nation of Fatherless Children*, claiming the book offered "an excellent contribution to the literature of the labor question and the labor movement."[25]

Before long, Gompers had a working relationship with several antisocialist groups. Gompers proudly supported the work of the Common Cause Society of Boston, a group that claimed "a Vote for *Socialism*" was a vote against "religion, family, the state, and trade unions."[26] He also worked with the German national church's Militia for Christ, a Catholic trade union organized by Peter Dietz. Father Dietz was a German Catholic priest, long an active member of the Ohio State Federation of Labor who sought Gompers's help in his efforts to suppress socialism within his diocese. In 1909, Dietz established what he hoped to become a national union of Catholic trade unionists, a project that anticipated the pope's statement that "confessional Catholic associations" should be formed in place of socialist trade unions.[27] In 1910, Gompers and Dietz started working with Archbishop Glennon of St. Louis to organize a national campaign for Catholic trade union membership, the Militia of Christ for Social Service. With the financial partnership of the AFL, the Militia of Christ published weekly newsletters to nearly three hundred labor newspapers and warned against a socialist takeover of the trade unions.[28]

As a young minister, Stelzle noted the work of Gompers and Dietz with a mixture of appreciation, envy, and foreboding. He was worried about the future strength of the Catholic Church in the United States, but he was more worried that socialism would render churches obsolete. Stelzle probably knew Dietz from his ministry in St. Louis. He hoped that through the Presbyterian Board of Home Missions, he, too, could work on swelling membership among the immigrant working classes while also mitigating the popularity of socialism in the labor movement. Stelzle ran a weekly press bureau that sent out press releases to 250 labor newspapers and one hundred monthly magazines around the country. His articles emphasized that Jesus supported the cause of the "working man" and that unions were consistent with the gospel message. The department also sponsored "conferences" for wage earners and employers to "talk," opportunities Stelzle always used to gain contacts with the working classes for further ministry.

For years, Stelzle had tried to convince labor unions to exchange delegates with city "ministerial associations," ostensibly for the sake of building community "solidarity." In 1905, inspired by Peter Dietz and operating on Sam Gompers's dime, Stelzle sent out an "Open Letter to Ministers of the Gospel," entreating both Catholic and Protestant clergy to see trade unionism as a bulwark against socialism and irreligion. He urged every trade union in the country to exchange delegates with area associations of clergy. More than one hundred cities participated in this practice within the next two years. In 1906, the AFL Executive Council, the highest level of leadership in the federation, created a position for a fraternal delegate from the ministry, and Stelzle got himself appointed to this esteemed body. He served as the ministerial delegate to the AFL 1906 to 1915.[29]

Stelzle entered leadership in the AFL at a high point in both the Great Migration and the influx of European immigrants. Industrial cities were brimming with single young men and young families, transplants eager to build some form of community in the midst of cramped living spaces and dangerous workplaces. Community was not hard to find; rather, transplants found themselves having to decide which types of communities to join. Bars and saloons offered food and entertainment, and frequently hosted unions and radical labor meetings. They also served as hosts for both prostitution and violence. Mutual aid societies, which formed the basis of community for many immigrants and African Americans, often sponsored their own newspapers, events, meeting halls, and banks.[30] Yet foremen in every industry pitted ethnic groups against one another to drive down wages. Ethnic societies could rarely address the problems of low wages and unsafe working conditions on their own. Stelzle observed wage earners' shifting affiliations and group formations as a student of sociology. His Department of Church and Labor sponsored social surveys within church neighborhoods and used their results for both fundraising and evangelism.

In partnering with Gompers, Dietz, and the AFL, Stelzle hoped to accomplish two things: first and foremost, he hoped to elevate the Christian, antisocialist messaging that the AFL had already begun to establish through emerging partnerships with the German national parish of the Roman Catholic Church.[31] Sam Gompers and other AFL executives knew that church leaders shared the goal of mitigating radicalism among the immigrant working classes.[32] In his syndicated articles and addresses to union members, now with even broader appeal because of his official AFL affiliation, Stelzle echoed the messaging of the Catholic hierarchy with regards to *Rerum Novarum*; he claimed that socialism was idolatry for the material world. Socialists, Stelzle claimed, rejected Jesus's assertion that "man cannot live by bread alone." "To its believers," he said, "socialism is their religion."[33]

However, dispelling socialist militancy was only a means toward an end, and Stelzle's broader goals were not simply to build a large, conservative trade union movement. After all, no matter what he told his trade union colleagues, he did not leave his life as a machinist for the ministry simply to serve the labor movement. Stelzle hoped that by partnering with the AFL, he could persuade wage earners to build their community within local Protestant churches. These goals are evident from early in his ministry. When speaking to audiences of middle-class Protestants, those from whom he garnered the donations upon which his ministry relied, Stelzle warned that the rise of socialist communities among wage earners threatened the future of Protestant America. As he put it in the *New York Observer* in 1904, "Socialism has become for thousands of workingmen a substitute for the church. . . . Socialists boldly declare that Jesus Christ was a Socialist. They insist that their system is nearer the ideal presented by Jesus than is Christianity, so-called. It may be true that a man can be a Christian and a Socialist too, but Socialism is avowedly materialistic. Its leaders despise the church because, they declare, the church stands for the present social system, and that is a barrier in the way of the advance of Socialism." The very "religious flavor" of Socialist open-air meetings was misleading, he continued, because unlike the second coming of Christ, its "beautiful ideal" could never be "put into force." "It would pay," he advised, for churches "to devote a whole department to the issuing of brief, practical pamphlets" refuting socialists' "fantastical doctrines."[34]

It was true that many American workers believed that Jesus would much sooner support a cooperative economic system than a profit-driven system. But Stelzle was quite presumptuous to suggest that Protestant churches held, or could hold, any significant authority within the lives of most wage earners. The statement deliberately overlooked the fact that most wage earners in urban settings hailed from Roman Catholic, Eastern Orthodox, Jewish, or African American church traditions, communities that had long held different positions on the meaning of the Sermon on the Mount and the purposes of church. Even white rural migrants, those familiar with Southern Baptist, Pentecostal, and independent church traditions, were more likely to spend time on Sunday with traveling evangelists than liturgical Protestants like Stelzle. Moreover, Stelzle seriously underestimated how many wage earners were skeptics, freethinkers, or atheists and actively opposed to any semblance of pastoral authority.

Nonetheless, Stelzle's plea to the executive committee of the AFL to invest money in his antisocialist work was successful. Trade unionists likely knew that their partnership with the Federal Council of Churches would strengthen the reach of their statements over the many ethnic communities within cities, many of whom held their own taverns, churches, and socialist labor newspapers. Hence, soon after he had assumed his official role as delegate to the AFL in 1906, Stelzle announced his plans for a deeper partnership with trade unionists. In an article called "Capturing the Labor Movement" Stelzle argued that the labor movement was growing so much more quickly than church membership, and serving so many purposes within working-class communities that were formerly held by churches, that either "the labor movement will capture the church, or the church shall capture the labor movement."

The article drafted a twofold strategy for making sure that churches retained their authority over urban space. First, they needed to end their history of "paternalism" within missions to the poor, and replace them with denominationally supported working people's churches that catered to the "every day life" of working people. Second, ministers needed to dispel the belief that socialism was a Christian concept. In its place, Stelzle nominated the kind of gospel of "Christian brotherhood" that the National Civic Federation, an arm of big business, liked to celebrate. Only "brotherhood," he claimed, led to "complete emancipation—physical, social, mental and moral."[35] The article garnered significant attention in the popular press. But most importantly for Stelzle, it effectively convinced the rest of the executive committee of the AFL to partner with him and the emerging Federal Council of Churches in a "union organizing" campaign. Soon after the Federal Council was formed in 1908, Stelzle made the MRFM its first major project.

This nationwide evangelistic campaign, which stretched from the fall of 1911 until the spring of 1912, involved a national crusade to visit hundreds of shop floors around the country and preach the twin gospels of trade unionism and church membership. It involved hundreds of volunteer workers, mostly pastors and church secretaries, to organize venues, coordinate with all the local trade unions in the area, and gain permission of employers to allow the ministers to come in and give their presentation. Employers were promised that the religious event would occupy only the lunch hour and would not impede on work time. Yet in many respects, that logistical work was the project. The planning alone brought together business leaders, religious leaders, and trade union leaders in almost every major city in the United States and Canada. In many cases, Roman Catholic, Jewish, and Protestant clergymen were also invited to participate.

The evangelistic event usually began on shop floors at precisely noon and lasted exactly fifty-five minutes. First, professional musicians played Christian hymns for about fifteen minutes; they invited workers to participate through singing along with the lyrics printed in their "souvenir programmes," pamphlets that contained lyrics, Bible verses, and trade union information. Next, a preacher gave a ten-minute address on the sympathy of Jesus for workingmen, "stopping promptly five minutes before the whistle calls the men to work." Stelzle had templates for such messages prepared. Trade union leaders would then pass out information about their locals. As Stelzle described them, these meetings were improvisational in character. "Not always was a Scripture lesson read, nor was prayer offered at every meeting," he wrote. "Neither were men always urged to give an outward manifestation of their acceptance of Christ. The [local] leaders were guided entirely by their circumstances and their judgment was good."[36] Usually, the meetings ran for three or four days consecutively in one shop and made Bibles available free to interested workingmen. The following Sunday, all workingmen and their employers were invited to a Saturday or Sunday evening service at a particular local church, according to their preferences.[37] Stelzle reported with satisfaction that seventy-five employers requested his evangelistic team to return on a weekly basis. Workers filled out forms with their religious background and curiosities, and Stelzle handed over lists of workers' names to local leaders "situated nearest factories" to follow up on his contacts.[38] Because all the shop floors they entered had only male workers, and because Stelzle was especially concerned with the lack of young men in churches, men were the focus of the campaign.

It is easy to see the ways Stelzle and his cooperating churches exploited their relationship with trade unionists for the sake of growing church membership rolls. Without the presence of trade union leaders, it is unlikely that workers would have sat through the program and shared their personal information. The evangelistic campaign made trade unions appear, especially to immigrant newcomers, like foundational national institutions. It also made Protestant ministers appear to be the nation's real moral authorities.[39]

Stelzle was especially proud of the work he did in western cities, where membership rolls for unions dwarfed church membership. Here especially, Stelzle worked with local ministers to organize "testimonies" (personal conversion stories) on the topic of "Christ, His Church, and the Workingman." In Portland, a city with a large socialist population, over one hundred men shared stories on how Christ favored economic justice. If they followed Stelzle's precise directions, they would insist that Jesus was a humble carpenter who very well knew that socialism would never work.[40] In Denver, the vice president of the local AFL presided while Stelzle preached on "A Square Deal," one characterized not by redistribution of power but "Christian brotherhood" in the relationship between God and Man.[41] In some cities, the evangelistic campaigns were accompanied by "midnight parades" through red-light districts.

The AFL and the New Social Christianity

Stelzle's deeper ambitions concerned the mission of American Protestantism within diverse urban centers. He not only wanted to see the demise of the socialist movement, but he wanted to see American wage earners trust both

Protestant church leaders and Christian businessmen as worthy stewards of American capital. In these early decades of the twentieth century, Henry Ford and others were experimenting with forms of welfare capitalism, incentive systems inside and outside of the workplace that encouraged workers to adopt certain behaviors in order earn the rewards of profit sharing. Stelzle, like his colleagues in the business community, was deeply attracted to these alleged solutions to the problem of "class warfare." As his committee had resolved on behalf of the New York Federation of Churches, a precursor to the Federal Council, "Private capital in every instance ought to be administered as a sacred trust for the common weal—this not merely in the distribution of surplus wealth, but also in all the active, productive uses of capital, the law of God requiring not only beneficence instead of corrupting extravagance, but also instead of greedy production, productive activities conducted on lines most considerate of the ultimate well-being of the whole community and the immediate welfare of the immediate workers."[42] Stelzle believed workers deserved nothing more from their employers than fair wages and decent working conditions. It was the responsibility of capitalists to administer their wealth responsibly.[43] We usually associate these statements with the gospel of wealth or the fundamentalist movement, but these ideas were also the foundation of the Federal Council's Social Gospel movement.

Not surprisingly, Stelzles's campaign was funded by many of the nation's biggest business owners, men with a tremendous amount of private capital that they did not want to be taxed to raise funds for public infrastructure. Stelzle's biggest funders were J. Pierpont Morgan, John Wanamaker, and Cyrus McCormick. This is not to say that Stelzle did not receive smaller sums of financial support from an array of Christian progressives like Edward Devine of *Survey* magazine, Graham Taylor of Chicago Commons, and Jane Addams. But, in refusing to even debate the principles of private enterprise, Stelzle was successfully attempting to move these progressives to the right.[44]

Stelzle's evangelical crusades for wage-earning men, what he called "Forward movements," reappropriated many of the same methods of evangelism that the CSF had utilized over the previous two decades. Both wrote their own hymns, leaflets, and sermons, collected cards with personal information for every participant, and followed up with attendees through newspapers or magazines sent in the mail. But Stelzle signaled that socialists were not the real Christians they claimed to be because they harbored false theology. He adopted terms popularized by socialists, including "Social Christianity," "Applied Christianity," and "Socialized Christianity." These confusingly close variations on the term "Christian Socialist" likely sparked confusion among those for whom English was a second language, and this was probably intentional. But Stelzle's new Social Christianity defanged socialists' spiritual critiques of the profit system.

Stelzle did not simply ignore socialists' many demands for public ownership and management of utilities, not to mention public works projects and a social safety net. Rather, with the backing of the AFL, he told both business leaders and wage earners that socialism, the enforced redistribution of wealth, was incompatible with natural law. It was hogwash, he said, to presume that it was possible to live in a cooperative commonwealth within the conditions of human nature. Stelzle thus weaponized his clerical authority to insist that socialists misunderstood both human nature and the concept of limited atonement. He held that selfish, sinful individuals could never overcome their depraved human nature and sustain a social system requiring selflessness. As he put it, "No society can do for a man what he will not do for himself."[45] Moreover, he said, the pursuit of Christ had little to do with social and economic equality. Jesus promised "contentment" in the world, not "satisfaction."[46] Stelzle wanted Christians to stop presuming that the demands of the labor movement were somehow holier than the demands of employers. As he put it, "It is only fair that the sinner at the top be given as much attention as the sinner at the bottom."[47]

Stelzle's bold statements representing the Federal Council of Churches implicitly disciplined the many left-leaning clergy within the newly-formed Federal Council. Indeed, he pointedly refuted Christian Socialist claims to history of the early church. In his *Gospel of Labor* (1912), Stelzle explained,

> First, the whole system was a purely voluntary one. No man was compelled to give up anything he was compelled to retain. Second, it was limited to the members of the Church—those who believed and were of "one heart and soul." . . . Fourth, the result of the plan was that it pauperized the Jerusalem Church and made it a great burden upon the weak churches elsewhere. The apostles were often called upon to take up special offerings for the church at Jerusalem. Fifth, the plan was a complete failure and was soon discontinued.

While Stelzle defined early believers' sharing as "generosity," he argued that the initial and unsuccessful practice of the first-century church could not be maintained in the fallen world of selfish human beings. He dismissed

Christian Socialist claims that corporate charity was "tainted," and identified personal decisions to dispense with material blessings as the universal application of Jesus's principles. He squarely endorsed corporate philanthropy as the support for millions of dollars' worth of "educational, social and religious work," and insisted that all arguments to the contrary should be "forever put out of the minds of the workingmen."[48]

Stelzle's MRFM led an international, theological crusade to take back the history of the first-century church from Christian Socialist commentators. The British antisocialist newspaper *Christian World Pulpit* echoed Stelzle, saying that the temporary collective of the early church "did not last. It was only a temporary expedient for dealing with poverty. Very soon the dishonorable poor became members of the Church in order to secure the means of livelihood without working for it, and in consequence, the poor were pauperized, and the rich found themselves unable to meet the demands made upon the common fund. It all went to prove the Communistic life impracticable." Furthermore, participation in the socialism of the early church was voluntary, private, and closed to Christian believers. The church, apart from the state, had and continued to retain "her own government, her own laws, her own life." Hence, affirmation that Christ is Lord and Savior was far more important than worldly focus upon reformatting systems to ensure "sensuous enjoyment, to feed and dress the body."[49]

Social Gospel as Personal Ethics

Thus, to the degree the Men and Religion Forward movement was the first action of the Federal Council of Churches to actualize this new commitment to social service, we can make several observations about the intent of this ecumenical crusade. First, it was driven by a clear opposition to Christian Socialist narratives about the history and purpose of the church and the degree to which capitalism was compatible with Christian praxis. Stelzle, true to his training at the Moody Bible Institute, emphasized personal salvation and rejected any sense of systemic sin. He echoed southern evangelicals in his claim that "there can be no social reform unless there be first of all some kind of spiritual reform, a regeneration of mankind." His working-class ministries suggested that the real lesson Christians should take from the first-century church was the fact that communal experiments do not last. Stelzle was a card-carrying member of the AFL, and his work had a meaningful impact on the mission of the Federal Council of Churches, but he was also a theological conservative by the standards of his own day.

Second, the movement denied socialists' moral claims that workers deserved a living wage.[50] Stelzle's movement held that it was the responsibility of Christian employers to treat their workers with dignity to "afford the worker the opportunity to develop all the possibilities of his manhood." He did not believe that employers should be hamstrung by any particular wage minimum, nor should they be limited in their wealth accumulation.[51] Quite to the contrary, Stelzle led a new generation of Protestant Social Gospel theologians, including Bertrand Thompson, Algernon Crapsey, and Francis Peabody, in suggesting that Jesus opposed wealth only when it was a hindrance to personal salvation. Thompson wrote, in a monograph filled with citations of Stelzle, that Jesus "had no sympathies with the poor, and he had no prejudice against wealth merely as wealth. He was not a reformer or a revolutionist of the external type; he had no economic or political programme; he was interested primarily in spiritual reformation."[52] Soon even Walter Rauschenbusch was feeling the pressure to agree to Stelzle's interpretation of the principles of natural law. Rauschenbusch's 1914 speech, "The Right and Wrong of Socialism," accused socialists of too little attention to personal morality and too much trust in the inherent Christianity of working-class people.[53] Shailer Matthews and Lyman Abbott soon raised similar critiques of Christian Socialism in their writing.

Finally, while Christian Socialists claimed that the church should be a radical organization and launch pad for social renewal, Stelzle and the Federal Council claimed the opposite. As Stelzle framed it, God never intended the church on earth to endorse the present political and social order, but he also never intended the church to transform it. Rather, he said, "We stand simply for the principles of Jesus Christ, applied to society in all its ramifications, and that we favor only so much of the present system as will stand the test of these principles."[54] In this respect, Stelzle adopted Roman Catholic understandings of ecclesiology. He insisted that a preacher "need not discuss social theories, but he must present, in the spirit of the prophet, the supreme laws of love, of justice, and of service, and apply them to present-day questions."[55]

Stelzle argued that socialists reduced the power of Christianity to spurn sin at every social and political level. He believed that "it is the business of the church to create healthy dissatisfaction with existing conditions" but that it could not and should not be confined to a particular economic philosophy. In

a column entitled "Why Workingmen Should Be Interested in the Church,"
Stelzle explained, "It was not the intention of the founder of the church that
it should become an annex to any social, industrial or political organization;
but by furnishing a Christian sentiment, it disturbs the wrong wherever it
exists."[56] Stelzle thus argued that Protestant churches needed to inhabit a
political space divorced from class and national politics. Of course, this argument was not without its contradictions. He wholeheartedly encouraged
ministers to speak out against child labor, prostitution, and saloons because
he claimed that these topics were specifically listed in the Bible.[57]

In sum, Stelzle offered the classic welfare capitalist argument that the
interests of labor and capital were identical. As he framed it, "Church and
Labor" should cooperate on the basis of "salvation of society, . . . emancipation of the individual . . . care of the human body," and "development of
the human soul."[58] This vision of "social regeneration" turned ideas about
reforming capitalism into individualized directives. Stelzle used premillen-
nial rhetoric in arguing that the "earthly utopia" Christ described would not
be the result of worldly agitation for justice, but of Christ "fulfilling the law."
Churches, he said, should stand with workingmen in disgust for the bro-
kenness of the present world and commit to improving working conditions.
But, he relied on personal ethics to bring about this change. When the spirit
of Christian brotherhood and "family affection" is fully awakened in the
hearts of believers, he argued, tenements would fall. The "so-called opposing
'classes' " will see their common Christian bonds and "churches will become
the center of inspiration and social activity as essential to the life of the people
as was the ancient Hebrew temple."[59]

William Easton's syllabus, which Stelzle commissioned for small-group
evangelistic meetings, reframed the mission of both Jesus and the historic Church. Students followed the Israelites from Genesis to the division
of the kingdoms and into the early church, learning of how Jews and early
Christians established the Kingdom of God through individual acts of personal morality. Easton quoted Christian Socialists like John Spargo, Austin
Bierbower, Washington Gladden, W. H. Freemantle, and Robert Hunter, but
only to refute their arguments.[60] Easton wanted workers to know that Jesus
was not a prophet of political change but an "agitator for personal and social
righteousness" and "an advocate of obedience to the law."[61] He said that Jesus
would have advocated for incremental reform, not "industrial war, competition, and labor-union strikes for shorter hours."[62] Drawing upon the rhetoric
of masculinity that already saturated the movement, Easton further argued

that Jesus valued male workers' commitment to faithful marriage and financial provision for one's family. He imagined the Church as a network of obedient and submissive male bodies.[63]

Socialist Response

Socialist workers immediately recognized the new Social Christianity as an attack on both collective bargaining rights and the definition of a good Christian worker. In November 1911, the Minneapolis Trades and Labor Assembly officially came out against the MRFM and initiated their own Union Labor Forward Movement, which would hold thirty to sixty meetings across the city, daily, in its two-week campaign the following April. Union leaders would "secure as many church pulpits and school houses as possible," and use the opportunity "not only to win members to the Labor Unions but also as a great educational work to demonstrate to the general public that organized labor stands for the Home, and peace in the industrial world, and also caring for the widows and orphans."[64] Mimicking its contenders' language, the ULFM valued "scattering the gospel of unionism to the uninformed and thus interesting them to a greater extent in the cause of toilers."[65] Sheet metal organizer Robert Byron called it "the biggest labor proposition ever inaugurated."[66]

Just like its competitor, the ULFM financed its nearly one hundred speakers with ten thousand buttons sold to advertise the movement throughout the city.[67] Minneapolis labor leaders, too, produced slides for moving picture theaters throughout the city.[68] In all this work, unionists referred to Federal Council ministers with terms like "labor fakir," someone who pretends to support the union but secretly supports management. At times, the response to the doctrine of personal restraint was sarcastic. As one writer put it, if only the wealthy business leaders professing Christianity and financing the movement had "denied themselves some of the dividends realized from their efforts in cutting the wages of working people down to the lowest possible figure," they might appreciate the "spiritual help." The MTLA discussed the possibility of inviting Stelzle to meet them, but Thomas Van Lear, a socialist, followed his address with the statement, "The Men and Religion Forward movement cannot make a $10.00 pay check look like $20.00." According to the newspaper, Van Lear's statement garnered four long minutes of applause.[69]

Many workers were upset that Stelzle was commandeering good Progressive reformers like Raymond Robins and Jane Addams against them. The Progressive reformer Raymond Robins, who served as head of the Social Service Department of the MRFM, received angry letters from workers in Paris, Illinois for forcing them back to work prematurely. The garment workers at Hart, Schaffner, and Marx orchestrated a strike of more than forty-thousand-employees. But, when the ministers came to town, one worker claimed, all were "forc[ed] . . . back to work" prematurely. Milwaukee socialists wrote to Robins, "Practically all the leading Protestant Preachers are with the Socialists. . . . If you were here I'm sure you would fight with us."[70] There were, of course, many socialist preachers in 1912, but none to be found within the MRFM.

Other socialist workers took the opposite tack and acted as whistle blowers on the capitalist, Christian propaganda that they believed drove the MRFM. In his book, *The Snare of the Men and Religion Forward Movement*, socialist William Coleman exposed Stelzle and Easton's educational propaganda as a misunderstanding of both Christianity and socialism. Coleman reiterated the party's official stance that "socialism does not in any manner, shape or form interfere with any man's private religious faith, nor attack any doctrine of any creed, nor make any religious belief a ground of objection to any party member." Coleman explained, "when a gang of capitalistic exploiters of labor put on the sacred garb of religion and endeavor to conceal their intent and purpose beneath the cloak of religion and to give Socialism a treacherous stab in the dark—why, then, Socialists must tear off their masks."[71] Similarly, William Prosser of the CSF responded to the claim that of the MRFM that "the class struggle is nothing but personal hatred and determinism, nothing but a belly philosophy that shut God and all moral motives and forces out of life," with a surprising declaration that socialism was merely "cooperation in industry, commerce, and all forms of human activity." The Church, he said, should enforce the actions that would make the Golden Rule central to modern society.[72]

To Coleman and Prosser, the MRFM was nothing but a ruse for the purpose of making a bull market "in the name of Jesus." Its aim, Coleman argued, was both to keep labor unions conservative, cleaving to their "old, safe, sound conservative ways," and to generally "suppress Socialism." Coleman argued that Stelzle "writes stupid reactionary articles for the bourgeois press and gets all the space he wants." In fact, he said, the capitalist system was not ordained by God, for it was not God's will that there should be a rich class on one hand and a "toiling . . . and a suffering class on the other."[73] "They have stolen Jesus from us and it is our task to retake him for ourselves as Socialists," said Coleman, "to which party he belongs, and of which party he was the founder and teacher."[74] However, despite Coleman's and Prosser's "testimonials," the MRFM had rendered socialists so far outside the tent of American Protestantism that even Christian Socialists began moving away from religion as a basis for organizing.

Conclusion

If we read the MRFM as the first major movement to actualize the ambitions of the Federal Council, we can deduce its priorities and measure its successes. The movement put into action a network of Protestant church leaders that would make "Christian" policy statements with regards to labor. While it had limited initial success in convincing immigrant wage earners to worship at middle-class Protestant churches, it had considerable success in directing middling- and middle-class parishioners to dismiss Christian Socialist theologies as unorthodox bunk. The most long-lasting effect of the MRFM was *not* any significant increase in Protestant church attendance among poor wage earners. Rather, Stelzle and the Federal Council of Churches collected data on poor communities and performed "social service" evangelism. This performance of "support" for the poor encouraged middling-class parishioners, including the emerging classes of foremen, to trust Protestant clerics, rather than socialist-leaning labor leaders, as the nation's primary authorities on the meaning of "church" and on Christian assessments of economics, social justice, and labor justice.

Observers noted a real change in the national conversation on the meaning and purposes of the Social Gospel after the MRFM. While socialists had used the terms "Social Gospel" and "Social Christianity" interchangeably with socialism for the previous two decades, the Federal Council's revival movement changed the common use of the term. Stelzle's celebration of wage earners' need for personal faith and orthodox church membership inspired many middle-class parishioners to follow his lead. Stelzle was convincing the new middling class of parishioners to entrust ministers of the Federal Council, rather than the labor movement, as esteemed and trustworthy agents of Christian justice in the modern republic. As progressive reformer Raymond Robins reflected later to the head of the World Council of Churches, the MRFM "came at a time when materialistic socialism was vigorously advancing" and soon after Debs had polled a million votes. He recalled, "There were socialist[s] in several state legislatures, some members of Congress, and a number of mayors of the socialist faith." Norman Thomas made a similar observation.[75] Both authors noted that the MRFM was a turning point. Robins reflected, "There has been a steady decline in the socialist vote and class cleavage of materialist socialism in this country since the Men and Religion campaign. Under the drive of Men and Religion, the workers, Progressives and Liberals found hope for the future inside the American system of law, economics and social order. This will be historically its most significant contribution to the social order of this country and the world."[76]

If socialists had convinced large numbers of wage earners and a growing middling class of clerks and managers to think critically about the system of private enterprise, the Federal Council illustrated that they could drive a wedge between the middling classes and the labor movement. The ministers of the Federal Council of Churches, standing in solidarity with Roman Catholic clerics, opposed any and all forms of socialism. They said that they stood with the AFL, but in fact these clerics only stood with the most conservative members of the nation's most conservative unions. In opposing socialism, these trade union leaders primarily defended skilled, white wage earners over and against the demands of immigrants and African Americans who worked in the lowest-paying and most dangerous jobs. The Federal Council offered no solidarity with the more radical wing of the labor movement—workers who were demanding industrial unions, public works projects, and cooperative ownership and management of farming, ranching, and factory production. Yet this selective support for labor was the point. The Federal Council made space for white Christians to call themselves supporters of the Social Gospel without taking seriously the moral claims of the immigrants and people of color who were the majority of the working classes.

At the heart of Stelzle's "Social Christianity" was the ministerial ambition to reject the idea of a "Christian Commonwealth," built through collective ownership of business, and reimagine the Christian nation as a network of politically neutral, procapitalist churches. This minister-led movement was not unlike other Progressive Era attempts to gain power and authority through expertise, but it was a bit more difficult to name. In the coming years, the Federal Council of Churches would sponsor myriad public statements, strike reports, and "investigations," all of which served primarily to defend its authority as the nation's moral leader. The radical labor movement would resist these attempts to speak on behalf of Christian workers, claiming that the profit system was, in itself, morally and spiritually corrupting. Ministers of the Federal Council would learn that despite their popularity with Anglo-Protestant men with some respected skills, they would have to work much harder to gain the approval of the increasing numbers of immigrants and African Americans who now dominated the ranks of the working class.

6

Reframing the Moral Lessons of the Labor Movement

In March and April 1914, Frank Tannenbaum, a twenty-one-year-old busboy in New York City, organized a massive break-in on a string of churches of New York. One after the other, he and fellow members of the Industrial Workers of the World entered sanctuaries and demanded food and shelter. Their point was to challenge ministers to take a side on the question of the poor. Were white, middle- and upper-class congregations who pretended to worship Jesus in favor, or not in favor, of support for the working classes? If they supported the poor, would they offer food and shelter to the unemployed? Would they offer sanctuary during strikes, and meeting spaces for organizing? Would they lobby for legislation that would support workers' rights to fair wages and working conditions, and broader national reforms that made democracy possible?

Some ministers offered shelter to IWW men and shocked the city with their shows of solidarity. Other ministers, like Father Schneider at St. Alphonsus, called the police and had the men arrested. The arrests were a ready-made spectacle for IWW leaders to illustrate the hypocrisy of American clergy. As Tannenbaum told the *New York Call*, "Do you call that the spirit of Christ, to turn hungry and homeless men away?" Newspapers and religious publications around the country referred to these break-ins as "church invasions."[1] Church leaders may have claimed that they were fervent supporters of social justice, but large numbers of wage earners were still not convinced that the churches stood behind the principles they preached. Indeed, in the period after the Men and Religion Forward movement and before the Red Scare, roughly 1912 to 1917, both radicals and more moderate unionists tested ministers' claims of support for the labor movement. In the process, they built a tentative alliance that became known as the Social Gospel.[2]

The Federal Council of Churches' primary mission was to grow churches and enhance the influence of ministers at the national level. In pursuing

The Gospel of Church. Janine Giordano Drake, Oxford University Press. © Oxford University Press 2024.
DOI: 10.1093/oso/9780197614303.003.0007

that goal, it offered broad statements of support for "labor" and cozied up to the executive committee of the American Federation of Labor, a group that shared their worries about the growing bulk of European immigrants who cheered on a more radical, more European, labor movement. When the Federal Council mass-distributed the *Social Creed of the Churches*, authored strike reports and investigations, and convened meetings on "Christian social work," it claimed its credentials as a friend of the labor movement. In many respects, it was. The Federal Council brought good publicity to strikes and publicly dignified workers' demands for better wages and working conditions. However, ministers' words and actions often undermined the authority of those in the radical labor movement to speak for themselves and grow their own moral authority in public space. As one IWW booklet framed it, "Every incident in the life of the union, every skirmish with employers is made the text for proletarian education."[3] Federal Council ministers claimed political neutrality, but they used the strategic sacrifices of wage earners to expand their own public influence and distract white Protestant attention away from actual labor leaders and their visions for social change.

The *Social Creed of the Churches*

A close analysis of the work of the Methodist minister Harry Ward, leading member of the Federal Council's Committee on Church and Social Service, illustrates some of the disconnects, big and small, between the goals of labor leaders and those of prominent Protestant ministers. In March 1914, just as Frank Tannenbaum was organizing "church invasions," the Boston University School of Theology invited the Methodist minister Harry Ward, author of the *Social Creed of the Churches*, to present a series of lectures on syndicalism and socialism at Ford Hall Forum. The talks were well attended by a broad cross-section of Boston and Ward boasted that the IWW Propaganda League praised the "unbiased, unprejudiced and able manner in which he presented the controversy between capital and labor and its causes." After all, Ward invited IWW members to share the podium with him.[4] However, while Ward went on to more radical Christian pacifism after 1919, his work on the Federal Council, and especially the *Social Creed*, is often interpreted as more radical than it really was.[5]

Ward, literally conceived by Victorian missionaries, never quite escaped the paternalistic evangelistic posture of his parents. Born in 1873 and raised in London, Ward took the social democratic ideals of Fabian reformers for granted about as much as the white supremacy and muscular Christianity of the Victorian British gaze. His German Baptist colleague Walter Rauschenbush, who preached among immigrants in New City, became re-nowned for the argument that the gospel demanded the remission not only of personal sins, but also of "societal sins," those injustices embedded in the functioning of corporations, cities, and other institutions.[6] Ward disagreed. While Rauschenbush became a noted public member of the Socialist Party and the Christian Socialist Fellowship, Ward did not.[7] Ward agreed with Rauschenbush that evangelizing cities needed to involve more than altar calls. He, too, argued that industry should be responsible not only to shareholders, but to God.[8] But, when Ward suggested that "socialism and Christianity could be partners," he meant that Christian clerics should lead socialists in morality and theology.[9] He believed in wealth distribution for the advancement of "civilization," but he thought that ordained Protestant clerics should preside over that process.[10]

Ward's evangelism never quite escaped Victorian British presumptions about the elevated authority of ministers, and of a universal Church, over all other offices and positions of power in the nation. In 1908, he reprised his *Social Creed of the Churches,* originally written in 1902 for his Methodist denomination, as a common creed for the Federal Council of Churches to endorse as the centerpiece of their social service mission. He said, and his fellow ministers agreed, that the churches stood

> For equal rights and complete justice for all men in all stations of life.
>
> For the right of all men to the opportunity for self-maintenance, a right ever to be wisely and strongly safe-guarded against encroachments of every kind.
>
> For the right of workers to some protection against the hardships often resulting from the swift crisis of industrial change.
>
> For the principle of conciliation and arbitration in industrial dissensions.
>
> For the protection of the worker from dangerous machinery, occupational disease, injuries and mortality.
>
> For the abolition of child labor.
>
> For such regulation of the conditions of toil for women as shall safeguard the physical and moral health of the community.

For the suppression of the "sweating system."

For the gradual and reasonable reduction of the hours of labor to the lowest practical point, and for that degree of leisure for all which is a condition of the highest human life.

For a release from employment one day in seven.

For a living wage as a minimum in every industry, and for the highest wage that each industry can afford.

For the most equitable division of the products of industry that can ultimately be devised.

For suitable provision for the old age of the workers and for those incapacitated by injury.

For the abatement of poverty.

These were powerful echoes of the AFL's platform principles, not to mention the key tenets of *Rerum Novarum*. But these principles were still far from the demands of the labor movement at the time. In 1912, as socialism became even more popular, Ward urged the Federal Council to revisit and expand the statement to address national conversations on unbearable working conditions and the extent to which Christianity was compatible with capitalist directives. The revised document called for the "the application of Christian principles to the acquisition and use of property, and for the most equitable division of the product of industry that can be ultimately devised." The revision also called for the "gradual and reasonable reduction of the hours of labor to the lowest practicable point, and for that degree of leisure for all which is a condition of the highest human life."[11] Ward's words were carefully chosen to encourage employers, his primary audience, to take the lead in reducing work hours while offering reasonable pay.

There were moments, however, when Ward's lack of commitment to socialist initiatives was irrelevant, even to the labor movement. As the IWW demonstrated in 1914, Ward's *Social Creed* could serve as a weapon in the hands of organized workers as they fought conservative ministers and business leaders on the righteousness of the profit system. In the year 1912, Harry Ward addressed audiences in seventeen states, including 347 special forums and thirty-six conferences. These numbers were surely boosted by the Men and Religion Forward movement, but Ward also visited twelve colleges, three normal schools, three theological schools, and a few high schools, all with the message that Christians needed to invest themselves in social reform.[12] Ward's 1917 *The Labor Movement, from the Standpoint of Religious Values* celebrated the church as the most important social movement, but it also patiently described the differences among trade unions, industrial unions, and syndicalist unions, and various other class-based strategies for compelling the action of employers and achieving industrial democracy. Ward showed that the "violence" in the labor movement more often derived from state militia and other strikebreakers than from resisting workers themselves.[13] By 1919, Ward had distributed fifteen thousand copies of the *Social Creed*, a feat for which he was deeply indebted to organized labor's endorsement of his work.[14]

The *Social Creed* and Socialism

However, there is a difference between support for the "remediation of poverty," as the *Creed* put it, and support for the actual labor movement. The *Creed* only endorsed the goals of labor insofar as they allowed ministers to claim that the movement for social justice resided in the churches. If we can deduce Ward's intentions through the records he kept during these busy years of *Social Creed* evangelism, his priorities become clear. Ward's records brim not with evidence of a better union contracts or municipal services, but with testimonials of workers who were so touched by his talks on the labor movement that they decided to join a church.[15]

Ward saved numerous notes of appreciation from other Methodist pastors who wrote to him on the ways that his work was increasing church attendance. One minister in a mill town in Massachusetts, and another in a steel town in Ohio, requested more copies of the *Social Creed*, "both in English and Italian."[16] The latter added that his initial canvass of the *Creed* "secured us many new S.S. [Sunday School] attendants."[17] Ward especially cherished reports that he had brought together socialists, unionists, and middle-class Christians to speak frankly with one another. One such wage earner in New York testified, "This is the first time I have been in a church for eighteen years. I would go regularly if I could hear such sermons as I heard tonight."[18] Both the Central Conference of American Rabbis and the National Catholic Welfare Council praised Ward for this support for trade unions.[19] And yet, if Ward received any notes from unions or socialists, he did not keep them in his clipping files. What was important about the *Social Creed* to him was that it functioned to invite wage earners, including women, immigrants, and skeptics, to attend church ministries.[20]

Ward's *Social Creed* arrived at a height of socialist popularity, but Ward refused to support labor leaders as moral authorities. He often invited union leaders to join him on forum platforms in support of better laws and even better labor contracts, but he did so to convince those workers to trust his leadership.[21] A comparison between the *Social Creed* and the priorities of the Socialist Party in 1908 is revealing. That year, the Socialist Party declared its primary concern to be public relief for the unemployed. Socialists demanded

> immediate government relief for the unemployed workers by building schools, by reforesting of cut-over and waste lands, by reclamation of arid tracts, and the building of canals, and by extending all other useful public works. All persons employed on such works shall be employed directly by the government under an eight-hour workday and the prevailing union wages.

Socialists wanted municipal reforms and public works projects. They also asked for significant expansions in the federal government, including the creation of a Department of Labor independent of the Department of Commerce, which would lead the charge to aggregate statistics about unemployment in every state and use this data to targeted public works projects. They demanded full and unrestricted suffrage for men and women, the abolition of the Senate, limitations placed on the power of the Supreme Court, and graduated income taxes.[22]

The *Social Creed of the Churches* made no reference to this problem of cyclical unemployment, poverty, free speech, or political representation for the masses of industrial workers. It made no reference to municipal socialism. The statement did not even mention demands for women's suffrage or working people's rights to the "freedom of the press, speech and assemblage." Again, while the 1912 revision and expansion of the *Social Creed of the Churches* affirmed support "for the right of all men to the opportunity for self-maintenance, for safeguarding this right against encroachments of every kind, and for the protection of workers from the hardships of enforced unemployment," the statement offered no suggestion as to who—business or the state—owed workers this living wage. In fact, the "Relief Measures" Ward offered in his explanatory booklet did not endorse any significant expansion of the welfare state. In his books, Ward argued that government-funded homeless shelters, employment bureaus, works projects, and unemployment insurance were all respectable ideas, but not solutions. Predictably, his section on the subject concluded with the subheading "Church Action" and a statement that churches should demand the "the proper regulation of private employment agencies" and encourage "local industries and public works to cooperatively plan the avoidance of any season of unemployment." In this statement, Ward signaled that he did not stand with socialists in the leadership of the public sector to address the problem of unemployment.[23]

The *Social Creed* also left out any commentary on workers' rights to collective bargaining or a legal minimum wage. Ward wrote that churches stood for "the right of employees and employers alike to organize and for adequate means of conciliation and arbitration in industrial disputes," an awkward statement that endorsed the theoretical right of workers to get a hearing from employers on their grievances, but nothing more. In his book by the same name, Ward elaborated, "There are other methods besides minimum wage laws by which a living wage can be secured for the workers." Collective bargaining, he for example, "often fails and leads to costly strikes. Trade unionism is limited in its power to obtain higher wages." Ward's preferred solution came down to "Church Action." He argued that Christians—by which he meant, white Christian businessmen—needed to rethink the endless desire to exploit poor people. As he put it, "Those who take money that is made at the cost of wasted health and moral destruction stand before God as those who live off the lives of their fellows."[24]

Ward liked the principal of distributed justice, but his *Social Creed* offered no mechanism, outside the "conscience" of Christian businessmen, for bringing it about. The *Social Creed* was silent on the proposition of nationalizing public utilities, a mandated eight-hour day, mandatory factory inspections for health and safety, and the public ownership of utilities. Ward obliquely addressed all this by stating that the problem of the day was the "acquisition and use of property." But, in refusing all specificity with regards to agents of change, his *Social Creed* was a statement of principles with vague and timid suggestions for action.

Unlike church officials, socialists did not ask for cultural shifts with the hope that action would follow. They demanded collective bargaining rights and offered legislative solutions with the intent that the culture would follow. The *Social Creed* left out the parts of the socialist agenda that would grant wage earners the authority to stand on their own before the public. In that respect, it was the hallmark of the Federal Council's agenda for social reform.

Strike Reports and Investigations

The Federal Council's "strike reports," publicly celebrated investigations into labor conflicts, similarly functioned to undermine wage earners' claims that the labor movement was an independent moral community that compelled action on its own. Though minsters described this work as sympathetic, closer examination illustrates that ministers undermined the moral communities that organized strikes and functioned to install white Protestants as the highest moral authorities over the diverse body of workers that populated the growing ranks of the de-skilled working classes.

Clergy involvement in strike reporting began unofficially in 1908, when the Federal Council of Churches' Committee on Church and Social Service began to brainstorm how to be truly useful to society.[25] Protestant ministers reached out to the Taft presidential administration in 1912 and "used [their] influence," as they officially put it, to urge Congress to appoint a Commission on Industrial Relations (USCIR), a research and arbitration body, to examine laboring and working conditions. Taft appointed Frank B. Walsh, a Kansas City labor lawyer, to head the commission. Fellow commissioners included a handful of men who represented "labor," drawn entirely from the leadership of the AFL, and a handful of men who represented "capital," including prominent businessmen from California, Kentucky, and New York. The commission held dozens of hearings with labor leaders and wage earners and published all its findings in an eleven-volume report in 1916.

The Committee on Church and Social Service lent "aid" to many, but not all, of the investigations that the commission undertook. It often conducted parallel investigations that ran alongside the official work of the commission. When ministers showed up, they usually directed interviews to reveal one of two things: (a) the degree to which workers' spiritual lives suffered because of poverty and the imperative for Sunday work, and (b) to the extent to which workers hungered for churches to defend their cause. None of this is surprising, of course; addressing these problems was the mission of the Federal Council. Nonetheless, in driving these federal investigations to reveal that working-class moral and spiritual life was inadequate and in need of moral guidance, ministers used their supposedly neutral influence to undermine and subordinate the moral authority of non-Protestant strikers.

The Federal Council helped investigate the 1910–1911 Bethlehem Steel strike, the 1912 Lawrence strike, the 1911–1912 Muscatine button workers

strike, the 1913 Patterson (New Jersey) silk strike, the glove cutters' strike
in Gloversville (New York) in 1914, and the experience of coal mining (especially in Colorado, West Virginia, and Michigan) in 1913–1914. Few
records remain of the Federal Council's work on most of these investigations,
evidence that clergy's presence in the study was sometimes symbolic.
Yet, in other cases, most notably Henry Atkinson's report on coal miners'
conditions, the Federal Council's presence registered public attention to
workers' struggles.[26]

However, each of these reports arrived too late to be helpful to workers at
the bargaining table. While strike reports functioned to keep a national spot-
light on particular kinds of workers for a middle-class reading audience, the
Federal Council was careful not to validate unions as independent, Christian
vehicles of justice. Consistently, reports emphasized the need for "neutral"
church leadership to intervene in the interest of justice. In a moment of rapid
growth in the number of socialists and syndicalists, especially as leaders
within these very strikes, the term "neutral arbitrators" signified the conservative branch of trades unionists. Nevertheless, AFL members, many of
whom were on the commission, jumped at the opportunity to take credit for
the "successful" settling of radical-led strikes. In partnering with ministers,
they appeared less partisan. They probably also eyed the Federal Council's
extensive data on immigrant communities and local churches; mailing lists
for churches in nearly every town in the United States would be an asset to
any labor movement.

The 1910 Bethlehem (Pennsylvania) Steel strike illustrates both the potential of ministerial support for the labor movement and some of the disconnect between the voiced mission of the Federal Council and the challenges of
putting that mission into practice. Overworked steelworkers in Bethlehem
disputed wages, the speed-up, and the length of the workday. Soon after
the strike began, the ministers called a meeting between the union and
employers. Workers refused to compromise. The ministers grew impatient
and publicly entreated the workers, but not the employers, for refusing to
reach a settlement. As they put it, "Is it reasonable to expect that by attacking
your employer openly and in secret, by trying to destroy his property and his
business, you can best persuade him to deal generously and magnanimously
with you?"[27] If this was the best that the Federal Council could offer workers,
the union condemned the whole council, including the *Social Creed,* as a
farce. Ward was embarrassed by his Bethlehem colleagues and used his office within the Federal Council's Committee on Social Service to authorize

another strike report, which borrowed heavily from the report issued by the US Department of Labor in 1910. In the new Federal Council report, ministers at the national level issued a formal apology to the workers, holding that Bethlehem ministers were "sincerely desirous to serve the interest of the workmen, . . . [but] too far aloof from the workingman to understand him and win his confidence."

Yet even Ward's Commission on Social Service, the very committee upon which Harry Ward sat and which distributed the *Social Creed*, was unwilling to support the strike as a moral action or the union as a respectable mouthpiece for workers. While the USCIR's report on the strike offered no comment on the need for external arbitration, the Federal Council's report demanded it. It began,

> When, on February 4, 1910, three machinists in the Bethlehem Steel Works were discharged for daring to protest in behalf of their fellows against Sunday labor, thus precipitating one of the most notable strikes in this country, they not only raised issues which concern the 9,000 men employed in the steel works, but brought to the attention of the American public certain industrial problems *which cannot be settled by capital and labor alone.* The American people must assume a distinct share in the responsibility of their solution. (Emphasis added.)

The report consistently emphasized the "large number of foreigners" that "made the strike difficult [for the union] to handle." Ministers nominated churches as the "ethical forces of the community" best suited to advocate for workers' real needs and added that churches could provide "opportunities for clean recreation," in contrast to that of taverns.[28]

Ultimately, the Federal Council report minimized the necessity for any union as a long-term solution to the problem.[29] In claiming that "organized labor had nothing to do with inaugurating the strike," the ministers stretched the truth. It was true that no union was recognized by the steel company at the start of the strike and that the strikers had sidestepped the possible demand for a closed shop in the interests of building support. However, the AFL was the entity that organized and initiated the work action. When the ministers claimed, "At no time did the labor union appear in the demands made upon the Steel Company, and the recognition of the union was not asked for in any of the demands of the men," they exploited a point of weakness in the labor movement to serve their own ends. Jacob Tazelaar, general organizer for the AFL, was angered by this distortion of the nature of the steel strike. As he put it, workers went on strike precisely because they were "denied the right of organization."[30]

Tazelaar took the opportunity to report on the farce of the *Social Creed* and the Social Gospel movement in a pamphlet he mass-distributed with the support of the AFL. "The Church, nearly as a whole, the Protestant as well as Catholic Church, gave no aid to the men who were fighting for a great moral issue," he explained.[31] Ministers felt betrayed by this claim, for they believed that they were supporting the labor movement in righting the wrongs of the Bethlehem ministerial association. However, Tazelaar noted that while Bethlehem workers had the moral and financial support of eight other unions around the country, they had no financial support from any churches.[32] Tazelaar added the other major grievance of Bethlehem strikers—the collusion of the Steel Corporation with ministers to garnish wages to pay ministers. This practice, strikers claimed, stole from workers and artificially boosted support for American clergy among wage earners. Yet the Federal Council denied this accusation, trusting the Steel Corporation reports that garnishing Protestant wages always took place *with permission*. This left room, of course, for mandatory garnishment with regards to the Roman Catholic Church.

The Federal Council's final "recommendations" based on the strike likely came as no surprise to workers. They recommended that Bethlehem ministers "organize an open forum for discussion" among workers, merchants, and Catholic priests wherein they could "discuss industrial conditions and civic problems openly and without fear." Of course, the Bethlehem Protestant ministers volunteered to moderate. Regular meetings of this kind, it was suggested, would create better harmony between "strikers and the ethical forces of the community." Strikers, therefore, were constructed as needy of "ethical" leadership.[33] Tellingly, when Charles Stelzle's committee reported back to the Federal Council, he raved that the report on the Bethlehem steel industry was "one of the most important utterances on the industrial situation that has been made up to that time by the Church."[34] He also carried a message from Frank Morrison, secretary of the AFL, which stated, "The moral effect of the visitation of fraternal delegates from the Federal Council of the Churches of Christ in America to the representatives of Labor . . . cannot be overestimated." AFL pundits celebrated the "fraternity and brotherhood" that ministers helped spread. In the long run, strikers gained very little from the intervention of Protestant ministers.

Federal Council intervention into the button strike in Muscatine, Iowa achieved similar ends. In the depths of winter in 1912, more than twenty-five hundred button workers in Muscatine, Iowa, organized a union and then found themselves laid off by their employers, allegedly for overproduction. The union, which contained a number of Socialist Party members recently elected to public office, insisted that the shutdown was "premeditated and without cause"; it was a lockout.[35] The *Muscatine News-Tribune* claimed that the shutdown was in retaliation for the fact that 65 percent of button workers registered as Socialist Party members, and the growing numbers who were now elected to citywide public office. Workers called on the US Commission on Industrial Relations to intervene, but negotiations came to a standstill when manufactures refused to recognize the union.[36] Manufactures called on the governor to send in militia for protection against angry workers. Iowa governor Beryl Carroll ordered workers back to work without a union, but workers only precipitated a boycott. John B. Lennon, AFL executive member and federally appointed arbitrator, wrote to Carroll, "I cannot get [Mr. Umlandt of the Automatic Button Company] to say anything definite. He will talk about matters that are past but as to the future of putting his people back to work, he simply says that he is not ready to say what he will do."[37]

This is when the Federal Council's ministers entered the scene, but their "help" involved rewriting the narrative of the strike to make themselves the heroes. Ministers zeroed in on the rising number of socialists and the degree to which these "young men" have "taken the leadership of the community out of the hands of both [church leaders and business leaders]."[38] Ministers were instructed to be more vigilant in keeping "informed" of "the teachings and character of all those who are attempting public leadership," a thinly veiled suggestion to avoid the heresy of Christian Socialists. Ministers' overall response to the conflict matched closely with recommendations offered at Bethlehem. They recommended "a permanent Arbitration Board," likely composed of business leaders, labor leaders, and ministers, to arbitrate future disputes, and they recommended that board members be "men who are prominent in in religious affairs, [and] who desire to treat their workers squarely." In other words, they supported workers' "collective voice" on the shop floor, but only insofar as that voice would offer a perspective from which ministers and other prominent community members could make their own, allegedly neutral, judgments.[39]

Federal Council ministers also participated in the US Commission on Industrial Relations, but instead of simply supporting the moral claims of workers, they often directed testimony to what they understood as the "problem" of low church attendance among the working classes. Frequently, commissioners called in ministers to witness to the ways that Sunday work expectations held back wage earners from joining a church. The Catholic bishop of Lead, South Dakota, for example, was called in to testify that he had "begged the [Homestake Mining] superintendent for a letter that would permit Catholics to be absent on Sunday without penalty," but to no avail. He watched numerous Catholic workers get fired in retaliation for attending his prolabor church. Several other ministers sounded an alarm at the mass exodus of immigrants, particularly Italians, from any form of church attendance, especially in western mining cities. Archbishop McFaul of Trenton, New Jersey, summarized these findings with the claim that "50,0000,000 [industrial workers] never go to church," and blamed business leaders' complete control over the social and cultural operations in their company towns. This was not simply a Catholic problem, he added; there were "6,000 empty Protestant churches in the Middle West."[40] McFaul's testimony before the commission, a message that he repeated publicly in many venues, tapped into deep American fears about the formation of a rebellious working class without any Christian moral and spiritual leadership.

Yet while commissioners were keen on uncovering obstacles to wage earners' participation in church, they made no effort to consider unions and workers' parties function as alternate Christian communities. The commission even issued a special hearing to explore differences among the various branches of the left wing of the labor movement, including socialists and syndicalists. But the interviews focused on differences in strategy; commissioners never probed the extent to which socialists identified capitalism itself as a moral problem. Morris Hillquit, representing the Socialist Party, identified the "object of the Socialist Party" as the "nationalization of industries," especially those industries with a "social function" that were essential to the public welfare. While his testimony made no use of the terms like "faith" or "morality," he emphasized the ways that capitalism robbed people of dignity. He said, "There are millions of citizens who stand in need of food, clothing, shelter, furniture, books, and so on, but we do not produce them, although we have the facilities to do so. We have the natural resources for it. We have the requisite skill for it, and we have millions of workers ready and eager to do the work required for their own sustenance."[41]

These were such classic socialist arguments that the Socialist Party reprinted the hearing in pamphlet form to clarify their strategies as they infiltrated the AFL. For, in stirring contrast to Hillquit, neither Gompers nor the ministers of the Federal Council had anything to say about the morality of capitalism.[42] In Iowa, as in Pennsylvania, the Federal Council cooperated with the AFL in suffocating socialists' moral and religious critiques of industrial capitalism.

The IWW and Lawrence

In many respects, Sam Gompers' opposition to socialism in 1912 was a very bold, not to mention deeply conservative, position. Socialists were electing officials to public office everywhere, especially within his own AFL locals and the leadership of many other industrial unions. In addition, radical socialists, largely immigrants, were successfully organizing massive strikes under the aegis of the AFL. The Federal Council's alliance with the AFL offered respectability to strikers, but it came with heavy costs. Without the funding the Federal Council of Churches brought in from big business, the executive leadership of the largest trade union might have had to take more seriously the goals of the Socialist Party or the IWW as the best partners it could find.

Gompers was firmly to the right of most of labor's rank and file in 1912. The left wing of the working classes were Wobblies, members of the IWW. As anarchists, Wobblies held out little hope that majority rule would ever support the most needy. They offered sharp critiques of state violence and the mystique of republicanism and believed that the only organizational leadership necessary was within workplaces. As they stated in their charter, Wobblies were united by the conviction that "trade unions foster a state of affairs which allows one set of workers to be pitted against another set of workers in the same industry . . . helping to defeat one another in wage wars." Some socialists were also Wobblies; other Wobblies critiqued socialists for their trust in the political system and the possibility of gradual reform. Wobblies had the most traction among immigrant workers, freethinkers, and those who worked in "proletarianized" industries—like mining—which required no previous training. Proletarians, the Marxist term that Wobblies sometimes used to describe themselves, performed simplified and rote tasks for which they were paid meagerly. In 1912, Wobblies organized for the right of workers to take ownership over farms and factories to share equally in the profits of their labor. Officially, they opposed "the wage system," preferring cooperative ownership of industry, and refused to recognize "that the

craft union movement is a labor movement."[43] They believed in the possibility of uniting all wage workers in "one big union," divided into "industrial
branches" within geographic districts. Their goal was to build local coalitions
of workers at all levels of skill and status.

The IWW, like the Socialist Party, had been acting like a religious com-
munity for years. Music was central to movement culture, and most of the
tunes were borrowed from familiar gospel hymns. "You'll Get Pie in the Sky
When You Die" was borrowed from "The Sweet Bye and Bye." Its author,
Ralph Chaplin, offered satirical commentary on the ways Christians prom-
ised rewards in heaven in place of rewards on earth. "Solidarity Forever,"
Chaplin's most famous song, borrowed from the Civil War hymn "The Battle
Hymn of the Republic."[44] According to the historian Donald Winters, the
IWW was united by faith in "solidarity," a term widely used in the labor
movement to connote belief in a cause greater than any one circumstance.
Their creed was summarized in the *Little Red Songbook*, the IWW preamble,
and the organization's pamphlets.[45]

But in 1911 and 1912, there were other reasons why the IWW was publicly
emphasizing its alternate Christianity. The Federal Council's procapitalist
Social Gospel had successfully persuaded some middling-class whites that
socialism was anti-Christian. At Lawrence, the left wing of the labor movement proceeded to test both ministers and churchgoers by placing the
Wobblies' most eloquent Christian preachers, Arturo Giovanitti and A. J.
Muste, at the helm of the strike.

The Lawrence strike began when the Massachusetts passed legislation
in 1910 ostensibly friendly to the young women and teenage girls who
comprised the majority of textile workers: they limited maximum work
hours from fifty-six to fifty-four per week. Employers in the Lawrence textile mills made clear that they would lower hourly wages to make up for lost
time. Within the Southern and Eastern European immigrant community of
Lawrence, largely composed of Catholics, priests were understood to have
significant influence over the working classes, and the church officially opposed socialism. However, Italian Americans were defecting from their
parishes and joining the Wobblies in great numbers.

Joseph Ettor, executive member of the IWW, sent Arturo Giovannitti, editor of *Il Proletario*, the Italian labor newspaper, and member of the Italian
Socialist Federation and the Socialist Party of America, to lead IWW
organizing in Lawrence. Giovannitti was born in Italy and migrated to North
America to work in Christian missions for the poor. He did coursework

in theology at Union Theological Seminary in New York before leaving to work full time in labor organizing. He would work alongside a team of local organizers in Lawrence, including Clark Carter, a Congregationalist minister at the Lawrence City Mission. Carter was in touch with the more than forty Catholic and Protestant churches in Lawrence and stood ready to conduct a left-wing "labor forward" movement through these church connections. He worked with Ettor to build a citywide "relief committee" to help finance the cost of striking.[46] Once Giovannitti and colleagues in the IWW had built momentum and a union local, the Amalgamated Textile Workers of America (an AFL affiliate) sent another Christian minister-turned-labor organizer, A. J. Muste, to join Giovannitti in strike communications. This intentionally Christian and socialist strategy for organizing Lawrence textile workers was, of course, carefully planned. Giovannitti's religious language succeeded in winning significant support within the community of clerics and social reformers, their most important allies in winning the strike. Yet, while Giovannitti initially accepted their partnership, he would not allow ministers to use him as a pawn in their own projects.

Over and over, Giovannitti emphasized the necessity of workers leading in building whatever coalition they might desire with middle-class churchgoers. His preached sermons like a minister, but instead of expounding on personal ethics, he inspired workers to take ownership of the power, and freedom from the wage system, that was deservedly theirs. As Giovannitti put it,

> Blessed are the rebels, for they shall reconquer the earth
> There is no destiny that they cannot break;
> There are no chains of iron that the other cannot destroy; . . .
> Arise, then, ye men of the plough and the hammer, the helm
> And the lever, and send forth to the four winds of the earth
> your new proclamation of freedom which shall be the last and shall
>   abide forevermore.[47]

The *Atlantic Monthly* immediately fell in love with the dashing anarchist poet. They reported that he "preached with missionary intensity the doctrine of Syndicalism."[48] Within days, Giovannitti found leading a strike of over twenty thousand young women of more than twenty-five nationalities. Clark Carter, testifying on behalf of the Lawrence City Mission, recounted that a large fraction of churches and mutual aid organizations in Lawrence supported the strike. He said, "It was my pleasure to refer various people who came to me for assistance—and whom I would gladly have assisted out of the funds at my disposal—to their own churches and their pastors, who were actively engaged in the work." When he was questioned by a Congressional committee a year later about which other churches supported the strike, Clark returned, "Do you want me to name about 40 churches?"[49] Giovannitti and Ettor forwarded the textile workers' demands to mill owners: an increase in wages, double pay for overtime work, and no discrimination against workers for their strike activity. The work action would become known as the "Bread and Roses" strike, for workers demanded not only sustenance ("bread"), but also spending money to buy things like flowers, dresses, and molasses ("roses").

Not surprisingly, the Citizens Association of Lawrence, a group of businessmen who owned the mills, interpreted the strike as a declaration of war upon Christian, American ideals. They called upon police, strikebreakers, and the state militia to resist the IWW by any means necessary.[50] Many strikers were jailed for the crime of disturbing the peace. Yet twenty-three thousand workers continued the strike even after workers had begun to fill up the jails. On January 29, 1912, the militia cornered a group of demonstrators on a street corner. After pushing and shoving, one striker, thirty-four-year-old Anna LoPezzi, was shot by police in a conflict blamed on the strikers. Despite the accepted fact that neither of the strike organizers, Giovannitti nor Ettor, was present at the murder, they were charged "accessories" to the "unlawful violence and riot" and jailed without bail from January 1911 until the following November.[51]

Without wasting time, Elizabeth Gurley Flynn and William Haywood took over communications.[52] When violence escalated, children were put on trains to wait out the strike with sympathetic families outside of Lawrence. Strikers staged parades and pageants with the IWW flag and songs from the IWW's *Big Red Songbook*, including parodies of, "Glory, Glory Hallelujah." The Citizens Association sponsored counterparades with the slogan "For God and Country! The Stars and Stripes Forever. The Red Flag Never." The parade featured a man who dressed up as Uncle Sam and a woman as the Statue of Liberty.[53] Such demonstrations attempted to pressure the immigrant strikers into breaking with the "foreign" politics and proving their Americanness, including a kind of American gender conformity. Lady Liberty, of course, did not protest. When, after more than six months on strike, Lawrence workers finally won the strike and went back to work, Giovannitti and Ettor still had not had their trial. The IWW raised $60,000 for their defense and held demonstrations around the country to illustrate the injustice of the arrest. On September 30, fifteen thousand Lawrence workers went on a one-day strike to demand their release. Italian supporters demonstrated in front of the American consulate in Rome.[54]

While in jail, Giovannitti and Ettor continued to craft their defense in Christian terms. They translated Emile Pouget's *Sabotage* into English, adding a foreword on their experience with the law in Lawrence. Giovannitti would represent the radical labor movement as heralds of a more Christian civilization that would soon displace the current one.[55] At his trial, his defense consisted largely in claims that he was, like Socrates and Jesus Christ, a "dreamer" and an idealist. Killing idealistic philosophers never actually eradicates those ideas but strengthens their power. As he put it at his trial, he challenged the judge to consider whether killing Christ, "who was adjudged an enemy of the Roman social order and put on the cross," solved the problem of insurrection in Rome. He continued, "Does he believe for a moment that the cross or the gallows or the guillotine, the hangman's noose, ever settled an idea? . . . If the idea can live it lives, because history adjudges it right."

He continued later,

It may be that we are dreamers, it may be that we are fanatics . . . but yet so was a fanatic Socrates, who instead of acknowledging the philosophy of the aristocrats of Athens preferred to drink the poison. And so was a fanatic the Savior Jesus Christ, who instead of acknowledging his submission to all the rulers of the times and all the priestcraft of the time, preferred the cross between two thieves. . . . We have been working in something that is dearer to us than our lives and our liberty; we have been working in what are our ideas, our ideals, our aspirations, our hopes—*you may say our religion* . . . we are now the heralds of a new civilization; we have come here to proclaim a new truth; *we are the apostles of a new evangel, a new gospel.*[56] (Emphasis added.)

Giovannitti hoped that Protestants and Catholics in Massachusetts would consider the radical labor movement within the American mythology of separatist religious traditions. In a final statement, he moved the jury to tears with the suggestion that if he must be put to death (like the Haymarket martyrs of a generation earlier), he would willingly embrace the opportunity to move the world closer to the truth. History, he argued, "shall have the last word to us."[57] The agitators, reaching into the broad appeal of Christian Socialism, were acquitted within two weeks.

As it turned out, the spectacle of the trial successfully convinced many middle-class, Anglo-Protestant sympathizers that the IWW was a good organization. "Why should Giovannitti, once a student at Union Theological Seminary and superintendent of the Methodist mission, be lost to the church?" wrote an editor for *The Continent*. Overlooking Giovannitti's support for the tactic of sabotage and his personal rejection of Jesus as messiah, the editor continued, "The man's basic beliefs are only Christian altruism— he learned his passion for humanity in the church at the feet of the best men's Brother." Moreover, "Why were his excess of ardor and immaturity of judgment allowed to force him outside the pale of organized Christianity? The man is a born dreamer and devotee, and a leader of men. He only needed ripening to be a great minister."[58] In that high noon of challenges on biblical orthodoxy, liberal Protestants raised few quibbles about the fact that Giovannitti was no longer an orthodox believer.[59]

A. J. Muste, graduate of Union Theological Seminary and former minister of the Ford Washington Collegiate Church in New York City—as well as a Christian pacifist labor organizer, praised Giovannitti. "It is of peculiar interest to one who is himself a graduate of a Protestant theological seminary, and who is having his own struggle trying to make what he learned there fit within the new scientific thought and social ideals, to learn that Giovannitti himself once began preparations for the Protestant ministry," he recounted.[60] When the noted "liberal" theologian of Union Theological Seminary, William Emerson Fosdick, publicly supported Giovannitti and the IWW, the IWW republished his commentary.[61] So many socialist Christians supported Giovannitti and the IWW that Federal Council leaders like Charles Stelzle and Harry Ward grew worried that they were losing their own moral high ground in the public square.

Sagamore Conference

The Presbyterian Reverend Charles Stelzle's response to all this was predictable; he would invite Giovannitti to the annual Sagamore Conference on Christian social work and try to suggest that Giovannitti was only an accessory to the Federal Council's larger Social Gospel project. Giovanitti would name this strategy and reject it.

"The Sagamore," started in 1907, was a yearly meeting of social workers, settlement house workers, professors, ministers, and other progressives interested in "Christian Sociology." Josiah Strong, Charles Stelzle, and Walter Rauschenbush, in addition to leaders of public forums like George Coleman, had all sat on the organizational board in years past. The previous Sagamore had "rejoiced at the signs of the times and the ever-multiplying evidences of the progress of the kingdom of God and the principles of fundamental democracy."

Inspired by Rauschenbush and Ward, if not by the abolitionist movement of their grandparents' era, participants discussed the ideals of "social salvation" and "complete emancipation of the individual man and the brotherly union of the entire race."[62] In inviting Giovannitti and Ettor, only recently released from jail, to the Sagamore, leaders probably hoped that they would offer good publicity for Giovannitti and Ettor that would be returned with public deference toward these white Anglo-Protestant social workers and ministers. All these members of the program committee, but most notably Josiah Strong, had presumed no change in the social, racial, and gendered hierarchies of the church, and the culture, of the nineteenth-century United States. They likely expected that their willingness to include the Italian anarchists would be returned with appreciation.[63] Yet in positioning Giovannitti within a spectrum of Christian radicals, capitalists, and unionists, the Sagamore Conference only stoked the rivalry between the churches and the labor movement for leadership in the new social crusade.

Charles Stelzle and Charles MacFarland, who gave speeches early in the event, set the stage for the debate by reminding the audience that the "Churches," described in that capitalized sense of universality, should lead the nation toward industrial democracy. Stelzle hoped that all Protestant churches would be more like the Presbyterian "Labor Temple" that he shepherded in New York City. They would make room for union meetings and women's social work ministries, and workers would patronize them in place of bars and saloons. Stelzle exhorted his audience that socialists were growing out of control. "About three or four years ago," he said, "socialists only had about one seventh of the delegates" to the AFL's convention. "At the last convention they represented fully one third." Stelzle hoped to "wipe out conditions which give rise to socialism," including poverty, unsafe working conditions, and alcohol, and support trade unions' attempts to grant (highly skilled) workers higher wages and improved working conditions.[64]

Essentially, Stelzle reiterated the Federal Council's agenda: he hoped to locate, or relocate, the movement for Christian social justice to the churches.

In this circle, Stelzle and the Federal Council stood out as conservatives for their dogged interest in increasing church membership. Richard Ely, the University of Wisconsin sociologist in attendance, had spent decades supporting socialists, populists, and union members in their struggles, including in their conflicts with conservative churches. Other social reformers, especially within the settlement house movement, believed in the possibility of what they called a "national religion," a civil religion of "solidarity" that would bind Americans together in a common morality and minimize theological and doctrinal distinctions. As Charles Zueblin of the Northwestern University settlement announced at the beginning of the conference, "The common morality of our common life promises to be a religious solvent."[65] To Zueblin, as well as Jane Addams of Hull House, every person could have a personal "creed," but Americans needed a common faith in "cooperation" that would bind them together outside of divisive religious debates.[66] By 1914, Arturo Giovannitti's vision of establishing Christian justice outside of the parameters of a church likely affirmed for the large number of socialist Christians and Christian Socialists in attendance that labor leaders might be best poised to establish the coming "national religion," a civic morality for the cooperative commonwealth.

Giovannitti's ability to capture the attention of both his audience and the media provides a window into the vast approval for a Christian, worker-led platform within the labor movement. The young labor leader's keynote speech, "The Constructive Side of Syndicalism," both christened syndicalism and defended the importance of having laborers speak for themselves. He explained that syndicalism was about worker-led reclamation of industrial capital and thus a rejection of compromise in the search for justice. "Ours is not a gospel of pacification," nor one of "harmony and brotherly love. So far as the economic conditions are concerned, ours is a struggle for the mastership and rulership of the earth." In case his message was unclear, Giovannitti explicitly rejected Federal Council investigations and arbitrations of industrial disputes and their accompanying messages, which entrusted business leaders with a decision to simply pay workers more. "Who is going to say what is a fair share for the laborer?" he queried, "Who is going to say what is a fair share for the capitalist? Who is going to say how many hours one should work and the other should sleep? We must have a neutral judge, an absolutely impartial judge."⁶⁷ As he emphasized, capitalism does not make room for churches to be neutral.

The only way to achieve the Kingdom of God, he claimed, was by enabling the poor to manage their own social and economic futures. As an anarcho-syndicalist, Giovannitti opposed efforts that relied upon the state to "dispense welfare to every member of the community by keeping them in subjection and slavery." In a syndicalist society, all people would, a priori, function as a unit of a larger whole.⁶⁸ The labor leader thus struck an uncommon chord of consensus within a union nearly torn apart by debates over the justice of sabotage as a defensive mechanism.⁶⁹ A. J. Portenar, labor leader and syndicalist in the printing trades, followed Giovannitti's address with another long critique of parliamentary socialism, entitled "Perversion of an Ideal." He said that syndicalists rejected the sluggishness of parliamentary methods but did not desire sabotage. The general strike was the only and most just way of achieving justice. To the quibble that such ideas were merely utopian, Portenar countered, "All that has been said of the IWW and of syndicalism has been said of trades unions in days gone by."⁷⁰

That summer day, Giovannitti won wide support for the Christian value of worker-led movements. Settlement House manager William Ewing, superintendent of the Wells Memorial Institute in Boston affirmed, "Mr. Giovannitti has said that only three or four persons in this audience would be in sympathy with him. I think he has found that a mistake. I think the audience is in deep sympathy with every man who is endeavoring to improve the position of people who are in such hard conditions as those for whom he is working." He strongly affirmed the antisabotage elements of the IWW, as he averred that violence was not warranted until all other methods of change were exhausted. But the settlement house leader and his colleagues agreed with Giovannitti and the IWW "in all places except where it differs from socialism."⁷¹ Giovannitti's radicalism had called into question the Socialist Party's vision for social democracy, but he made the socialist redistribution of the profits of industry seem both moderate and Christian.

Conclusion

In sum, starting in 1912, wage earners exposed pretentions to solidarity in the *Social Creed of the Churches* with evidence that their noncommittal "principles" meant nothing without support for the actual labor movement. Through their actions, trades unionists, socialists, and Wobblies illustrated that they had the same moral and spiritual authority to lead the working poor as those who called themselves professional ministers. Yet the labor movement did more than simply critique the *Social Creed of the Churches*; they *made* the *Social Creed of the Churches* into the document they wanted it to be. Trade unions, socialists, and even Wobblies distributed the *Social Creed of the Churches* widely and maintained close relationships with ministers like Harry Ward, Charles Stelzle, Henry Atkinson, and Clark Carter.

On the local as well as the national level, wage earners educated ministers on the problems with capitalism and pushed them to voice their support for labor, especially on matters that related to them, such as relief from Sunday work. According to an internal report of their social reform work in 1915, ministers reported with pride that "leaders of social movements expressed appreciation" for their service.[72] While this may be a stretch, it reflects labor leaders' facility in cultivating allies who felt respected. Workers used the moral, physical, and financial resources that churches offered them and largely accepted their solidarity graciously. If the Federal Council had more money and access to good publicity, the labor movement had members who could literally shut down whole industries and whole cities at a time. The two movements depended upon one another, and they knew it. However, while the labor movement only selectively used the resources that ministers brought to the table, those ministers' voices rung louder than some workers had hoped. When we turn from the national sphere to the local sphere, it becomes clearer that the labor movement's ministerial allies were taking a dominant role within the labor movement. Organized workers were growing reliant upon their ministerial allies for their sponsorship of the movement's cultural and social existence in urban space.

That is, as a result of the Men and Religion Forward movement, the widespread publicity of the *Social Creed of the Churches*, and the example of the Lawrence strike as credit to the "Social Gospel," Protestant ministers were moving from allies to unofficial spokesmen. These ministers appeared to welcome workers to use their churches with no strings attached, but in fact those strings were considerable. When labor leaders made use of churches and church property to host public discussions and organize strikes, those actions were read by other progressive reformers as church-based "ministry." Instead of entrusting labor leaders as the interlocutors of their own struggle, journalists and public officials sought supervising ministers for comment. Technically, organized workers had the power to withdraw from their partnerships with ministers at any time. But as the Great War began in Europe, ministers' latitude to define what was and was not an appropriate use of their ministries would turn out to determine the boundary between the Social Gospel and socialism.

7

Charles Stelzle's Labor Temple and the Contested Boundaries of American Religion

When he put out the four-foot-square electric sign at the corner of Fourteenth Street and Second Avenue in 1910, Charles Stelzle likely knew that the term "Labor Temple" would be confusing.[1] There was another building called "Labor Temple" not far from his, and this was not a church, but a building that provided meeting space for all the unions associated through the Central Labor Union within the city. The other New York Labor Temple was owned by a local labor federation and served as a social and political center for Jewish and Italian socialists. It regularly hosted union and socialist meetings, free public lectures, and rented space to host painting and music classes for neighborhood residents.[2] Stelzle's Labor Temple also offered union meeting space, free college courses, and public forums, but it was owned by the Presbytery of New York.[3] Were it not for the fact that the building was a beautiful Presbyterian church abandoned by Anglo-Americans who fled to the suburbs, one might have missed that Stelzle's intentions were explicitly ecclesiastical.

Stelzle's Labor Temple serves as a case study in Federal Council of Churches ministries and their ambitions at the local level. As ministers sought to "clean up" cities, an initiative that included shutting down the "vice districts," taverns, and dance halls that bred allegedly disorderly behavior and radical ideas, they hoped to replace these centers of immigrant life with their large churches. These ornate, semipublic complexes, they suggested, would serve a bit like settlement houses; they would create spaces within which wage earners could safely interact with public intellectuals, politicians, and middle-class professionals. And yet wage earners' use of the New York City Labor Temple in the 1910s reveals the extent to which church officials took advantage of the resource starvation of the working classes and used their churches to solidify their own authority and control over urban space.

The Gospel of Church. Janine Giordano Drake, Oxford University Press. © Oxford University Press 2024.
DOI: 10.1093/oso/9780197614303.003.0008

Wage earners used the Presbyterian Labor Temple as a labor temple or labor church in the Christian Socialist tradition. That is, its auditorium and meeting rooms served as a locus for union building, strike organizing, and recreation, even as only a handful attended the explicitly "religious" services. Wage earners especially made use of the protected ecclesiastical space during the Red Scare, when socialist conversations were proscribed by the state. But when pushed, church officials refused to protect the religious speech of their socialist members, as they would not admit that these radicals were a central part of their spiritual community.

Ministers of the Federal Council of Churches, especially those on the Committee on Church and Social Service, worked both nationally and locally to accomplish very similar goals. In making their churches into community centers, Protestant ministers put themselves at the center of urban community formation and rendered wage earners dependent, or at least desirous, of the resources they had to give away. However, these resources came with strings attached. New York City Labor Temple officials used their ministries as evidence that they were committed to social justice, but their priorities for those ministries remained different from those of many of their patrons. For example, when the Red Scare came to the Labor Temple, the New York Presbytery defended its own authority as ordained ministers to offer controversial, prophetic perspectives in the name of American Christianity. Meanwhile, they refused to grant that kind of immunity to the wage earners who had made that space their own. More broadly, Federal Council ministers encouraged the public to entrust them as leaders in the world of social service and to see their churches as public institutions that served the common good, but they also used their oversight to sharply limit the boundaries of the Christian faith.

Stelzle's Vision

The abandoned church that would become the Labor Temple sat in one of the most radical and anticlerical neighborhoods on the East Coast, if not the entire United States. This Lower East Side neighborhood, filled with Yiddish, Polish, Slovak, Magyar, and Italian immigrants, had very few white Protestants and a number of leading socialist institutions.[4] According to Stelzle's survey, a resounding 79 percent of its residents (429,000 of 542,000) spoke a primary language other than English.[5] In 1906, it became home to the Rand School of Social Science, a Socialist Party school aimed to educate workers in radical citizenship, and economics, for the coming revolution. In 1914, Bouck White would found the Church of the Social Revolution, a socialist church committed to a proletarian Jesus and hymns of the coming "Revolution," only a few blocks away. White, a Socialist Party member, wrote his own socialist hymns to popular American tunes and published them with a socialist press for wide distribution within socialist congregations around the country. Song titles included "The Commonwealth Is Coming," "We Speak a Manifesto," and "Workers of the World, Unite!," as well as moving meditations on child labor, industrial accidents, and "the profit takers," big business owners.[6] The neighborhood was also home to Morris Hillquit, a lawyer and Socialist Party leader who would win forty-five thousand votes for mayor of New York City in 1917. In addition to the socialist and Christian Socialist messages that filled the city streets, the (other) Labor Temple hosted feminists and anarchists like Emma Goldman, Margaret Sanger, Alexander Berkman, and Elizabeth Gurley Flynn, who also openly critiqued Catholic and Protestant ministers and preached of a much higher morality within their own causes.[7]

Stelzle told the New York Presbytery that the territory "bounded by Fourteenth Street, East River, Katherine Street, the Bowery and Fourth Avenue" was the most important mission field in New York City. In his first weekly installment of the *Labor Temple Bulletin* in 1912, Stelzle reflected, "The Church has its work, that of moral and religious teaching, which no other organization in the world can do for it." It was a thinly veiled way of saying that he would not let anarchists, feminists, and socialists lead in the revolution for working-class justice.[8]

Stelzle's vision for the Labor Temple was twofold: first, he hoped to reframe this Presbyterian building into an exciting, ecumenically Protestant church and to serve as an example that traditional Christian morality was hip. As an institutional church, the building was open weekdays for religious, social, and civic meetings. On weekends, from 2:30 p.m. to 10:00 p.m., it hosted Bible classes, organ recitals, literary clubs, concerts, (censored) film showings, and theatrical performances.

The auditorium, which doubled as a sanctuary, seated a thousand people and was designed to walk a modern boundary between religious worship and entertainment.[9] Stelzle recounted, "I had carefully studied the methods of motion picture houses and vaudeville houses to discover means for introducing life and snappiness into the program." Among his many acts of showmanship, after the sermon at the end of a service, "Almost at the snap of the finger, the curtain was pulled to one side, the lights were turned up, and the choir burst forth into an inspiring song." This, he found, minimized the number of people who left church early.[10] Historian Jean Kilde found that like many theatrical spaces, "evangelical auditoriums" often included stages, houselights, and stage lights. Because middle-class congregants valued talented public speakers, this space illuminated both the speaker's importance and his or her message.[11] Stelzle hoped his church would replace vaudeville-type theaters in his neighborhood, which likely included opportunities for drinking and extramarital sex.

Second, Stelzle wanted to increase the number of working-class men who attended churches. In 1910, seven hundred "working girls" used the Labor Temple for a mass meeting of the Book Binders' Union, and Stelzle was pleased that the space kept them safe from other meeting places that doubled as disreputable dancing halls.[12] However, his interest was primarily in men's membership in churches and in their ability to protect women from such disrepute. In the Labor Temple's Sunday afternoon forum, by far his most popular program, with five hundred people attending weekly, a series of lectures by prominent scholars in the auditorium were followed by extended questions and answers. Then, from 8:00 p.m. to 10:00 p.m., Stelzle set aside time for fellowship among young workingmen. He used the first hour as a traditional Presbyterian service with a sermon geared especially geared to working-class youth; the second hour featured a motion picture. If the young people wanted to see the movie, they were strongly urged to come first for the service. Of the unholy hour between nine and ten on Sunday evenings, he commented, "This is the zero hour in a big city. Perhaps more young people go wrong during that hour than any other."[13]

The goal of the Labor Temple and of Stelzle's church overall, he said, was to function as a politically neutral haven of believers.[14] Just like the network of politically neutral unions organized as the American Federation of Labor, Stelzle explained, "The Church may work with any other society, insofar as their purposes are similar, but there can be no just criticism against the Church if it declines to endorse the complete program of the organization with which it is for the time being cooperating . . . the Church must have the right to maintain a neutral position, just as the trades union would not be expected to take sides were the church to take up denominational differences."[15] He often acknowledged the popularity of the Christian Socialist and anticlerical positions. As he would mention, "some men are wont to say" that "the

Church has always been against the workingman." He even acknowledged the compelling historical arguments made by Christian Socialist Cyrenus Osborne Ward to earn esteem. "During the first centuries of its history," he wrote in the *Bulletin*, "the Church received its strongest support from the great labor guilds of the period—the labor unions we would now call them— and it is not impossible that Jesus himself was a member of the Carpenter's Guild of Nazareth." However, instead of agreeing with Ward's final argument that organized religion had been aligned against workers for hundreds of years, Stelzle used Ward's evidence as proof that Christianity is a working people's religion. He concluded the essay, "I confess that the Church has not done all that it should for humanity, because, after all, it is made up of poor, weak, mortals. But give it credit for what it has done. You would demand the same treatment for trades unionism, or any other society, and rightfully so."[16] Stelzle essentially conflated Christian Socialists with anticlerical atheists, arguing that both repeatedly failed to trust the churches as centers of moral justice.

Stelzle would invite prominent progressives and radicals to heavily moderated discussions in his large, glimmering auditorium. Yet he would interpret their statements as highly partisan and use every opportunity to remind his audience that the church had no official position on "social systems" or "economic systems."[17] For example, socialist George Strobel and Rev. John Haynes Holmes heatedly debated to what extent the "present social system . . . must be demolished."[18] Rev. Norman Thomas, Socialist Party member who was then only a Presbyterian pastor on the Upper East Side, was invited to give a talk on "God and the Social Hope," with a response by Stelzle himself.[19] Stelzle set up such events to make his argument that there is no single Christian perspective on economic change, and thus continually undercut the argument that Jesus was a socialist. "We may set it down as a fundamental principle that the Church cannot advocate any economic system, no matter what it may be," he wrote in January 1911: "The Church is purely a voluntary association and it is composed of all classes, including both employers and employees. The Church cannot assume to legislate for its members on matters which are clearly outside its province, and concerning which men have the right to disagree, and in which no direct moral principle is involved."[20]

When he did not expect to be successful in maintaining his authority as moderator, it is likely that Stelzle invited middle-class Presbyterian to join him by filling seats in the audience and giving credence to his conservative statements. One evening in 1910, for example, Stelzle hosted a debate between the Anthony Comstock and the anarchists and feminists Emma Goldman and Dr. Ben Reitman on the rights of individuals to birth control information and prophylaxis (condoms). In his memoir, Stelzle recalled that both Goldman and Reitman were shocked by the audience's reverence for his own authority.[21] After all, Goldman and Reitman knew the neighborhood well. Yet, in his weekly *Labor Temple Bulletin*, written for his immigrant neighbors, Stelzle rehashed the event by reminding his audience that Comstock did not really understand the neighborhood. He said that his "characterization of 'so-called liberals, free-thinkers and free-lovers'; had the effect of stirring up a lively time. . . . It scarcely needed the decisions of the presiding officer to control them—the audience attended to that, as usual."[22] It is likely that Stelzle planted his friends, a mixture of Union Theological Seminary students, social work volunteers, and middle-class ministry volunteers, in the audience to reinforce his messages.

Stelzle hoped that the Labor Temple's ministries would undermine the moral space that the labor and radical movements had begun to carve within this neighborhood. When he turned over leadership of the institution to Rev. Jonathan Day in 1912, he began a lecture series on the question, "Have We Use Any Longer for the Church?" The great utility of the Labor Temple for lectures, union meetings, and other events made the answer evident. Invited lecturers addressed this question from many disciplinary backgrounds, but their answer was always the same: modern America needed a Church with a capital C.

In early March 1912, a Dr. Thompson argued that the church must "concern herself with the social, moral, and physical welfare of the people of America. The Church has it in her power to keep the big moral issues before the people and to make men realize that they should not only be Christian men, but Christian citizens." The following week, Rev. R. C. Hull declared the same. Stelzle interpreted the large attendance, respect of visitors for Christianity, and clear message about the church at these meetings as evidence of the Labor Temple's success. He reflected in August 1912, "We expect in the future to bring to happy and organized culmination that earnest religious aim which has always been central in all plans for the development of the work of the Labor Temple."[23] By "religious aim," he meant an evangelism that led to both personal conversions and a more corporate, cultural realization of the importance of the church in modern America. Before long, the tension between these twin goals of Protestant churches would divide the Presbyterian denomination in controversy.

White Goods Strike, 1913–1914

When we look at the Labor Temple from the perspective of workers, however, we notice that Stelzle's hope for the space as an evangelical Protestant outreach was presumptuous. Many of the Jewish, Italian, Slavic, and Anglo-Protestant migrants who used the auditorium and recreational space on a regular basis had nothing to do with the explicitly religious ministries that Stelzle ran on Sunday evenings.

Some workers treated the space as the kind of Labor Temple that Upton Sinclair described in his 1922 *They Call Me Carpenter*. When Sinclair's Jesus returns to the world as a humble carpenter, he searches hard for his churches, but cannot find them. Eventually, he identifies the workers in the Labor Temple as the people who follow the commands of his Father. The Carpenter chooses to train and encourage his disciples there. When a film producer offers to broadcast the Carpenter's religious message for the poor to glorify church attendance, the idol of the day, Carpenter refuses. The businessman tries to tempt Jesus, saying that he could "bring de Japs and de Chinks and de ni***rs—de vooly headed savages. . . . I offer you the whole world, Mr. Carpenter, and you would be the boss!" But the Carpenter declines the offer.[24] In creating such an obvious interaction between good and evil, the humble Carpenter and the businessman filmmaker imperialist, Sinclair proposes that the true Jesus cares about and identifies with the poor, but not for the sake of building larger and more opulent dens of organized Christianity. Sinclair's Jesus is not at all concerned about church attendance. He compares wealthy Christians' regard for the poor to that of the Pharisees, a "pretense" for the sake of high regard within churches.[25]

To Sinclair and the host of socialists who were politically actualized by his work, Christianity was only found within the intentionally anticapitalist institutions of the labor temple, labor church, and labor movement. Since capitalism was part and parcel of the scheme of the devil to give some people unlimited and selfish power, Christian Socialists insisted that labor organizing must have a spiritual platform. Sinclair ended his modern-day parable, "We live in an age, the first in human history, when religion is entirely excluded from politics and politics excluded from religion." Sinclair thought this was a shame. The novel, he claimed, was "a literal translation of the life of the world's greatest revolutionary martyr, the founder of the world's first proletarian party," and to it he attached an appendix of references to Scripture corresponding to each scene in his story.

Similarly, between 1910 and 1918, the Labor Temple skyrocketed in its use as a neighborhood center for political, social, and, in some cases, spiritual life. Stelzle described the demographics of the Labor Temple membership as an ethnic and religious mirror of its neighborhood. Aside from being 95 percent male by design, the membership counted 75 percent "socialists and other radicals" and, among these, 50 percent Jews.[26] Likely, many of the radicals who were not Jewish were Italian.[27] Stelzle's goals for the space did not keep radical and Jewish workers outside. During the winter of 1912–1913, the building functioned as the base of strike operations for the white goods strike, a campaign led and executed by young women garment workers ("girls"). During these cold winter months, not only did the Labor Temple feed and house dozens of women, but organizers let strikers freely use their auditorium for mass meetings. Even though women led the strike, dozens of working-class men descended on the Labor Temple and tried to distribute socialist materials. Rev. Jonathan Day proudly reported on his system of guards at the door that kept out five hundred "young men who could give no bonafide evidence that they were entitled to entrance."[28]

The left-leaning young minister, Jonathan Day, made room for workers to use the space as they wished. During that cold winter, the white goods strikers met at the Labor Temple daily, except for Sundays. On Monday evenings, the space offered the girls the room to host speeches and rallies to maintain morale. One week, for an audience estimated between five hundred and six hundred, Day invited the renowned minster and Christian Socialist W. D. P. Bliss to give a short talk on their struggle for shorter hours and higher wages. His daughter Enid traveled with him and followed his talk with song, both in Russian and in Italian. One of the strike organizers, Louis Taylor, sang and recited poetry. Miss Last, another striker, recited Ella Wheeler Wilcox's poem, "Justice—Not Charity." Labor Temple personnel served the strikers ice cream and cake, and Day reported with satisfaction, "The strikers themselves helped splendidly in the distribution of the refreshments," which had to be distributed in the auditorium, both in the gallery and in the balcony." He rejoiced at the fact that so many strikers had made the Temple their own.[29]

And yet, as the Labor Temple came into national focus, Day backtracked on both his radical goals of the Labor Temple and his proud support for the white goods strikers. Initially, he reported on the strike with obvious solidarity, "We are so glad to have these hundreds and even thousands of girls feel that we are their friends to the extent that we want to give them a decent place in which to meet . . . we want to cooperate with them for social justice."[30] As local and national attention focused on the Labor Temple as a haven of radicals, however, Day stopped emphasizing his and the strikers' shared goals for social justice and emphasized instead the Labor Temple's function as a neutral, protective space. "We have attempted not only to protect these girls from invasion of undesirables, who do not belong in their Unions, and who seek them out with no good intent," Day wrote in February, "but we have tried, also, to inspire them with a desire for lawfulness and genuine civility."[31]

By the end of the winter, support from the International Ladies Garment Workers Union and the strong leadership of Rose Schneiderman brought these strikers success. They negotiated a "50 hour week, an increase in wages with a minimum of $5 per week, and an end to the practice of sending work out to sweatshops and home workers." However, manufacturers initially refused to recognize the union's bargaining power. The women stayed out on strike until the "preferential shop" was won, in part thanks to the organizing space of the Labor Temple.[32]

Unemployed Occupation of the Churches, 1914–1915

The following winter, 1914–1915, a record four hundred thousand men in New York City were unemployed, fifty thousand of whom were known to walk the streets at night to show their numbers. According to Stelzle's account, a group of workers began entering several churches in New York City to apprehend pew cushions, presumably for poor families to sleep upon during the cold winter. This was part of the ongoing strategy of IWW church invasions, efforts to test the principles set out in the Social Creed. Yet, despite his claims that he hoped the church would be a haven for neighborhood workers, Stelzle chastised workers for assuming "that they had a right to the 'soft cushions' which were not being used during the week by the members of the church." In the classic IWW test of whether the Labor Temple really belonged to the people, Stelzle's answer was no.[33]

In his open forum following the event in 1915, Stelzle insisted that the workers' claims on the space of the church as a house for the unemployed took improper advantage of the correct purposes of a church. Stelzle's speech gestured to the disdain and spitefulness that he understood among workers who sought to occupy churches for political movements. He recalled, "I told the audience that their boldness assumed that the preachers were afraid of being considered un-Christlike if they refused to permit the unemployed to crowd into their buildings. So they defiantly took possession of whatever church building they wished, disregarding all the courtesies and decencies of conduct which they themselves demanded of everyone else."

He continued that the churches were "never constructed to be used as lodging-houses" due to limited sanitary facilities and said that many churches found that after occupying workers left, "vile" remnants were left, "often due to pure maliciousness." Perhaps he referred to urine and feces. He went on to explain that such acts, in addition to the diseases that he understood many workingmen already carried, "defil[ed]" the church sanctuary. During the discussion after Stelzle's speech, however, workers vocally disagreed, trying to take back the forum as a space to spread their ideas about churches. Stelzle left us no specific records of what else the workers wanted to discuss, but perhaps they wanted to discuss birth control, the color line, or state entitlements to social insurance. Perhaps they discussed who should really set the terms for what was and was not permissible in the building. Whatever the topic was, the discussion erupted into a "free-for-all fight." Even though the New York Presbytery owned the land, the workers believed that they were entitled to use the space.[34]

At the Annual Convention of the American Federation of Labor later that year, socialist Thomas Van Lear, who had led protests against Stelzle's Men and Religion Forward movement three years earlier, raised the subject of unemployed workers occupying churches. He declared, "Most of the churches have big cushion seats, which are much better trappings than any lodging house can afford." He suggested that such seven-day churches ought to be owned and operated by the working classes. After all, he said sneeringly, "Our Christian church friends, who are always so deeply interested in labor conditions," had no reason not to oblige. Socialists around the country had been supportive of the idea of a seven-day church, for it meant clergymen took "interest in them seven days a week instead of one."[35] However, because Samuel Gompers and others on the AFL executive committee were close with Stelzle, the AFL did not push that churches be more open to occupying workers than they had been.[36] When AFL Vice President James Duncan responded, "In times of industrial depression, no other organization did more than the church in furnishing help of various kinds to the poor and un-employed," some delegates cheered and others hissed. Many radical workers still understood church leaders as hypocrites when they claimed that their churches were friendly to labor and open to use as public and civic space, but workers were not entitled to its space for sleeping during strikes.[37]

When, in 1919, the Lusk Committee investigated allegations of socialist activity in the Labor Temple on behalf of the New York Senate, they con-firmed the presence of many IWW members who regularly attended events. In fact, investigators found that many IWW members considered the Labor Temple their home base for strike organizing. Investigators reported that radical workers initially got involved to prove to church authorities that the church was opposed to their goals. Workers soon found, however, that the Labor Temple "was not only interested but had been doing some construc-tive things, of which the IWW was unaware." State investigators concluded that the Labor Temple authorities harbored IWW members throughout the 1910s because of their mutual goals of providing information and organizing. Continued socialist occupations of the church, according to the report, "turned out to be an opportunity for the IWW to find out some things the Church was interested in doing, and it gave the church at the same time the opportunity to find out some things that the IWW was thinking about needed reforms in society."[38]

According to the Lusk Committee, the Labor Temple functioned as a de facto community center for Jewish, secular and Christian socialists inter-ested in religious and philosophical discussions. This was evidenced by the fact that workers continued to attend the Labor Temple's activities, especially nonreligious forums, despite their repeated criticism that Stelzle was aligned with capitalism.[39] The committee found that the Presbyterian leaders who ran the Labor Temple were not complicit in radicalism. The church "is in the very heart of the congested, polyglot East Side, throbbing with life, burning with intellectual curiosity, intensely conscious of economic problems, the home of strong labor unions and social radicalism. The Jewish element, with its intellectual power and its marvelous combination of materialism and idealism, is very strong. In such a district the Christian approach must be unconventional, friendly, obviously sympathetic with human problems," and such, they found, it was. Approvingly, the committee reported that the Temple "ha[d] been of infinite value in affording a decent meeting place for these men and women, restraining from them violence and despair, and showing a spirit of fairness on the part of the Church."[40] Stelzle's ministry held up to the state litmus test of an anti-radical institution, but workers did not necessarily agree.

Workers Define "Christianity" for the Presbytery

Many of the wage earners who used the space thought they were redefining both Christianity and church for the modern era. Overwhelmingly, they constructed a definition of Christianity that was encompassing, universalist, and liberal. As Dave Burns has argued, it was socialists and other "infidels" whose conversation with Christians produced the rise of liberal Christianity.[41] Moreover, as Matthew Bowman has shown, the urban evangelical church was a sacramental community that invested "social work with spiritual power to convert by speaking of it in the same typological terms with which they described worship."[42] Indeed, many Labor Temple members were not baptized and did not profess the faith, but they were counted as "members" of the liberal evangelical church community in a broader sense.

In 1910, neighborhood workers interested in religion began informally holding prayer meetings and sharing their personal faith on Friday evenings at the Labor Temple. The club was supervised by ministry interns from Union Theological Seminary and Bible Teachers' Training School nearby, and its popularity supplemented by the high, daily attendance at the Labor Temple's nonreligious programs.[43] Meetings began with a series of talks given by members of the developing group, called "My Religion and Why I Believe It." Recalled Stelzle of the initial meetings,

The first man who spoke was a Jew who had become a Unitarian. He said that he had been won by the character and life of Christ. The second was also a Jew, a Socialist. He told how he had been taught religion by his Russian mother, but that he had since studied other religions. He said, "I believe that love is God, shown by mercy and kindness."

Then followed a man who said that he was a Quaker by training, but that he now believed in the religion of the "mind." He did not know where he came from, nor did he know where he was going, but he felt sure that the same power that had brought him into being would take care of his destiny.

"Do good and help your neighbor and consider all others as brothers, is my religion," said a plain-looking workingman.

A Roman Catholic gave an earnest testimony to the power of his religion, saying that, while we may disagree in dogma, there may still be unanimity in the broader matters of religion.

Following these testimonies, and joining them in working-class fellowship, were those Protestant workingmen who said they long "had known the power of Jesus in their lives." Stelzle distinguished between these two groups of workingmen, but the records of this fellowship show no such distinction. Stelzle counted a full 50 percent of the members of this fellowship as born Jews, but once again, the records of the fellowship minimized such ethnic differences.

Later that year, this informal spiritual community organized officially as the Labor Temple Fellowship; the financial cost of running the group was recorded in church records as $12,500 per year. Stelzle framed the fellowship to his donors and the Church Extension Committee as an urban mission. He said, "If, as we believe, the Labor Temple shall prove that people who have drifted away from churches can be won back . . . [it] would justify an indefinite cost."[44] However, workers understood the club differently. They listed no specific requirement to practice the Christian faith in a church, deciding instead to sign pledges stating that they would "share the purpose of Jesus, and . . . seek to bring in the Kingdom of God."[45] Religion scholars may categorize this doctrine as "liberal," but it is important to note that this ecclesiology was specifically socialist in nature. At this first incorporation, remembered Stelzle, the membership comprised 149 people, "almost one third of whom were Jews."[46]

When in 1912 Jonathan Day announced he was starting a Labor Temple Bible School, he framed the purpose of the Bible study as an adventure in understanding the expansiveness of the Social Gospel. He divided the work between himself, in the Adult Division, and Harvey Vaughan, in the Junior Department. "The purpose of the school is not only to deepen the religious sense and the spirit of worship in the lives of those who attend," he said, "but also to cultivate a sense of responsibility for social conditions. The Bible will be used, but there will be no sectarian teaching. The literature used in the Adult Department will be that issued by the American Institute of Social Service, entitled 'The Gospel of the Kingdom.' . . . There will be the very largest liberty given in the way of discussion in the classes and encouragement of a larger knowledge."[47] The very fact that he announced his philosophy of the Bible and methodology of studying it at the same time as announcing the program reveals how well he knew that these would be workers' concerns. However, Day willingly "liberalized" the meaning of Bible study and fellowship for the sake of stirring the attention of his working-class neighbors.

When the Labor Temple Fellowship introduced itself again in 1912, the workers in attendance began a tradition of redefining both "faith" and "Church" for the sake of this particular congregation. Day did not stop them but followed their lead with great interest. Similar to the Christian Socialists of the last generation, the group decided that membership in the Christian Fellowship was singularly dependent upon belief in the coming Kingdom of God. All must "share the purpose of Jesus" and work "to bring in the Kingdom of God," they repeated from their earlier charter. This was strikingly close to the work of William Prosser within his People's Church, affiliated with the Christian Socialist Fellowship. Day was happy that the community had reached this decision. He reported with satisfaction at the turnout, "It seems as if this is as broad as anyone who is humane could desire it. . . . It seems that anyone who desires to better his own personal life or to help the life of another could not object to the wording of this statement."[48]

Under this definition of a Christian and this definition of the fellowship of believers, ministry at the Labor Temple took off. Between 1912 and 1914, two non-English-speaking congregations were born, one under the direction of the Rev. L. Harsanyi, a Hungarian, and another under Rev. Agide Pirazzini, an Italian. Both were born overseas but trained as ministers in the United States.[49] In 1913, Rev. Harvey Vaughan was promoted to religious secretary at the Labor Temple, overseeing both religious education and citizenship education (sometimes called "English language services"). That year, two thousand children attended weekly motion pictures, story hour, singing classes, or Bible school, all activities that led back to the gospel message.[50] In 1915, Rev. Edward Chaffee replaced Vaughan and formed the American International Church, an English-speaking Presbyterian congregation that had its official headquarters at the Labor Temple.[51] Thanks to this redefinition of Christianity and church, this radical neighborhood became a vibrant center of Christian ministry.

When workers insisted that this space was essentially the equivalent to a socialist or European labor temple, more a center of labor union activity than an American church, Charles Stelzle took umbrage. Stelzle retorted in 1911, "This is not true. If the Temple were to be a church, it might, with perfect consistency, be conducted precisely as we are now doing it. Anyway, there is nothing in our program which would be contrary to the kind of a church in which we believe." Stelzle was trying to claim the heritage of labor temples as something particularly Protestant, denying the fact that they originated as a rebellion against the Protestant churches.

Ministers at the New York Presbytery likely knew better, but until the Great War changed everything, they fell silent and let Stelzle's point remain. Stelzle spoke for the denomination in arguing that a Presbyterian church requires no "particular form of worship" or "special method of work."

> The same thing is true about the kind of gospel we preach. At the Temple we are not compelled to believe everything about the Bible or about Christianity that everyone else believes. We thoroughly believe that our gospel is a universal gospel. It meets the needs of men of every nationality and of every temperament. . . . Such a gospel makes no distinction between so-called secular and religious activities. It embraces every aspect of a man's life. It is concerned with his physical, mental and moral needs; therefore, it is evident that the lectures and discussions, the music and the socials, the clubs and the classes are all a part of the gospel in which we believe.[52]

Stelzle took credit for the social and cultural work of the socialist Christians, freethinkers, Catholics and Jews in his neighborhood who were redefining the meaning of Christianity and the purpose of church.[53]

In 1915, Jonathan Day continued to expand Labor Temple ministries with educational opportunities, even as the expenses for running the building continued to rise. Free or very inexpensive lectures were still among the most popular events in New York City, so Day decided to change the nominal fee to twenty-five cents per lecture. Day hired William Durant, a renowned Columbia University philosopher, as the first director of the Labor Temple School. Durant had previously been principal of Ferrer Modern School, a freethinking grade school founded by New York anarchists. At the Labor Temple, Durant taught three or four college-level classes per week, mostly on history and philosophy, to anyone interested. His lectures at the Labor Temple became the basis of his most famous publication, *The Story of Civilization*. However, Durant was very expensive and never satisfied with his salary. When he asked the Presbytery for the funds for a research sabbatical, they returned that they simply could not afford it. Before long, Durant resigned out of frustration, dissatisfied because church leaders undervalued his work.

Limited funding from the New York Presbytery and the lack of a large, tithing base meant that the Labor Temple ministry was partially dependent on wealthy New York donors. Small fees for Bible education, dues for fellowships, rent for union meetings, and admission prices for college classes, public lectures, and forums all provided small revenue streams, and the New York Presbytery's Church Extension Committee offered no complaints before 1917 that the building was not functioning as an ordinary church. Little disrepute came to the Labor Temple during the tumult of 1912–1914, because as far as the Home Missions Committee was concerned, "Americanism" was preached in citizenship classes. Jonathan Day claimed that during the white goods strike in 1913, the Labor Temple represented a unique opportunity "to preach the Gospel to the people who do not ordinarily hear it." Even though the average weekly attendance at church services was 330, Day recommended later that year that the building maintain its flexibility as an "extension," and not be established separately, under the supervision of the New York Presbytery.[54]

Jonathan Day did not like the term "mission," but this is how he convinced the Presbyterian Church Extension Committee to view his ministry. Until the US entered the Great War, the committee largely praised Day, claiming he was "giving the people who attended, the majority being Hebrews, every bit of the Gospel they would stand for."[55] In 1915, even as the English-language congregation adopted the name "American International Presbyterian Church," they remained a subsidiarity of the Presbyterian Board of Home Missions.[56] However, the increasing militarization of the country for war in 1917 and 1918 profoundly affected the churches. When Day suddenly left the Labor Temple in 1918 to serve at Berea College, everything began to change.[57]

Labor Temple Rents to Socialists

One could have predicted the disorder that comes to an institution when its strong leader suddenly departs. The Espionage Act's antisocialist amendment in 1918 made every appointee of the Home Missions Committee subject to public scrutiny as a socialist or supporter thereof. Possibly for related reasons, that year the junior pastor Edmund Chaffee took a sabbatical to work with the Red Cross in Palestine, and the popular William Durant, the first director of the Labor Temple School, finally resigned and was replaced with G.K. Beck.[58] The Home Missions Committee appointed a Mr. Shriver to oversee the Labor Temple ministries immediately, but records show he floundered, even as he appointed others to help him shoulder the burden.

Beck was more antisocialist, less popular, and less familiar with the people in the neighborhood than his predecessor. Likely, the Home Missions Committee made this appointment because he was more conservative in his understanding of the church and its purposes. Probably to sustain both the building's finances and its use by the community, Shriver in 1918 decided to rent part of the facility to the Fine Arts Guild, an organization whose name did not let on that it was a socialist and freethinking organization and a well-known sponsor of Margaret Sanger's birth control movement. Under the sponsorship of the Guild, Sanger spoke to packed auditoriums at the Labor Temple several times.[59] When the Lusk Committee visited the Labor Temple in 1918 to investigate potentially seditious activities to the state of New York, its members found significant evidence of radicalism. Archibald Stevenson, a businessman-attorney who had worked as a lawyer for the Lusk Committee during their investigations and practiced privately as a Presbyterian, had a hard time believing that the Labor Temple was a Presbyterian institution.[60] In 1919, the attorney initiated a series of public letters and pamphlets that sought to expose the seditious and un-Presbyterian behavior within this congregation.

Before long, the Labor Temple became the public face of a percolating public debate over the boundaries of American Protestantism.[61] The sides various Presbyterian leaders took on these theological issues were informed to a great extent by their interest in sustaining relationships with self-identifying working-class believers who rejected formal and traditional doctrine. According to Stevenson, the very problem with the Labor Temple was the thing so many boasted about: its liminal space between a church and a missionary endeavor. He rejected the Presbytery's argument that the Labor Temple was a "Christianizing Center" and insisted that any such center should never be legally or religiously allowed to let socialists take the podium. Listing the radicalism of speakers who had used the space most recently, especially under the sanction of the Fine Arts Guild, Stevenson argued that the Labor Temple ought to lose its charter as a Presbyterian institution. Not only was it in violation of its tax-exempt status as a religious institution, but Stevenson felt "confident that the Presbyterian who originally . . . invested in this property and those who now contribute to its support would be astonished" that such activities were "permitted under the supervision of the New York Presbytery."[62]

Stevenson, a private member of the Fifth Avenue Presbyterian Church of New York City, thought the Presbyterian denomination needed to stick to its job. As Stevenson described it, the "legitimate function" of the church was the "the instruction of individuals, first, to their Creator; second, to the State under which they live; and third, to their fellows." He went on, "It is not the duty of the church to enter the fields of scientific research, to solve economic problems, or to indulge in the past time of discussing political economy. It has a greater duty—a more difficult task to perform—and that is to stimulate the individual's devotion to his faith, his honesty, his loyalty, and his clean moral living. These are tasks of sufficient difficulty to absorb the entire energies of ministers designated to serve a community such as surrounds the Labor Temple."

What Stevenson was most upset about was not just the theology of Labor Temple clergy but the new ecclesiology that defined church so broadly. Socialists, he could tell, had initiated this expansion in the definition of religion for the sake of legitimating their case. Stevenson was upset that some clergy had allowed this for the sake of their expanding ministry. He objected to the way the Labor Temple, like other broadly religious organizations in New York City, willingly provided a religious shelter for socialist discussions. "If carried out by a secular organization," Stevenson continued, "the program of the Labor Temple would be subject to condemnation."[63] In 1918, Stevenson was probably correct on this point. During World War I, the Sedition Act put many people in jail for "conspiracy to overthrow the government," and for this reason even more workers felt comfortable framing their moral platforms as Christian movements. Churches had long been protected, moral spaces within American culture.

However, while many left-leaning Christians wanted to continue to protect church spaces as a political sanctuary, conservative Presbyterian like Stevenson did not. Rev. Harry Ward, chair of the Methodist Federation for Social Action and member of the Federal Council Committee for Church and Social Service, simultaneously chaired the American Civil Liberties Union during World War I. Ward argued through the ACLU that "conscience" was as much a political as a religious perspective, and both needed to be protected in times of war. According to Ward and other liberal clergy, the Labor Temple was not simply one legitimate use of a church, but it was the ideal use of a church. That said, when they came under scrutiny by the state of New York, neither Ward, Jesse Forbes, Henry Sloane Coffin, nor William Adams Brown defended the radical socialists as practitioners of the Presbyterian faith. Socialists were simply identified as the "audience" or "mission field" in the Church's work. William Adams Brown even visited the Labor Temple during the investigations and presided over an open forum, wherein he asked the audience of "three or four hundred" to "have a part in the Church's work."[64] In limiting the right to speak prophetically to clergy themselves, New York City's liberal Presbyterian cut socialists out of the grounds of legitimate Christian authority.

Forbes Redefines Liberal Ecclesiology

Jesse Forbes of the New York Presbytery ultimately defended his own job and conscience, but not the jobs and consciences of the dozens of Christian Socialists who had been attending the New York Labor Temple. Forbes revised the narrative of the Labor Temple over the previous decade, insisting that the Presbyterian Church never promoted or harbored communists except to articulate the contrary, Christian position. In retrospect, he described the work of Dr. Durant, the philosophy professor who left in 1918, as a "man who has passed thru radicalism to a firm belief in our present representative institutions." He said his lectures jettisoned propaganda and exercised "a strongly conservative influence over men and women who would be impossible for us to reach otherwise." Forbes defended the right of radicals to speak from the Labor Temple platform, "provided always that we make sure that at the same time meeting the Christian position is presented and adequately defended."[65] This principle, he and the committee affirmed, has always been the guiding rationale behind famous, radical speakers in their auditorium, and would continue to be strictly enforced.

To enforce this principle more effectively, Jesse Forbes and the Church Extension Committee redesigned oversight of the Labor Temple in 1920 so that it would function more like a traditional, middle-class Presbyterian church. "Social Activities" were to be separated in form and function from "Religious Activities," each of which would be monitored carefully. "It may be well that in opening the Temple to meetings of the latter kind [social activities] we have made mistakes which should be guarded against in the future," the Extension Committee stated. In taking such a position, Forbes betrayed the people, and expressions of Christianity, which had comprised the Labor Temple for the previous decade. Upholding the older vision of a church mission, Forbes continued, the Labor Temple serves as a "point of contact between the churches and those estranged from them," and, for this reason alone, "Free discussion of opposing views is permitted and welcomed." In a telling final statement, the committee might have revealed its most important motive in issuing such a statement. "We would further charge the [Presbyterian Church Extension] Committee," Forbes entreated, "to see to it that every regulation of state or city is carefully observed and that no moneys are received which would invalidate our right to exemption from taxation."[66]

All that Forbes and his committee defended was the right of clergy to define the proper bailiwick of Christian teachings. In a public statement issued to the New York State legislature over the Lusk Committee report, Jesse Forbes remarked,

> With due deference, we would raise the question whether in this commonwealth it is a proper function of a committee in the legislature to pass judgment upon the teaching of ministers in the Church. We resent the classifying of ministers as "socialist and pacifist sympathizers" on evidence which says nothing of either socialism or pacifism. We would remind the Legislature that in the exercise of liberty of conscience our national life has been developed. And we would humbly suggest that any attempt to curtail freedom of thought on the part of the Church and its ministers is an attack upon that historic Americanism which we rejoice that your honorable body is attempting to foster.[67]

At the trial, Forbes refused to stand in alliance with the radicals who used the Labor Temple on a daily basis for the previous decade. He was willing to defend clergy's right to openly discuss social justice within churches, but not the right of laypeople to do the same. Forbes thus turned a national public referendum on socialism in 1918 and 1919 into a referendum on the purpose of a church. Turning down the opportunity to defend the legitimacy of Christian Socialism as a Christian movement for positive social change, Forbes instead defended the rights of clergy to speak with impunity. He was unwilling to risk accusations of sedition and a loss of tax-exempt status for the sake of the continued membership and active participation of socialist-leaning, working-class Christians within churches. The development of liberal Christianity was thus as much about the unwillingness of clergy to exercise a prophetic voice as it was about their theoretical right to do so.

Restructuring American Religion

Thus, if we take the New York City Labor Temple as a case study of the relationships between Social Gospel ministers and immigrant workers in the Progressive Era, we can make several concluding observations. As the historian Derek Chang illustrated in his study of Chinese Americans and African Americans in Pacific Coast churches, the church-based encounter between whites and people of color changed Anglo-Protestant thinking with regard to race.[68] The story of immigrant wage earners' participation in Labor Temple activities illustrates that this encounter also transformed ministers' understanding of "church" and forced them to articulate the boundaries around the Christian faith and the purposes of a church building.

By 1919, as the twin crises of the influenza epidemic and the Espionage Act pressured ministers to shut down all large gatherings of immigrants, Social Gospel ministers—even those recognized as "modernists"—refused to defend laypeople's demands that the churches directly serve the American democracy. Throughout its early years, the Labor Temple created semipublic spaces for workers to host discussions on collective bargaining rights, racial equality, women's suffrage, social insurance, and birth control. Yet, by 1918, its Presbyterian landlords claimed the freedom to offer prophetic critique of the culture as a unique privilege of clergymen and used their missions as object lessons in the authority of their ministerial office. Throughout the tenure of their Presbyterian mission to immigrant wage njearners, Federal Council leaders exploited the high demand for the resources they offered largely to exalt themselves as public authorities and police the boundaries of legitimate religious expression in their neighborhood.

If we take the Labor Temple as an example of the work of the Federal Council at the local level, we observe that ministers only stood in solidarity with workers insofar as their presence buttressed ministers' public esteem. This "modernist" conviction about the meaning of "church" derived in part from the work of ministering to and alongside immigrant wage earners and watching those wage earners stretch ministers' understanding of "church" and a Christian commonwealth. Ministers' defense of their own freedoms to speak prophetically from the pulpit appeared to some as a work of solidarity with wage earners, who had spent years making such claims themselves. Yet to the many wage earners in radical labor organizations, the Federal Council's refusal to sponsor such discussions as constitutionally protected in the name of American religion appeared as a rejection of any real commitment to social justice.

Examinations of the Federal Council's work with wage earners within national and local contexts between 1912 and 1919 reveals the Social Gospel as an imperious ministerial movement that allowed clergy's working-class partners little room to set the terms of their partnership, especially after the United States joined the Great War in Europe. Why were ministers so confident that their own version of Christian industrial justice would prevail over that of the labor movement? One cannot fully understand this attitude, much less the long-term vision of the Federal Council, without backing up a bit and revisiting the period between 1912 and 1919 at the national level. Ministers of the Federal Council had been cultivating a special relationship with the Democratic Party since at least 1912, when they helped put Wilson in the White House. Once Wilson was elected to a second term, Federal Council ministers were not just hopeful but quite certain that their future as public policymakers was secure in their special relationship with the president of the United States.

8

The Great War and the Victory of White Protestant Clergy

When Woodrow Wilson ran for election in 1912, he called himself a Christian. A Christian, as he defined it in his "New Freedom" campaign platform, was "more concerned about human rights than about property rights."[1] Wilson was a southern Presbyterian aristocrat, born and bred in a world of African American domestic workers and agricultural hired hands, and raised in a Protestantism of white supremacy and Black cultural deference. His was the party that ended Reconstruction and installed a strict system of racial apartheid in the South. Yet Wilson staked his election to the presidency in both 1912 and 1916 on the willingness of northern evangelicals to break with the party of "Big Business" and the tariff and join him in a party that celebrated "democracy," small businesses, labor, and "human rights." He knew that the Federal Council of Churches, only a young organization, earnestly wanted to become the nation's moral conscience on matters of foreign policy, immigration policy, and labor legislation. Wilson could use their growing database of churches and their big-tent rhetoric of "Christian Social Service." Ministers of the Federal Council could use his connections to the State Department, the War Department, and the Labor Department.

Protestant ministers' close relationship with the executive branch would test, and eventually break, the alliances Protestant ministers were building with the labor movement. Though working-class Americans had successfully resisted Protestant authority over public life throughout Wilson's first term, World War I made Protestant clergy into national statesmen and guardians of a global Christian empire. American victory in the war would spell the victory of white Protestant clergy over civic, moral, and spiritual affairs. It would invest white Protestants, more than any other interest group, with the authority to dictate the postwar terms of Christian nationhood and Christian industrial relations.

The Gospel of Church. Janine Giordano Drake, Oxford University Press. © Oxford University Press 2024.
DOI: 10.1093/oso/9780197614303.003.0009

It did not matter to Wilson that ministers of the Federal Council represented only a fraction of American Christians. In fact, he saw the Great War as another auspicious opportunity for white Protestants to evangelize and reform the white, foreign-born, and African American working classes, at home and abroad. After the war, Wilson charged American clergy, like clergy around the world, to draw up plans for "peace" in both domestic and international relations. Perhaps not surprisingly, American ministers stepped away from their tepid wartime support for wage and price controls, the nationalization of key industries, limitations on company profits, and even the continuation of legal rights of collective bargaining. This decision to break with the American Federation of Labor appeared strange if one had not followed closely the Federal Council's ambitions during the previous decade. Indeed, ministers of the Federal Council broke with the AFL because they now had the patronage of the president of the United States and recognized that they had the opportunity to revise the history of social reform to proclaim themselves the nation's historic saviors to American industry. The Great War catapulted the ministers of the Federal Council to a national stage and vested authority in their visions for explicitly Christian domestic and international policy. These ministers would claim that the hallmark of a Christian nation was not its social or economic relationships but the number of physical churches and the public authority of white Protestant ministers within them. In upholding this nineteenth-century vision of the Protestant missionary enterprise, the ministers of the Federal Council betrayed their working-class allies.

Woodrow Wilson's Federal Council of Churches

Before Wilson even took office, ministers of the Federal Council intended to negotiate a special relationship to the president wherein they would bring him a domestic and international Social Service agenda, and he would boost their public authority and aid in their church-planting efforts. Henry Carroll, director of the US Census of Religious Bodies in 1890 and 1906, was installed as Associate Secretary to the Federal Council and manager of the enormous church database. Carroll would work with Federal Council President Shailer Matthews, Secretary Charles Macfarland, and a small team of Protestant ministers across the white denominations in a project to make the nation, and the world, more Christian.

The executive committee of the Federal Council lost no time. Macfarland hand-delivered an official letter to Wilson in support of his "warm and sympathetic sense of our democracy" and his conviction, "both by utterance and execution, that our social order must be fashioned after the Kingdom of God as taught by Jesus Christ." The letter, which Macfarland proudly published, praised Wilson for his "personal faith" and pledged that ministers would muster "the political forces of the nation, and its moral forces as embodied in the churches of Christ," to "serve together for the social and spiritual well-being of the people."[2] He then offered a number of suggestions for bold foreign policy changes, including the recognition of the Republic of China and loosening of migration restrictions from Japan. In addition, Macfarland explained that the nation needed to dramatically increase the number of military chaplains on bases around the world, enough to secure "one chaplain for each battleship and cruiser, for each school ship and navy yard, and also one for each occupied army post." He added that the distribution of military chaplains should not necessarily concern itself with the proportions of membership in each denomination. After all, Roman Catholics were still numerically the largest denomination in the country. Rather, Macfarland maintained that the matter was so urgent that more Protestants should be issued "in the interest of providing adequate moral influence and spiritual help."[3]

President Wilson quickly reciprocated the Federal Council's offers of support and guidance. Within a week, Wilson wrote back, "I need not tell you how deeply I appreciate the address of confidence directly to me on the part of the [Federal Council] or of how greatly it adds to my sense of being supported and guided." He quickly passed on their requests to the War Department. Secretary of War Lindley Garrison wrote back that he could not increase the number of chaplains because the War Department was undergoing a reduction in "the number of garrisoned posts in the interests of tactical organization and command." It was, after all, officially peacetime. Yet Garrison and the president remained open to other suggestions. These included a resolution to maintain "friendly relations between the peoples of Japan and the United States" by reconsidering the immigration exclusion acts known as the Gentlemen's Agreement, and a resolution against the "bigotry and race hatred" evident within the czar of Russia's treatment of Jews. The ministers maintained "considerable correspondence" with several national churches, including those within the US possessions of Panama and the Philippines. Wilson not only accepted, but encouraged, this type of soft diplomacy. The following year, Wilson sent delegates to meet with the AFL and the Federal Council of Churches for further discussions on the US relationship with Japan. The Federal Council of Churches' Commission on Relations with Japan urged Congress to rethink the United States' "Oriental policy based on a just and equitable regard for the interests of all nations concerned" for the sake of protecting both Japanese and American labor "from dangerous competition." Wilson thanked the Federal Council for its work.[4]

Soon after war in Europe began, the Federal Council worked closely with Wilson in offering a set of principles for European peace that would become the foundation for Wilson's League of Nations. The Federal Council executive committee approved the eighteen "Bryan Peace Treaties," named after Secretary of State William Jennings Bryan, which provided structures for nations to deliberate diplomatically. In 1914, ministers urged "upon the governments of the world the need of a universal treaty," or permanent league, providing structures for diplomatic deliberation. They concluded with a firm declaration of the importance of neutrality, adding, "We believe that he who would attempt to drag this country into the present war not only sins against patriotism, but would destroy all hope of speedy peace. Only as this nation remains strictly neutral can she offer mediation. If she becomes involved there is no impartial court left to which the nations may appeal."

This language of mediation and neutrality in international relations matched their mission within industrial relations. Macfarland wanted the Federal Council to MacFarland become Christ's chosen instrument for deliberating justice. He wanted more ministers to serve as diplomats overseas. Shailer Matthews, as president of the Council, asked that Wilson consider declaring an International Day of Prayer to allow American ministers to act as international arbiters among the churches of the world. In September 1914, Wilson wrote to the Federal Council, "I need not tell you how sincerely I appreciate the approval expressed in that letter of the efforts I have made to bring about mediation and peace." Wilson knew that he depended on the Federal Council for his continued approval with the public. He agreed to make October 4 an International Day of Prayer "to bring all men to realize that the Gospel of Christ is a Gospel of peace and brotherhood and as binding on nations as on individuals." Churches in Germany, Austria, France, and China participated. The ministers believed that their spiritual diplomacy was working.[5]

Meanwhile, the Federal Council of Churches' Home Missions Council began to articulate plans for "World Redemption," a project that was explicitly tied to assumptions of white supremacy.[6] The committee offered surveys of poverty, literacy, and health conditions in the American colonies and sphere of influence, including Puerto Rico, Panama, Cuba, the Philippines, the Mexican/American borderlands of Texas, and the Deep South. In his 1903 *Souls of Black Folk*, W. E. B. Du Bois had called out the hypocrisy of white Christians who "cite the caste-leveling precepts of Christianity, or believe in equality of opportunity for all men," without offering any critique of the color line or the power dynamics inherent in white European colonialism.[7] This accusation was leveled, fairly, at the Federal Council and its ambitions for evangelism, both domestically and abroad.

As the Ku Klux Klan grew in size and power throughout the early decades of the twentieth century, the burning cross came to define the union of white Protestant Christianity and the necessity of excluding nonwhites and non-Protestants from the "Christian nation." Thomas Dixon's 1905 *The Clansman* circulated among white Protestants as a celebration of the "restoration" of white male leadership in the South. When it was made into a silent film, Woodrow Wilson screened *Birth of a Nation* in the White House. As the historian Kelly Baker has explained, the Klan issued an "appeal to white Protestant America" to believe that the world would be better served by white Protestant leadership over all social and civic institutions than by an inter-racial democracy. Imperial Wizard Evans later explained these goals: "Pre-eminence is enjoined upon us by God and by our obligations to the world. If the Klan aspires to purify America and make her impregnable, it is not any selfish reason."[8] The rising popularity of eugenics, the pseudoscience of racial genetics, added "scientific" credentials to white Protestants' desires to exercise dominion and authority over all the races of the world.

In 1914, the Black clergy of the Federal Council's Committee on Negro Churches issued a "Declaration of Principles, Aims and Methods" that timidly sought "more cordial relations between white and colored churches." Theirs was an understatement that highlighted the fact that African American communities were struggling for survival, especially within the poorest neighborhoods of the northern cities over the previous generation. When not facing lynching, Progressive Era African Americans faced heavy policing, racial segregation, and inequitable access to education and social services. Many Black Americans lived in neighborhoods with inadequate access to sanitation within crowded tenements. The statement, authored by white and Black clergy, meekly appealed to white ministers to exercise their "responsibility" to lead African Americans by opposing lynching and partnering with Black communities by funding ministerial training schools. It broadly recommended that "boards of white churches could also advise and help the boards of the corresponding colored denominations" with "courses in community betterment and sanitation, as well as in Bible study and ministerial work proper." On matters of race relations, the Federal Council essentially extended the work of Religious Reconstruction, wherein southern white ministers used their relationships with Black churches to extend their own authority on matters of race.[9]

It is important to note who was financially sponsoring the Federal Council's energetic commitment to the "uplift" of so-called civilization, domestic, and international. In 1914, steel magnate Andrew Carnegie made a $2 million donation to the Church Peace Union, which soon became known as the World Alliance for Promoting International Friendship through the Churches, and later the World Council of Churches. The organization sought to bring together national and international luminaries to broker "peace" in all sectors of the world, including through the institution of a League of Nations, World Court, and International Labor Organization.[10] As the millionaire capitalist proclaimed in the inaugural conference on the subject, "The peace of the world lies in the hands of the churches more than anywhere else."[11] "No city can be Christian until the nation is Christian. No nation can be Christian until the international order is Christian."[12] The World Alliance celebrated foreign missions, "the cultural and religious rights of minorities, the treatment of races, freedom of religious belief, and the cultivation of international brotherhood in labor organizations."[13] Privately, Carnegie continued his advocacy against socialism and for immigration restriction.[14] Through church-based diplomacy, he hoped, "men on both sides of the Atlantic" would "meet in groups for the purpose of devising plans whereby international relations could be influenced for good by the united forces of religion."[15] Carnegie, who had joined John Rockefeller in funding Federal Council initiatives, knew that the more he supported the moralistic work of ministers, the less they critiqued American enterprise. "Peacemaking" was always a front for power.

After all, this commitment to "peace" was short-lived. Soon after Germany's unchecked invasions of neighboring states, ministers of the Federal Council started talking about the terms on which they would support war. In 1916, while the president was campaigning on the fact that he had kept the United States out of war, Sidney Gulick's *The Fight for Peace*, prepared jointly by the Federal Council of Churches' Commission on Peace and

Arbitration and the Church Peace Union, began to take center stage. Gulick argued that the work of international peacemaking was central to the calling of Christ, but it sometimes involved laying down one's own life to fight injustice. As he put it, "A church that does not beget sacrificial living among its members is powerless." All Christians should be "ready to suffer with him in the redemption of the world, transforming it from what it is to what it ought to be."[16] Gulick, long active in international diplomacy through the Federal Council, was afraid of a premature peace. The Federal Council now identified all belligerence as wrong, but the prospect of making peace without justice seemed worse. Shailer Matthews, Charles MacFarland, and Frank Mason North cosigned a statement from the World's Evangelical Alliance in October 1916 suggesting that the prospect of a "divided Christendom" might be even worse than war. He said, "We are confronted with the unspeakable sorrow of a divided Christendom. Christians are grouped into many bands under different names suggesting the sway of the human spirit rather than that of the divine Spirit. Surely, praying people of every race and tongue in all the earth will fall down before our God in the opening of the new year and beseech Him for . . . Unity."[17]

The Federal Council came to see itself as the shepherd of a new world Christendom, led by white Anglo Saxon Protestants in the United States and administered by the American military. In late 1916, more than sixty ministers signed a statement to the president, rebuking him for his unwillingness to act militarily in Europe. As the historian Richard Gamble summarized, "What had been an implicit part of the logic of progressive Protestantism was now plainly spelled out: the distinction between the world and the church was now gone."[18] The Federal Council hoped to call upon their diplomats in Germany and Austria to inaugurate a new Christendom. They would serve as guardian to people of other faiths, including Catholics and people of color, at home and abroad. Insofar as an intra-European conflict had disrupted this plan, Federal Council ministers sought to become the leaders and mediators of that "permanent peace."[19]

Wilson's "Industrial Democracy"

It was therefore not shocking when ministers of the Federal Council joined American businessmen in becoming the nation's foremost war hawks in the spring of 1917. On March 2, the day after the intercepted Zimmerman telegram from Germany to Mexico, the Methodist minister Worth Tippy sent a memo to Newton Baker, Wilson's Secretary of War. Tippy claimed to speak on behalf of the Federal Council of Churches' Commission on Church and Social Service, an organization that represented twenty-two thousand American churches. He boldly addressed Wilson: "I regret to urge war but I think [the] time has come to go in with all our power. . . .The president needs to go in and lead resolutely."[20] Ministers around the country, receiving urgent messages from the Federal Council's news service, echoed Tippy's sentiments in sermons and syndicated columns. Rev. Randolph McKim preached a sermon called "America Summoned to Holy War," reprinted on Palm Sunday in the *New York Times* and *Literary Digest*. He claimed that "the crusades shrink into insignificance compared with the crusade to which we are summoned at present."[21]

Many expressed skepticism about this growing alliance among business leaders and war hawk ministers. House majority leader Claude Kitchin, Democrat of North Carolina, warned, "Allied with these war advocates of the pulpit . . . are many captains of our great corporations, who are wont in times of trouble to exploit foreign governments as well as their own countrymen with a deadly impartiality." Indeed, Federal Council minsters continued to spend time with self-identified "Christian businessmen," hoping to gain their patronage and partnership in the continued mission of the Federal Council. Almost overnight, the religious press, which had long expressed trepidations about the European conflict, offered enthusiastic support for the war.[22]

Immediately after Wilson signed Congress's declaration of war on Germany, he called upon the Federal Council of Churches to support the war from every pulpit in the country, with the message that entrance into the war would free "long oppressed subject nationalities," especially within Central and Eastern Europe, and make space for establishing a "permanent peace." The congressional chaplain prayed that God would "guide us in a just and righteous cause."[23]

The American working classes, however, like their comrades around the world, would be difficult to persuade. Many were first- or second-generation immigrants from the United States' adversaries in the war. Not only did many of these immigrants resist conscription to fight against family abroad, but many were part of international communities of socialists and communists who were more eager to see the "workers of the world" unite than to actualize a united Christendom under the tutelage of American Protestants. Even those immigrants whose home countries aligned with the Allies often fled religious persecution. As Eugene Debs put it in a speech in 1918 in Ohio, "The master class has always declared the wars; the subject class has always fought the battles. The master class has had all to gain and nothing to lose, while the subject class has had nothing to gain and all to lose—especially their lives."[24] His incitement of rebellion against the draft was so powerful that a jury declared he endangered the wartime aims of the United States. Debs was jailed for sedition. In a desperate effort to increase enlistments, Wilson accelerated eligibility for US citizenship, including voting rights, for any white male immigrant who declared his interest in cutting ties with the nation of his birth and becoming an American.[25] Wilson's Espionage Act empowered states and federal authorities to investigate, censor, attack, and deport anyone who spoke out against the war and in favor of socialist and communist ideas. When persuasion did not work, suppression always seemed to fix the problem.

Sam Gompers, president of the AFL, hesitantly offered support for the war effort as an olive branch of peace with both the Wilson administration and the Federal Council. He wanted to believe in the Federal Council's Wilsonian rhetoric of going to war to protect "human rights and the perpetuation of democratic institutions."[26] Gompers also wanted to believe that the president was an ally to labor and could not afford to break the partnership they had developed. After all, as immigration slowed, workers became scarcer, while many factories converted to military production. Even one strike would hamper military production and endanger troops who depended on supplies. In 1914, Wilson created the War Industries Board to collect data and mediate strikes. That year, the Bureau of Labor Statistics registered a record 979 strikes, but this was only the beginning. In 1915, the number rose to 1,246, and in 1916 it was 3,678. In the single month of May 1916, there were 617 strikes nationally. In 1917, strikes reached a height of 4,233, and the number leveled off at just above 3,000 for the next two years (Tables 8.1 and 8.2).[27] In small and large cities across the country, workers felt emboldened to claim their human rights to higher wages and better working conditions. The "War Boards," as they become known, granted new respect for the work of unions, and union leaders, as American patriots. In the emerging Union of Soviet Socialist Republics, state-sponsored arbitration boards were called "soviets." In the United States, Wilson referred to the close relationship among businesses, federal officials, and unions as "industrial democracy."[28]

Table 8.1 Strikes and lockouts, 1914–1919.

	Number of			Number of Employees Involved		
	Strikes	Lockouts	Total	Strikes	Lockouts	Total
1914	979	101	1080	**	**	**
1915	1246	159	1405	468983	35292	504275
1916	3678	108	3786	1546428	53182	1599610
1917	4233	126	4359	1193867	19133	1213000
1918	3181	104	3285	1192418	43041	1235459
1919	3253	121	3374	3950411	162096	4112507

Opposition to Industrial Democracy

Yet, "industrial democracy," as a concept, was growing less popular with white Protestant clergy. Their own influence over the labor movement was rapidly dissolving with every strike that was arbitrated without the influence of ministers, and this proved worrisome to their long-term plan. As Harry Ward reframed his perspective on the topic of unionization in 1916, "Nothing can be gained in an effort to bring about industrial peace by appeal to class."[29] Ward had met with other advocates of the Social Gospel to theoretically and theologically reconstruct what "Christian" workplace relationships should look like. They decided that a truly Christian nation should not be characterized by the hostility, selfishness, and jealousy encouraged in the sense of class war. All these qualities were un-Christian. In a reconstructed Christian nation, rather, all employees—from the managers to the workers— would be motivated by the Christian responsibility of selfless service.

By 1917, cheerleaders for the *Social Creed* were growing indignant at both Black radicalism and unions' growing sense of efficacy, entitlement, and independence, often born of successful organizing campaigns in the United States and successful nationalist campaigns within Europe. The Great Migration, the mass exodus of African Americans out of the sharecropping South, meant that hundreds of thousands of African Americans moved to northern cities, including Chicago, Detroit, New York, and Cleveland, only to find themselves invited into lower-paying jobs and segregated, poorer neighborhoods and schools. Black organizations, including the National Association for the Advancement of Colored People, the Urban League, and the National Association of Colored Women's Clubs cultivated a new

Table 8.2 Principal causes of strikes and lockouts 1914 to 1919.

Causes	1914 No.	1914 % of total	1915 No.	1915 % of total	1916 No.	1916 % of total	1917 No.	1917 % of total	1918 No.	1918 % of total	1919 No.	1919 % of total
Wages alone	294	36.4%	409	29.1%	1349	42.8%	1578	44.2%	1433	50.8%	1115	35.3%
Wages: with or without other demands	387	47.9%	623	44.3%	2110	66.9%	2260	63.4%	1906	67.6%	2087	66.0%
Hours alone	48	5.9%	81	5.8%	120	3.8%	521	14.6%	85	3.0%	122	3.9%
Hours: with or without other demands	96	11.9%	251	17.9%	725	23.0%	649	18.2%	427	15.1%	932	29.5%
General conditions	72	8.9%	39	2.8%	59	1.9%	99	2.8%	56	2.0%	65	2.1%
Conditions and other demands	110	13.6%	86	6.1%	145	4.6%	227	6.4%	125	4.4%	176	5.6%
Recognition of the union	63	7.8%	52	3.7%	366	11.6%	314	8.8%	221	7.8%	397	12.6%
Recognition and other demands	96	11.9%	96	6.8%	586	18.6%	564	15.8%	406	14.4%	748	23.7%
Discharge of employees	47	5.8%	73	5.2%	127	4.0%	206	5.8%	137	4.9%	141	4.5%
Total for which information was furnished	808		1405		3155		3567		2819		3161	

generation of Black lawyers and activists who demanded equal protection under the law and the end to segregated public accommodations.[30] In 1905, W. E. B. Du Bois joined with Black leaders across the country in the Niagara Movement; Black "race men" and women, largely educated in Black universities, demanded full civil rights for Black Americans, including voting rights and equal protection within public accommodations.[31] However, Black church leaders, including Black Social Gospel leaders in places like Howard University, were less willing to commit to such demands. Over the previous generation, white and Black church leaders had cooperated on the common ground of encouraging respectability, education, and gradual uplift for Black Americans.[32] Working class African Americans were growing frustrated with church leadership.

Across the country, working class African Americans were rebelling against their churches and redefining their relationships to Christianity. A new generation of Black nationalists offered critiques of European colonialism and celebrations of African heritage. Hubert Harrison, a West Indian socialist organizer, participated in Marcus Garvey's work for Black independence while also representing the Socialist Party in New York City politics. He denounced the Bible as a relic of slavery and refused to support a white Jesus. As he put it, "Christianity, as organized and made effective in all her institutions, from the church to the jail, insists that only white men are men and that Negroes especially must be treated like dogs, whether kindly or cruelly."[33] W. E. B. Du Bois, another socialist, did not dismiss the whole of Christianity, but he did publicly express his frustrations with Black ministers' unwillingness to speak more fervently against white Protestant racism. He also praised the Socialist Party's goal to provide essential community infrastructure for Black children and families, including better schools, safer policing, and more public service jobs.[34]

Ever since the US entered the war, Federal Council statements on racial and economic justice began to fade. Ministers spoke theoretically of workers' rights to "increased economic resources and enlarged participation in industrial control," but fell silent on the widespread persecution of both African Americans and labor radicals.[35] In 1917, Attorney General Mitchell Palmer worked with local police to raid all forty-eight local offices of the Industrial Workers of the World, in addition to the homes of major Wobbly leaders. Ostensibly, officers used the raid to confirm that Wobblies had no connection to the German war department. In fact, the raids supplied the materials to prosecute Wobblies for sedition and deport those immigrants without the legal rights to a trial in the United States. The IWW was at the leading edge of building interracial and interethnic alliances in some of the most dangerous professions, and Harry Ward—who had worked with Wobblies in Seattle— tried to convince Federal Council leaders to issue a statement in defense of Wobblies' civil rights. The executive leaders of the Federal Council, probably fearing their own public labeling as "reds," refused to offer any statement. As the war continued, many ministers who had previously supported unions now fundamentally disagreed that workers should become partners with their supervisors in adjudicating wages, working conditions, or future plans.

By 1917, socialists' vision of industrial democracy not only challenged the authority of white Protestant ministers but upheld a vision of "industrial democracy" that emboldened claims to integrated cities, powerful and independent unions, and equal pay for equal work. Wilson relied heavily on the Federal Council of Churches, in concert with the Committee on Public Information, both to rally workers behind the war and counter socialist, Black nationalist, feminist, and labor-driven narratives on the future of the American democracy.

Selling the New Christian Order

That year, Wilson entrusted the Federal Council of Churches' Commission on Church and Social Service with the responsibility of selling the war to both churches and the American labor movement. In doing so, the commission recycled the same messages it had used in selling Federal Council labor investigations and mediations. First, Protestant church leaders could be entrusted to dictate the terms of "industrial peace" precisely because of their neutrality. Worth Tippy, chair of the commission, asked "the religious press," including editors of denominational magazines and newsletters, to emphasize the League of Nations as a moral instrument. He also asked them to carry standing heads over their editorial columns reading "Never Again" and "The Last Time," to indicate that this war could really help establish a permanent peace. Second, the Federal Council commission emphasized the ways the war would open opportunities for church-planting and Christian diplomacy throughout Europe. As the commission framed it in a preliminary report on the ad campaign to the secretary of the Council, "[The war] will not only strengthen Protestant missions but will go far toward promoting the ends of federated action to which the Federal Council is devoted." These ends, of course, were "to establish a more Christian social order," both in the United States and around the world. In this vision, American missionaries would become diplomats in the cause of industrial democracy. They would "reinterpret the labor movement in spiritual terms."[36] It did not matter, of course, that the American labor movement had been attempting to do just this over the previous several decades. The commission claimed the labor movement's moral crusade as its own.

Soon, on the president's dime, the Federal Council issued "repeat mailings" to every minister in the United States with an explicit Christian endorsement of the decision to enter the war.[37] Each church received a hefty pile of materials that seamlessly combined the Federal Council's work in promoting peaceful international and industrial relations. Mailings included "strike reports, study courses and bibliographies, social service catechisms, and similar material for the guidance and instruction of pastors and church classes, covering social questions and presenting them from the point of view of the obligation and opportunity of the churches."[38]

In each of these reports, Federal Council ministers interpreted the work of labor movement and claimed its most popular demands—demands for better wages and working conditions—as their own. By 1918, when other national organizations had joined them in mass mailings, the Federal Council enhanced its dossier with self-published pamphlets that claimed it had long led the charge for a living wage and democracy in the workplace. Never mentioned were tangles with the labor movement, the extent to which their theology was borrowed from Christian Socialist writers, or that they lapsed in defending the many unions they claimed to represent. In these repeat mailings, church leaders were the nation's heroes.

Federal Council booklets offered new narratives of the labor movement that foregrounded arbitration, rather than organizing, as the heart of the Christian movement. *The Social Service Catechism*, for example, enumerated fifteen short questions implying that the labor movement, while noble in intention, was ultimately a quest for more money and power. Christians, identified in opposition to the labor movement, should focus on the task of "realiz[ing] the Christian ideal of human society, . . . and . . . make Jesus Christ a fact in the universal life of the world."[39] This catechism, like others, belied its pretenses to simplicity by appropriating Walter Rauschenbusch's term "social salvation," but defining it vaguely as a reconstructed social order.[40] Similar booklets included the very well-circulated *Social Creed*, Harry Ward's 1918 *The Gospel for the Working World*, and the Commission on Church and

Social Service's 1920 *Pocket Phrase Book: Economic and Industrial Terms in Common Use.*

Federal Council mailings also rewrote the relationship between the Federal Council and the labor movement. Wad's *Gospel for a Working World*, for example, acknowledged that the labor movement, including the radical IWW, was deeply committed to the Christian ideals of solidarity. Ward said that the IWW "reaches down and gathers the outcast and the rejected. It takes them in without regard to color or sex or creed or race. . . . This dream is a religious aspiration." Yet Ward now explicitly rejected the labor movement as an instrument of peacemaking and justice. He claimed that the Kingdom of God would be realized through the "complete transformation of the whole of human life, individual and social." For, "With the evil that is in the world there can be no truce or compromise. There is no other propaganda for social reconstruction which goes so far or demands such thoroughgoing change as the propaganda of Jesus."[41] Ward said he dedicated the book to the working people of Seattle, and the Federal Council paid for and distributed ten thousand free copies of the book to workers who were readying for a general strike.[42] His *Gospel* acknowledged the righteousness of their goals, but did not even mention the spiritual value of labor organizing, much less the particular agenda of the labor movement.[43]

Rather, the "gospel" that Ward proclaimed to the working world was the good news of a local church. Jesus, he said, did not seek to change society any more or at any faster rate than that slow process of redeeming individuals. Christianity "stirred a quest for social justice on the part of the people who profit by injustice as well as those who suffer from it." Workers in "the trade union movement" preached Christianity, but so also did "employers and investors seeking to express the standards of Christianity in industry." He entreated wage earners and middle-class parishioners to see "philanthropic welfare work" as "genuine attempts to realize justice and brotherhood.[44] In pushing his audience to see the labor movement as an imperfect attempt to secure worldly justice, Ward defanged the strongest moral platform of the movement.

Federal Council publications took advantage of the fact that the Sedition Act of 1918 had precluded use of the federal mail to narrate and defend the cause of socialism. Instead of defending wage earners, many of whom now found themselves jailed, ministers used this opportunity enhance their own public authority as "translators" between the labor movement and middle-class Anglo parishioners. The *Pocket Phrase Book*, for example, offered church-stamped commentary on political and economic philosophies. Terms of significance included "Bourgeoisie," "Christian Socialism," "Class Consciousness," "Capitalism," "Class Struggle," "Communism," "Materialism," "Syndicalism," and "Welfare Work."[45] While "collective bargaining," "profit sharing," and "shop committees" were listed as methods of industrial peace, syndicalism and socialism were conspicuously omitted. Students learned that the "industrial masses" needed fair treatment, and that justice would never be served through the exaggeration of class differences, as socialists taught. For, workers were taught as children, "we" ought to find opportunities for "cooperation of groups and classes."[46]

Other pamphlets were designed as study guides for adult Sunday School classes within middle-class and aspiring-class Anglo congregations, or perhaps even within Sunday evening programs in institutional churches like Stelzle's Labor Temple. These booklets, like William Easton's *The Church and Social Work*, reiterated the earlier message that Jesus would never support socialism.[47] Easton affirmed that the goals of Christian social work could be distilled down to personal virtue, not social justice. Similar arguments, also with extended bibliographies of social service literature, included Harry Ward's *Social Service for Young People* (1914), Paul Strayer's *Moral Reconstruction* (1915), the Federal Council's *Social Studies for Adult Classes, Study Groups and Church Brotherhoods, Christian Duties in Conserving Spiritual, Moral and Social Forces of the Nation in Time and War* (1917), and *Bibliography of Social Service* (1918).[48]

Yet the most popular kind of pamphlet was the report on living and working conditions in a particular place. When paired with the *Social Service Catechism* and *Pocket Phrase Book*, strike reports provided opportunities for ministers to retell and reinterpret the work of federal investigators by emphasizing unions' lack of moral leadership and their need for church leaders to offer guardianship. Each report concluded with the premise on which it began: religious communities needed to grow to displace radicalism. The Methodist minister Worth Tippy's social survey of logging communities in the Pacific Northwest in 1919, for example, used data he collected through surveys of IWW workers to conclude that logging workers appreciated moral and spiritual discussions of social issues but stubbornly refused to admit their need for churches. Most loggers, Tippy reported, "considered ministers parasites and the church unreal." They were insistent that the church in the United States stood behind the Mammon of employers. Tippy raved at the dangers of IWW propaganda, primarily because Wobblies "hold that the

churches are capitalistic and that there will be no church in the Revolution."
Not surprisingly, his final recommendation was to get companies to sponsor
"industrial chaplains" in the logging districts. This would derail the Wobblies'
antireligious and anti-American radicalism and also provide wage earners
with the social infrastructure they had come to rely upon.[49] In strongly paternalistic language that crowned men's leadership within the family and their
consequent leadership in the churches, Tippy recommended that industrial
chaplains mentor men within families to both "stabilize the industry" and
"emphasize the need of the church." This conclusion was tellingly much less
about loggers than the opportunity for white Protestant men reform working
class gender and family roles.[50] The Federal Council's *Pittsburgh Survey*
arrived at similar conclusions.[51]

A New Theology of Peace

As the Commission on Church and Social Service moved from defending
the war to defending the peace, its Christologies and theologies also shifted.
Depictions of Jesus shifted from emphasis on his muscularity, strength, and
determination to an emphasis on his more feminine characteristics, including his meekness, humility, and dedication to peacemaking.[52] This shift
was part of a larger effort to remake Jesus as a humble and submissive servant,
not a poor carpenter or vigorous champion of social equality. As one wartime pamphlet put it, "Can you imagine Jesus Christ, who embodies His own
commands, thrusting a bayonet into another man's side? Can you imagine
Jesus Christ touching the fires that would scatter the limbs and bodies over
the grass of Europe's plains?"[53] By 1918 and 1919, there were many Christian
Socialists who were pacifists, but their right to be conscientious objectors
and refuse conscription was denied by courts. The Federal Council's wartime
Jesus was not a pacifist but a good soldier who went where he was sent; he
was a church-planter, not a worldly and selfish rabble-rouser. Worth Tippy
imagined that the historical Jesus wandered out of the "wilderness" with "a
vision of the Kingdom."[54] His primary mission was to not to defend truth and
principles of justice, but to "urge . . . genuine cooperation."[55]

This new emphasis on Christ's love for peacemaking usually led to
assertions that Jesus wanted all Christians to overcome their worldly
differences according to race, gender, class, and culture. As Worth Tippy
now put it, "Jesus came to make a fellowship of all classes by annihilating

classes except for certain superficial workaday ways of getting on together. The Church is a benefactor of all classes and must aim to establish a brotherhood as broad as human life and extending to the lowest depths of human want."[56] Tippy claimed that the value of brotherhood, both internationally and intranationally, was ultimately more important to Jesus than the value of justice. In a 1919 speech, his fellow Presbyterian Reverend Robert E. Speer envisioned that in the future, "the principle of competition shall have given way to the principle of association and fellowship. It will be a new world where the principle of unity shall have replaced the principle of division." Speer claimed that the business of the church was merely to "release on man the divine power of renewal and redemption that will affect every area and department of life." The church should mediate, "class to class and . . . nation to nation."[57]

It is worth noting that these ministers' understanding of their role as a mediator did not involve standing up for African American protesters or other persecuted political radicals. The Federal Council fell silent on congressional legislation authorizing espionage, raids on the socialist and radical newspaper headquarters, and mass arrests of socialists as domestic terrorists. At the meeting of the Secretarial Council of the Federal Council of Churches in October 1917, Harry Ward again raised a question about the Federal Council's role in protesting the Red Scare. Yet, the council, which included Worth Tippy, Francis McConnell, Samuel Batten, and Henry Atkinson, must have disagreed. Minutes read, "It was decided inadvisable to do anything in the matter of the suppression of the IWW although it was recognized that they have grievances." In lieu of defending workers, the men agreed that "it is expedient to agitate on the political and economic reconstruction after the war; but, at present time we should be working at a program."[58] The decision represented self-aware complicity with the Red Scare. The council later agreed to endorse a proposal for "increase in the number of probation officers in New York Courts."[59] The ministers saw no contradictions between peacemaking and increased policing.

A central part of the Federal Council work during the Great War was their rewriting of the history of Protestant social service in the US. The Commission on the Church and Social Service titled their annual report in 1920, "The Enlarging Social Program of the Churches." They recounted that "The supreme teachings of Christ are of love and brotherhood. These express themselves in a democracy," resulting in "noble mutualism." The "doctrine of the class-conscious struggle," they now held "is opposed to this ideal. It is a reversion to earlier forms of competitive struggle," and "tends toward the breaking up of society, even of radical groups, into bitterly antagonistic factions, thus defeating its own ends." Even though congressional investigations listed some Federal Council members, especially Worth Tippy and Samuel McCrea Cavert, as potential communists, the pamphlet went to lengths to reiterate their distance from allyship with unions.[60]

Turning their back on the working-class Christian Socialists who had made their names famous at forums around the country, these pastors now claimed, "The dictatorship of the proletariat in practice is a new absolutism in the hands of a few men, and is as abhorrent as any other dictatorship. The hope of the world is in the cooperation of individuals and classes and the final elimination of classes in the brotherhood of a Christian society. To build up this cooperation should be the supreme endeavor of the churches."[61] Worth Tippy reiterated, "The church ought not allow itself be carried away into unrestrained attacks upon managers of industry. It should take a fair and sympathetic treatment of capital, managers, and technicians, and organizations of workers. The opposite policy is suitable only to the propaganda of revolutionary Socialism."[62] The committee effectively caved to exigencies of "Americanism" during wartime.

In their defense, most Social Gospel ministers did not necessarily intend to place workers at a disadvantage in the workplace. Most of these Federal Council leaders expected their influence in Congress, with the presidential office, and with "Christian Businessmen" would continue to grow into the postwar era. They thought, much like President Wilson with regards to the Great War, that they could trade concessions on short-term war measures to win the right to dictate the terms of industrial peace. Hence, though these ministers undermined the legitimacy of unionization and a social democratic state by supporting the Wilson administration, they did so with the expectation that the church, through their ambassadorship, would serve as the new mouthpiece and official arbiter of social and economic justice in the postwar world.

Postwar "Reconstruction"

Once again, the expectation that white Protestant church leaders should lead the world in establishing a permanent peace and lead the nation in establishing industrial justice was the product of a long Anglo-American tradition which celebrated ministers as public moral authorities. During the Great War in the United Kingdom, the archbishop of Canterbury entreated British lawmakers to respect collective bargaining rights and establish a welfare state. In his 1919 "Christianity and Industrial Problems," he echoed all the most important claims of Christian Socialists in arguing that capitalism was fundamentally opposed to the aims of Christianity. As he put it, "The fundamental evil of modern industrialism is that it encourages competition for private gain instead of cooperation for public service." He explained that this "perversion of motive" fosters both the abuse of workers "as hands rather than as persons" and workers' loss of control over their work processes. The archbishop accused business leaders of endorsing "economic Machiavellianism," a system that relieved "men of the moral restraints which control the strong and protect the weak" and said that lawmakers had to protect against this abuse. He recommended parliamentary support for public education, a minimum wage tied to a living wage, the end to child labor, limited weekly work hours, and continued public aide in "health and housing."[63] He even suggested limits to excessive profits within any single enterprise. This statement far surpassed the demands of the *Social Creed of the Churches*.

British and Canadian social workers echoed the archbishop's recommendations as they put further pressure on the UK and Canada to establish a welfare state. The International Conference of Social Service Unions of Britain encouraged the state—and not just churches—to provide funding for housing, health, and public education for children. They also called for national trade boards to fix prices and wages. The British Quaker Employees, who offered their own "Reconstruction Program," specifically demanded not just that workers should be paid a minimum wage, but that all "surplus profits" of the company should be reasonably distributed between workers and proprietors. The Methodist Church of Canada declared it "un-Christian to accept profits when laborers do not receive a living wage, or when capital receives disproportionate returns as compared with labor." Their public statements referred to Jesus as the "Carpenter of Nazareth" and endorsed the "nationalization of our national resources, such as mines, water-powers, fisheries, forests, the means of communication and transportation and public utilities on which all the people depend."[64]

That year, both the National Council of Catholic Bishops and the Federal Council of Churches set out to write or revise their own similar statements, but neither came close to the British or Canadian declarations on the management of capitalism for a postwar peace. The two American statements, the *Bishops' Plan for Social Reconstruction* and *Church and Industrial Reconstruction*, had a great deal in common. Each voiced theoretical support for a living wage, increased worker control over production and distribution, and workers' rights to childhood education, health, and leisure. The Catholic bishops' statement was released earlier than that of the Federal Council, and therefore the latter took the opportunity to affirm many aspects of the Catholics' statement. However, neither religious body was willing to entrust American lawmakers, not to mention the labor movement, with the power to define and enforce the provisions of social welfare.

John Ryan, author of the Catholic statement, argued that "the State should make comprehensive provision for insurance against illness, invalidity, unemployment, and old age."[65] He recommended "capitalists," or proprietors, distribute wages more equitably and allow worker participation in management. But, he did not call for state enforcement of these principles. A few years later, he would endorse the nationalization of public municipalities as a principle of moral theology, but he would never declare it a state imperative.

Ryan had been working for years to make Christian Socialist critiques of capitalism central to discussions on moral theology within seminaries. His 1916 book, *Distributive Justice: The Right and Wrong of Our Present Distribution of Wealth*, had foreshadowed this statement. It used principles of Christian Socialism and British and American visions of a Christianized state to critique the proper ownership of capital earned in rent, interest, and profits from business. For his 1923 book, *The Christian Doctrine of Property*, he went on to affirm Christian Socialists, including R. H. Tawney's renowned British bestseller, *The Sickness of an Acquisitive Society*. He suggested that increases in the valuation of property due to manufacture were not only entitled to stockholders, but also the users and improvers of that property on the shop floor. He even set a cap on reasonable profitability within industry, specifying that all surplus profits of an industry beyond the annual rate of return of six percent ought to be split between stockholders and workers as a reward for innovative enterprising and risk. Ryan's moral theology of the economy teetered on the edge of communism. As he put it,

Where the line should be drawn between State ownership of industries which is morally lawful and State ownership which encroaches on the right of private property, cannot be exactly described beforehand. The question is entirely one of expediency and human welfare. In any case, the State is obliged to respect the right of the private owner to compensation

for any of his goods that may be appropriated to the use of the public. . . .
the considerations which move the Church to oppose Socialist concentration of ownership are an argument against a concentration in the hands of
individuals and corporations."[66]

Ryan thought municipal ownership was a key tenet of moral theology.

Yet, while Ryan held these principles as high recommendations of the
Catholic church, he also strictly abided by the limits placed on Catholics as
a denomination in the secular nation.[67] At the end of the bishops' statement,
Ryan reiterated that while states and localities should provide social insurance, it was not the place of religious bodies to dictate policy but to nominate
moral principles.[68]

Protestant clergy, meanwhile, hardly nominated any moral principles.
Professor William Adams Brown, professor at Union Theological Seminary
and heir to a great New York fortune, served as secretary of the General
War Time Commission under President Wilson and authored the Federal
Council's statement on "Industrial Reconstruction." In that statement,
Brown spoke generally about the need to reform the wage system to pay
workers consistently with the profitability of their industry, but he offered no
critiques of capitalism itself. He said that the chief concern of the church was
to inspire a Christian spirit of cooperation, for he believed that this "spirit"
would reorganize relationships in the business world. After an extensive discussion on the principles of surplus profits and the justice of redistributing
them among workers, he stated, "How surplus profits can actually be made
available for the good of the public cannot yet be fully determined. The most
direct way is in making prices as reasonable as possible to the consumer. If
large surplus profits remain in private hands, they should be used in the spirit
of service to further worthy social ends." While public ministries in Europe
were established to set standards for wages and profits, Brown declined to endorse any recommendation that would compromise the latitude of business
proprietors.

The Federal Council ultimately endorsed a position that charity and welfare capitalism were equally legitimate methods of redistributing profits as
the payment of a living wage. Brown defended the rights of "social experts,"
but not union leaders, to determine the needs of workers.[69] In defending the
living wage in theory but offering no specific way to put this into practice,
Brown took a side in the simmering union battles over the necessity of an independent voice for labor. By 1919, Henry Ford was proclaimed as a national

hero for his "Five Dollar Day," a welfare capitalism scheme that paid workers well, in addition to "stock options," but also employed "social experts" to oversee and respond all workers' decisions, both on and off the shop floor. The National Civic Federation, a major lobby for industrial leaders, praised Ford's work as brilliant and encouraged more industrial proprietors to think of his work as a solution to labor conflict. Brown, siding with welfare capitalists like Ford, ultimately offered no actual support for either collective bargaining or labor-friendly legislation.[70]

Hence, in a moment of international solidarity among the working classes and international clerical statements on the incompatibility of capitalism with both human rights and democracy, the Federal Council declined to affirm any legislation to extend the rights of collective bargaining or the welfare state at the national level. The official Federal Council statement could be summarized in Brown's declaration that Christians, "in any position of control," should use their "influence to the fullest extent possible to secure Christian social ends."[71] Those "Christian social ends" were intentionally vague, for they would soon include abstinence from alcohol, thrifty spending habits, and white cultural mores, what Brown described as an "evangelism of what it means to live like a Christian." Instead of demanding their lawmakers support the working classes as such, ministers of the Federal Council lobbied for a world where white Protestant missions to the poor would remain indispensable.[72]

Conclusion

The Great War elevated Protestant ministers at every level into positions of public authority on both international and industrial justice. In the fall of 1919, as the United States won the war and the right to establish the peace, the Federal Council also won the right to "church" the United States through the multiplication of white, or white-supervised, brick-and-mortar churches. President Matthews and Secretary Macfarland, but also the many Protestant clerics who ran state and city-wide federations of Protestant churches, used their special position as Wilson's partners to speak authoritatively on Christian ideals relating to labor, race, and international relations. More often than not, their statements declined to support anticolonial movements, interracial democracy, or unions' vision of industrial democracy. The war put the Federal Council in a position to redefine American Protestantism as a strong and growing set of institutions wherein white men set the terms of justice for women and people of color.

It is important to recognize the degree to which the war changed Federal Council ministers, and through them the meaning of the Social Gospel. Shopfloor organizing campaigns, which had flowered under the War Industries Board, continued to grow in 1918 and 1919. During the summer of 1919, while ministers were socializing with business leaders and President Wilson in smoke-filled rooms, William Z. Foster had begun laying plans with the AFL for one of the largest labor campaigns of the century. He and the Sam Gompers, who bankrolled the organizing drive, had no reason to doubt that ministers would waver on their support for the collective bargaining rights.

Yet Federal Council ministers had always believed that churches, not unions, were God's chosen instruments for establishing democracy and a Christian commonwealth. They knew that the labor movement, especially the growing syndicalist movement, would no longer defer to their moral authority as ministers. Now that the labor movement had grown large and powerful, ministers feared that it might once again challenge the Federal Council's authority to serve as the nation's foremost arbiter of social and economic justice. Out of fear, but also an abundance of cash donations from business leaders, the Federal Council effectively switched sides against the labor movement in the year 1919. The white Protestant vision of the postwar world gambled on the expectation that clergy's civic authority and moral suasion among business leaders would remain in place; clergy expected they would continue to persuade business leaders to pay workers as much as they could afford. As it turned out, that moral suasion would last only long enough to dismantle the Christian moral authority of unions.

9

The Interchurch World Movement and the Christening of the Open Shop

In the spring of 1919, the American labor movement erupted in its largest organizing campaign of the century, and no industry seemed more important to surmount than steel. US Steel controlled mill towns and cities across Pennsylvania, Ohio, Indiana, Illinois, West Virginia, Alabama, and Colorado. Under the leadership of William Z. Foster, head of the AFL's National Committee for Organizing Iron and Steel Workers, more than one hundred thousand steel workers had signed up for the union by the spring of 1919. That summer, workers delivered twelve demands: increased wages, an eight-hour day, a seniority system, a weekly day off, the abolition of company unions, and most important of all, the right of collective bargaining. Judge Elbert Gary, president of US Steel, refused to meet with the union to discuss these grievances; he opposed "outside" unions (noncompany unions) on principle. In August, ninety-eight percent of union members voted to authorize a strike for the right of the Amalgamated Association of Iron, Steel and Tin Workers to represent the steelworkers.

President Wilson tried to gather Gary and the strike committee together to work out their interests and forestall a strike, but with no success. Gary refused to negotiate with anyone, including the president of the United States, and Wilson felt powerless to coerce him. On September 22, 1919, 350,000 steelworkers, about half of all steelworkers in the nation, walked off their jobs. Mills in Pueblo (Colorado), Chicago, Wheeling (West Virginia), Johnstown (Pennsylvania), Cleveland (Ohio), Lackawanna (Pennsylvania), and Youngstown (Ohio) were almost entirely shut down.[1] Wilson immediately proceeded to contact ministers from the Federal Council of Churches

The Gospel of Church. Janine Giordano Drake, Oxford University Press. © Oxford University Press 2024.
DOI: 10.1093/oso/9780197614303.003.0010

to investigate, report on, and help mediate the work action that would become known as the Great Steel Strike.

While Social Gospel clerics had been defending workers' rights for years, Protestant clerics now had much more authority as "experts" in negotiating settlements. Yet, in their reports, they shifted attention away from the central question of the strike—the right to collective bargaining—and focused on what they perceived were the real needs of workers: their need for provisions, moral authorities, churches, and order. Clerics upheld workers' rights to better pay, but they also supported the various versions of employee representation plans (company unions) that industrial magnates like Gary were holding out for as they refused to negotiate with the Amalgamated. Again, the organized workers explicitly opposed "company unions." However, bending their ear to the suggestions of John D. Rockefeller and other wealthy boosters for Protestant revival campaigns, the Federal Council of Churches broke the alliance it had built with the trade union movement since the founding days of the organization.

If Federal Council clerics had previously argued that that they were workers' mouthpiece, that their churches were nexuses of social justice, and that workers were entitled to a living wage, they now changed their tune. Progressive ministers now used their nationwide church revival movement, the Interchurch World Movement (IWM), to distract from the union focus of the strike. In their report and the lobbying that came after, they suggested that steelworkers lacked adequate provisions, but could not be trusted as independent moral agents. They argued that it was ultimately their employers' responsibility to provide for workers' social and moral welfare. To smooth this real transition from supporting unions to rejecting them, ministers shifted the focus of their reform from the "worker" to a working-class "family." Employee representation plans, ministers suggested, would function like the Christian family; they would establish "natural" hierarchy and means through which workers' concerns would be heard. These ministers elevated the concept of a "brotherhood of man" and argued that all anyone owed to one another was Christian "service." Thus, as Social Gospel leaders traveled the country proselytizing Rockefeller's "Christian" doctrine of antiunionism, they shifted the meaning of the *Social Creed of the Churches*. The Protestant vision of the postwar world gambled on the expectation that clergy's civic authority and ability to persuade business leaders to do the right thing would remain in place indefinitely. In fact, their moral suasion would last only long enough to dismantle the Christian moral authority of unions.

The Great Steel Strike

As soon as the war ended in November 1919, American workers realized they were in trouble. Prices were rising faster than wages, and union members were experiencing layoffs and violent retaliation in many industries, including steel mills throughout the nation. War boards, which had provided protection to union-organizing drives only a year earlier, had been created to ensure steady industrial production, not the "the mass organization of industry."[2] The National Civic Federation, a union of employers, was intent on using the rise in unemployment and growing affinities for white supremacy to establish a new, nonunion "normalcy" in industrial relations. Workers, however, had won so many strikes during the Great War, both in the United States and in Europe, that they would not back down easily. William Z. Foster, an American-born syndicalist, was one such example. In his book *Syndicalism*, he explained why an "industrial union" was the only method through which workers could address persistent problems in both deskilling and falling real wages. As he put it, "The labor unions in the various industries will take over the management of their particular industry." Independent shop organizations would be better at leading their industries and their communities than ordinary lawmakers within the corrupt American system. They would eventually come to lead "all social production, including education, medicine, criminology." Foster argued that syndicalism was fundamentally more democratic than "majority rule." Workers would elect their own foremen and superintendents based on their qualifications and excellence, not by their ability to "secure the support of an ignorant majority, through their oratorical powers."[3]

Following the Seattle general strike and the Boston police strike, and coinciding with syndicalist uprisings in Hungary, Germany, and Italy, it appeared to many American workers, and particularly immigrants from these countries, that syndicalism was the future. Foster's strike announcements suggested that the union would inaugurate a "golden era of prosperity" in industrial relations and warned that any hesitation would force workers into "miserable and hopeless serfdom."[4] Syndicalism offered a fundamentally more equitable distribution of "the social product" than capitalism; it was a moral system whose ends justified its means. He quoted the old Marxist saying, "From each according to his ability, to each according to his needs." In Foster's explanation, through the mechanism of the general strike and solidarity with "farmers, tenants and agricultural wage workers," all workers would eventually attain ownership over all production. Foster was also a pragmatist; he worked directly for, and alongside, Sam Gompers. Yet the fact that Gompers was willing to work with him reflected the widespread popularity of industrial unionism by 1919.

Gary, head of US Steel, conferenced regularly with other big business owners, including John Rockefeller, Andrew Carnegie, and Henry Ford, especially on the topic of thwarting "radicalism" through an "American Plan." In Pennsylvania, where a large fraction of steelworkers were of German, Italian, Eastern European, or African American descent, the term "American Plan" did vast rhetorical work. As its advocates explained it, this plan of industrial organization was far more efficient than those that held businesses hostage to union leaders, labeled "outside agitators." It was no coincidence that many union leaders were immigrants or ethnic Americans who spoke multiple languages; company managers, meanwhile, were more likely to be white, native-born Protestants. Aware of these differences between independent and company unions, Federal Council officials sided with the company's "open shop," later called "right to work," philosophy. In their report, they sympathetically summarized Gary's position:

> The steel companies were defending the right of every man to "engage in any line of employment that he selects, and under such terms as he and the employer may agree upon . . . depending on his own merit and disposition." The workmen were treated in accord with "the highest standards of propriety and justice."[5]

Open-shop advocates often cited President Teddy Roosevelt's 1902 declaration that "no person should be refused employment" because that person did not want to be part of a union.[6] Company unions, they argued, offered workers the opportunity to elect people who represented them to employers; it was more modern than independent union representation. In fact, there was more to this: shop-floor representation plans also came alongside plans to mechanize, or deskill, work that was previously held by trade unionists, specialists who brought particular knowledge of their craft to the workplace. In "simplifying" industrial organization, employers also hoped to create an interchangeable workforce that had much less leverage to make demands of management.[7]

Because this interruption in the production of steel impacted every other industry in the already slowing 1919 economy, Congress and President

Wilson intervened. The Senate Committee on Education and Labor undertook an investigation focused on the troubles with "radicals." President Wilson called upon church leaders, as well as John D. Rockefeller, to work closely with the Bureau of Industrial Research to conduct politically neutral research on the conditions in the steel industry and the fairness of the workers' claims. All this gave John D. Rockefeller Jr., one of the wealthiest men in the United States, an idea.

During the winter of 1919, while steelworkers were out on strike, Rockefeller planned a national Christian revival campaign, akin to the Men and Religion Forward Movement seven years earlier, to overlay and distract from the Great Steel Strike. He invited millionaires Edward Filene, Andrew Carnegie, John Wanamaker, and Paul Underwood Kellogg to donate funds to a traveling show that would plant churches, celebrate Christian family values, authorize research, and distract the media's focus away from strikers. As Rockefeller put it in his editorial in the *Saturday Evening Post*, there was an urgent need to forestall religious leadership from passing to "laymen outside of the church"—a thinly veiled reference to strikers—and save the nation "from its present chaos and unrest."[8] For his own part, Rockefeller wired his father a request for $50 million to $100 million to create a foundation that would help consolidate a central account through which all denominations' expenses could be paid. As he explained the request to his father, "I do not think we can overestimate the importance of the Movement. As I see it, it is capable of having a much more far-reaching influence than the League of Nations in bringing about peace, contentment, goodwill and prosperity among the people of the earth." Rockefeller Senior answered his son's call with a unidentified donation on the order of millions, in addition to a $1 million line of credit in case more was needed.[9] Robert Lansing, acting US secretary of state, would serve as chairman of the IWM board of directors, a subsidiarity of the Federal Council's ministries.[10]

The IWM would serve as a constant source of distraction from the fact that support for thousands of steelworkers were still out on strike to defend the rights of unions. In December 1919, twelve trained "teams" of ministers put on sixty-seven "training conferences" in forty-eight states, all of which celebrated the values of "Christian brotherhood" and family. At the end of this national tour, the IWM paid fifteen hundred actors, one thousand chorus members, and seventy-five musicians to put on a pageant called *The Wayfarer* at Madison Square Garden arena in New York City. The play centered on

an everyman industrial worker who despairs of his hard work with no reward and wonders if he should join the Revolution. Through a journey with
"Understanding," he learns that Christian joy wells only from the knowledge of Christ's resurrection, a much richer joy than worldly revolutions. In
trips through time resonant of *A Christmas Carol*, the Wayfarer visits ancient
Jews, and then Christ himself, practicing the virtues of patience and long-
suffering, in both life and death. Shepherds sing "Gloria in Excelsis," during
just the right season for Christmas celebrations, and the Wayfarer learns that
to participate in the Christian tradition is to suffer with Christ. As the head-
note to the play's program explained, "Revolution has shaken the industrial
and social fabric to its very foundation. . . . Not a few question the ability of
the Church to solve the problems of the new era. The Wayfarer represents
this discouraged element. He is guided from despair to faith and service by
Understanding, who interprets the presence of the living Christ in every age,
triumphant over doubt and adversity."[11] It was a Christmas pageant with a
union-busting message. The Methodist Centenary Exposition in Columbus
(Ohio), which coincided with the Chamber of Commerce's Open Shop festival, was similar.[12]

Throughout the winter of 1920, the IWM printed a daily bulletin that
described how the church stood primarily for interdenominational Christian
brotherhood. On one hand, articles claimed that this brotherhood would
be characterized by cross-class cooperation. As Worth Tippy explained it,
"The Church should . . . use its vast educational force, first uncompromis-
ingly against the class struggle; second, in the advocacy of the cooperation of
classes," for "Controversies over wages and hours never go to the root of the
industrial problem."[13] On the other hand, this brotherhood would be based
in a shared male camaraderie created through men's common leadership
over their families. It makes claims to universal camaraderie, yet that camaraderie is bought at the price of excluding women.[14] Ministers used the term
"brotherhood" to rationalize the category of male breadwinners without
discussing the implied deference of women and children. Ministers of the
Federal Council liberally made use of this terminology. Organizers argued
that "the men of America are the last reserve of the church."[15] Dr. William
Pierson Merrill, Presbyterian pastor in New York City, wrote that Christianity
was the only solvent for the urban problem of division among the masses because it was "a universal religion of brotherhood." After the strike had ended,
more than two hundred laymen affiliated with the IWM issued a statement
on the importance of the Christian home. They held that the movement was

characterized by the belief that "the Christian home should be exalted and its solidarity emphasized."[16]

Outside the limelight, US Steel launched a full attack on the union. In Gary, Indiana, where a large fraction of steelworkers were African Americans, the governor called in federal troops to protect strikebreakers and intimidate strikers. In other cities, the company called immigrant strikers "Bolsheviks" and contrasted them with the "red blooded Americans" who wanted to "keep America busy, and prosperous, and American." When the strike still did not abate, US Steel brought in an estimated thirty thousand African Americans to serve as strikebreakers throughout the nation's steel plants.[17] The battle would be won on maintaining the media narrative that US Steel was a good American company that really knew better than the union what was best for their workers.

In December 1920, 125 "leading ministers from all parts of the country" were paid to descend on Pittsburgh, the epicenter of the strike, to discuss the challenge of worldliness and the necessity of a local church. As the "Stewardship Department" of the IWM explained it, "Every man is a steward and must give account for all that is entrusted to him"; this rule applied to wealthy and poor alike. Another minister elaborated, "If men are right with men on the money question, the chances are good they will be right all around."[18] Business owners, they implied, could carry out justice so long as they willingly gave to charity.[19] That month, ministers would occupy cities, especially where workers were striking against US Steel, and celebrate the mission of the church and the necessity of membership for everyone. Poor churches, as they often explained, were inadequate to meet the challenges of the present day. A church should strive for a central location, well-built architecture, high ceilings, heating and ventilation, a fire protection system, indoor plumbing, bells, an auditorium, and a number of rooms both for religious education and for community use.[20] Between the IWM, the importation of strikebreakers, and Gary's violent repression, the strikers conceded to US Steel on January 8, 1920.

Exalting Churches as Centers of Worker Justice

When the IWM's *Strike Report* came out the following spring, the report drove home the same arguments these wealthy businessmen and their hand-selected clerics had pushed throughout the movement: workers were suffering, not from the nonrecognition of their union, but from a dearth of churches and from poverty-stricken "families." The Federal Council used the report, much like their revival messaging, to reinstall clerical leadership over the meaning of working-class justice and to make local churches, rather than unions, taverns, or the city streets, the new moral and intellectual centers of working-class community. The *Strike Report* held that "a fair and comprehensive history of the strike would not require mention of either the Protestant Church or the Catholic Church as organizations in Allegheny County." Moreover, "The great mass of steel workers paid no heed to the church as a social organization. . . . After the strike, workers generally were making no effort to make the church their church."[21]

These statements were patently false. Father Stephen Kazincy, for example, the "labor priest" in Braddock, Pennsylvania, rallied his church behind the steel strike. The *Strike Report* allowed him a single line: "He saw the strikes' cause as a protest against oppression, oppression represented by conditions in the steel mills, by the activities of the State Constabulary and the county authorities as well as the authorities of Braddock."[22] According to William Z. Foster, however, Father Kazincy and his Lutheran colleague, Rev. Charles Molnar, "constituted two of the great mainstays of the strike in their district."[23] Foster reported that the Kazincy opened his church to strikers, "turned his services into strike meetings, and left nothing undone to make the union men hold fast. The striking steelworkers came to his church from miles around, Protestants as well as Catholics. The neighboring clergymen who ventured to oppose the strike lost their congregations—men, women, and children flocked to Father Kazincy's, and all of them stood together, as solid as a brick wall."

In Foster's account, Kazincy and several of his Roman Catholic colleagues served as moral backbones to the steel strike in Pennsylvania. He argued that because Kazincy had such support among workers, steel managers "did not dare to do him bodily violence, nor to close his church by their customary 'legal' methods." His church had a long reputation for providing "leadership in other areas of the religious and institutional life of the East European community," especially during the Homestead Strike of 1892, forty years earlier. Instead, steel managers went after the Catholic hierarchy to muzzle the labor priest. When the Catholic bishops threatened to close his church in 1919 for insufficient tithing, Kazincy announced that if they did, he would place an enormous sign on his church steeple, "This church destroyed by Steel Trust." When they tried to foreclose on his church mortgage, Kazincy raised $1,200 from strikers' support the next day. Kazincy was later attacked on the steps of his parish, St. Michael's Catholic Church, during a nonviolent protest in which he participated.[24] Kazincy remembered it as "the most magnificent display of self-control manifested by the attacked ever shown anywhere." Kazincy contrasted the brutality of attacks on civil protesters as "iron-hoofed Huns" descending on civil society. He encouraged his flock not only to seek to "win the strike" but to use tactics that would "win the confidence of the public." Recognizing Kazincy's moral and spiritual leadership in this critical moment, Foster described the labor priest as a comrade and said of him and fellow left-leaning ministers, "They are men who have caught the true spirit of the lowly Nazarene." He also called out Bishop John Podea of the Roumanian Greek Catholic Church in Youngstown, Ohio and Rev. E. A. Kirby, pastor of the St. Rose Catholic Church in Girard, Ohio, as men who "realized that all true followers of the Carpenter of Nazareth had to be on the side of the oppressed steel workers."[25]

The strike report completely omitted these priests' leadership over the moral and spiritual lives of strikers. Though both Kazincy and Molnar testified before the strike commission about the working conditions of their parishioners, their questions and answers were confined to the discussion about Sunday labor. Neither was given the opportunity to tell his stories about how their congregations had responded to crisis. In the official, IWM report, the ministers concluded, "A fair and comprehensive history of the strike would not require mention of either the Protestant Church or the Catholic Church as organizations in Allegheny County."[26]

The Protestant pastors and the Bureau of Industrial Research set up their entire investigation to arrive at this claim that workers lacked a moral compass. That is, their research focused not on the legitimacy of the union's claim to collective bargaining rights, but on the legitimacy of their claim to higher pay. While the report found that workers lacked sufficient salary to maintain minimum standards of healthy food and housing, it did not affirm that workers deserved an independent advocate in their struggle for a justice.[27] To the contrary, the *Strike Report* concluded that workers needed ministers, now more than ever, to give them moral guidance. The report held, "We plead with the pulpit that it be diligent to discharge its legitimate prophetic role as advocate of justice."[28] Moreover, ministers recommended that "organized labor . . . [s]eek alliance and council from the salaried class known as brain workers."[29] In the recommendation of both the IWM evangelistic campaign and their research team, Protestant churches, not unions, were called to serve as the moral protectors of working-class families. By omitting the significant participation of Christian workers within the walkout and within the nonviolent protests of the strike, these ministers undermined the unions' platform that they should be trusted to represent unions independently.[30]

Gendered Rhetoric of the Family

The ministers of the Social Gospel also undermined workers by gendering them as female, or needy of Christian moral oversight. This occurred in two ways. First, the *Strike Report* marked working-class gender and sexual practices as inappropriate. Second, the ministers reframed the shop-floor ecosystem to suggest that all upstanding, Christian men join with one another in protection of women. While organized steelworkers demanded that Elbert Gary meet his employees at the bargaining table as equals, the publications of the Federal Council offered narratives that excused Gary for his unwillingness to meet his employees as equals. Ministers constructed white Protestant patriarchy as the marker of a "Christian civilization" and identified church leaders as the only legitimate Christian moral agents over the nation.[31]

In their *Strike Report*, ministers identified workers' fundamental grievance not in any of their twelve explicit demands, but in Gary's failure to provide workingmen the time, space, and resources to enact their ideal of a Christian family life. As ministers summarized, "Twelve-hour day workers, even if the jobs were as leisurely as Mr. Gary says they are, have absolutely no time for family, for town, for church or for self-schooling; for any of the activities that begin to make up full citizenship."[32] While chapters of the report emphasized the excessive workdays and repressive work atmosphere, the appendixes drew explicit attention to the very low wages Gary paid as compared to various assessments of the minimum salary required to sustain a family in a city.[33] Federal Council ministers turned workers' demands for the rights to dispose of their income as they wished into a plea to employers to exercise more precise paternalism over their workforce.

Harry Ward's rationale for the living wage followed a similar pattern. In his 1914 update to the *Social Creed*, Harry Ward affirmed that a living wage was necessary for the "defense of family and child."[34] For Ward, a living wage gave workers space to develop Anglo-Protestant home arrangements. He thought that children living in very close quarters with their parents left their parents little privacy for their sexuality, and thus, he said, children "cannot be expected to develop normal moral standards." Larger working-class homes, especially those with living rooms, would also allow young people room to bring their dates to their family home rather than spending time together admist the "unrecognized peril of the streets." Ward expected that greater pay to a male householder would allow him more power in relation to his family, especially his daughters.[35]

In fact, in his efforts to defend the authority of employers to exercise Christian leadership on the shop floor, Harry Ward feminized all workers as needy of a stronger man's protection and guidance. He argued that working-class men should focus, like women, on a life of sacrifice. They should "live for the sake of children yet unborn" and "teach the higher meaning and results of crucifying the flesh and lusts of the flesh." He hoped that Christian sexual purity, defined as monogamous relations between married people, should "become the social code and will lay the foundation of the Christian order."[36] By suggesting that employers were responsible for their workers beyond their shop-floor behavior, Ward effectively supported Gary's arguments that workers did not know what was best for them. "If Christianity intends to develop a civilization," Ward said, implying again that immigrants and African American migrants did not currently uphold the standards of civilization, then these poor Americans would have to learn the "chastity of both sexes, and loyalty in the marriage relationship." Aligning with temperance advocates but now against workers, Ward upheld Victorian, Anglo-Protestant standards of sexual propriety as a universal requirement of godly cultures. As he framed it, "This is no arbitrary decree of ecclesiastical organizations, it is a stern revelation of the divine decree in terms of the immutable laws of the physical universe."[37]

Worth Tippy, longtime member of the Committee on Church and Social Service, now marked working-class sexuality as a danger in itself and called upon both industrial employers and fellow Anglo-Protestant church members to address it. His book, *The Church and the Great War* argued that the chaos of war and industrial conflict (strikes) created the opportunity for employers to take responsibility for working-class mores. He criticized the "general attitude of lightness concerning the standards of relationships between the sexes" among workers and argued that religious organizations must nourish a "nobler conception of marriage so that it shall never be a mere legal and ecclesiastical sanction for lust, but shall be recognized as one of the chief means of social progress and as furnishing one of the greatest obligations for those individuals who enter it."[38]

As workers organized in unprecedented numbers, Tippy dedicated an entire chapter of his next book to the importance of promoting "sex morality." While he strongly supported monogamy and believed birth control should only be used sparingly, he also contended that prophylactics were an important technology to prevent the spread of venereal disease. Even though Tippy spent the early part of his career trying to connect with wage earners on their own terms, he now boldly declared that among the "permanent objectives of the churches" was "to sustain the monogamous family, to bring the sex instinct under control in a maximum number of persons, to keep the minds of youth clean and idealistic, to maintain the sanctity of sex relations, to lift up equal standards of morality for men and women, [and] to keep the home a sanctuary for childhood."[39] Tippy argued that young people ought to be educated in the "spiritual ideals of love and the relations of the sexes; the training of young men to be good husbands and fathers and young women to be good wives and mothers." He advocated open discussions among couples, married and unmarried, about sexuality, and even supported intentional efforts of churches to provide social outlets for young people to date. He pushed for younger marriage and shorter engagements as an antidote to sexual experimentation and supported widespread sex education.[40] This work raised the eyebrows of Christians everywhere and got him listed as author of "licentious discussions" for "people who would normally never hear [of] or become interested in . . . sexual trash" in the 1934 "Who's Who" for radicals.[41] But, for Tippy, a central purpose of churches was to provide the recreational space for courtship and appropriate family relationships. In a widely syndicated column called "The Church and Social Reconstruction" that he distributed in the IWM, Tippy argued that the Church (with a capital C), "which brings both sexes and all ages into normal relations, is admirably fitted to provide for this wholesome association of the sexes, and to do so should become an object of definite endeavor."[42]

These ministers' hope to reform the Christian family involved creating a strong patriarch who stood in camaraderie with other men in the workplace, and socializing young men to adopt this understanding of their role in the family through regular programming at local churches. In a widely syndicated article called "The Coming Seven Day Church," Tippy argued that churches should be open seven days a week, with religious, educational, and social activities which would socialize men to what a "Christian home" really was.[43] He now preached that workers were wrong in their suggestion that "wage slavery cannot be abolished except by a complete overturning of the present economic organization of society." Rather, he said, justice can be done "by assuring the workers, as rapidly as it can be accomplished with efficiency, a fair share in the management by collective bargaining and a share in control" through stock purchase, profit sharing, and company unions.[44] Because men were men, they did not need unions.

Tippy imagined that the relationship between workers and employers should mirror that of wives and husbands. The Interchurch Committee on Methods of Cooperation held, "In the home God has given us in miniature a picture of what He means His world to be—a society in which the welfare of each is the concern of all and the greatest who serves the most."[45] Tippy never imagined that a "fair share" in management had to imply equality in decision-making. By constructing workers as female and needy of ecclesiastical and managerial authority, he implied that workers were not fully capable of exercising the very leadership they demanded. The gendered metaphor of Christian service allowed pastors to imagine a Christian unit that instantiated power differentials but would not see differences in rank and power as obstacles to workplace harmony.

When Tippy argued that working-class men deserved a living wage, it was with the assumption that men should earn a family wage—enough money so that their wives could exit the workforce and stay home with children.[46] Tippy supported women's suffrage, but he did not support women's social and spiritual authority as evangelists and reformers. Several historians have illustrated the silencing of social workers and female ministers as the consequence of the fundamentalist movement.[47] Yet the Social Gospel movement was equally invested in limiting the authority of social workers in particular, and women's leadership in ministry overall. In the early twentieth century, women were conducting social surveys and carrying out citywide efforts to educate, distribute aid, help find employment, and share the gospel with immigrants and other newcomers. Tippy saw this type of social work as fundamental to Jesus's ministry, but also a fundamentally masculine enterprise.[48] In *The Church, a Community Force*, he argued that, for a church to "become a community force, its pastor must lead it there. . . . He must know its uplift forces and its social works, and, in order to know and to lead, he himself must be one of them."[49] Tippy worked with Cleveland city government on a plan for all the social workers in the city to receive their training under his guidance and to report to him as pastor of his Epworth Community

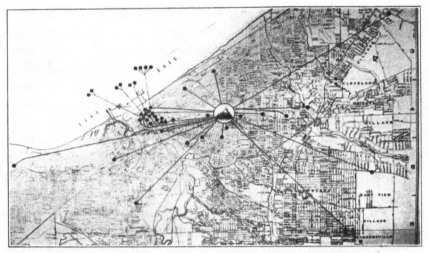

EPWORTH MEMORIAL CHURCH AND ITS RELATION TO THE WELFARE MOVEMENTS
OF THE CITY

Figure 9.1 Worth Tippy hoped his church would serve as the nerve center of all social services in Cleveland, Ohio.

Church (Figure 9.1). This is to say, Tippy did not respect the authority of the women social workers who ran his city's settlement house networks. In his book, which he used to sell this plan to Cleveland city government, he illustrated all social work in his city as an extension of his church's efforts for social reform.[50] He saw the work of all women engaged in ministry in his city as an extension of his own church's leadership.

Nominating the Rockefeller Plan

At his World Survey Conference in January 1920, Rockefeller invited ministers and fellow millionaires to discuss conditions for evangelism and industrial reconstruction in the United States and around the world. While Rockefeller did not direct the "American Industrial Relations Division," he worked as hard as he could to direct the team of ministers who were investigating the steel strike to consider the role of their report in light of his larger movement for brotherhood and the American family. He hired

Raymond Fosdick, his personal lawyer and brother to the noted "modernist" Harry Emerson Fosdick, to officially curate the history of the IWM and conceal the role that he had played in the organization.[51] He also revised the National Association of Manufacturers' "American Plan," called it the "Rockefeller Plan," and defended it at the conference.

However, by the time the *Strike Report* was published in late 1920, the ministers' strongest argument in favor of workers—the value of a living wage—already seemed passé. The IWM's evangelistic campaign had so convincingly changed the narrative to emphasize working-class "spirituality" and "stewardship" that the progressives who authored the *Strike Report* no longer found that their own denomination's ministers were willing to uncritically heed their demands for workplace justice. Starting in 1919, protofundamentalists had begun challenging the social and political authority of all those associated with the Federal Council, accusing them of sympathy with communists and with "higher critics" (Bible scholars who troubled the authorship and historical veracity of Scriptural claims). A new flank of evangelicals now subscribed to a competing set of religious authorities who also used direct mail. These emerging fundamentalists, too, were a group of ministers with partners in big business who seized a political crisis to exert their own authority and control religious messaging.[52]

The *Strike Report* served as a lightning rod to further divide Protestants according to which ministers, and which patrons within the business community, they supported. Many conservative ministers came out in support of the "bootstraps" gospel of "more religion," not higher pay, as a salve for poor steelworkers. The Reverend Frank Stevenson, a fundamentalist minister in Cincinnati, explained, "We are all laborers, and the only man who deserves censure today is the man who achieves wealth and then in the prime of life stops working, living off unearned income." He claimed that "every man has an equal chance to climb as far as his ability permits him," and all therefore all men could be capitalists. Instead of legislation or required mediation of strikes, he said, "We need more religion." In Stevenson's estimation, the "Christian religion put into actual practice alone can permanently reduce the cost of living, insure peaceful progress to every enterprise, and bring near the Kingdom of Heaven. It is the old-fashioned remedy for the old-fashioned sin of a troubled world."[53] Victor Bigelow, minister in Andover, Massachusetts, publicly agreed that steelworkers should stop making unnecessary demands of their employers. He addressed Boston-area ministers in 1920: "God never abandons justice in order to be merciful, and neither should we." The Federal Council of Churches, complacent about its leadership over Protestant America, was quickly losing its national and international authority on matters of industrial justice.

Further disrupting the authority of Federal Council ministers, the emerging fundamentalists were now receiving major corporate sponsors for their procapitalist and anti–Social Gospel sermons. Elbert Gary heard about Bigelow's message and paid for it to be mass-produced as a pamphlet, *Mistakes of the Interchurch Steel Report*. Bigelow, a cheerleader for welfare capitalism, argued that no corporation should be forced into negotiating with entities it deemed illegitimate. For, he held, the US Steel Corporation was "as anxious for the welfare of its employees as are members of our Interchurch Commission." The "poor workman," he continued, "has no escape from arbitrary treatments under the operation of labor union conferences . . . the vast majority of the two hundred thousand employees of the US Steel Corporation prefer the 'arbitrary' treatment of the Corporation than the arbitrary treatment by labor unions." Bigelow blamed the Interchurch Commission for its defense of the union at all, claiming that they endorsed the "hobo's doctrine" that "glorifies leisure and denounces toil." Jesus, the "Ceaseless Toiler of Galilee," he said, believed in "work as the greatest means of character building and as the demonstrator of the highest manhood." In protest of the eight-hour day, he said that "many generations of experience have proved that men have healthy capacity for more than eight hours of toil." He defended Gary's industrial spies as "sheer self-defense" against violence and condemned all agitation for union representation as a scheme of the AFL that "must be repudiated!"

Bigelow and the many conservative ministers he represented not only rejected unions' demands for a living wage, but insisted that white patriarchy was working properly under the industrial discipline of welfare capitalism. Ernest Young, another minister, explained in his *Comments on the Interchurch Report* that US Steel had the best interest of the workers in mind. Company managers, he said, had to "lower pay to workers when they must, in order to maintain their profits and the prices of their goods"; this was simply how business worked.[54]

When accounting for popularity, no publication matched that of Marshall Olds's *Analysis of the Interchurch World Movement Report*, a four-hundred-page tome published by Putnam and Sons, which excoriated every assertion of the *Strike Report* and especially the claims that workers were underpaid and that a twelve-hour day was too long. It eviscerated the concept that business leaders owed workers a living wage and emphasized that the Bureau of Industrial Research's research team, conducting the investigation alongside Federal Council ministers, included "biased" socialists.[55] Judging by the number of extant copies, Olds's book appears to have circulated more than the *Strike Report* itself.

American workers and socialist intellectuals fought back against Olds, Rockefeller, and the many Protestants hopeful of capturing the allegiance of the Christian working classes. In 1921, Upton Sinclair finally self-published his provocative book which argued that churches in the United States accepted, and even supported, capitalism because it provided the preconditions to make them needed for the poor. In *The Profits of Religion*, he argued that church leaders, Catholic and Protestant, betrayed "the revolutionary hope of Jesus, for a kingdom upon the earth" by suggesting that their "daily bread" would not come until they went to heaven. In return for exemption from all taxes with all the rights of taxpayers, churches kept silent on the injustices of society. Sinclair rebuked Gary, Bigelow, Olds, and their allies who refused to identify with the poor, and suggested that the class struggle was occurring "in the churches, as everywhere else in the world, and the social revolution is coming in the churches, just as it is coming in industry." Mimicking progressive Protestants, Sinclair, too, said "we need a new religion," one based on morality. The book sold 60,000 copies and served as the basis of Sinclair's 1934 run for governor of California.[56]

Yet, even 1921, most progressive Protestant ministers of the Federal Council wanted nothing less than to be identified with Sinclair and the socialist movement. That year, in another nationwide campaign, many of the same clergy who had worked for years on the Federal Council's Committee on Church and Social Service went on a national tour to support the Rockefeller Plan, a nonunion employee representation plan. In some respects, this endorsement was predictable in the evolution of the Social Gospel. Tippy, Ward, and Stelzle had always been against "class antagonisms" and in favor of "brotherhood." However, until 1919, they had done their best to maintain good relationships with trade unions.

By 1921, not only were all those ties broken but ministers denied they had ever existed. The Federal Council's Labor Sunday message of 1920 declared "a call through the churches to employers and workers to get together and to undertake to work out cooperative relations within industry."[57] Through male to male "brotherhood" in the workplace, churches would nurture in shops "an atmosphere of fairness, kindness and good will, in which those who contend, employer and employee, capitalist and workingman, may find both light and warmth . . . which will come to them not by outward pressure but from the inner sense of brotherhood."[58]

The reason these clerics could make such a shift from defending the labor movement to defying it was their conviction that all workers really wanted was a decent wage.[59] The pastors supported an industrial organization plan that upheld a single document, a *Book of Standard Practices and Rules*, which functioned like the US Constitution or the Bible, a higher set of principles above Stella any individual job contract.[60] As financier and philanthropist Sam Lewisohn defended the American Plan in middling-class churches across the country, "Dramatic experiments are interesting, but real progress will be made by slow but certain improvements in the technique of leadership and cooperation." Those leaders, he argued, were the "Enlightened employers," who, "by reason of their tactical position as administrators of industry, have the responsibility of blazing the trail." To Lewisohn, workers had neither the right nor privilege to secure safe working conditions, job security, and "adequate guarantees against sickness and disablement". Lewisohn had no real interest in shared power between workers and employers. He was much more concerned with selling middling-class white churchgoers on the prospect that his schematic for workplace organization was respectful and orderly. When pressed, he held it was "premature to ask labor to accept responsibilities on boards of directors. They can take an interest in matters affecting their own status or in the details of management, but they are not yet equipped to assume larger responsibilities."[61] The *Book of Standard Practices and Rules* would stand out as the holy book of the shop floor, since it was considered agreed upon by employees and employers.[62]

Once the Federal Council no longer saw itself in alliance with unions, it was also more free to support white supremacy and its regime of racial apartheid, especially in the South. In 1921, the Committee on Negro Churches offered a "A Constructive Program for Just Inter-racial Relations," claiming to represent the four million African American church members within the Federal Council. The committee argued that the vague ideals of "brotherhood" rung hollow and instead emphasized the imperative for Black wage earners, including both men and women, to earn equal pay for equal work. The statement also called out lynching and other violent attacks on African American communities as attacks not just on Black people, but on Christian homes. As the ministers framed it, "The home of the Negro should receive the same measure of respect and protection as that of other Americans, and the sanctity of his home relations should be safeguarded in every possible way." In laying claim to the same type of rhetoric of "home protection" as that used by the white Protestant majority, especially within the temperance movement, African Americans critiqued the white vision of Christian nationhood that centered white churches. The ministers concluded, "If we propose a democratic program for the protection and self-determination of the weak and oppressed people of Europe as a means of permanent peace and goodwill abroad, let us apply the same program at home."[63] While the Federal Council would go on to turn this committee into a commission and shepherd numerous "interracial commissions" into existence, in 1920 African American ministers fought against white ministers who largely allied with white segregationists.[64]

Robert Speer, newly-elected president of the Federal Council of Churches in 1921, was unwilling to take a public stand against racism. In a statement he made as president in 1921, he affirmed the doctrine of "separate but equal" as enshrined in Christian doctrine. As he put it, African Americans should receive access to "parks and playgrounds, equal wages for equal work, adequate and efficient schools, courteous and equal facilities and courtesy while traveling, [and] police protection and equality before the law." Speer opposed all forms of racial mixing. While W. E. B. Du Bois and his Niagara Movement continued to challenge the color line, the Federal Council now defended it.[65] While the Fellowship of Reconciliation opposed the continued use of force through the US military, the Federal Council now defended it. As Speer put it in his book *The Gospel and the New World*, which he published as president of the Federal Council, Protestant ministers were called to uphold the authority of white men to make any business decisions they saw fit and to move within a white society segregated from people of color.[66] The most they sought to offer African Americans, or any industrial workers, was "courtesy."

While the rising the fundamentalist movement would cast Social Gospel progressives as "modernists," "liberals," and even socialists, their doctrines of gender, family, nation, and economics were deeply conservative by the standards of their day. Between their wartime partnership with Wilson and their new alliance with John D. Rockefeller Jr., Federal Council leaders adopted the racial and economic positions of Lost Cause Christianity. American Protestants, north and south, now upheld the spirituality of the church (its nonpolitical nature), the sanctity of racial apartheid, and the righteousness of American business.[67] The perception of the Social Gospel as a radical or even liberal movement was largely a product of corporate messaging in the 1920s and beyond.

Conclusion

In the end, the Interchurch World Movement illustrated, both to ministers and to the business community, that money had more power than ministers to define the core principles of Christian justice. Through the Rockefeller-funded IWM, the very Social Gospel advocates who had publicly championed unionization in the 1910s became leaders in the campaign to break the biggest strike of the century and terminate collective bargaining rights for at least another decade. Through their endorsement of the Rockefeller Plan, the Federal Council of Churches rolled back the many gains that workers had made over the previous decade along the lines of racial, gender, and industrial democracy.

Ministers of the Federal Council supported welfare capitalism over collective bargaining rights because they believed that employers knew what was best for the non-white and non-Protestant wage earners who depended on them. The imagined "brotherhood of man," which they offered as the solution to industrial conflict, elevated the authority of the new middling-classes of foremen and clerks who supervised deskilled factory workers. These foremen were not professionals, but they were also not the deskilled workers who were most in need of unions. They were the well-to-do wage earning classes that joined Protestant churches (and, often, the Ku Klux Klan) in large numbers in the 1920s.

It is worth noting that Federal Council ministers conceded to the rhetoric of "cooperation" and "Christian brotherhood" without accepting the terms of ethnic, racial and gender egalitarianism—or a rejection of the profit system— that many socialists meant when they popularized these terms. They did so because they compared the Christian workplace to that of a Christian family unit, a partnership of unequals.

The IWM spelled the end of trust between the AFL and the Federal Council of Churches. Employee representation plans proved a weak solution to the industrial crisis. Henry Ford, who was wildly popular as an employer in the 1910s because of his high pay, benefits, stock options, and shop-floor representation for workers, reneged on his promise of treating his workers well after the Great War. When his own profits took a downturn in 1919 and again in the Depression, he made no excuses in laying off most of his work-force. By 1920, and surely by 1929, it became clear that plans for workplace "cooperation" offered workers no leverage in difficult times.[68] When the economy slowed, clerical support for "selflessness" and "submission" became weapons used to force wage earners to shoulder the financial risks of busi-ness. The year 1920 marked the end of the alliance between ministers and unions, a turning point one could mark as the end of the Social Gospel era. Both ministers and Wilson's Democratic Party had robbed unions, and the working-class religious left more broadly, of the moral platform of Christian justice.

It is important to recognize just why the Social Gospel era ended. It was not, as the historian Paul Carter notably claimed, just the violence of war or the lack of substantive theology that precipitated its decline.[69] Nor was the Red Scare, which ministers cooperated with and benefited from, en-tirely to blame for white Protestants' substantial change in course. Rather, white Protestant ministers gambled away the Christian moral necessity of an independent labor movement and a social democratic republic on the ex-pectation that they and their churches would continue to keep businessmen accountable. In insisting on their own "neutrality" and the public necessity of ministers in all arenas of life, they banked on the hope that immigrant wage earners and African Americans would be more likely to profess Christianity and develop "democratic virtues" under their tutelage than under the lead-ership of unions. They expected that so-called Christian businessmen would continue to need their support in order to rationalize their power. They were wrong about this.

Contrary to their hopes and expectations, the most well-resourced Protestant churches did not swell with immigrant and African American wage earners in the 1920s. The new middling classes who occupied most Protestant pews became only more intent on reforming, or "Americanizing" first-generation immigrants and people of color. Not only did the IWM and its accompanying "Christian service" messages close the Social Gospel era. The Rockefeller-funded infiltration of the Social Gospel movement ensured that modern churches—like those in the Gilded Age—would be indispensable to the poorest workers as social service agencies, but also dependent on the philanthropy of business for their survival.

Afterword

On the Heroic Narrative of Christian Social Service

From the perspective of organized labor, the minister-led Social Gospel movement, embodied in the Federal Council of Churches, was not only a rival but a traitor. At the height of the movement for social democracy in the United States, Protestant ministers weaponized both their theological expertise and the surplus capital of millionaires to protect business owners from the demands of the largest strike of the decade. These ministers were effective not only because the Federal Council of Churches had cultivated authority as leaders in social service, and had a massive database with the names and addresses of every church leader in the United States to prove it. But also, contrary to the myth of disestablishment, the president of the United States anointed these Protestant ministers as his agents, tasking them with the challenge of building his appeal as a president committed to a more Christian nation. Clergy of the Federal Council took the opportunity to exalt their own authority, even if it meant breaking with some of their historic partners.

As we consider the real rivalry between churches and the labor movement for moral authority, it is worth considering *why* this particular conservative religious lobby was so successful. It was executed by privileged, well-resourced men with spiritual authority, international diplomatic authority, and the powerful weapon of the Sedition Act to put down resistance. But, despite the new popularity of church buildings and ministries among the poor, the majority of wage earners still had limited reverence for the spiritual or political authority of white Protestant ministers. American wage earners had attempted to change both the political associations of a "Christian" and the meaning and purpose of a church body in the United States. How did these ministers so effectively suppress the grassroots movement for socialism and industrial unionism had that been predicted, only a few years earlier, to surmount the two-party system?

It is difficult to overstate the impact of both voter suppression and violence in US history. Voting registers were growing quickly throughout the

The Gospel of Church. Janine Giordano Drake, Oxford University Press. © Oxford University Press 2024.
DOI: 10.1093/oso/9780197614303.003.0011

1910s as new immigrants and southern migrants poured into northern cities and declared their intentions to participate in the American democracy. Many among these new voters were also union members, advocates for municipal services, and émigrés from countries with powerful labor movements. Many among the working-class residents of northern cities participated in the international print culture of the labor movement. The fact that the American Federation of Labor bankrolled William Z. Foster, a communist-leaning organizer, to create a massive industrial union in 1919 reminds us how mainstream the left wing of the labor movement became within the short duration of the Great War.[1] President's Wilson's Committee on Public Information and the Red Scare it provoked was not very successful in winning the ideological war for "democracy." It was successful in suppressing the circulation of socialist ideas and the eligibility of radical voters. The 1919 defeat of the Amalgamated Union, like the new waves of immigration deportation and the violent pogroms of white vigilantes on African American communities across the country, remind us that brute suppression, taking all its violent forms, was perhaps the most obvious reason that conservative progressives came to triumph within American politics.[2]

But brute suppression is only as powerful as its ideological justification. The other major reason this lobby was so successful revolves around the heroic narrative these ministers told about themselves. Leaders in the Federal Council effectively appropriated and imitated the grassroots movement for socialism. Not only did Federal Council ministers steal socialists' trained attention on the Beatitudes, their imagery of Jesus the Carpenter, and their terms like "Social Christianity" and the "Social Gospel." They also stole from their friends in the AFL and their mission to do justice for the poor. After the Great War, Social Gospel leaders declared victory for working people, giving the impression that the grassroots movement for social democracy had been accomplished. However, in the heroic narrative these ministers told about themselves, neither elite churches, nor the lack of collective bargaining rights, nor racial patriarchy was ever at the heart of the problems of the Gilded Age. As they described it, the problem was poverty, pure and simple. Social Gospel leaders not only exhorted business leaders to take seriously their responsibility to their employees but built a multiplicity of ministries that they believed would accelerate social mobility among the poor. They convinced many Americans that the welfare capitalism they endorsed carried on the fundamental mission of the labor movement.

In the absence of a powerful socialist movement, Social Gospel ministers represented themselves as the nation's prophets of social service. In 1920, Robert Speer, newly-elected president of the Federal Council of Churches, accepted an invitation to give a commencement address at Vassar College, a left-leaning liberal arts college. "It is only the teaching of Christ that can make the world perfect," he exhorted. "If He were to come today, He would substitute the principles of cooperation for the principles of competition."[3] In years past, this was the kind of statement that socialist stump preachers like Oscar Ameringer and George Washington Woodbey might have offered as critique for capitalism. However, over the previous dozen years, Speer and the Federal Council had appropriated these ideas and given the words new meaning. Speer used the language of "cooperation" to sacralize welfare capitalism and white racial patriarchy as Christian social structures. The Federal Council's definition of Christianity, which became the Democratic Party's definition of Christianity for the rest of the century, declared social democracy anathema to their faith.

The new "Social Christianity" that presided in the executive council of the Federal Council of Churches did not, again, stamp out all vestiges of socialism or Christian Socialism in America. Support for collective bargaining rights and a robust, secular welfare state still lingered in union halls, in the pews, and even in the pulpits of some churches, and within print culture. In fact, conservative Protestant ministers were coming to recognize that it would require a nearly continuous evangelistic campaign both to keep industrial workers compliant with their employers and to maintain the clergy's trust in business leaders. In May 1921, the new Republican president's secretary of labor, James J. Davis, called on the ministers of the Federal Council to continue to use their churches to celebrate the virtues of "social justice, economy and thrift" that they had proclaimed so loudly during the IWM. As Davis put it, "With both employer and employee sitting before the pulpit a complete understanding between the two becomes almost a church obligation." The very fact that the secretary of labor leaned on church leaders to suppress labor conflict spoke volumes of the success of the IWM (and the MRFM before it) in changing the national conversation on the needs of the working poor. "And above all," Davis continued, "let the church teach the practical application of the Golden Rule, not as a millennial theory, but as a vital principle for our daily guidance in all the business affairs of today—'Whatsoever ye should that men should do to you, do ye even to them.' The practical application of the text is real Christianity."[4]

Davis's rejection of the "millennial theory," George Herron's vision of a coming age of a cooperative commonwealth, reminds us that Christian Socialist ideals still lingered among public servants and in popular culture. Upton Sinclair's *They Call Me Carpenter* (1922), a drama of Jesus returning to the world and finding the labor temple was his church, experienced new popularity in the 1920s and 1930s. Sinclair's EPIC [End Poverty in California] Drama League" staged it dozens of times within his campaign for governor for California in 1934, and it remained a topic of discussion for decades thereafter.[5] Sinclair's *The Profits of Religion*, an analysis of how church leaders evaded taxes and hoodwinked and exploited the poor, enjoyed both popularity and fierce opposition into the 1950s.[6] Two generations of Americans had claimed that the foundational structures for a just republic consisted in the cooperative ownership and management of public utilities, joint stock corporations for production and distribution, a generous welfare state that taxed unearned wealth, collective bargaining rights, public works projects, and universal suffrage. Many among them insisted that *these* were the component parts of a Christian nation. And yet, despite the fact that these Christian Socialist ideals stuck around in the left wing of the Democratic Party and played a substantial role in erecting the New Deal, they lost control of the narrative about how to build a more "Christian America."[7]

It is easy to blame Socialist Party leaders for failing to anticipate, or fight back, at this glaring appropriation of their rhetoric with a very different legislative agenda. After all, the minority of self-identified Christian Socialists in the party had tried to turn these ideals into party doctrine in 1908, 1912, and again in 1919, and they had found themselves outvoted by "secularists" every time.[8] However, party leaders, a mixed group including Jews, Christians, agnostics, and atheists, wanted to play the long game. They maintained that a modern political party does not get stuck in the weeds of endorsing one religious perspective over another. As one party official eloquently reprised the party's official declaration that religion was a "private matter,"

When we say that religion "is a private matter" we do not mean that it has no social significance. Such a contention would be manifestly absurd. Religion is inseparable from conduct, from human relations, and hence it is a social force of the greatest importance. What is meant by the declaration is that religious belief or nonbelief is a matter for the individual conscience with which the State or political parties within the State can have nothing to do. Therefore the Socialists of all countries take their stand upon the broad

principle that Church and State should be entirely separate. This is, like-
wise, a fundamental provision of the Constitution of the United States, and
those who assail us for our strict adherence to it assail one of the basic principles of American democracy.[9]

American socialists gambled on the possibility that the public authority of
church leaders would eventually be struck down by the "free exercise" clause
of the Constitution. They expected that the place of religion in American
society would be gradually replaced, as it was in Europe, with an American
labor party, secular intellectuals, and the authority of science. They expected
that the Rockefeller-funded dogma that capitalism was a Christian practice
would eventually be exposed, perhaps along with the supposed "miracles" of
the Christian faith, for its obviously fraudulent claims.[10] Needless to say, the
twentieth century did not bring the vindication socialists anticipated.

Quite to the contrary, Secretary Davis's exhortations to the Federal Council
would reap a newly solidified syncretism between the doctrines of American
capitalism and the doctrines of American Christianity. Under the leadership of the majority of American Christian clergy of the mid-twentieth century, including liberals, fundamentalists, and Roman Catholics, opposition
to "socialism" would become part and parcel of practicing as a "Christian."
Opposition to socialism was literally one chapter of *The Fundamentals*,
the new compendium of fundamentalist social teaching. Charles Erdman,
a theologian at Princeton Seminary, took Charles Stelzle's words out of his
mouth when he held that first-century communism was "local, voluntary,
occasional, temporary" and "never admitted or established as an abiding
principle of Church life."[11] Opposition to socialism also remained central to
Roman Catholicism.[12] Despite the New Deal's massive expansion of the social security state, a project that brought the work of many social democrats
to fruition, socialists largely lost the rhetorical battle for the story of social
mobility in the United States.

Within evangelical Christian narratives of American "progress," socialism
and communism were construed as "secularist" and secularism as the greatest
enemy of the Christian nation.[13] By midcentury, American church leaders
and missionaries, like soldiers, were adorned as heroes inside and outside the
churches. Those who presided over Christian schools, orphanages, clinics,
and hospitals—in both the United States and Latin America—claimed
that their ministries had more effectively achieved the same goals as those
advocated by their socialist and communist adversaries.[14] After World War

II, evangelical Protestant church leaders appropriated the scruffy Jesus who spends time with the poor as the hallmark of their ministries. In the dominant narratives of social work throughout the Cold War, especially those celebrated within denominational women's societies, it was Christian missionaries, reformers, and social workers—not socialists, unions, public schools, or the Social Security system—who led the nation in remediating poverty in the twentieth century.[15]

The stories of the Social Gospel movement that we most often tell in seminaries and churches celebrate white Protestant men who listened hard to the needs of American wage earners and fought on their behalf. This narrative began in the founding of the Federal Council of Churches in 1908 when ministers offered Christian Socialists no credit for steering their ministries, not to mention serving as their greatest rivals. In 1934, as the Congress of Industrial Organizations was organizing allies among the American clergy to make a New Deal with Franklin Delano Roosevelt, Worth Tippy retold the history of Christian "Social Action" in the United States by crowning church leaders as the nation's perennial heroes for the poor. He said that it was the Methodist church, not the massive rebellion of the nation's working-classes, which "lifted the Second Commandment to its rightful place beside the first in the Gospel of Christ."[16]

Getting the Story Right

The Gospel of Church demonstrates that the Social Gospel narrative preserved in most Protestant seminaries and church annals needs a profound revision.[17] In highlighting the work of ministers without equal attention to the working-class leaders they worked with and against, these narratives reinscribe the paternalism at the heart of the American Christian faith. Early twentieth-century Social Gospel leaders were ordinary people with an elite, well-educated, or "progressive" sense of purpose. The many sung and unsung Charles Stelzles, Harry Wards, and Worth Tippies of the Federal Council's Social Gospel movement thought they were committing their careers to alleviating poverty and dignifying the social position of the poor. They genuinely believed that their churches and enhanced public influence over industrial relations would do more for workers than radical trade unions ever could. They rightly saw socialism as a challenge on the entire social order, including the systems of patriarchy, white supremacy, and Christian nationalism. But these ministers could not reconcile this much social transformation with the principles of their profoundly white and American imaginary. They trusted in the claims of their seminary professors and their fathers that "Christian justice" meant white men making prudent decisions on behalf of women, immigrants, poor people, and brown-skinned peoples. They had little regard for concepts of direct democracy, and they did not "give" working-class people a better life.

At its very best, this conservative Christian movement for corporate responsibility invested wage earners' struggles with renewed public attention. These ministers probably deserve credit for the modest improvement in wages and working conditions in the 1920s. Under welfare capitalism, a supposedly gentler version of capitalism, robber barons like Henry Ford and John Rockefeller capitulated to the argument that workers deserved better. New employee policies rewarded compliant workers with profit-sharing incentives, paid vacations, and other "benefits" that they could earn for "good" service. Both Harry Ward (Methodist) and John Ryan (Catholic) celebrated these new arrangements as "accountability" for both employers and employees. Welfare capitalism had some major flaws as a long-term solution to the labor problem. Investors, after all, chased profit, not ethical business practices. But by and large, Social Gospel–oriented clergy maintained their support for welfare capitalism until at least the Great Depression, when the best jobs were gone.[18]

Seen in the least favorable light, Social Gospel leaders duped both the labor movement and the American people. These ministers told their partners in the AFL that they truly supported the promise of the *Social Creed*: a living wage, safe working conditions, and the end to child labor. However, once they gained the audience of the president of the United States and the leading tycoons of industry, their understanding of labor justice shifted. One might argue that these ministers were bribed by Rockefeller and other millionaires into this about-face on collective bargaining rights. That perspective may also misunderstand their goals from the start. The ministers of the Federal Council were always more interested in church-planting and ministry-building than in empowering wage earners in the public sphere. Protestant and Catholic ministers should be remembered for failing to speak out against the power of money and white supremacy backing their ministries. They should be appropriately criticized for taking advantage of the struggles of the industrial era to grow the size and influence of their churches.

That said, we cannot understand the so-called Progressive Era and its decline without grappling with how profoundly white supremacy and patriarchy reached into every corner of social life. While these wartime ministers
of the Federal Council supported only a palliative solution to the industrial
crisis, they stood to the left of many other Christians, especially the emerging
fundamentalists and a good fraction of American Catholics within the period 1919–1929. Despite persecution, Worth Tippy continued to advocate
for comprehensive sex education and access to birth control. He would later
advocate for Black civil rights. Henry Churchill King, who had been an ad-
viser to President Wilson and defender of his colonial aims abroad, remained
president of Oberlin College, a perch from which he championed theological
"liberalism," interracial unity, and Christian social service. He too, labeled
a leftist, went on to advocate for the legal refugee status of undocumented
immigrants. After Harry Ward left the country in 1919 to tour the USSR,
he became a founding member of both the American Civil Liberties Union
and the Fellowship of Reconciliation and an advocate for justice for both
immigrants and people of color. For him and many other Social Gospel
leaders, the independently executed IWM was, even by the year 1921, a mistake. The postwar Federal Council of Churches was far less committed to
social justice.

But, the largest fraction of Protestant ministers in the Federal Council
of Churches dropped their interest in labor justice around 1920. Charles
Stelzle is one example. In the 1920s, he grew disheartened by the declining
size of immigrant communities in New York City and accepted that his old
days in ministry to a diverse group of new European immigrants would
never return. Publicly, he claimed that "the continued moral presence of the
churches" would itself "complete the reformation" of American industrial relations, but he did not stick around to make that happen. Stelzle took a job as
president of the Church Advertising Department within the International
Advertising Association, where he solicited donations for settlement houses
and other charities.[19] While each of these Social Gospel leaders was instru-
mental in suppressing social democracy during and after the Great War, they
did not together achieve much more than this. Their support for labor justice
was always only as consequential as the labor movements with whom they
partnered.

Contrary to our hagiographic biographies of Social Gospel leaders, most
working people with backgrounds outside of the Anglo-Protestant tradition
held out only cautious reverence for these Protestant ministers who "helped"

them. The US Census of Religious Bodies did not conduct a survey between 1916 and 1926, but Charles Stelzle noted that church membership rolls had increased at a rate of 3.6 percent per year from around 1912 until 1917, and then came to a screeching halt. In 1919, he observed, "Every great denomination actually lost in total membership." Stelzle noticed that working people continued to support "movements outside the church which have a distinctly religious value," a reference to Christian afterschool programs and rehabilitation programs, but even Stelzle knew that most immigrant and African American wage earners did not feel comfortable worshipping in liberal Protestant churches on Sundays.[20] By 1930, in the depths of the Great Depression, overall church attendance rates had fallen further still. In New York City, only 7 percent of the adult white population held membership in Protestant churches, while 34.1 percent were Roman Catholics and 27.1 percent counted themselves as Jewish. The reign of the Social Gospel movement made religious institutions into popular locations to park the profits of "Christian capital" and vital social welfare dispensaries for the poor. They were popular institutions among the aspirant middling classes. It is likely that Stelzle unwittingly contributed to the rising prominence of Catholic and Jewish schools, charities, social institutions, and hospitals in his city.[21] But by Charles Stelzle's own analysis, the Social Gospel had failed to in its efforts to substantially swell denominational Protestant churches with poor wage earners.

A more accurate history of the Social Gospel movement emphasizes the groundswell of Christians who refused to patronize the Gilded Age churches that trumpeted a wealthy white Christ and rationalized their accumulated wealth through their paltry charitable donations. This groundswell was bigger than the movement Eugene Debs could capture within his imperfect (and sometimes blatantly racist) Socialist Party. It was larger still than the network Rufus Weeks was able to build through his Christian Socialist Fellowship. Not all the more than three hundred socialist newspapers active in 1916 spoke of Jesus on a weekly basis, but each one, and their hundreds of thousands of subscribers, is testament to the massive rebellion against the collusion of Christianity and American capitalism. It is this largely disorganized groundswell of American socialism that precipitated the short-lived gains for the labor movement during the Great War. It was this groundswell that provoked almost all the richest men in the country to invest in seminaries, churches, and evangelical crusades that begged religious leaders to stop the socialist rebellion by imagining a kinder, gentler version of capitalism capable of sustaining their income streams without unions.

A more accurate history also observes that American churches, under the mystique of disestablishment, have been funded by the surplus capital of business owners for at least the last two hundred years. While we like to believe that nations without a state church can promote "religious freedom," we need to recognize that this "freedom" empowers the wealthy to invest in the ministries that suit them best. Under a capitalist system that offers few checks on the wealth of capitalists and no real floor to provide a living wage for the most deskilled workers, "religious freedom" gives liberty to wealthy businessmen to shape the meaning of every religious tradition. In the early twentieth century, the wealthiest men in the country united to undermine and suppress Christian critiques of capitalism. A more accurate history of the Social Gospel movement provokes questions about how churches should fund-raise and treat the gifts of millionaires. To the extent these challenges are still with us, they are the enduring legacy of late nineteenth-century Christian Socialist movement.

Perhaps most of all, a more accurate history of the Social Gospel movement observes the long marriage between Christian nationalist lawmakers and church leaders. In the Gilded Age, church missions, orphanages, and church-sponsored hospitals and schools provided the bulk of the nation's social safety net. Congressmen turned down opportunities to raise money for an alternate, public infrastructure when they knew that Christian organizations were content to carry out this work with private funding and small public grants. Despite the uproar of the early twentieth century for public and cooperatively owned infrastructure, church leaders and their ministry partners did their best to retain their monopolies on social services for the very poor. Many supported the creation of publicly owned and managed electricity, water, and transit systems. However, they also did their best to put home missionaries—including pastors, deacons, deaconesses, settlement house staff, teachers, and nurses—in the coveted positions of direct and daily influence over the moral and spiritual needs of the working poor. Elaborate "seven day" ministry programs, funded by the profits of big business, provided instruction in English, American customs, the rights and privileges of American citizens, and "healthy" recreation opportunities for children and adults. Social Gospel leaders jealously guarded their influence over working people's moral and spiritual development.

In making churches and church-related ministries—rather than the labor movement—the nation's primary dispensaries of social services and the nation's primary interpreters of American identity, lawmakers ensured the posterity of Protestant Christianity within a rapidly diversifying nation. Semipublic, essential ministries to the poor provided progressives the continuous data and points of contact to claim their own "expertise" as they spoke "on behalf" of the poor in their public advocacy. However, Social Gospel progressives rarely had the same intentions for a pluralist social democracy as those of the working poor, and this was precisely why progressives were so effective in winning the trust of elite lawmakers in the Republican and Democratic Parties. Social Gospel leaders convinced American elites that the poor needed to be treated better. However, they equally claimed that the nation's Protestant church leaders and business leaders, and not the heavily Catholic, Jewish, atheist, and agnostic labor movement, should retain the moral and cultural leadership over the rapidly diversifying nation.

This charitable work in the name of "Christian nationhood" came at a cost to the working people who wanted to extend the public ownership and management of utilities to the spheres of education, social services, and healthcare. In part because of the heroic narrative of Christian social services in our stories of the twentieth century, most of our nation's essential services to the poor remain privatized. Commercial insurance policies, employee-sponsored benefits, and Christian ministries for the very poor provide a significant fraction of the American social safety net.[22] Indeed, to this day, a large fraction of the nation's preschools, homeless shelters, pregnancy resource centers, mental health rehabilitation centers, food banks, soup kitchens, refugee relief and resettlement services, children's homes, and afterschool programs are owned and operated by private, religious ministries. Many such agencies do excellent work, but most retain their rights to shape their staffing and services around their ministry purposes. Offering rationales based in fiscal responsibility, the nation's lawmakers continue to resist efforts to "reduplicate" these private ministries with public agencies. However, in allowing private companies and private charities to shape the social safety net for the very poor, we maintain the cultural myth that businessmen and missionaries, rather than poor people themselves, know best how to create healthy communities.

Early twentieth-century social democrats and anarcho-syndicalists both identified this heroic narrative of Christian Social Service as their adversary.

This is precisely why Socialist Party leaders affirmed that the separation of church and state was at the core of the American socialist movement. Socialists believed that the wealthiest men in the country should not have the right to determine which churches survive and which are rendered illegal, which social services should exist and how they are managed. They recognized the Social Gospel movement as an effort to restore the dependence of the poor on wealthy benefactors, and they rejected the leadership of Christian ministers over the modern American commonwealth. In fact, clergy, the trade union movement, and the secular Left continued to work together for the next fifty years, in peacetime and in war, in the architecture of both the New Deal and the Great Society.[23] However, despite or perhaps because of their conflicting goals, antisocialist Christians have continued to label socialists and social democrats as selfish, atheist, and ultimately foreign agents, claiming that church leaders alone are not self-interested in their efforts to serve the poor.[24]

Now, more than a century after the Social Gospel movement, privately funded ministries remain at the heart of the nation's social safety net. The heroic narratives these ministries tell about themselves also serve to "remind" Americans that our capitalist economic system usually functions the way it should. Heroic Christian ministers and their extensive ministries to the poor continue to provide the excuse for why capitalism is a mostly functional economic system, and why public ownership of public services is unnecessary.

Notes

Acknowledgments

1. Rick Warren, *The Purpose Driven Church: Growth without Compromising Your Message and Mission* (New York: Zondervan, 1995), 17.

Introduction

1. Edward Bellamy, *Equality* (New York: Appleton, 1898), 264.
2. *Publisher's Weekly*, Sept. 1, 1945, 845; *Publisher's Weekly*, Apr. 21, 1934, 1504; *Publisher's Weekly*, Mar. 2, 1946, 1383. On the Social Gospel and popular books, see Erin Smith, *What Would Jesus Read? Popular Religious Books and Everyday Life in Twentieth-Century America* (Chapel Hill: University of North Carolina Press, 2015), 21–46.
3. A. A. Berle, "Religion and Ethics: What Is the Matter with Our Theological Schools?," *Current Literature* 4 (Oct. 1907): 410–11; "The Church's Growing Sympathy with Socialism," *Social Democrat* 11 (1907): 697–99.
4. "Plans and Resolutions Adopted at the 2nd Annual Conference of the Christian Socialist Fellowship," June 1–4, 1907, in *Christian Socialist* (Chicago) Aug. 15, 1907, 5–6, http://www.marxisthistory.org/history/usa/parties/csf/1907/0604-csf-resoluti ons.pdf.
5. Walter Rauschenbusch, *Christianizing the Social Order* (New York: Macmillan, 1912), 405.
6. Norman Thomas, *A Socialist's Faith* (New York: Norton, 1951), 22.
7. Henry May, *Protestant Churches and Industrial America* (New York: Harper Torchbooks, 1967); Richard White and C. Howard Hopkins, *The Social Gospel: Religion and Reform in Changing America* (Philadelphia: Temple University Press, 1976), 5; Paul Carter, *The Decline and Revival of the Social Gospel: Social and Political Liberalism in American Protestant Churches, 1920–1940* (Hamden: Archon Books, 1971), 12–14.
8. Ken Fones-Wolf, *Trade Union Gospel: Christianity and Labor in Industrial Philadelphia, 1865–1915* (Philadelphia: Temple University Press, 1989); Heath Carter, *Union Made: Working People and the Rise of Social Christianity in Chicago* (New York: Oxford University Press, 2015); Matthew Pehl, *The Making of Working-Class Religion* (Urbana: University of Illinois Press, 2016).
9. As religious studies scholars have recently emphasized, the definition of "religion" is contingent on historical and social circumstances. See Kathryn Lofton, "Why

Religion Is Hard for Historians (and How It Can Be Easier)," *Modern American History* 3, no. 1 (2020): 74; Tisa Wenger, *Religious Freedom: The Contested History of an American Ideal* (Chapel Hill: University of North Carolina Press, 2017). On the labor/radical tradition as a religion, see Dan McKanan, *Prophetic Encounters: Religion and the American Radical Tradition* (Boston: Beacon Press, 2012).

10. Edward Blum, *Reforging the White Republic: Race, Religion, and American Nationalism, 1865–1898* (Baton Rouge: LSU Press, 2015).

11. Ken Fones-Wolf has used the term "trade union gospel." See Fones-Wolf, *Trade Union Gospel.*

12. Tobias Higbie, *Labor's Mind: A History of Working-Class Intellectual Life* (Urbana: University of Illinois Press, 2019), 54–55.

13. David Brody, *Steelworkers in America: The Nonunion Era* (Urbana: University of Illinois Press, 1998), 125–46; James Green, *The World of the Worker: Labor in Twentieth-Century America* (New York: Hill and Wang, 1980), 70–73.

14. Marc Karson, *American Labor Union and Politics: 1900–1918* (Carbondale: Southern Illinois University Press, 1958), 224–43.

15. Jacob H. Dorn, "The Oldest and Youngest of Idealistic Forces at Work in Our Civilization: Encounters between Christianity and Socialism," in *Socialism and Christianity in Early Twentieth Century America*, ed. Jacob H. Dorn (Westport, CT: Greenwood Press, 1998), 3–5.

16. On science and American socialism, see David Burns, *Life and Death of the Radical Historical Jesus* (New York: Oxford University Press, 2013); and Mark Pittenger, *American Socialists and Evolutionary Thought, 1870–1920* (Madison: University of Wisconsin Press, 1993).

17. Dale Soden, *Outsiders in a Promised Land: Religious Activists in Pacific Northwest History* (Stillwater: Oklahoma State University Press, 2015); Philip Foner, *The Policies and Practices of the American Federation of Labor, 1900–1909* (New York: International Publishers, 1964), 111–35.

18. Rabbi Isaac Marcuson, ed., *Central Conference of American Rabbis 34th Annual Convention*, vol. 23 (Richmond, VA: Old Dominion Press, 1923), 71, 244, 280; Harry F. Ward, *A Year Book of the Church and Social Service in the United States* (New York: Fleming Revell, 1916), 11; Robert E. Speer, "The World's Challenge to Christianity Today," *Record of Christian Work*, vol. 41, ed. W. R. Moody (East Northfield: Record of Christian Work Company, 1922), 811.

19. *Federal Council of Churches Unshaken in Its Stand for American Prohibition* (Westerville, OH: Federal Council of the Churches of Christ in America, 1925); Diane H. Winston, *Red-Hot and Righteous: The Urban Religion of the Salvation Army* (Cambridge, MA: Harvard University Press, 2000). On churches and vice districts, see Kevin J. Mumford, *Interzones: Black/White Sex Districts in Chicago and New York in the Early Twentieth Century* (New York: Columbia University Press, 1997), 33, 46.

20. Allison Greene, *No Depression in Heaven: The Great Depression, the New Deal, and the Transformation of Religion in the Delta* (New York: Oxford University Press, 2016); Dorothy Brown and Elizabeth McKeown, *The Poor Belong to Us: Catholic Charities and American Welfare* (Cambridge, MA: Harvard University Press, 1997); Maureen

Fitzgerald, *Habits of Compassion: Irish Catholic Nuns and the Origins of New York's Welfare System, 1830–1920* (Urbana: University of Illinois Press, 2006).

21. Charles Wood, "Soon We May Have to Go to Church," *Collier's*, Nov. 24, 1923, 7, DC 1, folder 12, Marion Worth Tippy Papers (DePauw University, Greencastle, IN).

22. "Religion Cheaper Than Candy," *Literary Digest*, Jan. 15, 1927, 26–32.

Chapter 1

1. Josiah Strong, *New Era, or, The Coming Kingdom* (New York: Baker and Taylor, 1893), 204.

2. Department of the Interior, Census Office, *Report on the Population of the United States*, vol. 2 (Washington, DC: Government Printing Office), xvi, xvii; Carroll Wright, *Abstract from the Eleventh Census* (Washington, DC: Government Printing Office, 1894), 42–43.

3. S. L. Loomis, "Modern Cities and Some of Their Problems," [Andover] *Theological Seminary Bulletin* 8 (June 1887): 9.

4. Tisa Wenger, "The God in the Constitution Controversy: American Secularisms in Historical Perspective," in *Comparative Secularisms in a Golden Age*, ed. Linell Cady and Elizabeth Shakman Hurd (New York: Palgrave Macmillan, 2010), 87.

5. "Religion and Schools," in US Congress, Senate, Religion and Schools: Notes of Hearings before the Committee on Education and Labor, U.S. Senate, on Joint Resolution S.R. 86, 50th Cong., 1st Sess., Feb. 15, 1889–Feb. 22, 1889, 8.

6. U.S. Congress, Senate, *Religion and Schools*. See also Joseph P. Viteritti, "Blaine's Wake: School Choice, the First Amendment, and State Constitutional Law," *Harvard Journal of Law and Public Policy* 21, no. 3 (Summer 1998): 657–71; and Steven K. Green, "Blaming Blaine: Understanding the Blaine Amendment and the No-Funding Principle," *First Amendment Law Review* 2 (Winter 2003): 107–51.

7. Robert T. Handy, *Undermined Establishment: Church-State Relations in America, 1880–1920* (Princeton: Princeton University Press, 2016); Robert Gross, *Public vs. Private: The Early History of School Choice in America* (New York: Oxford University Press, 2018), 38.

8. According to Carroll, in 1880 a very detailed census was commissioned, but the data was disorganized and ultimately lost. H. K. Carroll, *The Religious Forces of the United States* (New York: Christian Literature Company, 1893), xi. For more on Henry Carroll, see *Proceedings, Sermons, Essays and Addresses of the Centennial Methodist Conference, Held in Mt. Vernon Place Methodist Episcopal Church, Baltimore, Md., December 9–17, 1884: With a Historical Statement* (Cincinnati: Cranston and Stowe, 1885), 46.

9. Carroll, *Religious Forces*, xiv, xxx.

10. Ibid., lvi, xxix.

11. Carroll notes only one category that he knows is underreported. Native religions—which he identifies as "pagan"—do not factor into his survey at all because the US census had not traditionally counted Indians on their own territory within US census reports.

12. Mark Noll, *America's God: From Jonathan Edwards to Abraham Lincoln* (New York: Oxford University Press, 2002), 53–72; Ralph Luker, *The Social Gospel in Black and White: American Racial Reform, 1885–1912* (Chapel Hill: University of North Carolina Press, 1991), 9–30.

13. John Aspinwall Hodge, *What Is Presbyterian Law as Defined by the Church Courts?* (Philadelphia: Presbyterian Board of Publication, 1882), 155–56.

14. Carroll, Religious Forces, xli.

15. Carroll wavers on his exact numbers. He says that the "proportion varies with the denominations, and is probably much smaller when more obscure denominations are brought into consideration." Ibid., xxxv.

16. Indirectly, he assessed the multiplier for Catholics at around 1.17 additional communicants orbiting the church.

17. Carroll, *Religious Forces*, xxx–xxxii.

18. Bishop Harris, ed., *Doctrines and Disciplines of the Methodist Episcopal Church* (Cincinnati: Walden and Stowe, 1880), 38–39.

19. Hodge, *Presbyterian Law*, 139, 151–54.

20. Thomas Rzeznik, *Church and Estate: Religion and Wealth in Industrial-Era Philadelphia* (University Park: Penn State University Press, 2013), 64.

21. See the frequent citations of Charles Stelzle, *American Social and Religious Conditions* (New York: Fleming Revell Company, 1912), especially his charts in the appendix. See, for example, Seymour Martin Lipset, *The First New Nation: United States in Historical and Comparative Perspective* (New Brunswick: Transaction Publishers, 1963), 147; Michael Zuckert and Thomas Engerman, *Protestantism and the American Founding* (South Bend: University of Notre Dame Press, 2004), 181; Roger Finke and Rodney Stark, "Turning Pews into People: Estimating 19th Century Church Membership," *Journal for the Scientific Study of Religion* 25, no. 2 (June 1986): 180–92.

22. On the weakness of northern evangelicalism in the nineteenth century, see Luke Harlow, "The Civil War and the Making of Conservative American Evangelicalism," in *Turning Points in the History of American Evangelicalism*, ed. Heath W. Carter and Laura Rominger Porter (Grand Rapids: Eerdmans, 2017), 107–32.

23. Matthew Frye Jacobson, *Barbarian Virtues: The United States Encounters Foreign Peoples at Home and Abroad, 1876–1917* (New York: Hill and Wang, 2001), 53–54; Ian Tyrell, *Reforming the World: The Creation of America's Moral Empire* (Princeton: Princeton University Press, 2013); David Hollinger, *Protestants Abroad: How Missionaries Tried to Change the World but Changed America* (Princeton: Princeton University Press, 2017); William Hutchinson, *Errand to the World: American Protestant Thought and Foreign Missions* (Chicago: University of Chicago Press, 1987); Barbara Reeves-Ellington, Kathryn Kish Sklar, et al., *Competing Kingdoms: Women, Nation and the American Protestant Empire, 1812–1960* (Durham: Duke University Press, 2010).

24. Walter Rodney, *How Europe Underdeveloped Africa* (Washington, DC: Howard University Press, 1974), 252–53; Catherine Ceniza Choy, *Empire of Care: Nursing and Migration in Filipino American History* (Durham: Duke University Press, 2003); Mary Renda, *Taking Haiti: Military Occupation and the Culture of US Imperialism, 1915–1940* (Chapel Hill: University of North Carolina Press, 2001); Ambrose Mong, *Guns and Gospel: Imperialism and Evangelism in China* (Cambridge: Lutterworth Press, 2016); Sung-Deuk Oak, *The Making of Korean Christianity: Protestant Encounters with Korean Religions, 1876–1915* (Waco: Baylor University Press, 2013).

25. Elizabeth Esch, *The Color Line and the Assembly Line: Making Race in the Ford Empire* (Berkeley: University of California Press, 2018); Daniel Immerwahr, *How to Hide an Empire: A History of the Greater United States* (New York: Farrar, Straus and Giroux, 2018).

26. Rzeznik, Church and Estate, 8.

27. George Marsden, *Religion and American Culture* (New York: Harcourt Brace Jovanovich, 1990), 153.

28. H. Richard Niebuhr, *The Social Sources of Denominationalism* (New York: Henry Holt, 1929), 82–83.

29. Sven Beckert, *The Monied Metropolis: New York City and the Consolidation of the American Bourgeoisie, 1850–1896* (Cambridge: Cambridge University Press, 2003); E. Digby Baltzell, *Philadelphia Gentlemen: The Making of a National Upper Class* (London: Routledge, 1989), 108–9; Rzeznik, Church and Estate, 25.

30. Paul Oslington, *Oxford Handbook of Christianity and Economics* (New York: Oxford University Press, 2014), 107.

31. On Christianity and the "invisible hand" in the Gilded Age, see Daniel Bell, "What Is Wrong with Capitalism? The Problem with the Problem with Capitalism," *Other Journal: An Intersection of Theology and Culture*, issue 5 (Apr. 2005); and Matthew T. Eggenmeier, *A Sacramental-Prophetic Vision: Christian Spirituality in a Suffering World* (Collegeville, MN: Liturgical Press, 2014), 115.

32. Andrew Carnegie, *The Gospel of Wealth and Other Timely Essays* (New York: Century Co., 1900), 4, 6.

33. Eugene McCarraher, *Enchantments of Mammon: How Capitalism Became the Religion of Modernity* (Cambridge, MA: Belknap Press, 2019), 190.

34. Russell Conwell, *Acres of Diamonds* (New York: Harper and Brothers, 1915), 19; McCarraher, *Enchantments of Mammon*, 190–95.

35. Timothy Gloege, *Guaranteed Pure: The Moody Bible Institute, Business, and the Making of Modern Evangelicalism* (Chapel Hill: University of North Carolina Press, 2015), 24, 44–51; Nicole Kirk, *Wanamaker's Temple: The Business of Religion in an Iconic Department Store* (New York: NYU Press, 2018), 7–28.

36. Rzeznik, Church and Estate, 32–33; Kirk, Wanamaker's Temple, 16.

37. McCarraher, Enchantments of Mammon, 191; Kirk, Wanamaker's Temple, 24–28.

38. Gloege, *Guaranteed Pure*, 34, 44, 173.

39. Department of the Interior, Census Office, *Report on the Population of the United States*, vol. 2 (Washington, DC: Government Printing Office), xvi, xvii; Carroll, *Religious Forces*, xli.

40. Evelyn Higginbotham, *Righteous Discontent: The Women's Movement in the Black Baptist Church, 1880–1920* (Cambridge, MA: Harvard University Press, 1993), 56.

41. Higginbotham, *Righteous Discontent*, 14–15, 19–46, 185–89; Glenda Gilmore, *Gender and Jim Crow: Women and the Politics of White Supremacy* (Chapel Hill: University of North Carolina Press, 1993), 191.

42. See, for example, Charlene Fletcher, "Confined Femininity: Race, Gender, and Incarceration in Kentucky, 1865–1920" (PhD diss., Indiana University, 2020).

43. Eugene McCarraher, *Christian Critics: Religion and the Impasse in Modern American Social Thought* (Ithaca: Cornell University Press, 2000), 21.

44. Rzeznik, *Church and Estate*, 95–99.

45. James Barrett, *The Irish Way: Becoming American in the Multiethnic City* (New York: Penguin Books, 2013).

46. Robert Orsi, *The Madonna of 115th Street: Faith and Community in Italian Harlem, 1880–1950* (New Haven: Yale University Press, 1985), 54–55.

47. "Testimony of Nicola di Alve," July 30, 1888, *Report of the Select Committee of the House of Representatives, to Inquire into the Alleged Violation of the Laws Prohibiting the Importation of Contract Laborers, Paupers, Convicts, and Other Classes* (Washington, DC: Government Printing Office, 1889), 133.

48. Barbara Dobschuetz, "Fundamentalism and American Urban Culture: Culture and Religious Identity in Dwight Moody's Chicago, 1864–1914" (PhD diss., University of Illinois, Chicago, 2002), 23; Callum Brown, "The Costs of Pew-Renting: Church Management, Church-Going and Social Class in Nineteenth-Century Glasgow," *Journal of Ecclesiastical History* 38 (July 1987): 347–61.

49. On social class and the architecture of churches, see Jeanne Halgren Kilde, *When Church Became Theatre: The Transformation of Evangelical Architecture and Worship in Nineteenth Century America* (New York: Oxford University Press, 2005), 101–4, 143.

50. Charles Sheldon, *In His Steps: What Would Jesus Do?* (Ulrichsville: Barbour Publishing, 2005), 152, 98–100, 125, 135, 142–44; Clay Motley, "Making over Body and Soul: *In His Steps* and the Roots of Evangelical Popular Culture," in *The Great American Makeover*, ed. Dana Heller (New York: Palgrave Macmillan, 2006), 85–103.

51. Edward Bellamy, *Equality* (New York: Appleton, 1897), 260–61, 228, 258–59, 344, 401–2.

52. Richard Heath, "The Waning of Evangelicalism," *Contemporary Review* 13 (May 1898); Richard Heath, *The Captive City of God* (London: A. C. Fifield, 1904), 13.

53. Quoted in Robert Doherty, "Thomas Hagerty, the Church and Socialism," *Labor History* 3, no. 1 (Winter 1962): 45–46.

54. Rev. Francis Howard, "Socialism and Catholicism," *Catholic World* 65 (Sept. 1897): 725.

55. On church as a means for social climbing, see Christopher Cantwell, "The Bible Class Teacher: Piety and Politics in the Age of Fundamentalism" (PhD diss., Cornell University, 2012).

56. See David Roediger, *Working toward Whiteness: How America's Immigrants Became White* (New York: Basic Books, 2005), 57–92.

57. Dobschuetz, "Fundamentalism," 30.

58. Edward Blum, "'Paul Has Been Forgotten': Women, Gender and Revivalism during the Gilded Age," *Journal of the Gilded Age and Progressive Era* 3 (July 2004): 247–70; Edward Blum, *Reforging the White Republic: Race, Religion, and American Nationalism, 1865–1898* (Baton Rouge: LSU Press, 2007). On Ruth Wood, see Dobscheuetz, "Fundamentalism," 178.

59. David Mislin, *Washington Gladden's Church: The Minister Who Made Modern American Protestantism* (Lanham, MD: Rowman and Littlefield), 54; Washington Gladden, *Recollections* (Boston: Houghton-Mifflin, 1909), 159–61.

60. On social class in the Gilded Age, see Stuart Blumin, *The Emergence of the Middle Class: Social Experience in the American City, 1790–1900* (Cambridge: Cambridge University Press, 1989); Sven Beckert, "Propertied of a Different Kind: Bourgeoisie and Lower Middle Classes in Nineteenth Century United States," in *The Middling Sorts: Explorations in the History of the American Middle Class*, ed. Burton Bledstein and Robert Johnston (New York: Routledge, 1993), 285–95.

61. Jacob H. Dorn, *Washington Gladden: Prophet of the Social Gospel* (Columbus: Ohio State University Press, 2016), 288, 291.

62. Ibid., 292; David Reimers, *White Protestantism and the Negro* (New York: Oxford University Press, 1965); Richard Knudten, *The Systematic Thought of Washington Gladden* (New York: Humanities Press, 1968), 165–78.

63. Derek Chang, *Citizens of a Christian Nation: Evangelical Missions and the Problem of Race in the Nineteenth Century* (Philadelphia: University of Pennsylvania Press, 2010), 132–52; Thomas Winter, *Making Men, Making Class: The YMCA and Workingmen, 1877–1920* (Chicago: University of Chicago Press, 2002), 6, 7, 12–13, 116, 142.

64. Heath Carter, *Union Made: Working People and the Rise of Social Christianity in Chicago* (New York: Oxford University Press, 2015), 52.

65. Ibid., 66.

66. Chang, *Citizens*, 99–131.

67. "Methodism and the Wage Earners: A Study of the Situation in Indianapolis," 1904, DC 615, folder 2 (Archives of Indiana Methodists, DePauw University, Greencastle, IN).

68. Henry Carroll, *Report on Statistics of Churches in the United States at the Eleventh Census* (Washington, DC: Government Printing Office, 1894), xxvi.

69. Josiah Strong, *Our Country: Its Possible Future and Its Present Crisis* (New York: Baker and Taylor, 1885), 138.

70. Strong, *New Era*, 75–76, 207, 205–9.

71. Ferenc Morton Szasz, *The Protestant Clergy in the Great Plains and Mountain West, 1865–1915* (Albuquerque: University of New Mexico Press, 1988), 153–74; Thomas Alexander, *Mormonism in Transition: A History of the Latter-Day Saints, 1890–1930* (Urbana: University of Illinois Press, 1986), 159.

72. Dale Soden, *Outsiders in a Promised Land: Religious Activists in Pacific Northwest History* (Corvallis: Oregon State University Press, 2015), 23.

73. Irene Mahoney, *Lady Blackrobes: Missionaries in the Heart of Indian Country* (Golden: Fulcrum Publishing, 2006), 8, 173; Anne Butler, *Across God's Frontiers: Catholic Sisters in the West, 1850–1920* (Chapel Hill: University of North Carolina Press, 2012).

74. *Sadlier's Catholic Directory* (New York: D. & J. Sadlier Company, 1889), 256–58.

75. Handy, *Undermined Establishment*, 39; Thomas McAvoy, *A History of the Catholic Church in the United States* (Notre Dame: University of Notre Dame Press, 1969), 255–62.

76. Szasz, *Protestant Clergy*, 58–59.

77. Ferenc Morton Szasz, *Religion in the Modern American West* (Tucson: University of Arizona Press, 2000), 53.

78. *The Official Catholic Directory and Clergy List, 1906* (Milwaukee: M.H. Wiltzius Co, 1906), 3.

79. *Sadlier's Catholic Directory*, 256–58.

80. Szasz, *Protestant Clergy*, 41–42.

81. Ibid., 44; Miriam B. Murphy, "Arrival of the Episcopal Church in Utah, 1867," *History Blazer*, Oct. 1995, https://historytogo.utah.gov/episcopal-church/.

82. Szasz, *Protestant Clergy*, 25.

83. Michael Piore, *Birds of Passage: Migrant Labor and Industrial Societies* (New York: Cambridge University Press, 1979); F. Tobias Higbie, *Indispensable Outcasts: Hobo Workers and Community in the American Midwest, 1880–1930* (Urbana: University of Illinois Press, 2003), 108–16.

84. Szasz, *Protestant Clergy*, 75.

85. *Seventy-First Anniversary of the American Baptist Publication Society* (Philadelphia: ABPS, 1895), 15; Salvatore Mondello, "Baptist Railroad Churches in the American West, 1890–1946," in *Religion and Society in the West*, ed. Carl Guarneri and David Alvarez (Lanham, MD: University Press of America, 1987), 111.

86. *Seventieth Anniversary of the American Baptist Publication Society* (Philadelphia: ABPS, 1894), 58–59; Mondello, "Baptist Railroad Churches," 115.

87. Mondello, "Baptist Railroad Churches," 116.

88. On the history of working-class religion, see Robert Mapes Anderson, *Vision of the Disinherited: The Making of American Pentecostalism* (New York: Oxford University Press, 1979); Vinson Synan, *The Holiness-Pentecostal Tradition: Charismatic Movements in the Twentieth Century* (Grand Rapids: Eerdmans, 1997); and Grant Wacker, *Heaven Below: Early Pentecostals and American Culture* (Cambridge, MA: Harvard University Press, 2009).

89. Szasz, *Protestant Clergy*, 84; Andrew Reiser, *The Chautauqua Moment: Protestants, Progressives and the Culture of Modern Liberalism* (New York: Columbia University Press, 2003); James R. Green, *Grass-Roots Socialism: Radical Movements in the Southwest, 1895–1943* (Baton Rouge: LSU Press, 1978), 40–41, 153–56.

90. Roger Finke and Rodney Stark, *The Churching of America, 1776–2005: Winners and Losers in Our Religious Economy* (New Brunswick: Rutgers University Press, 2005), 166.
91. Anderson, Vision of the Disinherited, 39.
92. Pentecostalism is usually traced through Charles Parham, a Holiness evangelist in Topeka Kansas, and his student William Seymour, a Black preacher who preached in Los Angeles for the Azusa Street Revival in 1906. Edith Blumhofer, *The Assemblies of God: A Chapter in the Story of American Pentecostalism* (Springfield, MO: Gospel Publishing House, 1989), 97–112.
93. Priscilla Pope-Levison, *Building the Old Time Religion: Women Evangelists in the Progressive Era* (New York: NYU Press, 2014), 11; Randall Stephens, "'There Is Magic in Print': The Holiness-Pentecostal Press and the Origins of Southern Pentecostalism," *Journal of Southern Religion* 5 (Dec. 2002), http://jsr.fsu.edu/2002/Stephens.htm.
94. Strong, *New Era*, 5, 204, 207; Strong, *Our Country*, 87, 109–10; Washington Gladden, "The Outlook for Christianity," *North American Review* 172 (June 1901): 919–33.
95. David Dawson, "Mission and Money in the Early Twentieth Century," *Journal of Presbyterian History* 80 (Spring 2002): 29–42.
96. Carroll, *Religious Forces*, xxxvi.
97. David Burns, *The Life and Death of the Radical Historical Jesus* (New York: Oxford University Press, 2013), 15–16, 205.
98. Walter Rauschenbusch, *Christianizing the Social Order* (New York: Macmillan, 1913), 405; George Shipman Payson, "Will Socialism Be Established in America? At Present an Economic Force of No Small Magnitude," *New York Observer and Chronicle* 85 (Aug. 1907): 137–39.
99. "The Church's Growing Sympathy with Socialism," *Current Literature*, Nov. 1907, 537.

Chapter 2

1. Charles Coe, *The Coming Nation*, Oct. 30, 1897.
2. On the Knights of Labor and its function as a working-class church, see Robert Weir, *Beyond Labor's Veil: The Culture of the Knights of Labor* (University Park: Penn State University Press, 2006); and Leon Fink, *Workingmen's Democracy: The Knights of Labor and American Politics* (Urbana: University of Illinois Press, 1985).
3. William Fitzhugh Brundage, *A Socialist Utopia in the New South: The Ruskin Colonies in Tennessee and Georgia, 1894–1901* (Urbana: University of Illinois Press, 1996); Charles Pierce Lewarne, *Utopias on the Puget Sound, 1885–1915* (Seattle: University of Washington Press, 1995); Robert Sutton, *Communal Utopias and the American Experience: Secular Communities, 1824–2000* (Westport, CT: Praeger, 2004).
4. On the particularly religious elements of these reform efforts, see Gaines Foster, *Moral Reconstruction: Christian Lobbyists and the Federal Legislation of Morality, 1865–1920* (Chapel Hill: University of North Carolina Press, 2002); and Kristin Kobes Du Mez, *A New Gospel for Women: Katharine Bushnell and the Challenge of Christian Feminism* (New York: Oxford University Press, 2015).

5. "Christianity and Workingmen: The Inter-denominational Congress," *Christian Union*, Dec. 17, 1885, 6.

6. Émile Durkheim, *The Elementary Forms of Religious Life*, trans. Joseph Ward Swain (Mineola: Dover Publications, 2008), 47. See also Dan McKanan, "The Implicit Religion of Radicalism: Socialist Party Theology, 1900–1934," *Journal of the American Academy of Religion* 78 (Sept. 2010): 750–89; Vanessa Cook, *Spiritual Socialists: Religion and the American Left* (Philadelphia: University of Pennsylvania Press, 2019); Dave Burns, *Life and Death of the Radical Historical Jesus* (New York: Oxford University Press, 2013).

7. Jason Martinek, *Socialism and Print Culture in America, 1897–1920* (London: Routledge, 2016), 4–5; Gregory Jackson, "What Would Jesus Do?" Practical Christianity, Social Gospel Realism, and the Homiletic Novel," *PMLA* 121 (May 2006): 641–61.

8. Martinek, *Socialism and Print Culture*, 4; David Paul Nord, "Working Class Readers: Family, Community, and Reading in Late Nineteenth-Century America," *Communications Research* 13 (Apr. 1986): 162.

9. Laurence Gronlund, *The Cooperative Commonwealth* (London: Modern Press, 1885), 165, 214.

10. Robert Blatchford, *Merrie England: A Plain Exposition of Socialism* (New York: Commonwealth Company, 1895), 94; Jason Martinek, "'The Workingman's Bible': Robert Blatchford's *Merrie England*, Radical Literacy, and the Making of Debsian Socialism, 1895–1900," *Journal of the Gilded Age and Progressive Era* 2 (July 2003): 326–46.

11. *Publisher's Weekly*, Sept. 1, 1945, 845.

12. Elizabeth Sadler, "One Book's Influence—Edward Bellamy's *Looking Backward*," *New England Quarterly* 17, no. 4 (1944): 530–55.

13. *Publisher's Weekly*, Apr. 21, 1934, 1504; *Publisher's Weekly*, Mar. 2, 1946, 1383. On the Social Gospel and popular books, see Erin Smith, *What Would Jesus Read? Popular Religious Books and Everyday Life in Twentieth-Century America* (Chapel Hill: University of North Carolina, 2015), 21–46.

14. Charles Sheldon, "What Would Jesus Do?," *Coming Nation*, Nov. 26, 1898. For more on Charles Sheldon's role in the Social Gospel movement, see Cara Burnidge, "Charles Sheldon and the Heart of the Social Gospel" (MA thesis, Florida State University, 2007).

15. Howard H. Quint, The Forging of American Socialism: Origins of the Modern Movement (Indianapolis: Bobbs-Merrill, 1964), 197; Elliot Shore, *Talkin' Socialism: J. A. Wayland and the Role of the Press in American Radicalism, 1890–1912* (Lawrence: University Press of Kansas, 1988), 26.

16. Shore, *Talkin' Socialism*, 1, 194.

17. "A Little World," *Appeal to Reason*, Dec. 5, 1914; "Race Equality," *Appeal to Reason*, Oct. 21, 1916; Shore, *Talkin' Socialism*, 104.

18. William Pratt, "Jimmie Higgins and the Reading Socialist Community: An Exploration of the Socialist Rank and File," in *Socialism and the Cities*, ed. Bruce Stave (Port Washington: National University Publications, 1975), 41–56; and James Green,

"The 'Salesmen Soldiers' of the 'Appeal' Army: A Profile of Rank-and-File Socialist Agitators," in *Socialism and the Cities*, 13–40.

19. Department of Labor Research, *The American Labor Year Book 1916* (New York: Rand School of Social Science, 1916), 146.

20. *N.W. Ayer and Son's American Newspaper Annual and Directory* (Philadelphia: N.W. Ayer and Son, 1899), 1390. In 1899, the Knights of Labor was waning in popularity as a labor organization, but its continued newspaper readership indicates that its writers still retained perspectives that others paid to hear. See also Edward Blum, "'By the Sweat of Your Brow': The Knights of Labor, the Book of Genesis, and the Spirit of the Gilded Age," *Labor* 11 (Summer 2014): 29–34.

21. Ayer and Sons Directory, 1915, 1257.

22. *Rowell's American Newspaper Directory* (New York: Printers' Ink Publishing Company, 1907), 384.

23. See Christo Aivalis, "In Service of the Lowly Nazarene Carpenter: The English Canadian Labour Press and the Case for Radical Christianity, 1926–1939," *Labour / Le Travail* 73 (Spring 2014): 97–126.

24. William Stead, *If Christ Came to Chicago!* (Chicago: Caird and Lee, 1894), 276.

25. Joseph Baylen, "A Victorian's 'Crusade' in Chicago, 1893–1894," *Journal of American History* 51 (Dec. 1964): 418–34; Timothy J. Guilfoyle, "If Christ Came to Chicago," *Encyclopedia of Chicago*, http://www.encyclopedia.chicagohistory.org/pages/624.html.

26. Bouck White, *Call of the Carpenter* (New York: Doubleday, Paige and Company, 1911), 312, 314.

27. Ibid., 339.

28. Advertisement, *International Socialist Review* 15, no. 1 (July 1914), inside front cover.

29. Sir Robert Seeley, *Ecce Homo: A Survey of the Life and Works of Jesus Christ* (New York: E. P. Dutton and Co, 1893), 4, 43, 48, 80.

30. Ibid., 80.

31. Timothy Messer-Kruse, *The Yankee International: Marxism and the American Reform Tradition, 1848–1876* (Chapel Hill: University of North Carolina Press, 1998), 104, 183, 250.

32. Cyrenus Osborne Ward, *A Labor Catechism of Political Economy: A Study for the People* (self-published, 1877), 45–47.

33. Cyrenus Osborne Ward, *Ancient Lowly, or A History of the Ancient Working People from the Earliest Known Period to the Adoption of Christianity by Constantine* (Washington, DC: W. H. Lowermilk and Co., 1889), x, 43–45, 51, 63. The Ancient Lowly was advertised for decades in both International Socialist Review and Appeal to Reason.

34. Shailer Matthews, "Christian Sociology," *American Journal of Sociology* 1, no. 1 (July 1895): 69–78; J. Graham Morgan, "The Development of Sociology and the Social Gospel in America," *Sociology of Religion* 1 (Spring 1969): 42–53.

35. George Herron, *The Christian State* (Chicago: Fleming H. Revell Company, 1895), 91, 153; George Herron, *A Plea for the Gospel* (Boston: Thomas Crowell, 1892); George Herron, *Between Caesar and Jesus* (Boston: Thomas Crowell, 1899).

36. George Herron, *The Christian Society* (New York: Fleming H. Revell Company, 1894), 82.

37. George Herron, *The Larger Christ* (Chicago: Fleming H. Revell Company, 1891), 99.

38. Jackson Stitt Wilson, "The Message of Christ to the Churches," in *How I Became a Socialist and Other Papers* (self-published, 1912), 7.

39. Jama Laserow, *Religion and the Working Class in Antebellum America* (Washington, DC: Smithsonian, 1995), 166, 219–20; Dan McKanan, *Prophetic Encounters: Religion and the American Radical Tradition* (Boston: Beacon Press, 2011), 214–15.

40. John Humphrey Noyes, *History of American Socialisms* (Philadelphia: Lippincott, 1870); Quint, *Forging of American Socialism*, 5–6.

41. George Allen White, "The Unity of Socialism and Christianity," *Coming Nation*, May 14, 1898.

42. John Peter Warbasse, *Cooperative Democracy* (New York: Macmillan, 1923).

43. Cyrus Camp, *Labor, Capital and Money, Their Just Relations* (Bradford, PA: Lerch, 1887), 139, 98–99.

44. Richard Ely, *Report of the Organization of the American Economic Association* (Baltimore: J. Murphy and Company, 1887), 458–61; Claire Goldstene, *The Struggle for America's Promise: Equal Opportunity at the Dawn of Corporate Capital* (Jackson: University of Mississippi Press, 2014), 47–67.

45. Bradley Bateman, "Between God and the Market: The Religious Roots of the American Economic Association," *Journal of Economic Perspectives* 13 (Fall 1999): 254; "Christianity and Workingmen," *Christian Union*, Dec. 17, 1885, 6; Leon Fink, *Progressive Intellectuals and the Dilemmas of Democratic Commitment* (Cambridge, MA: Harvard University Press, 1997), 52–79.

46. Albert Shaw, *Cooperation in a Western City* (Baltimore: American Economic Association, 1886), 102–4.

47. Walter Rauschenbusch, *Christianizing the Social Order* (New York: Macmillan, 1913), 233.

48. William Kerby, "Aims in Socialism," *Catholic World* 85 (July 1907): 510.

49. "John Trevor's My Quest for God," *Coming Nation*, July 9, 1898; John Trevor founded the first labor church in late 1891. By 1895, the number of local congregations had increased to fifty-four within Britain. D. F. Summers, "The Labour Church and Allied Movements of the Late 19th and Early 20th Centuries" (PhD. diss., University of Edinburgh, 1958), 311; Stanley Pierson, "John Trevor and the Labor Church Movement in England, 1891–1900," *Church History* 29 (Dec. 1960): 463–78.

50. For more on the Berkeley Temple, see Berkeley Temple, Threescore Years and Ten, 1827–1897: Pine Street Church (1897); Charles Albert Dickinson, *The Work of Berkeley Temple, Boston: Organized for City Evangelization, Christian Nurture, and Practical Christianity* (Boston: Berkeley Temple, 1888); and Charles Albert Dickinson, *The Berkeley Temple Year Book, 1890* (Boston: Berkeley Temple, 1890).

51. Katherine Pearson Woods, "Progressive Methods of Church Work: The Church of the Carpenter," *Christian Union*, Aug. 27, 1892, 383; *Convention of the Protestant Episcopal Church in the Diocese of Massachusetts, May 3–4, 1893* (Boston: Damrell and Upham, 1893).

52. Convention of the Protestant Episcopal Church in the Diocese of Massachusetts; Brundage, Socialist Utopia.

53. W. D. P. Bliss, "Christian Socialism," *Zion's Herald*, Dec. 17, 1890, 1.

54. W. D. P Bliss, "The Labor Church," *Encyclopedia of Social Reform* (New York: Funk and Wagnalls, 1897), 780–81.

55. Bradley Bateman and Ethan Kapstein, "Retrospectives: Between God and the Market: The Religious Roots of the American Economic Association," *Journal of Economic Perspectives* 13 (Fall 1999): 249–58.

56. Richard Dressner, "William Dwight Porter Bliss's Christian Socialism," *Church History* 47 (Mar. 1978): 66–82.

57. The history of this city becoming organized is described in Mary Blewett, *Men, Women and Work: Class, Gender and Protest in the New England Shoe Industry, 1780–1910* (Urbana: University of Illinois Press, 1988). Blewett writes that Casson inspired E. Wetherell to write *After the Battle; or, A Lesson from the Lynn Strike by a Fellow Worker* (1903); Quint, *Forging of American Socialism*, 126. On friction with DeLeon, see *People*, May 2, 1899.

58. Leslie Wharton, "Herbert N. Casson and the American Labor Church, 1893–1898," *Essex Institute Historical Collections* 117 (Feb. 1981): 119–37.

59. Eltweed Pomeroy, "Herbert N. Casson and the Lynn Labor Church," *Coming Nation*, Jan. 8, 1898; Bliss, "The Labor Church"; H. Roger Grant, "Portrait of a Workers' Utopia: The Labor Exchange and the Freedom, Kansas Colony," *Kansas Historical Society* 43 (Spring 1977): 56–66.

60. Quint, Forging of American Socialism, 168–69, 244, 252.

61. Herbert Casson, "Lynn Labor Church," *Coming Nation*, Mar. 20, 1897; James Taylor Rogers, "The Economic Law of the Sermon on the Mount," *Coming Nation*, July 30, 1898.

62. Casson, "Lynn Labor Church," *Coming Nation*, Aug. 15, 1898.

63. T. E. Longshore, "Primitive Christianity and Socialism Identical," *Coming Nation*, July 16, 1898; James Taylor Rogers, "The Economic Law of the Sermon on the Mount," *Coming Nation*, July 16, 1898.

64. See Neil Johnson, *The Labour Church: The Movement and Its Message* (New York: Routledge, 2018).

65. "Ingersoll in a Pulpit," *The Freethinker*, May 3, 1896; Burns, *Life and Death*, 31–33.

66. *Outlook*, Nov. 9, 1895, 760.

67. "Ingersoll's Chicago 'Sermon," *Chicago Press Dispatch*, Apr. 12, 1895;

68. "Rusk Told to Get Out," *Chicago Tribune*, Mar. 6, 1896, 3; "Dr. Rusk Must Quit," *Chicago Times Herald*, Mar. 6, 1896; *Christian Observer*, May 13, 1896, 13; *Chicago Letter*, June 18, 1896, 28.

69. "Ingersoll's Chicago 'Sermon': His Proposals for Elevating Mankind," *Public Opinion*, May 14, 1896; *Cleveland Plain Dealer*, Apr. 12, 1895.

70. "Ingersoll's Chicago 'Sermon': His Proposals for Elevating Mankind," *Public Opinion*, May 14, 1896; *Kansas City Times*, Apr. 12, 1895.

71. *Omaha World Herald*, Apr. 12, 1895.

72. Longshore, "Primitive Christianity"; "The First M. P Church Service under the Pastorate of Rev J. W. H. Brown," *Plow and Hammer*, Sept. 24, 1890.

73. Priscilla Pope-Levison, *Building the Old Time Religion: Women Evangelists in the Progressive Era* (New York: New York University Press, 2014), 78, 134.

74. Campbell J. Gibson and Emily Lennon, "Historical Census Statistics on the Foreign-Born Population of the United States: 1850 to 1990," Working Paper no. 29, US Census Bureau, Washington, DC, 1999, https://www.migrationpolicy.org/programs/data-hub/charts/immigrant-population-over-time.

75. Department of Commerce and Labor, *Religious Bodies: 1906* (Washington, DC: Government Printing Office, 1910), 334–35.

76. Ibid., 18–26, 55–56, chart adapted from data on p. 26, image from p. 56. On immigration, see *Statistical Abstract of the United States* (Washington, DC: Government Printing Office, 1907), 47–48, 55.

77. "Municipal Socialism," *The Times* (London), Aug. 19, 1902; Fred Reid, "Socialist Sunday Schools in Great Britain, 1892–1939," *International Review of Social History* 11 (1966): 18–47; Jacqueline Turner, *The Labour Church: Religion and Politics in Britain, 1890–1914* (New York: I. B. Tauris, 2018), 148–54, 168–69, 214–16.

78. Department of Labor Research, American Labor Year Book, 153; *Christian Advocate*, Jan. 11, 1912, 1.

79. Henry Meyer, "The Socialist Sunday School Union," *Sunday School Journal*, Nov. 1912, 812.

80. John T. McFarland, Benjamin Winchester, eds., *The Encyclopedia of Sunday Schools and Religious Education: Giving a World-Wide View of the History and Progress of the Sunday School and the Development of Religious Education* (New York: T. Nelson & Sons, 1915), 973–74.

81. Richard Heath, "The Waning of Evangelicalism," *Contemporary Review* 12 (May 1898); Richard Heath, *The Captive City of God* (London: Arthur C. Fifield, 1904), 13–35.

82. H. M. Books, *The Church Impeached*, 55, 50, as quoted in Heath, *Captive City of God*, 19.

83. Hugh McCloud, *Piety and Poverty: Working-Class Religion in Berlin, London and New York, 1870–1914* (New York: Holmes and Meier, 1996), 23–28.

Chapter 3

1. William Mailly, ed., *National Convention of the Socialist Party, May 1–6, 1904* (Chicago: National Committee of the Socialist Party, 1904), 1.

2. *The World Almanac, 1893* (New York: Press Publishing, 1893), 83–85, reprinted in *A Populist Reader: Selections from the Works of American Populist Leaders*, ed. George Brown Tindall (New York: Harper & Row, 1966), 90–96.

3. Walter Dean Burnham, "The System of 1896: An Analysis," in *The Evolution of American Electoral Systems*, ed. Paul Kleppner et al. (Westport, CT: Greenwood Press, 1981), 147–202.

4. Joe Creech, *Righteous Indignation: Religion and the Populist Revolution* (Urbana: University of Illinois Press, 2006), 170–75.

5. Eugene Debs, "Labor Strikes and Their Lessons," in *Striking for Life: Labor's Side of the Labor Question: The Right of the Workingman to a Fair Living*, by John Swinton (New York: Western Wilson, 1894), 315–26; Nick Salvatore, *Eugene Debs: Citizen and Socialist* (Urbana: University of Illinois Press, 1982), 137.

6. On Debs's personal faith, see Eugene Debs, *Walls and Bars* (Charles H. Kerr and Company, 1927, 1973), 265–69; Dave Burns, "The Soul of Socialism: Christianity, Civilization, and Citizenship in the Thought of Eugene Debs," *Labor: Studies in the Working-Class History of the Americas* 5, no. 2 (2008): 83–116; Jacob Dorn, "'In Spiritual Communion': Eugene V. Debs and the Socialist Christians," *Journal of the Gilded Age and Progressive Era* 2 (July 2003): 303–25; Salvatore, *Eugene Debs*.

7. George Herron, "The Christian State," *Los Angeles Times*, May 2, 1895, 2.

8. David Karsner, *Debs: His Authorized Life and Letters from Woodstock Prison to Atlanta* (New York: Boni and Liveright, 1918), 165–66; *Chicago Evening Press*, Nov. 23, 1895.

9. George Herron, *The Christian State* (New York: Thomas Crowell, 1895), 215, 174.

10. Karsner, *Debs*, 157–59; James Francis Darsey, *The Prophetic Tradition in Radical Rhetoric in America* (New York: NYU Press, 1999), 91.

11. Salvatore, *Eugene Debs*, 160–61.

12. "Declaration of Principles of the Social Democracy of America," *Social Democrat* (Terra Haute, Ind.), July 1, 1897, 1, 4. Biblical allusion to Genesis 3:19.

13. Burns, "Soul of Socialism"; Salvatore, *Eugene Debs*, 161.

14. Eugene Debs, "To the Hosts of Social Democracy in America," *Social Democrat* (Chicago), Sept. 2, 1897, 2.

15. "Evangelist Varley," *Boston Daily Globe*, Oct. 25, 1897, 2.

16. "New View of Socialism," *Chicago Tribune*, Mar. 28, 1897, 40.

17. Howard H. Quint, The Forging of American Socialism: Origins of the Modern Movement (Indianapolis: Bobbs-Merrill, 1964), 291.

18. Morris Hillquit, *History of Socialism in the United States* (New York: Funk and Wagnalls, 1906), 321.

19. "Why Christians Should be Socialists," *The Dawn*, May 1890, 29, 30, 40.

20. E. E. Carr, "The Christian Socialist Fellowship: A Brief Account of Its Origins and Progress," *Christian Socialist*, Aug. 15, 1907, 5.

21. William Howe Tolman, *Municipal Reform Movements in the United States* (New York: Fleming Revell Co., 1895), 139–40.

22. Advertisement, Chicago School of Social Economy, *International Socialist Review* 2 (Mar. 1901): 592.

23. Ira Kipnis, *The American Socialist Movement, 1897–1912* (Greenwood, IN: Greenwood Press, 1952), 51.

24. William Fitzhugh Brundage, *A Socialist Utopia in the New South: The Ruskin Colonies in Tennessee and Georgia, 1894–1901* (Urbana: University of Illinois Press, 1996); Theodore Kallman, *The Kingdom of God Is at Hand: The Christian Commonwealth in Georgia, 1896–1901* (Athens: University of Georgia Press, 2021).

25. *Railway Times*, June 15, 1897; Salvatore, *Eugene Debs*, 163.

26. "Debs: To the Hosts of the Social Democracy of America," *Social Democrat*, Aug. 20, 1897, 2.

27. Frederic Heath, *Social Democracy Red Book* (Chicago: Debs Publishing Company, 1900), 59; *Rock Island Argus*, June 26, 1897, 3; "Debs Social Democracy," *Arizona Republican*, Oct. 30, 1897, 7; "Eugene Debs' Social Democracy," *Seattle Post-Intelligencer*, Nov. 27, 1897, 1. On the "500 charters," see "Spreading Like Magic," *Labor World* (Duluth, MN), July 17, 1897, 2.

28. Heath, Social Democracy Red Book, 61.

29. "Debs Tells His Dream," *Chicago Tribune*, June 20, 1897; "Debs Writes to J. D. Rockefeller," *Chicago Tribune*, June 20, 1897; Quint, *Forging of American Socialism*, 293; "Eugene Debs' Social Democracy," *Seattle Post-Intelligencer*, Nov. 27, 1897, 1; "Debsiana," *Kansas City Journal*, June 21, 1897.

30. "Eugene Debs' Dream," *Kansas City Journal*, June 21, 1897.

31. Fredrich Engels, *Socialism: Utopian and Scientific*, trans. Edward Aveling (Chicago: C. H. Kerr, 1907 [first published in French, 1880]), 27.

32. The People, June 13, 1897; Quint, Forging of American Socialism, 297.

33. The People, June 13, 1897; Quint, Forging of American Socialism, 297.

34. Salvatore, *Eugene Debs*, 165; Mark Pittenger, *American Socialists and Evolutionary Thought, 1870–1929* (Madison: University of Wisconsin Press, 1993); Hillquit, *History of Socialism*, 321.

35. Laurence Gronlund, "A Weak Argument," *Social Democrat*, June 23, 1898, 1.

36. Victor Berger, "American Socialism," *Social Democratic Herald*, July 9, 1898.

37. Heath, Social Democracy Red Book, 61, 63.

38. "Declaration of Principles of the Social Democratic Party," 3.

39. "To Study London Slums," *Chicago Daily*, Feb. 9, 1899.

40. "Tells of London Slums," *Chicago Daily Tribune*, May 14, 1899, 3.

41. James Connolly, "Wages, Marriage and the Church," *The People*, Mar. 23, 1904.

42. Jacob H. Dorn, "The Oldest and Youngest of the Idealistic Forces at Work in Our Civilization: Encounters between Christianity and Socialism," in *Socialism and Christianity in Early 20th Century America*, ed. Jacob H. Dorn (Westport, CT: Greenwood Press, 1998), 8.

43. James Connolly, "The New Evangel: Socialism and Religion," *Workers' Republic*, June 17, 1899.

44. Kipnis, American Socialist Movement, 101–6; Quint, Forging of American Socialism, 374–75.

45. George Herron, "A Plea for Unity of American Socialists," Nov. 18, 1900, *International Socialist Review* 1 (Dec. 1900): 321–28.

46. Proceedings of the Socialist Unity Convention, Held at Indianapolis, Indiana, beginning July 29, 1901 [n.p.], 275; Quint, Forging of American Socialism, 381–83.

47. "The Socialist Party: Indianapolis Convention Effects Union of All Parties . . . ," *Social Democratic Herald* (Milwaukee), Aug. 17, 1901, 2–3.
48. "A Catholic View of Socialism," *International Socialist Review* 2 (Oct. 1901): 262–64; George Herron, "The Social Opportunity," *International Socialist Review* 5 (Apr. 1904), 577–95.
49. E. E. Carr, "The Christian Socialist Fellowship: A Brief Account of Its Origins and Progress," *Christian Socialist*, Aug. 15, 1907, 5.
50. "The Socialist Party," *Social Democratic Herald* (Milwaukee), Aug. 17, 1901, 2–3.
51. James Connolly, "The American SDP: Its Origins, Its Press, and Its Policies," July 1903, in *The Lost Writings*, by Connolly (London: Pluto Press, 1997), 74.
52. "Negro Resolution Adopted by Indianapolis Convention," *Missouri Socialist*, Aug. 10, 1901; "The Socialist Platform," *The Representative*, Oct. 10, 1901, 2; A. T. Cunzer, "The Negro or the Race Problem," *International Socialist Review* 3 (Nov. 1903): 261–64; Sally M. Miller, "Red and Black: The Socialist Party and the Negro," in *Race, Ethnicity and Gender in Early Twentieth-Century American Socialism*, by Miller (New York: Garland Publishing, 1996), 33–46; Oakley Johnson, *Marxism in the United States before the Russian Revolution* (New York: AIMS Humanities, 1974), 68–84.
53. J. B. Webster, "A Farmer's Criticism of the Socialist Party," *International Socialist Review* 2 (May 1902): 770.
54. William Jones, "'Nothing Special to Offer the Negro': Revisiting the 'Debsian View' of the Negro Question," *International Labor and Working-Class History* 74, no. 1 (Fall 2008): 213.
55. On Black locals as a foundation for interracial organizing, see Joseph Gerteis, *Class and the Color Line: Interracial Class Coalition in the Knights of Labor and the Populist Movement* (Durham, NC: Duke University Press, 2007); Eraste Vidrine, "Negro Locals," *International Socialist Review* 5 (Jan. 1905): 389–92; E. F. Andrews, "Socialism and the Negro," *International Socialist Review* 5 (Mar. 1905): 524–26.
56. Eugene Debs, "The Negro in the Class Struggle," *International Socialist Review* 3 (Nov. 1903): 257–67.
57. Karl Kautsky, "Socialist Agitation among Farmers in America," *International Socialist Review* 3 (Sept. 1902): 148–60; Webster, "Farmer's Criticism," 772; Donald Marti, "Answering the Agrarian Question: Socialists, Farmers, and Algie Simons," *Agricultural History Society* 65, no. 3 (Summer 1991): 53–69.
58. Algie Simons, "The Socialist Party and the Farmer," *International Socialist Review* 2 (May 1902): 777.
59. Webster, "Farmer's Criticism," 770.
60. Clarence Meily, "Socialism and the Negro Problem," *International Socialist Review* 3 (Nov. 1903): 266.
61. Clarence Meily, *Puritanism* (Chicago: C. H. Kerr, 1911), 126.
62. William Noyes, "Some Proposed Solutions of the Negro Problem," *International Socialist Review* 1 (Dec. 1901): 401–13; Oscar Edgar, "A Study of Race Prejudice," *International Socialist Review* 4 (Feb. 1904): 462–65.

63. For example, see Charles Dobs, "The Farmer and the Negro," *International Socialist Review*, Apr. 1904; and William Dalton, "An Official Program Separate from Platform," *International Socialist Review*, Apr. 1904, 612–14.

64. R. Laurence Moore, "Flawed Fraternity—American Socialist Response to the Negro, 1901–1912," *The Historian* 32 (Nov. 1969): 1–18; Sally Miller, "For White Men Only: The Socialist Party of America and Issues of Gender, Ethnicity and Race," *Journal of the Gilded Age and Progressive Era* 2 (July 2003): 298.

65. "The Souls of Black Folk," *International Socialist Review* 3 (Nov. 1903): 316.

66. Moore, "Flawed Fraternity"; James Green, *Grass-Roots Socialism: Radical Movements in the Southwest, 1895–1943* (Baton Rouge: Louisiana State University Press, 1978), 47; Marti, "Answering the Agrarian Question," 56.

67. "Letter to the Editor," *Broad Ax* (Salt Lake City), Dec. 21, 1901, 1.

68. Eugene Debs, "On the Color Question," *Indianapolis World*, June 20, 1903; William Dalton, "An Official Program Separate from Platform," *International Socialist Review* 4 (Apr. 1904): 612; Jones, "Nothing Special."

69. Brad Paul, "Rebels of the New South" (PhD. diss., University of Massachusetts, 1999), 42, 54; Josh Honn, "Coming to Consciousness: Eugene Debs, American Socialism, and the Negro Question" (MA thesis, Lehigh University, 2003), 23]; see also George Washington Woodbey, *Why the Negro Should Vote the Socialist Ticket* ([Chicago]: National Office of the Socialist Party, [1914]).

70. "Socialist Platform," *Estancia News* (Torrance County, NM), Oct. 9, 1908, 6.

71. Miller, "White Men Only," 285; William English Walling, "The Founding of the NAACP," *Crisis* 36 (July 1929): 226; Mary White Ovington, "Closing the Little Black Schoolhouse," *Survey*, May 28, 1910, 343.

72. Mari Jo Buhle, *Women and American Socialism, 1870–1920* (Urbana: University of Illinois Press, 1981), 60–63.

73. William Frederich Ries, *Men and Mules* (Toledo, OH: W. F. Ries, [1908]), 24.

74. "Socialist Platform," *Estancia News* (Torrance County, NM), Oct. 9, 1908, 6.

75. May Wood Simons, *Woman and the Social Problem* (Chicago: Charles H. Kerr, 1899), 3, 24.

76. "Will Speak on White Slave Topic," *El Paso Herald*, June 13, 1913; "Woman to Speak on Woman's Suffrage," *El Paso Herald*, May 22, 1915.

77. Oscar Ameringer, *Socialism for the Farmer Who Farms the Farm* (St. Louis: National Rip-Saw Pub., 1912), 13–14.

78. Mary Kules, *The Religion of a Socialist* (Pittsburgh: self-published, 1908), 41, 17.

79. Green, *Grass-Roots Socialism*, 49.

80. Dorn, "Oldest and Youngest," 2; Robert Handy, "Christianity and Socialism in America, 1900–1920," *Church History* 21, no. 1 (Mar. 1952): 43; Richard Dressner, "William Dwight Porter Bliss' Christian Socialism," *Church History* 47, no. 1 (Mar. 1978): 78; Handy, "Christianity and Socialism," 44; *The Christian Socialist*, May 15, 1909, 1.

81. John D. Long (DD), "[Letter] 1908 April 18, Brooklyn, N.Y. [to] Comrade Markham," *Wagner College Digital Collections*, accessed Jan. 31, 2012, http://wagnercollections. omeka.net/items/show/5069.

82. Dorn, "Oldest and Youngest."
83. Philip Foner, ed., *Black Socialist Preacher: The Teachings of Reverend George Washington Woodbey and His Disciple, Reverend G.W. Slater, Jr.* (San Francisco: Synthesis Publications, 1983), 16; George Washington Woodbey, *The Bible and Socialism: A Conversation between Two Preachers* (San Diego: self-published, 1903), n. 30.
84. Foner, Black Socialist Preacher, 251–55.
85. Philip Foner, "From Slavery to Socialism: George Washington Woodbey, Black Socialist Preacher," in *Socialism and American Christianity*, ed. Jacob H. Dorn (Westport, CT: Greenwood Press, 1998), 65–92.
86. James Hennessey, *American Catholics: A History of the Roman Catholic Community in the United States* (New York: Oxford University Press, 1981), 214; Thomas McGrady, *Beyond the Black Ocean* (Terra Haute: Standard Publishing Co., 1901), 232–34, 260; Eugene Debs, "Thomas McGrady," *Appeal to Reason*, Dec. 14, 1907, in *Debs: His Life, Writings and Speeches*, by Eugene Debs (Chicago: Charles H. Kerr, 1908), 277–82; Thomas McGrady, *Socialism and the Labor Problem: A Plea for Social Democracy* (Terra Haute: Standard Publishing Co., 1903).
87. Toby Terrar, "Catholic Socialism: The Reverend Thomas McGrady," *Dialectical Anthropology* 34 (Jan. 1983): 216, 231; Mary Haritta Fox, *Peter Dietz, Labor Priest* (South Bend: Notre Dame University Press, 1953), 27; Dominic Sibilia, "Thomas McGrady: American Catholic Millennialist," *American Catholic Historical Society* 12 (Spring 1994): 32–46; Jacob H. Dorn, "Comrade Father Thomas McGrady: A Priest's Quest for Equality through Socialism," *Fides et Historia* 22 (Summer 2014): 1–27.
88. Debs, "Thomas McGrady."
89. Jay P. Dolan, *The American Catholic Experience: A History from Colonial Times to the Present* (New York: Doubleday, 1985), 339–45.
90. Thomas Hagerty, *Economic Discontent and Its Remedy* (Terre Haute: Standard Publishing Company, 1902), 45–46.
91. Robert Doherty, "Thomas Hagerty, the Church, and Socialism," *Labor History* 3 (Winter 1962): 43; Gregory Kiser, "The Socialist Party in Arkansas, 1900–1912," *Arkansas Historical Quarterly* 40 (Summer 1981): 124.
92. On Maynard, see Cynthia Tucker, *Prophetic Sisterhood: Liberal Women Ministers of the Frontier, 1880–1930* (Boston: Beacon Press, 1990), 174; John Sillito, "Conflict and Contributions: Women in Utah Churches, 1847–1920," in *Women in Utah History*, ed. Patricia Lyn Scott and Linda Thatcher (Boulder: University Press of Colorado, 2005), 112; "Writer to be Buried Tomorrow," *Los Angeles Times*, Nov. 14, 1926, 11.
93. Kiser, "Socialist Party in Arkansas," 132; "Socialist Case Is Set for Trial," *Birmingham Age-Herald*, Dec. 3, 1903, 5.
94. For a partial list of the most popular literature of the Socialist Party of America, see "Literature Department," *Party Builder*, Jan. 21, 1914, 7.
95. "Debs Discusses Campaign before Leaving West," *New York Call*, June 2, 1908, 4.

96. "Fatherhood of God and Brotherhood of Man" and "The Jubilee of Labor," in Charles Kerr, *Socialist Songs and Music* (Chicago: Charles Kerr and Company, 1901).

97. "Socialists in Secret," *New York Tribune*, Apr. 25, 1908, 2; "Socialist Ministers Unite," *Owosso Times*, May 8, 1908, 3.

98. "Socialist Camp Meetings," *New York Sun*, June 3, 1908, 2; "New Socialist Move," *New York Tribune*, May 20. 1908, 8; "Socialists Reaching Out: Clerical Ones Would Gather in All Intellectual Proletarians," *New York Sun*, May 20, 1908, 8.

99. "Ministers and Socialism," *Waxahachie Daily Light*, Sept. 17, 1908, 2.

100. Daniel DeLeon, *Unity: An Address Delivered by Daniel DeLeon at New Pythagoras Hall, February 21, 1908* (New York: New York Labor News Company, 1914), 6.

101. *Information Department and Research Bureau of the Socialist Party of America* (Chicago: National Office, Socialist Party, 1913), 27, 34.

Chapter 4

1. Frederick Guy Strickland, "A New Spiritual Awakening," *Miami Valley Socialist*, Mar. 22, 1912; "That Chautauqua Debate: Is Socialism Practicable?," *Miami Valley Socialist*, Aug. 16, 1912. See also "Senator Urges Church to Meet Socialist Challenge," *American Socialist*, July 18, 1914; Frederick Guy Strickland, "Working Class Ethics," *Miami Valley Socialist*, Feb. 23, 1912; Herman Stern, *A Socialist Catechism* (Berkeley: University of California Press, 1912), 16.

2. Hermann Cutter, *They Must, or God and the Social Democracy: A Frank Word to Christian Men and Women* (Chicago: Cooperative Printing Company, 1908), 8.

3. Richard Heath, *The Captive City of God, or The Churches Seen in the Light of the Democratic Ideal* (London: Arthur C. Fifield, 1904), 29–30.

4. Richard Heath, *Social Democracy, Does It Mean Darkness or Light? A Summary of the Works of Hermann Kutter* (n.p., 1910), 2.

5. Bertrand Thompson, *Churches and the Wage Earners: A Study of their Cause and Cure for Their Separation* (New York: Charles Scribner's Sons, 1908), 129.

6. William Pitts, *The Reception of Rauschenbusch: The Responses of his Earliest Readers* (Macon: Mercer University Press, 2018), 81.

7. Walter Rauschenbusch, *Christianity and the Social Crisis* (New York: Macmillan, 1907), 10, 348; Jacob H. Dorn, "In Spiritual Communion: Eugene V. Debs and the Socialist Christians," *Journal of the Gilded Age and Progressive Era* 2 (July 2003): 303–25; Gary Dorrien, "Thy Kingdom Come: Walter Rauschenbusch, Vida Scudder, and the Social(ist) Gospel," in *The Making of American Liberal Theology: Idealism, Realism and Modernity*, by Dorrien (Louisville: Westminster John Knox Press, 2003), 82.

8. Rauschenbusch, Christianity, 330.

9. Clarence Andrew Young, "The Downtown Church: A Study of a Social Institution in Transition" (PhD diss., University of Pennsylvania, 1912), 11.

10. Donald Winters, *The Soul of the Wobblies: The IWW, Religion, and American Culture in the Progressive Era, 1905–1917* (Westport, CT: Greenwood Press, 1985), 21;

Robert Handy, "Christianity and Socialism in America, 1900–1920," *Church History* 21, no. 1 (Mar. 1952): 50.

11. Charles Stelzle, *A Son of the Bowery: The Life Story of an East Side American* (New York: George Doran, 1926), 80.

12. Kenneth Hendrickson, "George R. Lunn and the Socialist Era in Schenectady, New York, 1909–1916," *New York History* 47, no. 1 (Jan. 1966): 22–40; Stephen Barton, *J. Stitt Wilson: Socialist, Christian, Mayor of Berkeley* (Berkeley, CA: Berkeley Historical Society, 2021); James Denton, *Rocky Mountain Radical: Myron Reed, Christian Socialist* (Albuquerque: University of New Mexico Press, 1997).

13. Strickland, "New Spiritual Awakening"; "That Chautauqua Debate: Is Socialism Practicable?," *Miami Valley Socialist*, Aug. 16, 1912. See also "Senator Urges Church to Meet Socialist Challenge," *American Socialist*, July 18, 1914; Strickland, "Working Class Ethics"; Stern, *A Socialist Catechism*, 16.

14. See especially Eugene Wood, *Socialism, the Hope of the World* (New York: Wilshire Book Company, 1906), 11; Gaylord Wilshire, *Socialism: A Religion* (New York: Wilshire Book Co., 1906); Mary Babbit, *If Christ Should Come* (New York: Wilshire Co., n.d.); and William Frederich Ries, *Men and Mules* (Toledo: Kraus and Schreiber, [1908]).

15. Kate Richards O'Hare, *The Church and the Social Problem* (St. Louis: National Rip Saw Company, 1911), 2, 9, 33.

16. "Rerum Novarum, Encyclical of Pope Leo XIII on Capital and Labor," *Vatican*, http://www.vatican.va/holy_father/leo_xiii/encyclicals/documents/hf_l-xiii_enc_ 15051891_rerum-novarum_en.html, accessed Apr. 28, 2023.

17. William Form, "Italian Protestants: Religion, Ethnicity, and Assimilation," *Journal for the Scientific Study of Religion* 39, no. 3 (Sept. 2000): 307–20; James Barrett, *The Irish Way: Becoming American in the Multiethnic City* (New York: Penguin Press, 2012), 93; James Hennessey, *American Catholics* (New York; Oxford University Press, 1981), 189.

18. Jacob H. Dorn, "Comrade Father Thomas McGrady: A Priest's Quest for Equality through Socialism," *Fides et Historia* 22 (Summer 2014): 1–27.

19. Form, "Italian Protestants"; Michael Miller Topp, *Those without a Country: The Political Culture of Italian American Syndicalists* (Minneapolis: University of Minnesota Press, 2001), 67–71.

20. Winters, Soul of the Wobblies.

21. Josiah Strong, *The Twentieth Century City* (New York: Baker and Taylor, 1898); Dorothea Muller, "The Social Philosophy of Josiah Strong: Social Christianity and American Progressivism," *Church History* 28, no. 2 (June 1959): 183–201.

22. Shailer Matthews, *The Church and the Changing Order* (New York: Macmillan, 1907), 171–72; Shailer Matthews, "The Development of Social Christianity in America during the Past Twenty-Five Years," *Journal of Religion* 7, no. 4 (July 1927): 376–86.

23. Jacob H. Dorn, "The Social Gospel and Socialism: A Comparison of the Thought of Francis Greenwood Peabody, Washington Gladden, and Walter Rauschenbusch," *Church History* 62, no. 1 (Mar. 1993): 82–100.

24. Gustav Cohn, "Municipal Socialism," *Economic Journal* 20, no. 80 (Dec. 1910): 561–68; John Sheldrake, *Municipal Socialism* (Brookfield, VT: Avebury, 1989); Jules Gehrke, "A Radical Endeavor: Joseph Chamberlain and the Emergence of Municipal Socialism in Birmingham," *American Journal of Economics and Sociology* 75, no. 1 (Jan. 1916): 23–57.

25. Robert Rives LaMonte, "The New Socialism," *International Socialist Review* 2 (Sept. 1912): 209.

26. Carl Thompson, *The Constructive Program of Socialism* (Milwaukee: Social-Democratic Publishing Company, 1908), 12, 23.

27. Edward Devine, "The New View of Charity," *Atlantic Monthly*, Dec. 1908, 739.

28. Thompson, Constructive Program of Socialism, 8.

29. "This Is Why," *National Rip-Saw*, Apr. 1908, 15.

30. Robert Hoxie, "The Rising Tide of Socialism: A Study," *Journal of Political Economy* 19 (Oct. 1911): 611.

31. Thompson, Constructive Program of Socialism, 23.

32. Robert Johnston, *The Radical Middle Class: Populist Democracy and the Question of Capitalism in Progressive Era Portland, Oregon* (Princeton, NJ: Princeton University Press, 2003); Michael McGerr, *A Fierce Discontent: The Rise and Fall of the Progressive Movement in America, 1870–1920* (New York: Oxford University Press, 2005).

33. *Information Department and Research Bureau of the Socialist Party of America* (Chicago: Socialist Party of America, 1913), 26.

34. Julie Greene, *Pure and Simple Politics: The American Federation of Labor and Political Activism, 1881–1917* (New York: Cambridge University Press, 1998), 113.

35. Philip Taft, "Attempts to 'Radicalize' the Labor Movement,'" *ILR Review* 1, no. 4 (July 1948); Dorothee Schneider, *Trade Unions and Community: The German Working Class in New York City, 1870–1900* (Urbana: University of Illinois Press, 1994); David Montgomery, "The 'New Unionism' and the Transformation of Workers' Consciousness in America, 1909–1922," *Journal of Social History* 7 (Summer 1974): 509–29.

36. Department of Labor Research, *The American Labor Year Book, Prepared by the Department of Labor Research of the Rand School of Social Science* (New York: Rand School of Social Science, 1916), 146–51.

37. Joshua Specht, *Red Meat Republic: A Hoof-to-Table History of How Beef Changed America* (Princeton, NJ: Princeton University Press, 2019); Neil Foley, "Mexicans, Mechanization, and the Growth of Corporate Cotton Culture in South Texas: The Taft Ranch, 1900–1930," *Journal of Southern History* 62, no. 2 (May 1996): 277.

38. On western labor radicalism, see David Brundage, *The Making of Western Labor Radicalism: Denver's Organized Workers, 1878–1905* (Urbana: University of Illinois Press, 1994); Greg Hall, *Harvest Wobblies: The Industrial Workers of the World and Agricultural Laborers in the American West, 1905–1930* (Corvallis: Oregon State University Press, 2001); Verlaine Stoner McDonald, *The Red Corner: The Rise and Fall of Communism in Northeastern Montana* (Helena: Montana Historical Society Press, 2011).

39. ,Wilson E. McDermut, stenographic report, *National Congress of the Socialist Party Held in Masonic Temple, Chicago, Ill,, May 15 to 21, 1910* (Chicago: Socialist Party, 1910), 29–30.

40. Green, Grass-Roots Socialism, 26.

41. Oscar Ameringer, *Socialism for the Farmer Who Farms the Farm* (St. Louis: National Rip-Saw Pub., 1912), 13–14, 20; James R. Green, *Grassroots Socialism: Radical Movements in the Southwest, 1895–1943* (Baton Rouge: Louisiana State University Press, 1978), 45–48.

42. Garin Burbank, *When Farmers Voted Red: The Gospel of Socialism in the Oklahoma Countryside, 1910–1924* (Westport, CT: Greenwood Press, 1976), 15–17.

43. McDermut, National Congress, 222.

44. Kyle Wilkison, *Yeomen, Sharecroppers, and Socialists: Plainfolk Protest in Texas, 1870–1914* (College Station: Texas A & M University Press, 2008), 134.

45. *The Rebel* (Hallettsville, TX), Mar. 22, 1913; Tom Hickey, "The Land Renter's Union in Texas," *International Socialist Review*, Sept. 12, 1912, 240.

46. Elizabeth Sanders, *Roots of Reform: Farmers, Workers, and the American State, 1877–1917* (Chicago: University of Chicago Press, 1999), 62.

47. *The Constitution of the United People's Church*, American Left Ephemera Collection (Digital Collections, University of Pittsburgh, Pittsburgh, PA); Clarence Blachly, *The Treatment of the Problem of Capital and Labor in Social-Study Courses in the Churches* (Chicago: University of Chicago Press, 1920), 3–4; *Christian Century* 32 (June 1915): 10.

48. Bessie Wormsley to S. R. Stephens, United People's Church of Pittsburgh, Nov. 12, 1916, American Left Ephemera Collection.

49. "Taking the Bible as the Textbook of the Social Revolution," *Current Opinion* 57 (June 1914): 22, 447.

50. Bouck White, *Church of the Social Revolution* (New York: Church of the Social Revolution Publishers, 1914), 40–41.

51. Ibid., 56. He followed up these books with *Carpenter and the Rich Man*, a fierce critique of the churches for misleading their congregants about the central purposes of Christ's ministry. Bouck White, *The Carpenter and the Rich Man* (New York: Church of the Social Revolution Publishers, 1914).

52. Justin Akers Chacon, *Radicals in the Barrio: Magonistas, Socialists, Wobblies, and Communists in the Mexican American Working Class* (Chicago: Haymarket, 2018), 209.

53. "Entrevista con el Arzobispo Bourgade," *El Nuevo Mexicano*, Nov. 23, 1901, 1; "El Socialismo!," *Revista Catolica* (Las Vegas, NM), Nov. 22, 1891; "El Papa y el Socialismo," *Revista Catolica*, May 31, 1891; "La Nueva Enciclica," *Revista Catolica*, Apr. 19, 1891.

54. Emilio Zamora, "Chicano Socialist Labor Activity in Texas, 1900–1920," *Aztlán* 6, no. 2 (1975): 223, 229; Winters, *Soul of the Wobblies*, 15–36.

55. Chacon, Radicals in the Barrio, 206–24.

56. "El Reino Socialista," *El Nuevo Mexicano*, Mar. 30, 1912, 2; "Mr. Bryan Discute el Crecimiento del Socialismo," *El Voz del Pueblo*, Dec. 26, 1908, 2. Translation by author.
57. Zamora, "Chicano Socialist Labor Activity," 223, 229.
58. "Socialista Desenganado," *La Revista de Taos*, Aug. 30, 1912, 4.
59. Sally Miller, "For White Men Only: The Socialist Party of America and Issues of Gender, Ethnicity and Race," *Journal of the Gilded Age and Progressive Era* 2, no. 3 (July 2003): 299; Philip Foner, ed., *Black Socialist Preacher: The Teachings of Reverend George Washington Woodbey and his Disciple, Reverend G.W. Slater, Jr.* (San Francisco: Synthesis Publications, 1983), 1–38.
60. "Negroes Becoming Socialists," Sept. 15, 1908, in Foner, *Black Socialist Preacher*, 301.
61. George Slater, "Emancipation," *Chicago Daily Socialist*, Dec. 10, 1908; George Slater, "The New Abolitionists," *Chicago Daily Socialist*, Jan. 4, 1909; George Slater, "The Colored Man Welcome," in Foner, *Black Socialist Preacher*, 328–30, 334–35, 336–38.
62. Sally Miller, ed., *Race, Ethnicity, and Gender in Early Twentieth Century American Socialism* (New York: Garland Publishing, 1996), 7.
63. On religious ideologies on racial separatism, see Fay Botham, *Almighty God Created the Races: Christianity, Interracial Marriage, and American Law* (Chapel Hill: University of North Carolina Press, 2013).
64. Miller, "For White Men Only," 285.
65. Philip Foner and Sally Miller, *Kate Richards O'Hare: Selected Writings and Speeches* (Baton Rouge: Louisiana State University Press, 1982), 46; Sally Miller, *From Prairie to Prison: The Life of Social Activist Kate Richards O'Hare* (Columbia: University of Missouri Press, 1993), 57–58, 73, 179–80.
66. Department of Labor Research, *American Labor Year Book*, 129.
67. James Barrett, "American Socialism and Social Biography," *International Labor and Working-Class History* 26 (Fall 1984): 76.
68. McDermut, National Congress, 126.
69. Ibid., 129.
70. Eugene Debs, "A Letter from Debs on Immigration," *International Socialist Review* 11 (July 1910): 11, in Miller, *Race, Ethnicity, and Gender*, 232.
71. Miller, Race, Ethnicity, and Gender, 11; Department of Labor Research, American Labor Year Book, 129–50.
72. *N.W. Ayer and Son's American Annual Newspaper and Directory* (New York: N.W. Ayer and Son, 1915), 1257.
73. Early elected delegates to the WNC included Josephine Conger-Kaneko, Caroline Lowe (Kansas), Winnie Branstetter (Oklahoma), Lena Morrow (California), Esther Laukki (Minnesota), Elizabeth Thomas (Wisconsin), Theresa Malkiel (New York), Marguerite Prevey (Ohio). McDermut, *National Congress*.
74. Ibid., 210.
75. Josephine Conger-Kaneko, "Does a Woman Support Her Husband's Employer?," *Progressive Woman*, Aug. 1913; Miller, *Race, Ethnicity, and Gender*, 18.
76. Ida Husted Harper, ed., *History of Women's Suffrage*, vol. 6, *1900–1920* (New York: National American Women's Suffrage Association, 1922), 169; *Indiana*

Socialist Party Bulletin 3, no. 3 (Sept. 1913); "Women's Department," *Marion Socialist*, Oct. 27, 1912; Caroline Lowe, "Work of Women in the Socialist Party," *Progressive Woman* 5 (May 1912); Ora Ellen Cox, "Socialist Party in Indiana since 1896," *Indiana Magazine of History* 12 (June 1916): 95–130; Stephanie Mihalik, "Lilith Martin Wilson: Berks County's First Female State Politician," Apr. 24, 2019, *BCTV.org*, https://www.bctv.org/2019/04/24/lilith-martin-wilson-berks-countys-first-female-state-politician/.

77. Martha Solomon, *Emma Goldman* (Boston: Twayne, 1987), 74–77; Christine Stansell, *American Moderns: Bohemian New York and the Creation of a New Century* (Princeton, NJ: Princeton University Press, 2000), 276–81.

78. Stansell, American Moderns, 274; Lawrence Langner, *The Magic Curtain: The Story of a Life in Two Fields, Theatre and Invention* (New York: Dutton, 1951), 68.

79. Floyd Dell, *Homecoming: An Autobiography* (New York: Farrar, Straus, and Giroux, 1933), 289.

80. Mari Jo Buhle, *Women and American Socialism, 1870–1920* (Urbana: University of Illinois Press, 1983), 260.

81. On Catholic and Protestant distaste for sexual libertinism, see David Goldstein, *Socialism: The Nation of Fatherless Children* (Boston: Union News League, 1903); Kathleen Tobin, *The American Religious Debate over Birth Control, 1907–1937* (Jefferson: McFarland, 2007); Marie Griffith, *Moral Combat: How Sex Divided American Christians and Fractured American Politics* (New York: Basic Books, 2017); and Carl Weinberg, *Red Dynamite: Creation, Culture Wars, and Anticommunism in America* (Ithaca, NY: Cornell University Press, 2021), 109.

82. Kate Richards O'Hare, *The Sorrows of Cupid* (St. Louis: National Rip-Saw Publishing Company, 1912), 203.

83. Ibid., 168; Eli Zaretsky, "Capitalism, the Family, and Personal Life," *Socialist Revolution* 15 (Jan.–June 1973): 22; Green, *Grass-Roots Socialism*, 93.

84. John M. Work, ed., *National Convention of the Socialist Party, Held at Chicago, Illinois, May 10 to 17, 1908* (Chicago: [Allied Print. Trades Council], 1908), 193. For more on the way that women's liberation was considered secondary to arty goals at this time, see Miller, "For White Men Only," 286.

85. Meta Stern Lilienthal, *Women of the Future* (New York: Rand School of Social Science, 1916), 18.

86. O'Hare, *Sorrows of Cupid*, 215.

87. Ibid., 24–25.

88. Buhle, Women and American Socialism, 113–15.

89. On Emil Herman, see Solon DeLeon and Irma Hayssen, eds., *The American Labor Who's Who* (New York: Hanford Press, 1925), 102–5. On freethinkers, see Susan Jacoby, *Freethinkers: A History of American Secularism* (New York: Holt, 2004).

90. Work, National Convention, 192. For more on Mila Tuper Maynard, see Cynthia Grant Tucker, *Prophetic Sisterhood: Liberal Women Ministers of the Frontier, 1880–1930* (Bloomington: Indiana University Press, 1994), https://nevadawomen.org/research-center/biographies-alphabetical/mila-tupper-maynard/.

91. Work, National Convention, 192.

92. Ibid., 192, 195, 200–201, 204–5.
93. On the Church Socialist League, see Phyllis Amenda, "God Bless the Revolution: Christian Socialism in the Episcopal Church, 1885–1940" (PhD diss., Binghamton University, 2009).
94. Work, *National Convention*, 197–98.
95. Ibid., 203–4.

Chapter 5

1. Josiah Strong, *Social Progress: A Yearbook and Encyclopedia* (New York: Baker and Company, 1904); Charles Stelzle, *American Social and Religious Conditions* (New York: Fleming H. Revell, 1912).
2. Strong, Social Progress, 186.
3. Charles Stelzle, *A Son of the Bowery: The Life Story of an East Side American* (New York: George H. Doran, 1926), 65.
4. Ibid., 77–78.
5. Ibid., 86.
6. Elias B. Sanford, *Origin and History of the Federal Council of Churches* (Hartford: S. S. Scranton Co., 1916), 69, 75; Robert Handy, "Charles Thompson— Presbyterian Architect of Cooperative Protestantism," *Journal of the Presbyterian Historical Society* 33, no. 4 (Dec. 1955): 209. On this work in Milwaukee, see "Church to Lead Labor," *Chicago Daily*, Nov. 23, 1895, 9; David Thelen, *The New Citizenship: Origins of Progressivism in Wisconsin, 1885–1900* (Columbia: University of Missouri Press, 1972), 71.
7. Charles Stelzle, "Presbyterian Department of Church and Labor," *Annals of the American Academy of Political Science* 12 (Nov. 1907): 28.
8. Charles Stelzle, ed., *The Social Application of Religion* (New York: Eaton and Mains, 1908), 20–25.
9. Charles Stelzle, "Greatest Need of the Churches Facing the People's Problems," *Labor Advocate* (Nashville, TN), Oct. 27, 1911, Clipping Files, box 6, Charles Stelzle Papers (Columbia University, New York).
10. Charles Stelzle, "Labour and the Churches, 1: The Fact of Alienation," *British Congregationalist*, Oct. 6, 1910, Clipping Files, box 6, Charles Stelzle Papers (Columbia University, New York).
11. Sanford, Origin and History, 342.
12. James Barrett, *The Irish Way: Becoming American in the Multiethnic City* (New York: Penguin Press, 2012), 65; Jay P. Dolan, *The American Catholic Experience* (New York: Doubleday, 1985), 295–303.
13. James Barrett and David Roediger, "The Irish and the 'Americanization' of the 'New Immigrants' in the Streets and Churches of the Urban United States, 1900–1930," *Journal of American Ethnic History* 24, no. 4 (Summer 2005): 3–33.

14. Philip Foner, *History of the Labor Movement*, 10 vols. (New York: International Publishers, 1964), 3:18–132.

15. John Piper, "The Formation of the Social Policy of the Federal Council of Churches," *Journal of Church and State* 11, no. 1 (Winter 1969): 65, 70.

16. On Confederate teachings for children, see, for example, "UDC Catechism for Children (1904)" Dec. 7, 2020, *Encyclopedia Virginia*, https://encyclopediavirginia.org/entries/u-d-c-catechism-for-children-1904/.

17. On religious reconstruction and "reconciliation," see Edward Blum, *Reforging the White Republic: Race, Religion, and American Nationalism, 1865–1898* (Baton Rouge: LSU Press, 2005); Edward Blum, *Vale of Tears: New Essays on Religion and Reconstruction* (Macon: Mercer University Press, 2005).

18. Piper, "Formation of Social Policy," 74; W. E. B. Du Bois, *The Souls of Black Folk* (Chicago: A. C. McClurg and Co., 1903); Edward Blum, *W. E. B. Du Bois: American Prophet* (Philadelphia: University of Pennsylvania Press, 2012). Most studies of the Federal Council of Churches leave out any mention of race. See, for example, Donald Gorrell, *The Age of Social Responsibility: The Social Gospel in the Progressive Era, 1900–1920* (Macon: Mercer University Press, 1988), 105–7; Christopher Evans, *The Social Gospel in American Religion: A History* (New York: NYU Press, 2017), 72–73, 108–9.

19. Frank Mason North, *The Church and Modern Industry* (New York: Federal Council of Churches of Christ in America, 1908), 2.

20. On the Catholic church and union activity in the Gilded Age, see Marc Karson, *American Labor Unions and Politics, 1900–1918* (1958; Boston: Beacon Press, 1965), 212–84.

21. Sanford, Origin and History, 270, 466.

22. Conversations on the topic were boosted by the work of Josiah Strong's National Advisory Committee for Studies in the Gospel of the Kingdom, a group that included W. D. P. Bliss, Washington Gladden, and Frank Mason North. See Josiah Strong, "Studies in the Social Gospel: What Must Society Do to Be Saved?," *Gospel of the Kingdom* 1, no. 8 (May 1909): 57–64.

23. John Ireland, *The Church and Modern Society*, vol. 1 (Chicago: D. H. McBride, 1896), 190.

24. Karson, *American Labor Unions*, 212–20; Philip Foner, *The Policies and Practices of the American Federation of Labor, 1900–1909* (New York: International Publishers, 1964), 114; Eltweed Pomeroy, "Two Kinds of Government," *American Federationist* 9 (Dec. 1902): 917–19.

25. David Goldstein, *Autobiography of a Campaigner for Christ* (Boston: Catholic Campaigners for Christ, 1936), 52–53; David Goldstein and Maria Moore Avery, *Socialism: A Nation of Fatherless Children* (Boston: Thomas Flynn and Co., [1911]), 12, 18, 20, 22.

26. Priscilla Pope-Levison, *Building the Old Time Religion* (New York: NYU Press, 2014), 31–34.

27. In 1912, the pope clarified these sentiments (1892) with the announcement that "confessional Catholic associations" should be formed "where it can be presumed that they can sufficiently assist the various needs of their members," but mixed

organizations were permissible where it served "the common good." Pope Pius X, "Singulari Quadam on Labor Organizations," Sept. 24, 1912, *Papal Encyclicals Online*, http://www.papalencyclicals.net/Pius10/p10lab.htm.

28. Foner, History of the Labor Movement, 3:120–22.
29. *An Open Letter to Ministers of the Gospel* (Washington, DC: American Federation of Labor, [1905]); Foner, *Policies and Practices*, 129; *Report of the Proceedings of the Twenty-Fifth Annual Convention of the American Federation of Labor, 1905* (Bloomington, IN: Pantagraph, 1905), 154. Minutes of the American Federation of Labor Executive Council, June 21, 1906, American Federation of Labor Correspondence, available on HathiTrust.
30. See Oscar Handlin, *The Uprooted* (New York: Grosset and Dunlap, 1951); Richard M. Linkh, *American Catholicism and European Immigrants, 1900–1924* (Staten Island: Center for Migration Studies, 1975).
31. On the Militia of Christ, see David Montgomery, *Fall of the House of Labor: The Workplace, the State, and American Labor Activism* (New York: Cambridge University Press), 307; Marc Karson, "Catholic Anti-socialism," in *Failure of a Dream: Essays in the History of American Socialism*, ed. John H. M. Laslett and Seymour Martin Lipset (Garden City, NY: Anchor Press, 1974), 88–90.
32. Kenneth Fones-Wolf, *Trade Union Gospel: Christianity and Labor in Industrial Philadelphia, 1865–1915* (Philadelphia: Temple University Press, 1990); Kenneth Fones-Wolf, "Revivalism and Craft-Unionism in the Progressive Era: Syracuse and Auburn Labor Forward Movements of 1913," *New York History* 63, no. 4 (Oct. 1982): 389; Montgomery, *House of Labor*, 304; *Labor News*, Sept. 20, 1912; Melissa Turkstra, "Constructing a Labour Gospel: Labor and Religion in Early 20th Century Ontario," *Labour / Le Travail* 57 (Spring 2006): 93–130.
33. Charles Stelzle, *Messages to Workingmen* (Chicago: Fleming H. Revel Company, 1906), 15, 57; "Calls Socialism Church Usurper," *Chicago Daily Tribune*, Mar. 25, 1908, 9.
34. Charles Stelzle, "Socialism and the Church," *New York Observer* 82, no. 11 (Mar. 17, 1904): 327.
35. Charles Stelzle, "Church and Labor: Capturing the Labor Movement," *Christian Observer* 19, no. 40 (Sept. 26, 1906): 14–15.
36. Stelzle, *Christianity's Storm Centre: A Study of the Modern City* (New York: Fleming H. Revell, 1907), 205.
37. "The Evangelistic Movement," *Christian Observer* 93, no. 26 (June 28, 1905): 4.
38. Stelzle, *Christianity's Storm Centre*, 206; Harry Ward, *A Yearbook of the Church and Social Service* (New York: Fleming H. Revell Company, 1914), 35.
39. Stelzle, Christianity's Storm Centre, 208.
40. "The Gospel in the Shops: Scores of Ministers Speaking to Workingmen This Week," *New York Observer and Chronicle* 86, no. 6 (Feb. 7, 1907): 188.
41. "Church and Labor Mass Meeting," *Zion's Herald* 87, no. 25 (June 23, 1909): 798. For more on Christian Socialism and public politics in Denver, see James Denton, *Rocky Mountain Radical: Myron Reed, Christian Socialist* (Albuquerque: University Press of New Mexico, 1997).

42. Charles Stelzle, "Is the Church Indifferent to Labor?" *The International Bookbinder* 8, no. 11 (November 1906): 376.

43. Charles Stelzle, "Unionists Not Anarchists: Not Fair to Judge an Organization by a Few Individuals," *New York Observer and Chronicle*, 85, no. 9 (Feb. 28, 1907): 272; "Evangelizing the Workingman," *New York Observer and Chronicle*, 85, no. 6 (Feb. 7, 1907): 167.

44. Frederick Smith, "The Forward Movement," *New York Times*, June 4, 1911, SM14. Though no list is ever complete, more participating individuals and organizations are listed in the *New York Observer*, June 15, 1911.

45. Stelzle, *Messages to Workingmen*, 22 (articles originally syndicated a few years earlier).

46. Ibid., 33–35; Charles Stelzle, *Gospel of Labor* (New York: Fleming H. Revell Company, 1912), 83–85.

47. Charles Stelzle, *The Church and Labor* (New York: Houghton Mifflin Company, 1910), 51, 59.

48. Stelzle, *Gospel of Labor*, 89–94.

49. S. D. Jackson, "Socialism and Christianity," *Christian World Pulpit*, Dec. 6, 1911, 364; Fisher Robson, "Individuality and Cooperation," *Christian World Pulpit*, June 9, 1915, 364.

50. On religion and the "private" domain, see Anne Braude, "Women's History Is American Religious History," in *Religion and American Culture*, ed. Thomas Tweed (New York: Routledge, 2003), 166; Ann Douglas, *The Femininization of American Culture* (New York: Knopf, 1977).

51. Howard Brierley, "The Church and a Living Wage," *Christian World Pulpit*, Mar. 20, 1912, 155.

52. Bertrand Thompson, *The Churches and the Wage Earners*, 95.

53. Jacob H. Dorn, "The Social Gospel and Socialism," *Church History* 62, no. 1 (Mar. 1993): 94; Walter Rauschenbush, lecture notes for "The Right and Wrong of Socialism," 1914, box 20, Walter Rauschenbush Papers (Burke Library, Columbia University, New York).

54. Stelzle, Messages to Workingmen, 22; Dale Soden, *The Reverend Mark Matthews: An Activist in the Progressive Era* (Seattle: University of Washington Press, 2013), 84.

55. Ibid., 33.

56. Ibid., 15, 57; "Calls Socialism Church Usurper," *Chicago Daily Tribune*, Mar. 25, 1908, 9.

57. Stelzle, *Messages to Workingmen*, 33–35; Stelzle, *Gospel of Labor*, 83–85.

58. Stelzle, *Gospel of Labor*, 85–89.

59. "In the World of Religious Thought," *Current Literature* 38, no. 3 (Mar. 1905): 269.

60. William O. Easton, *The Church and Social Work: A Syllabus* (Philadelphia: Social Service Committee of the Men and Religion Forward Movement, 1912), 4.

61. Ibid., 9–10.

62. Ibid, 11.

63. Ibid., 13–15. On the MRFM and muscular Christianity, see Orrin G. Cocks, "The Scope and Value of the Men and Religion Movement," *Proceedings of the Academy of Political Science in the City of New York* 2, no. 4 (July 1912): 543; and Gail Bederman,

"The Women Have Had Charge of the Church Long Enough: The Men and Religion Forward Movement, 1911–1912, and the Masculinization of Middle-Class Protestantism," *American Quarterly* 41, no. 3 (Sept. 1989): 423–65.

64. "Union Labor Forward Movement," *Labor Review*, Dec. 22, 1911, 1.

65. "Union Labor Forward Movement," *Labor Review*, Feb. 16, 1912, 2.

66. "Union Labor Forward Movement Starts April 21," *Labor Review*, Nov. 3, 1911, 1.

67. "One Hundred Speakers Here Next April," *Labor Review*, Feb. 23, 1912.

68. "Union Labor Forward Movement Closing," *Labor Review*, May 3, 1912, 1.

69. "Men and Religion Forward Movement," and "Is Stelzle a Fakir? Inquires C. Fischer," *Labor Review*, Sept. 29, 1911, 4.

70. *Labor Review*, Oct. 6, 1911; Neil Salzman, *Reform and Revolution: The Life and Times of Raymond Robins* (Kent, OH: Kent State University Press, 1991), 95, 108–13.

71. William Coleman, *The Snare of the Men and Religion Forward Movement* (Washington, DC: self-published, [1912?]), 5.

72. William Prosser, *An Open Letter to Raymond Robins of Chicago: An Exposition of Socialism, Answering Mr. Robins' Attack on the Socialist Movement* (Pittsburgh: Christian Socialist Fellowship of America, 1912), 12, 17–18, 22; "Men and Religion Forward Movement" and "Organized Labor's Relation to Men and Religion Forward Movement," *Labor Review*, Oct. 6, 1911, 1.

73. Coleman, Snare, 7, 9.

74. Ibid., 10.

75. Norman Thomas, *A Socialist's Faith* (New York: Norton, 1951), 22–24.

76. Quoted in Salzman, *Reform and Revolution*, 112; Raymond Robins to Harry N. Holmes of the World Council of Churches, n.d., Raymond Robins Papers (State Historical Society of Wisconsin, Madison).

Chapter 6

1. *New York Call*, Mar. 5, 1914, quoted in Philip Foner, *History of the Labor Movement*, vol. 4, *The Industrial Workers of the World* (New York: International Publishers, 1965), 444–45; "Religious Press on the IWW Invaders: Religion and Social Service," *Literary Digest* 48 (Apr. 4, 1914), 760–62.

2. On the labor movement as a product of unions' education of ministers in an earlier period, see Heath Carter, *Union Made: Working People and the Rise of Social Christianity in Chicago* (New York: Oxford University Press, 2015).

3. *Revolutionary Industrial Unionism: Tactics and Plan of the Workers International Industrial Union* (Melbourne: Literature of the Education Bureau of the International Industrial Union, 1918), 19.

4. Harry Ward, *The Labor Movement, from the Standpoint of Religious Values* (New York: Sturgis and Walton, 1917), ix.

5. Christopher Evans, *The Social Gospel in American Religion* (New York: New York University Press, 2017), 109.

6. Harry Ward, *A Year Book of the Church and Social Service* (New York: Fleming Revell, 1914), 15, 47.

7. Jacob H. Dorn, "The Social Gospel and Socialism: A Comparison of the Thought of Francis Greenwood Peabody, Washington Gladden, and Walter Rauschenbush," *Church History* 62, no. 1 (Mar. 1993): 82–100.

8. Eugene Link, *Labor-Religion Prophet: The Times and Life of Harry Ward* (Boulder, CO: Westview Press, 1984), 38.

9. David Nelson Duke, *In the Trenches with Jesus and Marx: Harry Ward and the Struggle for Social Justice* (Tuscaloosa: University of Alabama Press, 2003), 64.

10. Ibid., 177, 192.

11. Harry Ward, *The Social Creed of the Churches* (New York: Abingdon, Press, 1914), 6–7; Duke, *In the Trenches*, 81; Link, *Labor-Religion Prophet*, 50.

12. Ward, Year Book, 46.

13. Ward, *Labor Movement*, 133–41.

14. Ward, Social Creed.

15. For example, "Social Service Campaign in Troy Conference" [*New York Christian Advocate*], Oct. 30, 1913, Methodist Federation for Social Action Papers (United Methodist Archives and History Center, Drew University, Madison, NJ); Samuel Zane Batten, *The Social Task of Christianity: A Summons to the New Crusade* (New York: Fleming H. Revell Company, 1911), 80.

16. W. F. Whitney to Harry Ward, Sept. 22, 1914, folder 4, box 11, Methodist Federation for Social Action Papers.

17. W. H. Spybey (Ripley, Ohio) to Ward, Mar. 19, 1914, box 11, Methodist Federation for Social Action Papers.

18. "Social Service Campaign in Troy Conference" [*New York Christian Advocate*], Oct. 20, 1913, Methodist Federation for Social Action clippings, box 11, Methodist Federation for Social Action Papers.

19. Ibid., 50.

20. Minutes of Meeting of Committee of Direction, Jan. 25, 1918, Committee on Christ and Social Service, folder 1, box 88, Henry Churchill King Papers (Oberlin College, Oberlin, OH); Florence Simms, "The Industrial Policies of the Young Women's Christian Association," *Annals of the American Academy of Political and Social Science* 103 (Sept. 1922): 138–40.

21. Link, Labor-Religion Prophet, 58.

22. John M. Work, ed., National Convention of the Socialist Party, Held at Chicago, Illinois, May 10 to 17, 1908 (Chicago: [Allied Print. Trades Council], 1908), 322–24.

23. Ward, Social Creed, 118–19.

24. Ibid., 176.

25. Elias B. Sanford, *Origin and History of the Federal Council of Churches in America* (Hartford: S. S. Scranton Co., 1916), 242.

26. Henry A. Atkinson, *The Church and Industrial Welfare, a Report on the Labor Troubles in Colorado and Michigan* (New York: Federal Council of the Churches of Christ in America, 1914); Upton Sinclair, *King Coal* (New York: Macmillan, 1917), 385; "Agent for Churches Assails Mine Heads," *New York Times*, Nov. 24, 1914; Charles Stelzle, "King Coal," *World Outlook*, Jan. 20, 1920, 27–33.

27. *South Bethlehem Globe*, Apr. 20, 1910; Federal Council of Churches of Christ in America, *Report of the Special Committee of Investigation* (New York: The Council, 1910), 10–11, folder 8, box 53, Federal Council of the Churches of Christ in America Records (Presbyterian Historical Society, Philadelphia, PA).

28. Federal Council of Churches of Christ in America, *Report of Special Committee*, 10–11, 15–25.

29. See Charles Neill, *Report on the Strike at Bethlehem Steel Works* (Washington, DC: Government Printing Office, 1910), 7.

30. Ibid., 131.

31. See, for example, Robert Hessen, "The Bethlehem Steel Strike of 1910," *Labor History* 15, no. 1 (1974): 3–18; Charles Stelzle, *A Son of the Bowery: The Life Story of an East Side American* (New York: George H. Doran, 1926), 161–66.

32. Neill, Report on the Strike, 132.

33. Federal Council of Churches of Christ in America, *Report of Special Committee*, 20.

34. *The Report of the Commission on the Church and Social Service to the Federal Council of the Churches of Christ in America as Adopted by the Council, December 9, 1912 in the Quadrennial Session at Chicago, Ill* (New York: Federal Council of the Churches of Christ in America, 1912), 7.

35. Kate Rousmaniere, "The Muscatine Button Workers Strike of 1911–1912," *Annals of Iowa* 46, no. 4 (1982): 252.

36. Ibid., 256.

37. Ibid., 259; John Lennon to Beryl F. Carroll, May 22, 1911, Military Correspondence, Governor Beryl F. Carroll Papers (State Library of Iowa, Des Moines).

38. *Report on the Industrial Situation at Muscatine, Iowa* (New York: Federal Council of the Churches of Christ, 1911), 8.

39. Ibid., 13.

40. *Industrial Relations: Final Report and Testimony Submitted to Congress by the Commission on Industrial Relations, Created by the Act of August 23, 1912*, vol. 4 (Washington, DC: Government Printing Office, 1916), 3596–600.

41. US Commission on Industrial Relations, *The Double Edge of Labor's Sword* (New York: Socialist Literature Company, 1914), 24.

42. Ibid., 160.

43. Vincent St. John, *IWW—Its History, Structure, and Methods* (New Castle, PA: IWW Publishing Bureau, [1913]).

44. Kenneth Fones-Wolf, *Trade Union Gospel: Christianity and Labor in Industrial Philadelphia, 1865–1915* (Philadelphia: Temple University Press, 1990), 148–49.

45. Donald Winters, *The Soul of the Wobblies: The IWW, Religion, and American Culture in the Progressive Era, 1905–1917* (Westport, CT: Greenwood Press, 1985), 11, 9.

46. US House of Representatives, Hearings before the Committee on Rules, of the House of Representatives on House Resolutions 409 and 433, doc. 671, p. 363, 62 Cong., 1 sess., Mar. 2–7, 1912.

47. Bruce Watson, *Bread and Roses: Mills, Migrants, and the Struggle for the American Dream* (New York: Viking, 2005), 218; Arturo M. Giovannitti, *The Collected Poems of Arturo Giovannitti* (New York: Arno Press, 1975), 193, 197–98.

48. "The Poetry of Syndicalism," *The Forum*, Oct. 1914, 853, quoted in Kerri Harney, "Bread and Roses in United States History: The Power of Constructed Memory" (honors thesis, State University of New York, Binghamton, 1999).

49. United States Congressional Serial Set No. 6320, p. 365.

50. Foner, History of the Labor Movement, 329.

51. Melvyn Dubofsky, *We Shall Be All: A History of the Industrial Workers of the World* (Chicago: Quadrangle Books, 1969), 248; Foner, *History of the Labor Movement*, 337 (the spelling of the name of striker who died differs in different accounts: Watson has "Lopizzo" [*Bread and Roses*, 218]; Foner has "LoPezzo" [336]); "Bread and Roses Strike of 1912: Two Months in Lawrence, Massachusetts, That Changed Labor History," *Digital Public Library of America*, https://dp.la/exhibitions/breadandroses/strike/arrested.

52. Dubofsky, *We Shall Be All*, 249.

53. Foner, History of the Labor Movement, 332–33; Watson, Bread and Roses, 228.

54. "Bread and Roses Strike of 1912."

55. Marcella Bencivenni, *Italian Immigrant Radical Culture: The Idealism of the Sovversivi in the United States, 1890–1940* (New York: NYU Press, 2011), 162.

56. Joseph Ettor, *Ettor and Giovannitti before the Jury at Salem, Massachusetts, November 23, 1912* (Chicago: Industrial Workers of the World, 1912), 38, 59; Peter Ciano, "The Moral Imprint of Early Twentieth Century Italian-American Radical Labor," *Proteus* 7, no. 1 (1990): 27.

57. Foner, *History of the Labor Movement*, 346; "The Social Significance of Arturo Giovannitti," *Current Opinion* 54 (Jan. 1913): 24–26.

58. "The Wayfarer," *The Continent*, July 31, 1913, 1055.

59. "Arturo Giovannitti," *The Survey*, Nov. 2, 1912, 163–66.

60. "Arturo Giovannitti," *The Survey*, Nov. 30, 1912, 264.

61. Fred Thompson, *The IWW: Its First Fifty Years* (Chicago: Industrial Workers of the World, 1955), 58.

62. Ibid., 84.

63. Sagamore Sociological Conference, Sixth Year, Sagamore Beach, Massachusetts, June 26–28, 1912 (n.p., n.p.), 83.

64. Sagamore Sociological Conference, Seventh Year, Sagamore Beach, Massachusetts, June 26–28, 1913 (n.p., n.p.), 48.

65. Sagamore Sociological Conference, Sixth Year, 6.

66. Sagamore Sociological Conference, Seventh Year, 5, 9.

67. Ibid., 38.

68. Ibid., 42.

69. On debates over sabotage, see David Shannon, *The Socialist Party of America: A History* (New York: Macmillan, 1955), 70–78.

70. Sagamore Sociological Conference, Seventh Year, 43, 47.

71. Ibid., 47.

72. *Annual Report of the Federal Council of Churches* (New York: Federal Council of Churches, 1915), 22.

Chapter 7

1. Charles Stelzle, *A Son of the Bowery: The Life Story of an East Side American* (New York: George H. Doran, 1926), 121.

2. Christine Stansell, *American Moderns: Bohemian New York and the Creation of a New Century* (Princeton, NJ: Princeton University Press, 2000), 96.

3. Stelzle, *Son of the Bowery*, 120.

4. On this section of the city, see Tony Michels, *Fire in Their Hearts: Yiddish Socialists in New York* (Cambridge, MA: Harvard University Press, 2005); and Melvyn Dubofsky, *When Workers Organize: New York City in the Progressive Era* (Amherst: University of Massachusetts Press, 1968).

5. This is just one such estimate, as quoted by Stelzle. He conducted extensive surveys to monitor the changes in this neighborhood center over the years. It should also be noted, however, that in this year, 1913, the neighborhood saw the highest population density of the entire life of the Labor Temple. Stelzle estimated that there were 68 percent (371,000) foreign-born whites, and only two percent (12,000) native-born whites of native parentage. *Labor Temple Bulletin* 3, no. 23 (Mar. 3, 1913).

6. On Bouck White and socialist Christianity, see Bouck White, *Church of the Social Revolution* (New York: Church of the Social Revolution Publishers, 1914); Bouck White, *Songs of the Fellowship: For Use in Socialist Gatherings, Propaganda, Labor Mass Meetings, the Home, and Churches of the Social Faith* (New York: Socialist Literature Company, 1912); Mary Kenton, "Christianity, Democracy and Socialism: Bouck White's Kingdom of Self-Respect," in *Socialism and Christianity in Early 20th Century America*, ed. Jacob H. Dorn (Westport, CT: Greenwood Press, 1998), 165–98; David Burns, *The Life and Death of the Radical Historical Jesus* (New York: Oxford University Press, 2013), 83–87.

7. For more on labor activity in this section of town, see Stelzle's description of the neighborhood: "The Labor Temple bordered the most congested area in New York. . . . Less than two blocks away was Tammany Hall. . . . The saloons, several of them run by famous sporting men, were crowded to the doors. Here, too, was one of New York's 'red light' districts." See Stelzle, *Son of the Bowery*, 121. On the Rand School of Social Science, a correspondence course in socialism that offered forty classes at twenty-five cents each, by mail, see *Appeal to Reason*, June 23, 1915.

8. Labor Temple Bulletin, Jan. 13, 1912.

9. Charles Stelzle, "Getting the Facts: A Fundamental Task," *Presbyterian Banner*, Jan. 11, 1934, Clipping Files, box 6, Charles Stelzle Papers (Columbia University, New York).

10. Stelzle, *Son of the Bowery*, 125; "Labor Temple Opened in NYC," *Christian Work*, Aug. 24, 1912, Clippings Files, box 6, Stelzle Papers; Charles Stelzle, "Vaudeville Show of the Church Service?," *The Continent*, n.d., Clippings Files, box 6, Stelzle Papers.

11. Jeanne Halgren Kilde, *When Church Became Theatre: The Transformation of Evangelical Architecture and Worship in Nineteenth-Century America* (New York: Oxford University Press, 2002), 114, 132, 143, 145.

12. Labor Temple Bulletin, Oct. 29, 1910.

13. Stelzle, *Son of the Bowery*, 126.

14. "Union Pastor Has a Plan," *Chicago Daily Journal*, Mar. 9, 1904, 4; David Montgomery, *Fall of the House of Labor* (Cambridge: Cambridge University Press, 1987), 304.

15. Charles Stelzle, *The Gospel of Labor*, 85.

16. Charles Stelzle, "Is the Church Opposed to Workingmen?," *Labor Temple Bulletin* 1, no. 26 (Apr. 22, 1911).

17. Charles Stelzle, "Religion in the Present Industrial Crisis," *Biblical Review*, Oct. 1920, Clippings Files, box 6, Stelzle Papers.

18. *Labor Temple Bulletin* 1, no. 14 (Jan. 28, 1911).

19. *Labor Temple Bulletin* 2, no. 6 (Dec. 9, 1911).

20. Charles Stelzle, "Can the Church Stand for Organized Labor?," *Labor Temple Bulletin* 1, no. 14 (Jan. 28, 1911).

21. Stelzle, Son of the Bowery, 128.

22. *Labor Temple Bulletin* 1, no. 2 (Nov. 5, 1910).

23. *Christian Work*, Aug. 24, 1912, Clippings Files, box 6, Stelzle Papers.

24. Upton Sinclair, *They Call Me Carpenter* (Pasadena, CA: self-published; Chicago: Paine Book Co, 1922), 101.

25. Ibid., 140.

26. Stelzle, *Son of the Bowery*, 123. In Day's notes on the ethnic composition of children's Hebrew/Bible classes, he also noted that 50 percent of the children attending were "Hebrew."

27. On radical Italian garment workers in the area, see Jennifer Guglielmo, *Living the Revolution: Italian Women's Resistance and Radicalism in New York City, 1880–1945* (Chapel Hill: University of North Carolina Press, 2010).

28. *Revolutionary Radicalism: Its history, purpose and tactics with an exposition and discussion of the steps being taken and required to curb it: being the report of the Joint Legislative Committee Investigating Seditious Activities, filed April 24, 1920, in the Senate of the state of New York*, pt. 2, vol. 3 (Albany: New York State Legislature, 1920), 2712.

29. *Labor Temple Bulletin* 3, no. 19 (Feb. 3, 1913).

30. *Labor Temple Bulletin* 3, no. 17 (Jan. 20, 1913).

31. *Labor Temple Bulletin* 3, no. 19 (Feb. 3, 1913).

32. Carrie Brown, *Rosie's Mom: Forgotten Women Workers of the First World War* (Boston: Northeastern University Press, 2002), 39.

33. Stelzle, Son of the Bowery, 126.

34. Stelzle, A Son of the Bowery, 125–27.

35. N. D. Cochran, "Is the Church the Best and Truest Friend Labor Ever Had?," *Chicago Day Book*, Dec. 4, 1912.

36. They together coordinated the Men and Religion Forward movement, and he did not wish to lose the alliance they had built. That year, Gompers announced from the podium that Stelzle's addresses "included many of the very best things said in the labor assembly." Charles Stelzle, "Religion Not Interdicted in Labor Convention," Nov. 28, 1912, n.p., Clippings Files, box 6, Stelzle Papers.

37. "Presbyterian Assembly's Forward-Looking Program," *Religious Weekly*, May 17, 1917, Clippings Files, box 6, Stelzle Papers. This conversation does not appear in the meeting minutes of the AFL convention that year.

38. *Revolutionary Radicalism*, 2713.

39. Ibid., 2705.

40. Ibid., 2704–5.

41. Burns, *Life and Death*, 11, 205.

42. Matthew Bowman, *The Urban Pulpit: New York City and the Fate of Liberal Evangelicalism* (New York: Oxford University Press, 2014), 129.

43. For more on seminary students, see *Labor Temple Bulletin* 1, no. 2 (Nov. 5, 1910).

44. "Labor Temple Opened in NYC," *Christian Work*, Aug. 24, 1912, Clippings Files, box 6, Stelzle Papers.

45. *Labor Temple Bulletin*, Apr. 22, 1911, 1, no. 26.

46. Stelzle, *Son of the Bowery*, 128–31.

47. *Labor Temple Bulletin*, 3, no. 1 (Sept. 29, 1912).

48. *Labor Temple Bulletin* 2, no. 30 (June 8, 1912).

49. Rev. Harsanyi was soon replaced by Rev. Gabriel Dokus, Magyar pastor and graduate of Bloomfield Seminary in New Jersey. He started Hungarian Sunday school classes in addition to vibrant foreign-language worship services. *Labor Temple Bulletin* 3, no. 5 (Jan. 6, 1915); *Records of the Committee on Church Extension of the Presbytery of New York* (Presbyterian Historical Society, Philadelphia, PA).

50. Douglas G. M. Herron, "The Story of the Labor Temple: An Experiment in the Communication of the Gospel" (master's thesis, Princeton Theological Seminary, 1956), 29–34.

51. "Administrative History," folder 1, box 1, RG 14 (Presbyterian Historical Society).

52. *Minutes of the Home Missions Committee*, Presbytery of New York (Jan. 16, 1913).

53. For more on Presbyterian theological controversies during this era, see Harry Emerson Fosdick, "Shall the Fundamentalists Win?," *Christian Work* 102 (June 10, 1922):716–22; J. Gresham Machen, *Christianity and Liberalism* (Grand Rapids: William Eerdmans, 1946); D. G. Hart, *Defending the Faith: J. Gresham Machen and the Crisis of Conservative Protestantism in Modern America* (Phillipsburg, NJ: P & R Publishing, 2003); Bradley Longfield, *The Presbyterian Controversy: Fundamentalists, Modernists, and Moderates* (New York: Oxford University Press, 1993); Lefferts Loetscher, *The Broadening Church: A Study of Theological Issues in the Presbyterian Church since 1869* (Philadelphia: University of Pennsylvania Press, 1954); and William Weston, *Presbyterian Pluralism: Competition in a Protestant House* (Knoxville: University of Tennessee Press, 1997). I am referring here to debates over the veracity of Scriptures, literal interpretation of Scriptures, the virgin birth of Christ, and other theological questions at the root of the fundamentalist/modernist controversy.

54. *Minutes of the Home Missions Committee*, Presbytery of New York (Jan. 16, 1913), (Presbyterian Historical Society).

55. Ibid. (Feb. 13, 1913).

56. Ibid. (Apr. 9, 1915).

57. On the sudden resignation of Day, see ibid. (Mar. 7, 1918).

58. On Edmund Chaffee's trip to Palestine, see his own work and *Minutes of the Presbytery of New York* (Mar. 11, 1918), vol. 22, p. 361.

59. Margaret Sanger, ed., *Birth Control Review* 5 (Jan. 1921): 2.

60. On the Red Scare of World War I, see Robert Murray, *Red Scare: A Study in National Hysteria, 1919–1920* (St. Paul: University of Minnesota Press, 1955).

61. See, for example, Gary Dorrien, *The Making of American Liberal Theology: Imagining Progressive Religion, 1805–1900* (Louisville: Westminster John Knox Press, 2001); Jean Miller Schmidt, *Souls or the Social Order: The Two Party System in American Protestantism* (New York: Carlson Publishing, 1991), 197–206; Donald Meyer, *The Protestant Search for Political Realism, 1919–1941* (Berkeley: University of California Press, 1960); George Marsden, *Fundamentalism and American Culture* (New York: Oxford University Press, 2006). All these scholars trace the development of Social Gospel theology in the United States, but they pin the developing universalism on theological liberalism rather than Christian socialist praxis.

62. *Correspondence Relative to the Conduct of the Labor Temple*, folder 2, box 1, RG 14 (Presbyterian Historical Society).

63. Correspondence Relative to the Labor Temple, Letter (reprinted) from Archibald Stevenson of Union League Club to Jesse Forbes, Clerk of the New York Presbytery, Nov. 30, 1920, folder 2, box 1, RG 14 (Presbyterian Historical Society).

64. Ibid., 6–10.

65. Ibid., 12.

66. Church Extension Committee, Statement of Policy at Labor Temple, Dec. 9, 1920, Edward Chaffee scrapbook, Edward Chaffee Papers, vol. I-1 (Syracuse University, Syracuse, NY).

67. Unidentified newspaper clipping, Chaffee scrapbook, Chaffee Papers, XX VII-1.

68. Derek Chang, *Citizens of a Christian Nation: Evangelical Missions and the Problem of Race in the Nineteenth Century* (Philadelphia: University of Pennsylvania Press, 2010), 99–131.

Chapter 8

1. *New York World*, Aug. 2, 1912, Oct. 30, 1912; Woodrow Wilson, *The New Freedom: A Call for the Emancipation of the Generous Energies of a People* (New York: Doubleday, Page and Company, 1913), 274.

2. Federal Council of Churches to President-Elect Woodrow Wilson, Feb. 20, 1913, reprinted in *Federal Council of Churches of Christ in America Annual Report 1913* (New York: Federal Council of Churches, 1913), 4.

3. Ibid., 5–6.

4. *Federal Council of Churches of Christ in America Annual Report 1914* (New York: Federal Council of Churches, 1914), 18–19.

5. Ibid., 35–38.

6. Cara Burnidge, *A Peaceful Conquest: Woodrow Wilson, Religion, and the New World Order* (Chicago: University of Chicago Press, 2016), 99.

7. W. E. B. Du Bois, *The Souls of Black Folk* (1903; New Haven: Yale University Press, 2015), 140; Edward Blum, *W. E. B. Du Bois: American Prophet* (Philadelphia: University of Pennsylvania Press, 2007), 121–22.

8. Kelly Baker, *Gospel according to the Klan: The KKK's Appeal to Protestant America, 1915–1930* (Lawrence: University Press of Kansas, 2011), 76; Glenn Michael Zuber, "Onward Christian Klansmen!": War, Religious Conflict, and the Rise of the Second Ku Klux Klan, 1912–1928" (PhD diss., Indiana University, 2004).

9. Charles S. Macfarland, *Library of Christian Cooperation*, vol. 5 (New York: Federal Council of Churches of Christ in America, 1919), 176–77, 211–15;

10. Charles Macfarland, *Pioneers for Peace through Religion* (New York: Fleming H. Revell, 1946), 96.

11. "The American Council of the World Alliance for International Friendship through the Churches," *World Friendship* 1, no. 1 (Apr. 1920), folder 2, box 108, Henry Churchill King Papers (Oberlin College, Oberlin, OH).

12. Ibid. See also Paul Carter, The Decline and Revival of the Social Gospel: *Social and Political Liberalism in American Protestant Churches, 1920–1940* (Ithaca, NY: Cornell University Press, 1954), 106–7.

13. Macfarland, Pioneers for Peace, 101.

14. "Bill for Better Protection of Aliens and the Enforcement of Treaty Rights," *World Friendship* 1, no. 2 (May 1920), folder 2, box 108, King Papers; "Bill for Better Protection of Aliens and the Enforcement of Treaty Rights," *World Friendship* 1, no. 3 (June 1920), folder 2, box 108, King Papers.

15. World Alliance of the Churches, *The World Alliance for Promoting International Friendship through the Churches*, undated pamphlet, folder 2, box 108, King Papers.

16. *The Church and International Relations: Report of the Commission on Peace and Arbitration* (New York: Federal Council of Churches, 1917), 174; Richard Gamble, *The War for Righteousness: Progressive Christianity, the Great War, and the Rise of the Messianic Nation* (Wilmington: ISI Books, 2003), 131–32.

17. Charles Macfarland, ed., *The Churches of Christ in Council*, 4 vols. (New York: Federal Council of Churches, 1917), 4:169.

18. Gamble, War for Righteousness, 143.

19. *Federal Council of Churches of Christ in America Annual Report 1916* (New York: Federal Council of Churches, 1916), 8; Gamble, War for Righteousness; Burnidge, Peaceful Conquest.

20. Arthur Link, ed., *Papers of Woodrow Wilson*, 69 vols. (Princeton, NJ: Princeton University Press, 2017), 41:353–54; Gamble, *War for Righteousness*, 145.

21. Gamble, *War for Righteousness*, 148; *Literary Digest* 54 (Apr. 14, 1917): 1064; *New York Times*, Apr. 2, 1917.

22. Albert Schenkel, *The Rich Man and the Kingdom: John D Rockefeller Jr., and the Protestant Establishment* (Cambridge, MA: Harvard University Press, 1996); Ronald Rogers, *The Struggle for the Soul of Journalism: The Pulpit versus the Press, 1833–1923* (Columbia: University of Missouri Press, 2018).

23. Gamble, War for Righteousness, 149.

24. Eugene Debs, "The Canton Ohio Anti War Speech," June 16, 1918, *Marxist Internet Archive*, https://www.marxists.org/archive/debs/works/1918/canton.htm.

25. Christopher Sterba, *Good Americans: Italian and Jewish Immigrants during the First World War* (New York: Oxford University Press, 2003), 57.

26. Samuel Gompers to Woodrow Wilson, Dec. 14, 1917, "Echoes of the Great War," *Library of Congress*, https://www.loc.gov/exhibitions/world-war-i-american-experiences/about-this-exhibition/over-here/war-industry/we-pledge-our-undivided-support/.

27. Alexander Bing, *War Time Strikes and Their Adjustment* (New York: Dutton, [1921]), 293.

28. See Joseph McCartin, *Labor's Great War: The Struggle for Industrial Democracy and the Origins of Modern American Labor Relations, 1912–1921* (Chapel Hill: University of North Carolina Press, 1998); Lizabeth Cohen, *Making a New Deal: Industrial Workers in Chicago, 1919–1939* (Cambridge: Cambridge University Press, 1990).

29. *Social Service Review*, Oct. 1916, Methodist Federation for Social Action, folder 4, part 1, box 11, Harry Ward Papers (University Archives, Drew University, Madison, NJ).

30. Cameron McWhirter, *Red Summer: The Summer of 1919 and the Awakening of Black America* (New York: St. Martin's Griffin, 2012).

31. W. E. B. Du Bois, "Denounced Republicans: Leaders of the Niagara Movement Succeed in Carrying Resolutions," *Oberlin Tribune*, Sept. 4, 1908; Angela Jones, *African American Civil Rights: Early Activism and the Niagara Movement* (Santa Barbara: Praeger, 2011), 153–59.

32. On the Black Social Gospel and respectability politics, see Ralph Luker, *The Social Gospel in Black and White: American Racial Reform, 1885–1912* (Chapel Hill: University of North Carolina Press, 1991); Evelyn Higginbotham, *Righteous Discontent: The Women's Movement in the Black Baptist Church, 1880–1920* (Cambridge, MA: Harvard University Press, 1994); Gary Dorrien, *The New Abolition: W. E. B. Du Bois and the Black Social Gospel* (New Haven: Yale University Press, 2018); and Anthea Butler, *White Evangelical Racism: The Politics of Morality in America* (Chapel Hill: University of North Carolina Press, 2021).

33. Jeffrey Perry, *Hubert Harrison: The Struggle for Equality, 1918–1927* (New York: Columbia University Press, 2020), 308.

34. W. E. B. Du Bois, "The Negro Party," *The Crisis*, Oct. 16, 1916; W. E. B. Du Bois, "Some Reasons Why Negroes Should Vote the Socialist Ticket," in *Race, Ethnicity, and Gender in Early Twentieth-Century American Socialism*, ed. Sally Miller (New York: Garland Publishing, 1996), 184–85; Hubert Harrison, "Socialism and the Negro," *International Socialist Review* 34 (July 1912): 65.

35. Meeting Minutes, Conference on the Relation of the Churches to Industrial Peace, Oct. 16–17, 1920, New York, Committee on the Church and Social Service, 1917–1921, folder 2, box 88, King Papers.

36. "The Churches and the Problems of Reconstruction: A Preliminary Report by the Research Secretary," Commission on the Church and Social Service, 1917–1921, folder 1, box 88, King Papers.

37. On the direct mail campaign and what it included, see "Commission on Church and Social Service," pamphlet, [1918], Commission on Church and Social Service, folder 1, box 88, King Papers. The Industrial Relations committee of the Federal Council first took initiative in issuing direct mail to "every pulpit, every church school and every

society," entreating leaders to learn more about how the Social Gospel was being ful-
filled at home and abroad during the war. "Report on Reconstruction," Dec. 5, 1918,
folder 1, box 88, King Papers; Harry Ward, *A Year Book of the Church and Social Service
in the United States, Prepared for the Commission on the Church and Social Service
of the Federal Council of the Churches of Christ in America* (New York: Missionary
Education Movement,)1915), 35. For more on this trend among church leaders, see
Bradley Bateman, "Make a Righteous Number: Social Surveys, the Men and Religion
Forward Movement and Quantification in American Economics," *History of Political
Economy* 33 (Winter 2011): 57–85.

38. Ward, Year Book, 35.
39. Commission on the Church and Social Service, *A Social Service Catechism*
(New York: Federal Council of Churches in America, 1913).
40. See, for example, Gary Scott Smith, *The Search for Social Salvation: Social
Christianity and America, 1880–1925* (Lanham, MD: Lexington Books, 2000); Walter
Rauschenbusch, *Christianity and the Social Crisis* (New York: Macmillan, 1910).
41. Harry Ward, *The Gospel for a Working World* (New York: Missionary Education
Movement of the United States and Canada, 1918), 148–49.
42. E. I. Chamberlain of Seattle District Defense Committee to Department of Evangelism
of the Methodist Episcopal Church, n.d., folder 6, part 2, box 11, MFSA Papers, Drew
University.
43. Ward, Gospel, 148–49.
44. Ibid., 94–95.
45. Ibid.; Commission on Church and Social Service, *Pocket Phrase Book: Economic and
Industrial Terms in Common Use* (New York: Federal Council of Churches, 1920).
46. *Industrial Democracy, for Labor Sunday, Aug. 31, 1919*, Committee on Christ and
Social Service, folder 1, box 88, King Papers. *The Church and Social Reconstruction*
[1919], DC 618, folder 2, Worth Tippy Papers (DePauw University, Greencastle, IN).
47. William Easton, *The Church and Social Work* (New York: Federal Council of Churches
of Christ in America, 1912), folder 8, box 53, RG 18 (Presbyterian Historical Society).
48. Harry Ward, *Social Service for Young People* (New York: Federal Council of Churches,
1914); Paul Strayer, *Moral Reconstruction: The Reconstruction of the Church with
Regard to Its Message and Program* (New York: Macmillan, 1915); *Social Studies
for Adult Classes, Study Groups and Church Brotherhoods* (New York: Federal
Council of Churches, [1914]).; F. Ernest Johnson, *A Bibliography of Social Service*
(New York: Federal Council of Churches, 1918); Commission on Church and Social
Service, *Christian Duties in Conserving Spiritual, Moral and Social Forces of the Nation
in Time of War* (New York: Federal Council of Churches, [1917]).
49. Worth Tippy, *Report of the Logging Camps of the Pacific Northwest with
Recommendations* (New York: Commission on Church and Social Service, Joint
Committee on the Church and Social Service, 1919), folder 2, box DC 618, Tippy
Papers.
50. Ibid., 27.
51. *The Strip: A Sociological Survey of a Typical Problem Section of Pittsburgh*
(Pittsburgh: Methodist Episcopal Church Union, 1915).

52. See Carter, *Decline and Revival*; Clifford Putney, *Muscular Christianity: Manhood and Sports in Protestant America, 1880–1920* (Cambridge, MA: Harvard University Press, 2003); Jonathan Ebel, *Faith in the Fight: Religion and the American Soldier in the Great War* (Princeton, NJ: Princeton University Press, 2010), and sources cited therein.

53. World Alliance of the Churches, *The Church and Permanent Peace, a Summary of the First Annual Conference of the National Council of the World Alliance for Promoting International Friendship through the Churches* (Garden City, NY: n.p., 1916), folder 1, box 108, King Papers.

54. Worth Tippy, "The Organization of a Church for Social Ministry," 5, 9, folder 1, DC 618, Tippy Papers.

55. Commission on the Church and Social Service, "Democracy in Industry," Aug. 31, 1919, folder 2, DC 618, Tippy Papers.

56. Federal Council of Churches, *The Church and Modern Industry* [1917] National Council of Churches Collection, Presbyterian Historical Society, folder 9, box 53, pp. 22–23, RG 18.

57. Robert E. Speer, "The Witness Bearing of the Church to the Nations," address delivered May 6, 1919, to a Special Meeting of the Federal Council of Churches in Cleveland, Ohio, folder 2, box 82, RG 18 (Presbyterian Historical Society).

58. Secretarial Council Minutes, Federal Council of Churches, Oct. 3, 1917, Meeting Held in Pittsburgh, folder 20, box 53, RG 18 (Presbyterian Historical Society).

59. Meeting minutes, Committee of Direction and Secretarial Council, Oct. 1, 1919, p. 6, folder 20, box 53, RG 18 (Presbyterian Historical Society).

60. Samuel McCrea Cavert, *The Churches Allied for Common Tasks: Report of a Third Quadrennium of the Federal Council of Churches in America, 1916–1920* (New York: Federal Council of Churches, 1921), 109; *Monthly Labor Review* 9 (1919): 369. See also Ray White, *The False Christ of Communism and the Social Gospel* (Zarephath, NJ: Pillar of Fire International, 1946), 242.

61. *Federal Council and Industrial Relations: Summary of Its Position and Practical Work since Its Foundation in 1908* (New York: Commission on Church and Social Service, 1920), 3, folder 9, box 53, RG 18 (Presbyterian Historical Society).

62. Folder 6, DC 2, Tippy Papers.

63. *Christianity and Industrial Problems* (London: Society for Promoting Christian Knowledge, 1919), 1, 10.

64. For a review and comparison of each of these more prominent statements, see Samuel Zane Batten, "The Churches and Social Reconstruction," *Biblical World* 53, no. 6 (Nov. 1919): 594–617; "Reconstruction Suggestions: The National Catholic War Council," *Federal Employee*, 4, no. 27 (Dec. 13, 1919), 725; *Bishops Program of Social Reconstruction* (Washington, DC: National Catholic War Council, 1919), http://www.stthomas.edu/cathstudies/cst/aboutus/bishopsprogram.html; William Adams Brown, *Church and Industrial Reconstruction* (New York: Committee on the War and Religious Outlook, 1920).

65. Bishops Program of Social Reconstruction. See also Jay P. Dolan, American Catholic Experience: *A History from Colonial Times to the Present* (New York: Doubleday, 1985), 344; James Hennessey, *American Catholics: A History of the Roman Catholic Community in the United States* (New York: Oxford University Press, 1981), 243–44.

66. John Ryan, *The Christian Doctrine of Property* (New York: Paulist Press, 1923), 11; John Ryan, *Distributive Justice: The Right and Wrong of Our Present Economic System* (New York: Macmillan, 1916). John Ryan pursued a PhD in theology in the early 1900s and argued in his dissertation that *Rerum Novarum* implied the rights of workers to ownership of a sustainable amount of personal property. The dissertation became his first book, *A Living Wage*, which was published in 1906.

67. Robert Handy argues that while John Ryan wanted to put pressure on the state, he was also concerned about being a cultural minority and working toward religious tolerance for Catholics. He often reiterated the pope's 1885 message concerning religious toleration and public protection around the world. See Robert Handy, *The Undermined Establishment: Church-State Relations in America, 1880–1920* (Princeton, NJ: Princeton University Press, 1991), 188–89.

68. Ryan, Christian Doctrine of Property, 46.

69. Brown, *Church and Industrial Reconstruction,* 139, 168–69.

70. On the effort during this period to steal craft secrets and mechanize them through scientific management, see David Montgomery, *Workers' Control in America: Studies in the History of Work, Technology, and Labor Struggles* (New York: Cambridge University Press, 1979), 48–101; David Brody, *Steelworkers in America: The Nonunion Era* (Urbana: University of Illinois Press, 1960); Jennifer Delton, *The Industrialists: How the National Association of Manufacturers Shaped American Capitalism* (Princeton, NJ: Princeton University Press, 2020).

71. Brown, *Church and Industrial Reconstruction,* 193, 210.

72. Ibid., 229–31.

Chapter 9

1. James Barrett, *William Z. Foster and the Tragedy of American Radicalism* (Urbana: University of Illinois Press, 1999), 89; David Brody, *Steelworkers in America: The Non-union Era* (New York: HarperCollins, 1970), 242.

2. Joseph McCartin, *Labor's Great War: The Struggle for Industrial Democracy and the Origins of Modern American Labor Relations, 1912–1921* (Chapel Hill: University of North Carolina Press, 1997), 172.

3. William Z. Foster, *Syndicalism* (Chicago: William Z. Foster, 1913), 6, 14; David Brody, *Labor in Crisis: The Steel Strike of 1919* (Urbana: University of Illinois Press, 1987); Barrett, *William Z. Foster.*

4. Quoted in Brody, *Labor in Crisis,*111.

5. Quoted in Brody, *Steelworkers in America,* 243; *Manufacturers' Record,* Sept. 19, 1919.

6. *Why the Open Shop?* (New York: National Association of Manufacturers, [1921]).

7. On "rationalizing" this work process, see Brody, *Steelworkers in America*; Lamar Beman, *Selected Articles about the Closed Shop* (New York: HW Wilson, 1922); David Montgomery, *Workers' Control in America: Studies in the History of Work, Technology, and Labor Struggles* (New York: Cambridge University Press, 1979).

8. Charles Harvey, "John D. Rockefeller Jr and the Interchurch World Movement of 1919–1920: A Different Angle of the Ecumenical Movement," *Church History* 51, no. 2 (June 1982): 203.

9. Ibid. I have searched IWM financial records at Union Seminary; the debt problem was significant, but I am unable to verify the amount of John D. Rockefeller Jr.'s donation.

10. Philip Ensley, "The Interchurch World Movement and the Steel Strike of 1919," *Labor History* 72, no. 3 (Spring 1972): 218.

11. J. E. Crowther, *The Wayfarer*, presented by the Interchurch World Movement (New York: HW Gray Co, 1919), 3.

12. Eldon Ernst, "A Moment of Truth for Protestant America: Interchurch Campaigns Following World War I" (PhD diss., Yale University, 1968), 98–99.

13. Worth Tippy, "The Cleveland May Day Riot," *Christian Advocate*, May 15, 1919.

14. Thomas Winter, *Making Men, Making Class: The YMCA and Workingmen, 1877–1920* (Chicago: University of Chicago Press, 2002).

15. "257 of the Nation's Leading Laymen Vote Approval of Interchurch World Movement," *Interchurch World Movement Bulletin*, Feb. 7, 1920, quoted from Jan. 31, 1920. William Adams Brown Ecumenical Archives, series 1, box 1, Interchurch World Movement Records (Burke Library at Union Theological Seminary, Columbia University, New York).

16. "Dr. Merill Pleads for World View, Indorsing Interchurch World Movement," *Interchurch World Movement Bulletin*, Jan. 24, 1920, Brown Archives, series 1, box 1.

17. Barrett, William Z. Foster, 97–98; Thomas Mackaman, *New Immigrants and the Radicalization of American Labor, 1914–1924* (Jefferson, NC: McFarland, 2017); Ruth Needleman, *Black Freedom Fighters in Steel: The Struggle for Democratic Unionism* (Ithaca, NY: Cornell University Press, 2003); Brody, Labor in Crisis, 162.

18. *Report of the Committee on Findings at the Interboard Convention at Cleveland April 30 and May 1, 1919* (New York: Interchurch World Movement [1920]), 8; *Diamond Points!* (New York: Interchurch World Movement of North America, 1919); *Report of the Committee of Twenty Concerning Plans for the Interchurch Movement of North America* (New York: Interchurch World Movement, 1919), in series 1, box 3, Interchurch World Movement Records.

19. *New Era Magazine*, June 1920, as quoted in Ernst, "Moment of Truth," 99–100.

20. *Standards for City Church Plants* (New York: Interchurch Press, 1920).

21. Commission of Inquiry, *Report on the Steel Strike of 1919* (New York: Bureau of Industrial Research, 1920), 243.

22. Bishop McConnell, *Public Opinion and the Steel Strike: Supplementary Reports of the Investigations to the Commission of Inquiry, the Interchurch World Movement* (New York: Bureau of Industrial Research, 1919), 276.

23. William Z. Foster, *The Great Steel Strike and Its Lessons* (New York: B.W. Huebsch, 1920), 118; Paul Krause, *The Battle for Homestead, 1880–1892: Politics, Culture and Steel* (Pittsburgh: University of Pittsburgh Press, 1992), 223–24. A large number of Kazincy's congregants were Slovak and Carpatho-Rusyn Catholic immigrants.

24. Foster, *Great Steel Strike*, 122; Colston Estey Warne, *The Steel Strike of 1919* (New York: Heath, 1963), 65; Krause, *Battle for Homestead*, 223.

25. Foster, Great Steel Strike, 117, 122, 178.
26. Commission of Inquiry, *Report on the Steel Strike*, 70. Father Kazincy has been hailed as a leader by later Catholic social justice advocates, most notably Dorothy Day. See Nancy L. Roberts, "Dorothy Day: Editor and Advocacy Journalist," *A Revolution of the Heart: Essays on the Catholic Worker*, ed. Patrick Coy (Philadelphia: Temple University Press, 1988), 121.
27. Foster, *Great Steel Strike*, ii.
28. Commission of Inquiry, *Report on the Steel Strike*, 250.
29. Ibid., 249.
30. Warne, *Steel Strike of 1919*, 9; Foster, *Syndicalism*; Barrett, *William Z. Foster*, 47.
31. On the relationships between radical labor organizations and sexual libertinism, see Christine Stansell, *American Moderns: Bohemian New York and the Creation of a New Century* (New York: Holt Paperbacks, 2001); and Helen Camp and Ellen Chesler, *Woman of Valor: Margaret Sanger and the Birth Control Movement in America* (New York: Simon and Schuster, 2007).
32. Interchurch World Movement, "Conclusions and Recommendations of Interchurch World Movement Report," in *The Steel Strike of 1919* (Boston: D.C. Heath, 1963), 85, 88, 97.
33. Commission of Inquiry, *Report on the Steel Strike*, ii.
34. Harry Ward, *The Social Creed of the Churches* (New York: Abington Press, 1914), 16.
35. Ibid., 22.
36. Ibid., 24.
37. Ibid., 23.
38. Ibid., 18, 20.
39. Worth Tippy, *The Church and the Great War* (New York: Fleming H. Revell Company, 1918), 68.
40. Two of the more important concerns Tippy discussed in his journal on his trip to European churches during World War I were the degree to which European churches accepted socialism and the family values of churchgoers. He noted in his diary on August 20, 1919, "Sex Problems (Belgium). . . . The war has brought dangerous laxity. The Protestant churches taking up sex matter." Commission on the Church and Social Service, *Message for Labor Sunday 1919* (New York: Federal Council of Churches of Christ in America), folder 2, box DC 618, Tippy Papers.
41. Elizabeth Dilling, *The Red Network: A "Who's Who" and Handbook of Radicalism for Patriots* (Chicago: self-published, 1934).
42. Interchurch World Movement, *The Church and Social Reconstruction*, 21, folder 2, box DC 618, Tippy Papers.
43. Worth Tippy, "The Coming Seven-Day Church: Axioms in Church Building," folder 11, box DC 615, Tippy Papers.
44. Tippy, "Cleveland May Day Riot."
45. *Report of the Committee on Methods of Cooperation* (Quadrennial Meeting of the Federal Council of Churches, Dec. 4, 1920), 3, folder 3, box 82, RG 18 (Presbyterian Historical Society).

46. On living wage campaigns and male breadwinning status, see J. Daniel Hammond, "Strange Bedfellows: John A. Ryan and the Minimum Wage Movement," *Life and Learning* 14 (2010): 123–48; Murphy, "Indestructible Right."

47. See May Mapes, "Vision of a Christian City: The Politics of Religion and Gender in Chicago's City Missions and Protestant Settlement Houses, 1886–1929" (PhD diss., Michigan State University, 1998); Betty Deberg, Ungodly Women: Gender and the First Wave of Fundamentalism (Minneapolis: Fortress Press, 1990); Thelka Ellen Joiner, *Sin in the City: Chicago and Revivalism, 1880–1920* (Columbia: University of Missouri Press, 2007).

48. Worth Tippy, "The Place of Social Work in the Ministry of Christ," folder 4, box DC 618, Tippy Papers. Tippy wrote two books about this very subject. See Worth Tippy, ed., *The Socialized Church: Addresses before the First National Conference of the Social Workers of Methodism* (New York: Eaton & Mains; Cincinnati: Jennings & Graham, 1909); and Worth Tippy, *The Church: A Community Force* (New York: Missionary Education Movement of the United States and Canada, 1914).

49. Tippy, The Church, 13–14.

50. Ibid., 35.

51. Raymond Fosdick, "History of the Interchurch World Movement of North America," [1923], Special Collections, University of Chicago, Chicago..

52. Tim Gloege, *Guaranteed Pure: The Moody Bible Institute and the Making of Modern Evangelicalism* (Chapel Hill: University of North Carolina Press, 2015).

53. Frank Stevenson, "Christ and Labor: A Sermon Preached in the Church of the Covenant by the Minister Frank Stevenson" (Cincinnati: The Church, [Oct. 26] 1919), Presbyterian Historical Society.

54. Victor Bigelow, *Mistakes of the Interchurch Steel Report: Address before the Boston Ministers Meeting, Pilgrim Hall* [New York: E. H. Gary, 1920], 2, 7–8, 19, 20, 23; E. Victor Bigelow, *Unfairness of the Interchurch Steel Report: Address by E. Victor Bigelow Before the Congregational Club, Worcester, Massachusetts, March 14, 1921* (Scranton, PA: C. F. Miller, 1921). See also Charles Hill, "Fighting the Twelve-Hour Day in the American Steel Industry," *Labor History* 15, no. 1 (Winter 1974); Ernest W. Young, *Comments on the Interchurch Report on the Steel Strike of 1919* (Boston: Gorham Press, 1921), 17–42.

55. Marshall Olds, *Analysis of the Interchurch World Movement Report on the Steel Strike* (New York: G. P. Putnam and Sons, 1922).

56. Upton Sinclair, *The Profits of Religion: An Essay in Economic Interpretation* (Pasadena: self-published, 1918), 217–18, 197, 294, 311; On sales figures, see Adele Parker, "Profits of Religion" (book review), *Seattle Record* (5 July 1997).

57. Secretarial Council minutes, Apr. 21, 1920, Federal Council of Churches, folder 20, box 53, RG 18 (Presbyterian Historical Society).

58. *The Federal Council and Industrial Relations: Summary of Its Position* (New York: Federal Council of Churches, 1920), folder 9, box 53, RG 18 (Presbyterian Historical Society).

59. Most of the pastors involved in this strike report and its reception revise the meaning of the strike to its place within the Protestant revival movement. Lyman Powell, *The Social Unrest: Capital, Labor and the Public in Turmoil* (New York: Review of Reviews Company, 1919), 759–72.

60. *Profitism, Slackism and You: A Constructive Study of the Labor Problem* (Seattle: Committee on Labor Relations of Seattle Chamber of Commerce and Commercial Club, 1920), folder 3, box 82, RG 18 (Presbyterian Historical Society). In this booklet given to the Federal Council by the Seattle Chamber of Commerce, many different schematic diagrams attempted to render proper relations in a more "Christian" work environment.

61. Sam Lewisohn, "Recent Tendencies in Bringing about Improved Relations between Employer and Employee in Industry," *Economic World* (1920), included in the *Report of Committee on Methods of Cooperation*.

62. Profitism, Slackism and You.

63. Samuel McCrea Cavert, ed., *The Churches Allied for Common Tasks* (New York: Federal Council of Churches, 1920), 145; *Church Council Calls for Justice to the Negro* (New York: Federal Council of Churches, 1919).

64. W. E. B. Du Bois, "Race Relations in the United States, 1917–1947," *Phylon* 9, no. 3 (1948): 234–47; R. M. Miller, "The Protestant Churches and Lynching, 1919–1939," *Journal of Negro History* 42, no. 2 (Apr. 1957): 118–31.

65. Edward Blum, *W. E. B. Du Bois: American Prophet* (Philadelphia: University of Pennsylvania Press, 2007); Gary Dorrien, *The New Abolition: W. E. B. Du Bois and the Black Social Gospel* (New Haven: Yale University Press, 2015).

66. Robert Speer, *The Gospel and the New World* (New York: Fleming H. Revell, 1919); John Piper, "Robert E. Speer on Christianity and Race," *Journal of Presbyterian History* 61 (Summer 1983): 237.

67. Charles Reagan Wilson, *Baptized in Blood: The Religion of the Lost Cause, 1865–1920* (Athens: University of Georgia Press, 2009); Gaines Foster, *Moral Reconstruction: Christian Lobbyists and the Federal Legislation of Morality, 1865–1920* (Chapel Hill: University of North Carolina Press, 2002).

68. On welfare capitalism, see Stephen Meyer, *The Five Dollar Day* (Binghamton: State University of New York Press, 1982); Andrea Tone, *The Business of Benevolence: Industrial Paternalism in Progressive America* (Ithaca, NY: Cornell University Press, 1997).

69. Paul Carter, *Decline and Revival of the Social Gospel: Social and Political Liberalism in American Protestant Churches, 1920–1940* (Ithaca, NY: Cornell University Press, 1954).

Afterword

1. Robert Friedheim, *The Seattle General Strike* (Seattle: University of Washington Press, 2018); Paul Buhle and Dan Georgakas, eds., *The Immigrant Left in the United States* (Albany: State University of New York Press, 1996); Bryan Palmer, *James P. Cannon*

and the Origins of the American Revolutionary Left, 1890–1928 (Urbana: University of Illinois Press, 2010).

2. David Krugler, *1919, The Year of Racial Violence: How African Americans Fought Back* (New York: Cambridge University Press, 2015); Cameron McWhirter, *Red Summer: The Summer of 1919 and the Awakening of Black America* (New York: Henry Holt, 2011); Barbara Foley, *Spectres of 1919: Class and Nation in the Making of the New Negro* (Urbana: University of Illinois Press, 2003).

3. "Denies Need of Radicalism," *New York Times*, June 7, 1920.

4. "Information Service, Research Department, Commission on the Church and Social Service, June 1, 1921, folder 2, Henry Churchill King Papers (Oberlin College, Oberlin, OH).

5. Upton Sinclair, *They Call Me Carpenter* (Pasadena, CA: self-published; Chicago: Paine Book Co, 1922); Upton Sinclair, *We the People of America, and How We Ended Poverty: A True Story of the Future* (Pasadena, CA: EPIC League, [1935]), 31.

6. See the extensive exchanges on the publication of the book, folder 4, box 20, Upton Sinclair Papers (Lilly Library, Indiana University, Bloomington); and folder 1, box 22.

7. There is a large scholarship on Christian businessmen's opposition to the New Deal in the 1930s–1950s. See Kimberly Phillips-Fein, *Invisible Hands: The Businessmen's Crusade against the New Deal* (New York: Norton, 2009); Bethany Moreton, *To Serve God and Wal-Mart: The Making of Christian Free Enterprise* (Cambridge, MA: Harvard University Press, 2009); Darren Dochuk, *From Bible Belt to Sunbelt: Plain-Folk Religion, Grassroots Politics, and the Rise of Evangelical Conservatism* (New York: Norton, 2011); Sarah Hammond, *God's Businessmen: Entrepreneurial Evangelicals in Depression and War* (Chicago: University of Chicago Press, 2017).

8. For a concise summary of these struggles, see Jacob H. Dorn, "The Oldest and Youngest of the Idealistic Forces at Work in Our Civilization: Encounters between Christianity and Socialism," in *Socialism and Christianity in Early 20th Century America*, ed. Jacob H. Dorn (Westport, CT: Greenwood Press, 1998), 1–23.

9. John Spargo to Fred Warren, July 4, 1912, box 1, Haldeman Manuscripts II (Lilly Library); "The Socialist Party and Religion: An Address to the Citizens of Religious Beliefs and Affiliations" [1919], Haldeman Manuscripts II.

10. This consistent leftist critique of "religion" as a farce is evident in the work of Upton Sinclair as well as the publications of Emanuel Haldeman-Julius. See Susan Jacoby, *Freethinkers: A History of American Secularism* (New York: Henry Holt, 2004); R. Alton Lee, *Publisher for the Masses, Emanuel Haldeman-Julius* (Lincoln: University of Nebraska Press, 2017); and Anthony Arthur, *Radical Innocent: Upton Sinclair* (New York: Random House, 2007.

11. Charles Erdman, "The Church and Socialism," in *The Fundamentals: A Testimony to the Truth*, ed. R. A. Torrey and A. C. Dixon, 4 vols. (Los Angeles: Bible Institute of Los Angeles), 4:99.

12. See, for example, Ken Fones-Wolf, "Religion and Trade Union Politics in the United States, 1880–1920," *International Labor and Working-Class History* 34 (Fall 1988): 39–55; Kenneth Heineman, "Catholics, Communists, and Conservatives: The Making of Cold War Democrats on the Pittsburgh Front," *US Catholic Historian* 34, no. 4 (Fall 2016): 25–54.

13. Carl Weinberg, *Red Dynamite: Creationism, Culture Wars, and Anti-communism in America* (Ithaca, NY: Cornell University Press, 2021), 220, 221, 278; D. G. Hart, *American Catholic: The Politics of Faith during the Cold War* (Ithaca, NY: Cornell University Press, 2020).

14. Glowing accounts of Christian missionaries' overseas work in infrastructure building are telling. See, for example, Alva Taylor, *The Social Work of Christian Missions* (Cincinnati: Foreign Christian Missionary Society, 1912); Robert Speer, Samuel Inman, and Frank Sanders, *Christian Work in South America: Official Report of the Congress of Christian Work in South America at Montevideo, Uruguay,* 2 vols. (New York: Fleming Revell, 1925), 1:354–58; David Hollinger, *Protestants Abroad: How Missionaries Tried to Change the World but Changed America* (Princeton, NJ: Princeton University Press, 2019).

15. On the centrality of social workers, see Jessica Lyn Gladden, *Social Work Leaders through History* (New York: Springer Publishing, 2018); John Holland, "Love's Directions," *Montana Farmer-Stockman*, Mar. 15, 1952, 29. For one example of the ongoing fetish for Christian missionaries as builders of infrastructure, see Alvin Schmidt, *Under the Influence: How Christianity Transformed Civilization* (Grand Rapids: Zondervan, 2001).

16. Worth Tippy, "Church Social Work in 1934," Feb. 1, 1935, folder 12, box DC 615, Worth Tippy Papers (DePauw University, Greencastle, IN).

17. See, for example, Gary Dorrien, *Soul in Society: The Making and Renewal of Social Christianity* (Minneapolis: Fortress Press, 1995); Christopher Evans, *The Kingdom Is Always but Coming: A Life of Walter Rauschenbusch* (Grand Rapids: Eerdmans, 2004); Harlan Beckley, *Passion for Justice: Retrieving the Legacies of Walter Rauschenbusch, John Ryan, and Reinhold Niebuhr* (Louisville: Westminster John Knox Press, 1992).

18. Darren Grem, *Blessings of Business: How Corporations Shaped Conservative Christianity* (New York: Oxford University Press, 2016), 13–48; Elizabeth Fones-Wolf, *Selling Free Enterprise: The Business Assault on Labor and Liberalism, 1945–1960* (Urbana: University of Illinois Press, 1994), 189–256.

19. Federal Council of Churches, *Labor Sunday Message, 1922* (New York: Federal Council of Churches, [1922]), 8; Charles Stelzle, "America and Religion: A Message to the People of the United States from One Hundred American Clergymen," *Men of New York* [1928], Clippings Files, box 6, Stelzle Papers; Charles Stelzle, "What Has the Church to Offer through Advertising?," *Associated Advertising*, Sept. 1924,, Clippings Files, box 6, Stelzle Papers.

20. Charles Stelzle, "Religion in the Present Industrial Crisis," *Biblical Review*, Oct. 1920, Clippings Files, box 6, Stelzle Papers.

21. Charles Stelzle, "What's Wrong with the Church?," *Survey Graphic*, Oct. 1933, 516–17, Clippings Files, box 6, Stelzle Papers.

22. On the history of the religious welfare state, see Dorothy Brown, *The Poor Belong to Us: Catholic Charities and American Welfare* (Cambridge, MA: Harvard University Press, 1997); and Jennifer Klein, *For All These Rights: Business, Labor and the Shaping of America's Public-Private Welfare State* (Princeton, NJ: Princeton University Press, 2003).

23. Kenneth Heineman, *A Catholic New Deal: Religion and Reform in Depression Pittsburgh* (University Park: Penn State University Press, 1999); Alison Collis Greene, *No Depression in Heaven: The Great Depression, the New Deal, and the Transformation of Religion in the Delta* (New York: Oxford University Press, 2016); David Swartz, *Moral Minority: The Evangelical Left in an Age of Conservatism* (Philadelphia: University of Pennsylvania Press, 2014); Doug Rossinow, *The Politics of Authenticity: Liberalism, Christianity, and the New Left in America* (New York: Columbia University Press, 1998).

24. Cheryl Chumley, *Socialists Don't Sleep: Christians Must Rise or America Will Fall* (New York: Humanix Books, 2020); Trent Horn and Catherine Pakaluk, *Can a Catholic Be a Socialist? The Answer Is No—Here's Why* (El Cajon, CA: Catholic Answers, 2020); Ellen Schrecker, *Many Are the Crimes: McCarthyism in America* (Princeton, NJ: Princeton University Press, 1998), 73–75.

Select Bibliography

Archives / Special Collections

American Catholic Trade Unionists Oral Histories, Notre Dame University
Edmund Chaffee Papers, Syracuse University
Eugene Debs Manuscripts, University of Chicago
Peter Dietz Papers, Notre Dame University
Kermit Eby Papers, University of Chicago
Papers of the Federal Council of Churches, Presbyterian Historical Society, Philadelphia
Minutes of the Federal Council of Churches, Henry Churchill King Collection, Oberlin College Archives
Papers of the Methodist Federation for Social Action, Drew University
Pastor John O'Brien Pamphlets, Notre Dame University
Charles Stelzle Papers, Columbia University
Worth Tippy Papers, Archives of Indiana Methodists, DePauw University
Haldeman-Julius Family Papers, University of Illinois at Chicago
Haldeman-Julius Manuscripts, Lilly Library, Indiana University
Committee on Christ and Social Service of the Federal Council of Churches Papers, Henry Churchill King Collection, Oberlin College
Haldeman-Julius Manuscripts, Lilly Library, Indiana University
Pamphlets on Socialism and the Socialist Party in the United States, University of Illinois
Frances Willard Clipping Files, 1890s, Frances Willard House, Evanston, IL
Upton Sinclair Papers, Lilly Library, Indiana University

Digital Archives

Early American Marxism: A Repository of Source Material, 1864–1946. www.marxisthistory.org.
Marxists Internet Archive. www.marxists.org.
American Left Ephemera Collection, Digital Collections, University of Pittsburgh
Wagner College Digital Collections, Women's Christian Temperance Union

Periodicals

The Appeal to Reason, 1895–1917
Coming Nation, 1910–1913
Chicago Daily Socialist, 1906–1912
The Christian Evangelist (Disciples of Christ, St. Louis and Chicago), 1882–1883
Christian Socialist (Danville, IL), 1904–1918

Christian World Pulpit (1913–1914)
Current Literature (1900–1912)
The Dawn, Journal of Christian Socialism (W. D. P. Bliss), 1890
The Day Book (Chicago), 1911–1917
The Gospel Echo (Disciples of Christ, St. Louis and Chicago), 1879–1882
Haldeman-Julius Weekly, 1922–1929
Labor Review (Minneapolis), 1911–1914
Miami Valley Socialist (Dayton, OH), 1912–1918
Plow and Hammer (Tiffin, Ohio), 1889–1893
Social Democrat (Terra Haute, IN) 1897–1898
Social Democratic Herald (Chicago, IL, St. Clair, IL, and Milwaukee, WI), 1898–1913
The Worker (Stelzle), 1917–1918

Primary Sources

Abbott, Lyman. *Christianity and Social Problems*. New York: Houghton Mifflin Company, 1899.
Abbott, Lyman. "The Ethical Teachings of Jesus." *Outlook* 94, no. 1 (1910): 576.
"Agent for Churches Assails Mine Heads." *New York Times*, Nov. 24, 1914.
"Arturo Giovannitti." *The Survey*, Nov. 2, 1912, 163–66.
Batten, Samuel Zane. "The Churches and Social Reconstruction." *Biblical World* 53 no. 6 (Nov. 1919): 594–617.
Batten, Samuel Zane. *The Social Task of Christianity: A Summons to the New Crusade*. Grand Rapids: Fleming H. Revell Company, 1911.
Beckwith, Clarence Augustine. *The Church, the People, and the Age*. New York: Funk & Wagnalls, 1914.
Behrends, Adolphus Julius Frederick. *Socialism and Christianity*. Charlotte: Baker & Taylor, 1886.
Berle, A. A. "Religion and Ethics: What Is the Matter with Our Theological Schools?" *Current Literature* 4 (1907): 410–11.
Bigelow, E. Victor. *Mistakes of the Interchurch Steel Report: Address Before the Boston Ministers Meeting, Pilgrim Hall*. New York: E.H. Gary, 1920.
Bigelow, E. Victor. *Unfairness of the Interchurch Steel Report*. Scranton, PA: C.F. Miller, 1921.
Bishops Program of Social Reconstruction. Washington, DC: National Catholic War Council, 1919. https://cuomeka.wrlc.org/exhibits/show/bishops/background/1919-bishops-reconstruction (accessed June 22, 2023).
Blachly, Clarence. "The Treatment of the Problem of Capital and Labor." PhD diss., University of Chicago, 1920.
Blachly, Clarence. *The Treatment of the Problem of Capital and Labor in Social-Study Courses in the Churches*. Chicago: University of Chicago Press, 1920.
Bliss, W. D. P. "Christian Socialism." *Zion's Herald*, Dec. 17, 1890, 1.
Bliss, W. D. P. "The Church and the Carpenter Thirty Years After." *Social Preparation for the Kingdom of God* 9, no. 1 (Jan. 1922): 12–15.
Bliss, W. D. P. *The Encyclopedia of Social Reform*. New York: Funk & Wagnalls Company, 1897.

Brierley, Howard. "The Church and a Living Wage." *Christian World Pulpit*, Mar. 20, 1912, 155.

Brown, William Adams. *Christian Theology in Outline*. C. Scribner's Sons, 1919.

Brown, William Adams. *Church and Industrial Reconstruction*. New York: Association Press, 1920.

Brown, William Adams. *The Church in America*. Macmillan, 1922.

Brown, William Adams. *Is Christianity Practicable? Lectures Delivered in Japan*. Scribner, 1919.

Brown, William Adams. *Modern Theology and the Preaching of the Gospel*. C. Scribner's Sons, 1914.

Bryan, William Jennings. *The First Battle: A Story of the Campaign of 1896*. Chicago: W.B. Conkey Company, 1897, 601. Wikipedia. http://en.wikipedia.org/wiki/File:Wjb1896.jpg (Sept. 7, 2012).

Bureau of Industrial Research and Interchurch World Movement of North America. *Public Opinion and the Steel Strike: Supplementary Reports of the Investigators to the Commission of Inquiry, the Interchurch World Movement*. Harcourt, Brace and Company, 1921.

"Calls Socialism Church Usurper." *Chicago Daily Tribune*, Mar. 25, 1908, 9.

Carey, James F. *The Menace of Socialism*. Boston: Boston Socialist Party Clubs, 1911.

Carr, E. E. "The Fellowship and the Parties." *Christian Socialist*, Sept. 1, 1907, 3.

Carroll, H. K. *Federal Council Yearbook, Covering the Year 1915*. New York: Missionary Education Movement of the United States and Canada, 1916.

Christianity and Industrial Problems, Being a Report of the Archbishop's Fifth Committee on Inquiry, Part I. London: Society for Promoting Christian Knowledge, 1919.

"Christianity and Workingmen." *Christian Union*, Dec. 17, 1885, 6.

"Church and Labor Mass Meeting." *Zion's Herald* 87, no. 25 (June 23, 1909): 798.

"The Church's Growing Sympathy with Socialism." *Current Literature* 43, no. 5 (Nov. 1907): 537.

"Clergymen Talk of Church and Labor: Patronizing Attitude toward the Workingman Is Severely Criticized." *New York Times*, Mar. 5, 1907, 8.

Cocks, Orrin G. "The Scope and Value of the Men and Religion Movement." *Proceedings of the Academy of Political Science in the City of New York* 2, no. 4 (July 1912): 543.

Coleman, George William. *Open Forum Movement*. Boston: Little, Brown, and Company, 1917.

Coleman, George William. *The Story of Ford Hall and the Open Forum Movement*. Boston: Little, Brown and Company, 1915.

Coleman, William Macon. *The Snare of the Men and Religion Forward Movement* (n.p.) [1912].

"Constitution of the Christian Socialist Fellowship." *Christian Socialist*, June 18, 1906, 5.

Convention of the Protestant Episcopal Church in the Diocese of Massachusetts, May 3–4, 1893. Boston: Damrell and Upham, 1893.

Cope, Henry Frederick. *Religious Education in the Church*. Charles Scribner's Sons, 1918.

Debs, Eugene. *Debs: His Life, Writings And Speeches*. Kessinger Publishing, 2009.

Debs, Eugene. *Walls and Bars*. Charles H. Kerr and Company, 1927, 1973.

Deitz, Peter. *Social Service: A Summary of the Social Position of Catholicism*. Oberlin, OH: N.P., 1911.

Denton, James. *Rocky Mountain Radical: Myron Reed, Christian Socialist*. Albuquerque: University Press of New Mexico, 1997).

Devon, Charles. "The Religious Possibilities of Manhood." *New York Observer and Chronicle* 89, no. 34 (Aug. 24, 1911): 235.

Drake, Durant. "Widening the Church's Invitation." *American Journal of Theology* 18, no. 2 (Apr. 1914): 257–65.

Easton, William O. *The Church and Social Work: A Syllabus.* Philadelphia: Social Service Committee of the Men and Religion Forward Movement, 1912.

"The Evangelistic Movement." *Christian Observer* 93, no. 26 (June 28, 1905): 4.

"Evangelizing the Workingman." *New York Observer and Chronicle* 85, no. 6 (Feb. 7, 1907): 167.

Federal Council Bulletin. Religious Publicity Service of the Federal Council of the Churches of Christ in America, 1920.

Foster, William Z. *The Great Steel Strike and Its Lessons.* B.W. Huebsch, 1920.

General War-Time Commission of the Churches. *War-time Agencies of the Churches: Directory and Handbook.* Federal Council of the Churches of Christ in America, 1919.

George, Henry. *Progress and Poverty: An Inquiry into the Cause of Industrial Depressions, and of Increase of Want With Increase of Wealth: The Remedy.* New York: D. Appleton & Co, 1886.

Getting at the Heart of the Downtown Problem: A Concrete Illustration of What the Church is Doing in One of the Most Difficult Fields in the World. New York: Department of Church and Labor, [1912].

Gilkey, Charles Whitney. "The Function of the Church in Modern Society." *American Journal of Theology* 18, no. 1 (Jan. 1914): 1–23.

"The Gospel in the Shops: Scores of Ministers Speaking to Workingmen This Week." *New York Observer and Chronicle* 86, no. 6 (Feb. 7, 1907): 188.

Gronlund, Laurence. *The Co-operative Commonwealth: An Exposition of Socialism.* Lee and Shepard Publishers, 1900.

Harney, Kerri. "Bread and Roses in United States History: The Power of Constructed Memory." Honors thesis, SUNY Binghamton, Spring 1999.

Herron, George Davis. *Between Caesar and Jesus.* Thomas Y. Crowell, 1899.

Herron, George Davis. *The Call of the Cross: Four College Sermons.* Fleming H. Revell Company, 1892.

Herron, George Davis. *The Christian Society.* Fleming H. Revell Co., 1894.

Herron, George Davis. *The Christian State: A Political Vision of Christ.* Kessinger Publishing, 2004.

Herron, George Davis. *The Larger Christ.* F. H. Revell Co., 1891.

Herron, George Davis. "A Plea for Unity of American Socialists." Address Nov. 18, 1900. *International Socialist Review,* Dec. 1900, 321–28.

Hughan, Jessie Wallace. *The Facts of Socialism.* New York: John Lane Co., 1913.

"In the World of Religious Thought." *Current Literature* 38, no. 3 (Mar. 1905): 269.

Jackson, S. D. "Socialism and Christianity." *Christian World Pulpit* 80, no. 2092 (Dec. 6, 1911): 364.

Leach, William. "The Weakness of Protestantism in American Cities." *Journal of Religion* 2, no. 6 (Nov. 1922): 616–23.

Lennon, John Brown. "Labor's Interest in World Peace." *American Federationist* 27, no. 6 (June 1910): 492.

Lloyd, Henry Demarest. *Wealth Against Commonwealth.* New York: Harper & Bros., 1894.

Macfarland, Charles, ed. *The Churches of Christ in Council: Their History, Organization, and Distinctive Characteristics, and a Statement of the Development of the Federal Council.* Fleming Revell Company. Vol. 1. New York: Federal Council of Churches, 1916.

Macfarland, Charles. *The Progress of Church Federation to 1922.* New York: Fleming Revell Company, 1921.

Macfarland, Charles. "The Social Program of the Federal Council of Churches in America." *Proceedings of the Academy of Political Science in the City of New York*, July 1912, 174.

Matthews, Shailer. "The Church and the Labor Movement." *Homiletic Review: International Monthly Magazine of Current Religious Thought, Sermonic Literature and Discussion of Practical Issues* 54 (July 1907): 148.

McFarland, John T., and Benjamin S. Winchester. *The Encyclopedia of Sunday Schools and Religious Education: Giving a World-wide View of the History and Progress of the Sunday School and the Development of Religious Education . . .* T. Nelson & Sons, 1915.

McGrady, Thomas. *Beyond the Black Ocean.* Terra Haute: Standard Publishing Co., 1901.

McGrady, Thomas. *Socialism and the Labor Problem: A Plea for Social Democracy.* Terra Haute: Standard Publishing Co., 1903.

Men and Mules. Toledo, OH: W.F. Ries, [1908].

"Men and Religion Forward Movement" and "Is Stelzle a Fakir? Inquires C. Fischer." *Labor Review*, Sept. 29, 1911, 4.

"Men and Religion Leaders Tell Aims." *New York Times*, Dec. 9, 1911, 13.

"Men and Religious Movement." *New York Observer and Chronicle* 89, no. 24 (June 15, 1911): 762.

"Men of Churches Begin a Campaign." *New York Times*, June 10, 1911, 22.

Mitchell, John. "The Workingman's Conception of Industrial Liberty." *American Federationist* 27 (May 1910): 410.

National Convention of the Socialist Party: Held at Chicago, Illinois, May 1 to 6, 1904. Allied Printing Trades Council, 1904.

National Convention of the Socialist Party: Held at Chicago, Illinois, May 10 to 17, 1908. Allied Print. Trades Council, 1908.

National Convention of the Socialist Party: Held at Indianapolis, Ind., May 12 to 18, 1912. M.A. Donohue & Co., 1912.

North, Frank Mason. *The Church and Modern Industry.* New York: Federal Council of Churches of Christ in America, 1908.

O'Hare, Kate Richards. *The Church and the Social Problem.* St. Louis: National Rip Saw Company, 1911.

O'Hare, Kate Richards. *The Sorrows of Cupid.* The National Rip-Saw, 1912.

Olds, Marshall, and Haskins & Sells. *Analysis of the Interchurch World Movement Report on the Steel Strike, Quigg, Murray Townsend.* New York: G.P. Putnam's Sons, 1923.

Payson, George Shipman. "Will Socialism Be Established in America? At Present an Economic Force of No Small Magnitude." *New York Observer and Chronicle* 85, no. 31 (Aug. 1, 1907): 137–39.

Phifer, Charles Lincoln. *The Road to Socialism: What Has Been Gained and What Is Yet to Win* Girard: Appeal to Reason, 1913.

Prosser, William. *An Open Letter to Raymond Robins of Chicago: An Exposition of Socialism, Answering Mr. Robins' Attack on the Socialist Movement.* Pittsburgh Center: Christian Socialist Fellowship of America, 1912.

Rauschenbusch, Walter. *Christianity and the Social Crisis.* Macmillan, 1911.

Rauschenbusch, Walter. *Christianizing the Social Order.* Macmillan, 1913.

Rauschenbusch, Walter. *Dare We Be Christians*. Pilgrim Press, 1914.

Rauschenbusch, Walter. *The Social Principles of Jesus*. Association Press, 1916.

Rauschenbusch, Walter. *A Theology for the Social Gospel*. Macmillan, 1917.

Robinson, William J. "Men and Religion Forward Movement." *New York Observer and Chronicle* 89, no. 43 (Oct. 26, 1911): 518.

Ryan, John. *The Christian Doctrine of Property*. New York: Paulist Press, 1923.

Ryan, John. *Distributive Justice: The Right and Wrong of our Present Economic System*. New York: Macmillan, 1916.

Sagamore Sociological Conference. *Sagamore Sociological Conference, Sagamore Beach, Massachusetts*. N.p., 1916.

Scudder, Vida Dutton. "Religion and Socialism." *Harvard Theological Review* 3, no. 2 (Apr. 1910): 230–47.

Sears, Charles. *Socialism and Christianity: Being a Response to an Inquirer Concerning Religion and the Observance of Religious Forms at the North American Phalanx*. The Phalanx, 1854.

Seeley, Sir Robert. *Ecce Homo: A Survey of the Life and Works of Jesus Christ*. New York: E. P Dutton and Co, 1893.

"Senator Urges Church to Meet Socialist Challenge." *American Socialist*, July 18, 1914.

Sheldon, Charles Monroe. *The Heart of the World: A Story of Christian Socialism*. F.H. Revell Company, 1905.

Simms, Florence. "*The Industrial Policies of the Young Women's Christian Association*." *Annals of the American Academy of Political and Social Science*, Sept. 1922, 138–40.

Simons, Algie Martin. *Class Struggles in America*. C. H. Kerr & Company, 1906.

Sinclair, Upton. *The Jungle*. Forgotten Books, 1935.

Sinclair, Upton. *King Coal: A Novel*. New York: Macmillan, 1917.

Sinclair, Upton. *Mammonart: An Essay in Economic Interpretation*. Simon Publications, 2003.

Sinclair, Upton. *The Profits of Religion: An Essay in Economic Interpretation*. Self-published, 1918.

Smith, Frederick. "The Forward Movement." *New York Times*, June 4, 1911.

Smith, Gerald Birney. "Christianity and the Spirit of Democracy." *American Journal of Theology* 21, no. 3 (July 1917): 339–57.

Social Service Message: Men and Religion Movement. New York: Association Press, 1914.

"The Social Significance of Arturo Giovannitti." *Current Opinion*, Jan. 1913, 24.

Spargo, John. *Americanism and Social Democracy*. Harper & Brothers, 1918.

Spargo, John. *The Bitter Cry of the Children*. New York: Macmillan, 1909.

Spargo, John. *The Jew and American Ideals*. Harper & Brothers, 1921.

Spargo, John. *Karl Marx: His Life and Work*. B.W. Huebsch, 1912.

Spargo, John. *Sidelights on Contemporary Socialism*. B.W. Huebsch, 1911.

Spargo, John. *Socialism: A Summary and Interpretation of Socialist Principles*. Macmillan, 1912.

Spargo, John. *Socialism and Motherhood*. B.W. Huebsch, 1914.

Spargo, John. *The Spiritual Significance of Modern Socialism*. B.W. Huebsch, 1908.

Spargo, John. *The Substance of Socialism*. B.W. Huebsch, 1911.

Stang, William. *Socialism and Christianity*. Benziger Brothers, 1905.

Stead, William. *If Christ Came to Chicago!* Chicago: Caird and Lee, 1894.

Stelzle, Charles. *American Social and Religious Conditions*. Fleming H. Revell Company, 1912.

Stelzle, Charles. "Applied Christianity: A Correspondence Course Provided by the Presbyterian Home Board." *New York Observer and Chronicle* 85, no. 37 (Sept. 12, 1907): 339.

Stelzle, Charles. *Boys of the Street: How to Win Them.* F.H. Revell Co., 1904.

Stelzle, Charles. *The Call of the New Day to the Old Church.* Fleming H. Revell Co., 1915.

Stelzle, Charles. *Christianity's Storm Centre: A Study of the Modern City.* Fleming H. Revell Co., 1907.

Stelzle, Charles. *The Church and Labor.* Houghton Mifflin Co., 1910.

Stelzle, Charles. "Church and Labor: Capturing the Labor Movement." *Christian Observer* 19, no. 40 (Sept. 26, 1906): 14–15.

Stelzle, Charles. *The Gospel of Labor.* Fleming H. Revell Company, 1912.

Stelzle, Charles. *If I Had Only One Sermon to Preach: Sermons by Twenty-One Ministers.* Harper & Brothers, 1927.

Stelzle, Charles. "King Coal." *World Outlook*, Jan. 20, 1920, 27–33.

Stelzle, Charles. *Letters from a Workingman.* F.H. Revell Co., 1908.

Stelzle, Charles. *Messages to Workingmen.* New York: Revell, 1906.

Stelzle, Charles. "Mission of the Church." *New York Observer* 79: 11 (Mar. 14, 1901): 351.

Stelzle, Charles. "Preaching to Workingmen." *The Independent* 54 (Sept. 4, 1902): 21–34.

Stelzle, Charles. "Presbyterian Department of Church and Labor." *Annals of the American Academy of Political Science*, Nov. 1907, 28.

Stelzle, Charles, *The Social Application of Religion: The Merrick Lectures for 1907–08, Ohio Wesleyan University.* Cincinnati: Jennings and Graham, 1908.

Stelzle, Charles. "Socialism and the Church." *New York Observer* 82, no. 11 (Mar. 17, 1904): 327.

Stelzle, Charles. *A Son of the Bowery: The Life Story of an East Side American.* George H. Doran Co., 1926.

Stelzle, Charles. "Unionists Not Anarchists: Not Fair to Judge an Organization by a Few Individuals." *New York Observer and Chronicle* 85, no. 9 (Feb. 28, 1907): 272.

Stelzle, Charles. *Why Prohibition!* George H. Doran Company, *1918.*

Stelzle, Charles. *The Workingman and Social Problems.* F.H. Revel Company, 1903.

Stelzle, Charles. "The Workingman's Church." *Outlook* 71, no. 4 (May 24, 1902): 266.

Stelzle, Charles. "Workingmen and the Church." *New York Observer and Chronicle* 79, no. 7 (Feb. 14, 1901): 213.

Stern, Herman Isidore. *A Socialist Catechism.* Herman I. Stern: Berekley, 1912.

"Taking the Bible as the Textbook of the Social Revolution." *Current Opinion*, June 1914, 447.

Thompson, Bertrand. *Churches and the Wage Earners.* New York: Charles Scribner's Sons, 1909.

Thompson, Carl. *The Constructive Program of Socialism.* Milwaukee: Social-Democratic Publishing, 1908.

Tippy, Worth Marion. *The Church, a Community Force: A Story of the Development of the Community Relations of Epworth Memorial Church, Cleveland, Ohio.* Missionary Education Movement of the United States and Canada, 1914.

Tippy, Worth Marion. *The Church and the Great War.* Fleming H. Revell Company, 1918.

Tippy, Worth Marion. *The Cleveland May Day Riot: What to Do.* New York: N.p., 1919.

Tippy, Worth Marion. *The Socialized Church: Addresses Before the First National Conference of the Social Workers of Methodism, St. Louis, November 17–19, 1908.* Eaton & Mains, 1909.

Tippy, Worth Marion, and Frederick Ernest Johnson. *The Church and Women in Industry*. Commission on the Church and Social Service of the Federal Council of the Churches of Christ in America, 1918.

Tippy, Worth Marion, and Paul Bentley Kern. *A Methodist Church and Its Work*. Methodist Book Concern, 1919.

US Congress, House Committee on Labor. *Investigation of Wages and Working Conditions in the Coal-Mining Industry: Hearings before the United States House Committee on Labor, Sixty-Seventh Congress, Second Session, on Mar. 30, 31, Apr. 1, 3–7, 10, 1922*. Washington, DC: US GPO, 1922.

Ward, Cyrenus Osborne. *Ancient Lowly: A History of the Ancient Working People from the earliest known period to the adoption of Christianity by Constantine*. Washington, DC: W.H. Lowermilk and Co., 1889.

Ward, Cyrenus Osborne. *A Labor Catechism of Political Economy: A Study for the People*. New York: n.p., 1878.

Ward, Harry Frederick. *The Labor Movement, from the Standpoint of Religious Values*. Sturgis & Walton Company, 1917.

Ward, Harry Frederick. *The New Social Order: Principles and Programs*. New York: Macmillan, 1922.

Ward, Harry Frederick. *Our Economic Morality and the Ethic of Jesus*. New York: Macmillan, 1929.

Ward, Harry Frederick. *The Social Creed of the Churches*. Abingdon Press, 1914.

Ward, Harry Frederick. *Social Evangelism*. Missionary Education Movement of the United States and Canada, 1915.

Ward, Harry Frederick. *A Yearbook of the Church and Social Service*. New York: Fleming Revel Company, 1914.

Ward, Harry Frederick, Federal Council of the Churches of Christ in America, and Commission on the Church and Social Service. *A Year Book of the Church and Social Service in the United States*. New York: Fleming H. Revell Co., 1914.

Warne, Colston E. 1900–1987. *The Steel Strike of 1919*. Boston: Heath, 1963.

"The Wayfarer." *The Continent*, July 31, 1913, 1055.

White, Bouck. *The Call of the Carpenter*. Doubleday, Page, 1914.

White, Bouck. *The Carpenter and the Rich Man*. Doubleday, Page, 1914.

White, Bouck. *Church of the Social Revolution: A Message to the World*. Church of the Social Revolution, 1914.

White, Bouck. *Songs of the Fellowship, for Use in Socialist Gatherings, Propaganda, Labor Mass Meetings, the Home, and Churches of the Social Faith*. Socialist Literature, 1912.

Willard, Frances Elizabeth, and Mary Artemisia Lathbury. *Woman and Temperance: Or, The Work and Workers of the Woman's Christian Temperance Union*. Park Publishing Co., 1888.

Wilshire, Gaylord. *Socialism, a Religion*. New York: Wilshire Book Co., 1906.

Wilson, J. Stitt. *The Bible Argument for Socialism*. ATLA Fiche 1990–1057. Berkeley, CA: J.S. Wilson, 1911.

Wilson, J. Stitt. *How I Became a Socialist and Other Papers*. Jackson Stitt Wilson, 1912.

Wood, Eugene. *Socialism, the Hope of the World*. New York: Wilshire Book Company, 1906.

Woods, Katherine Pearson. "Progressive Methods of Church Work: The Church of the Carpenter." *Christian Union*, Aug. 27, 1892.

"Would Working Men Draw the Line in Benevolence." *Congregationalist and Christian World*, Sept. 16, 1905, 376.

Secondary Sources

Amenda, Phyllis. "God Bless the Revolution: Christian Socialism in the Episcopal Church, 1885–1940." PhD diss., Binghamton University, 2009.

Anderson, Robert Mapes. *Visions of the Disinherited: The Making of American Pentecostalism.* New York: Oxford University Press, 1979.

Armstrong, James. "The Labor Temple, 1910–1957: The Social Gospel in Action in the Presbyterian Church." PhD diss., University of Wisconsin, 1974.

Arthur, Anthony. *Radical Innocent: Upton Sinclair.* Random House Digital, 2006.

Bailey, Beth. *From Front Porch to Back Seat: Courtship in Twentieth Century America.* Baltimore: Johns Hopkins University Press, 1988.

Barrett, James R. *The Irish Way: Becoming American in the Multiethnic City.* New York: Penguin, 2012.

Barrett, James R. "Was the Personal Political?: Reading the Autobiography of American Communism." *International Review of Social History* 53, no. 3 (2009): 395–423.

Barrett, James R. *William Z. Foster and the Tragedy of American Radicalism.* Urbana: University of Illinois Press, 2001.

Bateman, Bradley. "Between God and the Market: The Religious Roots of the American Economic Association." *Journal of Economic Perspectives* (Fall 1999): 249–58.

Bederman, Gail. "'The Women Have Had Charge of the Church Work Long Enough': The Men and Religion Forward Movement of 1911–1912 and the Masculinization of Middle-Class Protestantism." *American Quarterly* 41, no. 3 (Sept. 1, 1989): 432–65.

Bencivenni, Marcella. *Italian Immigrant Radical Culture: The Idealism of the Sovversivi in the United States, 1890–1940.* New York: NYU Press, 2011.

Bisset, James. *Agrarian Socialism in America: Marx, Jefferson and Jesus in the Oklahoma Countryside, 1904–1920.* Norman: University of Oklahoma Press, 2002.

Blewett, Mary. *Men, Women and Work: Class, Gender and Protest in the New England Shoe Industry, 1780–1910.* Urbana: University of Illinois Press, 1988.

Blum, Edward. "'Paul Has Been Forgotten': Women, Gender and Revivalism during the Gilded Age." *Journal of the Gilded Age and Progressive Era* 3, no. 3 (July 2004): 247–70.

Blum, Edward. *Reforging the White Republic: Race, Region, and American Nationalism, 1865–1898.* Baton Rouge: Louisiana State University Press, 2007.

Blum, Edward. *W. E. B. Du Bois: American Prophet.* University Park: University of Pennsylvania Press, 2007.

Blum, Edward J., and Paul Harvey. *The Color of Christ: The Son of God and the Saga of Race in America.* Chapel Hill: University of North Carolina Press, 2012.

Blumhofer, Edith Wadvogel. *Restoring the Faith: The Assemblies of God, Pentecostalism, and American Culture.* Urbana: University of Illinois Press, 1993.

Bohlmann, Rachel. "Drunken Husbands, Drunken State: The Woman's Christian Temperance Union's Challenge to American Families and Public Communities in Chicago, 1874–1920." PhD. Diss., University of Iowa, 2001.

Braude, Ann. *Radical Spirits: Spiritualism and Women's Rights in Nineteenth-Century America* Bloomington: Indiana University Press, 2001.

Brody, David. *Labor in Crisis: The Steel Strike of 1919.* Urbana: University of Illinois Press, 1965.

Brown, Dorothy, and Elizabeth McKeown. *The Poor Belong to Us: Catholic Charities and American Welfare.* Cambridge, MA: Harvard University Press, 1997.

Brundage, William Fitzhugh. *A Socialist Utopia in the New South: The Ruskin Colonies in Tennessee and Georgia, 1894–1901*. Urbana: University of Illinois Press, 1996.

Buhle, Mari Jo. *Women and American Socialism, 1870–1920*. Urbana: University of Illinois Press, 1981.

Buhle, Paul. *Marxism in the United States: Remapping the History of the American Left*. New York: Verso, 1987.

Burbank, Garin. *When Farmers Voted Red: The Gospel of Socialism in the Oklahoma Countryside, 1910–1924*. Westport, CT: Greenwood Press, 1976.

Burnidge, Cara. "Charles Sheldon and the Heart of the Social Gospel." MA thesis, Florida State University, 2007.

Burns, Dave. *Life and Death of the Radical Historical Jesus*. New York: Oxford University Press, 2013.

Burns, Dave. "The Soul of Socialism: Christianity, Civilization and Citizenship in the Thought of Eugene Debs." *Labor* (Spring 2008): 83–116.

Burwood, Stephen. "Debsian Socialism Through a Transnational Lens." *Journal of the Gilded Age and Progressive Era* 2, no. Special Issue 3 (2003): 253–82.

Butler, Jon. "Forum: American Religion and the Great Depression." *Church History* 80, no. 3 (Sept. 1, 2011): 575–78.

Callahan, Richard J. *Work and Faith in the Kentucky Coal Fields: Subject to Dust*. Bloomington: Indiana University Press, 2009.

Callahan, Richard, Kathryn Lofton, and Chad Seales. "Allegories of Progress: Industrial Religion in the United States." *Journal of the American Academy of Religion* 78, no. 1 (Mar. 2010): 1–39.

Calverton, V. F. "Left Wing Literature in America." *English Journal* 20, no. 10 (Dec. 1931): 789–98.

Cantwell, Christopher. "The Bible Class Teacher: Piety and Politics in the Age of Fundamentalism." PhD diss., Cornell University, 2012.

Carroll, Bret. *The Routledge Historical Atlas of Religion in America*. New York: Routledge, 2000.

Carroll, Bret. *Spiritualism in Antebellum America*. Bloomington: Indiana University Press, 1997.

Carter, Heath. *Union Made: Working People and the Rise of Social Christianity in Chicago*. New York: Oxford University Press, 2015.

Carter, Paul Allen. *The Decline and Revival of the Social Gospel: Social and Political Liberalism in American Protestant Churches, 1920–1940*. Ithaca, NY: Cornell University Press, 1956.

Chacon, Justin Akers. *Radicals in the Barrio: Magonistas, Socialists, Wobblies, and Communists in the Mexican American Working Class*. Chicago: Haymarket, 2018.

Ciano, Peter. "The Moral Imprint of Early Twentieth Century Italian-American Radical Labor." *Proteus* 7 (1990): 25–31.

Clark, Ana. *Struggle in the Breeches: Gender and the Making of the British Working Class*. Berkeley: University of California Press, 1995.

Clayton, Joseph. *Robert Owen: Pioneer of Social Reforms*. London: A.C. Fifield, 1908.

Coffman, Elesha. "Constituting the Protestant Mainline: The Christian Century, 1908–1947." PhD diss., Duke University, 2008.

Commission of Inquiry. *Report on the Steel Strike of 1919*. Vol. 2. New York: Harcourt, Brace and Howe, 1920.

Craig, Robert. *Religion and Radical Politics: An Alternative Christian Tradition in the United States*. Philadelphia: Temple University Press, 1995.

Creech, Joe. *Righteous Indignation: Religion and the Populist Revolution*. Urbana: University of Illinois Press, 2006.

Crunden, Robert Morse. *Ministers of Reform: The Progressives' Achievement in American Civilization, 1889–1920*. Urbana: University of Illinois Press, 1985.

D'Agostino, Peter. *Rome in America: Transnational Catholic Ideology from the Risorgimento to Fascism* Chapel Hill: University of North Carolina Press, 2004.

D'A Jones, Peter. *The Christian Socialist Revival, 1877–1914: Religion, Class and Social Conscience in Late Victorian England*. Princeton, NJ: Princeton University Press, 1968.

DeBerg, Betty A. *Ungodly Women: Gender and the First Wave of American Fundamentalism*. Mercer University Press, 2000.

Deichmann, Wendy, and Carolyn DeSwarte Gifford, eds. *Gender and the Social Gospel*. Urbana: University of Illinois Press, 2003.

Dickinson, Charles Albert. *The Berkeley Temple Year Book, 1890*. Boston: Berkeley Temple, 1890.

Dickinson, Charles Albert. *The Work of Berkeley Temple, Boston: Organized for City Evangelization, Christian Nurture, and Practical Christianity*. Boston: Berkeley Temple, 1888.

Dillon, Mary Earhart. *Frances Willard: From Prayers to Politics*. Chicago: University of Chicago Press, 1944.

Dochuk, Darren. *From Bible Belt to Sunbelt: Plainfolk Religion, Grassroots Politics, and Evangelical Conservatism*. New York: Norton, 2011.

Dolan, Jay P. *The American Catholic Experience: A History from Colonial Times to the Present*. New York: Doubleday, 1985.

Dombrowski, James. *The Early Days of Christian Socialism in America*. Octagon Books, 1977.

Dorn, Jacob H. "'In Spiritual Communion': Eugene V. Debs and the Socialist Christians." *Journal of the Gilded Age and Progressive Era* 2, no. 3 (July 1, 2003): 303–25.

Dorn, Jacob H. "The Social Gospel and Socialism: A Comparison of the Thought of Francis Greenwood Peabody, Washington Gladden, and Walter Rauschenbusch." *Church History* 62, no. 1 (Mar. 1, 1993): 82–100.

Dorn, Jacob H. *Socialism and Christianity in Early 20th Century America*. Westport, CT: Greenwood Press, 1998.

Dorn, Jacob H. *Washington Gladden: Prophet of the Social Gospel*. Columbus: Ohio State University Press, 1968.

Dorrien, Gary. *The Making of American Liberal Theology: Idealism, Realism, and Modernity, 1900–1950*. Knoxville, TN: Westminster John Knox Press, 2003.

Dorrien, Gary. *The Making of American Liberal Theology: Imagining Progressive Religion, 1805–1900*. Knoxville, TN: Westminster John Knox Press, 2001.

Dorrien, Gary. *Social Ethics in the Making: Interpreting an American Tradition*. New York: John Wiley & Sons, 2008.

Douglas, Ann. *The Feminization of American Culture*. New York: Macmillan, 1998.

Dressner, Richard B. "Christian Socialism: A Response to Industrial America in the Progressive Era." PhD diss., Cornell University, 1972.

Dressner, Richard B. "William Dwight Porter Bliss's Christian Socialism." *Church History* 47, no. 1 (Mar. 1, 1978): 66–82.

Dubofsky, Melvyn. *We Shall Be All: A History of the Industrial Workers of the World*. Abridged ed. Urbana: University of Illinois Press, 2000.

Dubofsky, Melvyn. *When Workers Organize: New York City in the Progressive Era*. Amherst: University of Massachusetts Press, 1968.

Duke, David. *In the Trenches with Jesus and Marx: Harry F. Ward and the Struggle for Social Justice*. Tuscaloosa: University of Alabama Press, 2003.

Dumez, Kristin. *Jesus and John Wayne: How White Evangelicals Corrupted a Faith and Fractured a Nation*. New York: Liveright, 2020.

Ebel, Jonathan. *Faith in the Fight: Religion and the American Soldier in the Great War*. Princeton, NJ: Princeton University Press, 2010.

Evans, Christopher H. *The Social Gospel in American Religion: A History*. New York: NYU Press, 2017.

Evans, Ellen Lovell. *The German Center Party, 1877–1930: A Study in Political Catholicism* Carbondale: Southern Illinois University Press, 1981.

Fink, Leon. "A Memoir of Selig Perlman and His Life at the University of Wisconsin: Based on an Interview of Mark Perlman and Edited by Leon Fink." *Labor History* 32, no. 4 (Feb 2007): 503–25.

Fink, Leon. *In Search of the Working Class*. Urbana: University of Illinois Press, 1994.

Fink, Leon. *Progressive Intellectuals and the Dilemmas of Democratic Commitment*. Cambridge, MA: Harvard University Press, 1997.

Flanagan, Maureen A. *Seeing with Their Hearts: Chicago Women and the Vision of the Good City, 1871–1933*. Princeton, NJ: Princeton University Press, 2002.

Fones-Wolf, Elizabeth, and Kenneth Fones-Wolf. "Sanctifying the Southern Organizing Campaign: Protestant Activists in the CIO's Operation Dixie." *Labor* 6, no. 1 (Mar. 20, 2009): 5–32.

Fones-Wolf, Kenneth. *Religion and Sexuality: The Shakers, Mormons and Oneida Community*. New York: Oxford University Press, 1981.

Fones-Wolf, Kenneth. "Revivalism and Craft-Unionism in the Progressive Era: Syracuse and Auburn Labor Forward Movements of 1913." *New York History* 63, no. 4 (Oct. 1982): 389.

Fones-Wolf, Kenneth, and Elizabeth Fones-Wolf. "Trade Union Evangelism: Religion and the AFL in the Labor Forward Movement." In *Working Class America: Essays on Labor, Community, and American Society*, ed. Michael Frisch and Daniel Walkowitz. Urbana: University of Illinois Press, 1983, 153–84.

Fones-Wolf, Kenneth. *Trade Union Gospel: Christianity and Labor in Industrial Philadelphia, 1865–1915*. Philadelphia: Temple University Press, 1990.

Foster, Gaines. *Moral Reconstruction: Christian Lobbyists and the Federal Legislation of Morality, 1865–1920*. Chapel Hill: University of North Carolina Press, 2007.

Foster, Lawrence. *Women, Family and Utopia: Communal Experiments of the Shakers, the Oneida Community, and the Mormons*. Syracuse: Syracuse University Press, 1991.

Fourier, Charles. *Selections from the Works of Fourier*. London: Swan Sonnenschein and Co, 1901.

Frederick, Peter. *Knights of the Golden Rule: The Intellectual as Christian Social Reformer in the 1890s*. Lexington: University Press of Kentucky, 1976.

Frey, Donald. *America's Economic Moralists: A History of Rival Ethics and Economics*. Albany: SUNY Press, 2009.

Furey, Hester L. "The Reception of Arturo Giovannitti's Poetry and the Trial of a New Society." *Left History* 2, no. 1 (1994): 27–50.

Gaffney, Mason. "Henry George, Dr. Edward McGlynn, and Pope Leo." self-published paper delivered at Cooper Union (Nov. 1, 1997), available: http://masongaffney.org/publications/K18George_McGlynn_and_Leo_XIII.pdf.

Gellman, Erik S., and Jarod Roll. *The Gospel of the Working Class: Labor's Southern Prophets in New Deal America*. Urbana: University of Illinois Press, 2011.

Gifford, Carolyn De Sware, and Amy R. Slagell. *Let Something Good Be Said: Speeches and Writings of Frances E. Willard*. Urbana: University of Illinois Press, 2007.

Gilmore, Glenda Elizabeth. *Gender and Jim Crow: Women and the Politics of White Supremacy in North Carolina, 1896-1920*. Chapel Hill: University of North Carolina Press, 1996.

Gloege, Tim. *Guaranteed Pure: The Moody Bible Institute and the Making of Modern Evangelicalism*. Chapel Hill: University of North Carolina Press, 2015.

Goodwyn, Lawrence. *Populist Moment: A Short History of the Agrarian Revolt in America*. New York: Oxford University Press, 1978.

Gorrell, Donald K. *The Age of Social Responsibility: The Social Gospel in the Progressive Era*. Atlanta: Mercer University Press, 1988.

Graham, John. *"Yours for the Revolution": The Appeal to Reason, 1895-1922*. Lincoln: University of Nebraska Press, 1990.

Grant, H. Roger. "Portrait of a Workers' Utopia: The Labor Exchange and the Freedom, Kansas Colony." *Kansas Historical Quarterlies* 43, no. 1 (Spring 1977): 56-66.

Grant, Percy Stickney. *Socialism and Christianity*. Brentano's, 1910.

Green, James. *Grass-Roots Socialism Radical Movements in the Southwest, 1895-1943*. Baton Rouge: Louisiana State University Press, 1978.

Greene, Alison Collis. "The End of 'The Protestant Era'?" *Church History* 80, no. 3 (Sept. 1, 2011): 600-610.

Greene, Alison Collis. *No Depression in Heaven: The Great Depression, the New Deal, and the Transformation of Religion in the Delta*. New York: Oxford University Press, 2016.

Gutman, Herbert. "Protestantism and the American Labor Movement: The Christian Spirit in the Gilded Age." *American Historical Review* 72, no. 1 (Oct. 1966): 74-101.

Hackett, David G., Laurie Maffly-Kipp, R. Laurence Moore, and Leslie Woodcock Tentler. "Forum: American Religion and Class." *Religion and American Culture* 15, no. 1 (Winter 2005): 1-29.

Hamilton, Mike. "Willow Creek's Place in History." *Christianity Today*, Nov. 13, 2000. http://www.christianitytoday.com/ct/2000/november13/5.62.html.

Hammond, Sarah R. "'God Is My Partner': An Evangelical Business Man Confronts Depression and War." *Church History* 80, no. 3 (Sept. 1, 2011): 498-519.

Handy, Robert T. "Christianity and Socialism in America, 1900-1920." *Church History* 21, no. 1 (Mar. 1, 1952): 39-54.

Handy, Robert T. "George D. Herron and the Kingdom Movement." *Church History* 19, no. 2 (June 1, 1950): 97-115.

Handy, Robert T, "George D. Herron and the Social Gospel in American Protestantism, 1890-1901." PhD diss., University of Chicago Divinity School, 1949.

Handy, Robert T. "The Influence of Mazzini on the American Social Gospel." *Journal of Religion* 29, no. 2 (Apr. 1, 1949): 114-23.

Handy, Robert T. *The Social Gospel in America, 1870-1920*. New York: Oxford University Press, 1966.

Handy, Robert T. *Undermined Establishment: Church-State Relations in America, 1880-1920*. Princeton, NJ: Princeton University Press, 1991.

Hardesty, Nancy. *Women Called to Witness: Evangelical Feminism*. Knoxville: University of Tennessee Press, 1999.

Harrell, David Edwin. *The Social Sources of Division in the Disciples of Christ, 1865-1900* Nashville: Disciples of Christ Historical Society, 1966.

Hart, D. G. *Defending the Faith: J. Gresham Machen and the Crisis of Conservative Protestantism in Modern America*. P & R Publishing, 2003.

Harvey, Paul. *Freedom's Coming: Religious Culture and the Shaping of the South from the Civil War through the Civil Rights Era*. Chapel Hill: University of North Carolina Press, 2005.

Hawley, Joshua. *Theodore Roosevelt: Preacher of Righteousness*. New Haven: Yale University Press, 2008.

Hendrickson, Kenneth. "Tribune of the People: George R. Lunn and the Rise and Fall of Christian Socialism in Schenectady." In *Socialism and the Cities*, ed. Bruce Stave. Port Washington: Kennikat Press, 1974, 72–98.

Hennessey, James. *American Catholics: A History of the Roman Catholic Community in the United States*. New York: Oxford University Press, 1981.

Hessen, Robert. "The Bethlehem Steel Strike of 1910." *Labor History* 15, no. 1 (1974): 3–18.

Holland, Joe. *Modern Catholic Social Teaching: The Popes Confront the Industrial Age, 1740–1958*. New York: Paulist Press, 2004.

Holloway, Mark. *Heavens on Earth: Utopian Communities in America, 1680–1880*. Dover, 1966.

Jacobson, Matthew Frye. *Barbarian Virtues: The United States Encounters Foreign Peoples at Home and Abroad, 1876–1917*. New York: Hill and Wang, 2001.

Jacoby, Susan. *Freethinkers: A History of American Secularism*. New York: Henry Holt, 2004.

Johnpoll, Bernard. *Pacifist Progress: Norman Thomas and the Decline of American Socialism*. Quadrangle Books, 1970.

Johnson, Graham. "British Social Democracy and Religion, 1881–1911." *Journal of Ecclesiastical History* 51, no. 1 (Jan. 2000): 94–115.

Johnson, Paul. *A Shopkeeper's Millennium: Society and Revivals in Rochester, New York, 1815–1837*. New York: Hill and Wang, 1979.

Johnston, Robert. *The Radical Middle Class: Populist Democracy and the Question of Capitalism in Progressive Era Portland, Oregon*. Princeton, NJ: Princeton University Press, 2006.

Joiner, Thelka Ellen. *Sin in the City: Chicago and Revivalism, 1880–1920*. Columbus: University of Missouri Press, 2007.

Karsner, David. *Debs: His Authorized Life and Letters from Woodstock Prison to Atlanta*. New York, 1918.

Karson, Marc. *American Labor Unions and Politics, 1900 1918*. Carbondale: Southern Illinois University Press, 1958.

Kazin, Michael. "A Difficult Marriage: American Protestants and American Politics." *Dissent*, Winter 2006. http://www.dissentmagazine.org/article/?article=159 (accessed Feb. 21, 2008).

Kazin, Michael. *A Godly Hero: The Life of William Jennings Bryan*. New York: Alfred A. Knopf, 2006.

Kazin, Michael. *The Populist Persuasion: An American History*. New York: Basic Books, 1995.

Kern, Kathi. *Mrs. Stanton's Bible*. Ithaca, NY: Cornell University Press, 2002.

Kilde, Jeanne Halgren. *When Church Became Theatre: The Transformation of Evangelical Architecture and Worship in Nineteenth-Century America*. New York: Oxford University Press, 2005.

Kipnis, Ira. *The American Socialist Movement, 1897–1912*. New York: Columbia University Press, 1952.

Knox, W. W. "Religion and the Scottish Labour Movement: 1900–39." *Journal of Contemporary History* 23, no. 4 (Oct. 1988): 609–30.

Kostlevy, William. *Holy Jumpers: Evangelicals and Radicals in Progressive Era America*. New York: Oxford University Press, 2010.

Laslett, John, and Seymour Lipset. *Failure of a Dream: Essays in the History of American Socialism*. Garden City, NY: Anchor Press, 1974.

Laszerow, Jama. *Religion and the Working Class in Antebellum America*. Washington, DC: Smithsonian, 1995.

Laubenstein, Paul. "A History of Christian Socialism in America." PhD diss., Union Theological Seminary, 1925.

LeWarne, Charles Pierce. *Utopias on Puget Sound, 1885–1915*. Seattle: University of Washington Press, 1975.

Loetscher, Lefferts. *The Broadening Church: A Study of Theological Issues in the Presbyterian Church Since 1869*. Philadelphia: University of Pennsylvania Press, 1954.

Longfield, Bradley. *The Presbyterian Controversy: Fundamentalists, Modernists, and Moderates*. New York: Oxford University Press, 1993.

Luker, Ralph. *The Social Gospel in Black and White: American Racial Reform, 1885–1912*. Chapel Hill: University of North Carolina Press, 1991.

Lurie, Reuben Levi. *The Challenge of the Forum; the Story of Ford Hall and the Open Forum Movement, a Demonstration in Public Education*. Boston: R.G. Badger, 1930.

Mackaman, Thomas. "The Foreign Element: New Immigrants and American Industry, 1914–1924." PhD. diss., University of Illinois, 2009.

Magee, Malcom. *What the World Should Be: Woodrow Wilson and the Crafting of a Faith-Based Foreign Policy*. Waco, TX: Baylor University Press, 2008.

Maher, P. E. "Laurence Gronlund: Contributions to American Socialism." *Western Political Quarterly* (Dec. 1962): 618–24.

Mapes, Mary. "Visions of a Christian City: The Politics of Religion and Gender in Chicago City Missions and Protestant Settlement Houses, 1886–1929." PhD diss., Michigan State University, 1998.

Marks, Lynne. "Challenging Binaries: Working-Class Women and Lived Religion in English Canada and the United States." *Labor* 6, no. 1 (Mar. 20, 2009): 107–25.

Marsden, George. *Fundamentalism and American Culture*. New York: Oxford University Press, 2006.

Martinek, Jason D. "'The Workingman's Bible': Robert Blatchford's Merrie England, Radical Literacy, and the Making of Debsian Socialism, 1895–1900." *Journal of the Gilded Age and Progressive Era* 2, no. Special Issue 3 (2003): 326–46.

Mason, Patrick. *The Mormon Menace: Violence and Anti-Mormonism in the Postbellum South*. New York: Oxford University Press, 2011.

Matinova, Timothy. "The National Parish and Americanization." *US Catholic Historian* 17, no. 1 (Winter 1999): 45–58.

McCartin, James, and Joseph A. McCartin. "Working Class Catholicism: A Call for New Investigations, Dialogue, and Reappraisal." *Labor* 4, no. 1 (Spring 2007): 99–110.

McCartin, Joseph A. "Building the Interfaith Worker Justice Movement: Kim Bobo's Story." *Labor* 6, no. 1 (Mar. 20, 2009): 87–105.

McCartin, Joseph A. "The Force of Faith: An Introduction to the Labor and Religion Special Issue." *Labor* 6, no. 1 (Mar. 20, 2009): 1–4.

McCartin, Joseph A. *Labor's Great War: The Struggle for Industrial Democracy and the Origins of Modern American Labor Relations, 1912–1921*. Chapel Hill: University of North Carolina Press, 1998.

McCloud, Hugh. *Piety and Poverty: Working Class Religion in Berlin, London and New York 1870–1914*. New York: Holmes and Meier, 1996.

McConnell, Bishop. *Public Opinion and the Steel Strike: Supplementary Reports of the Investigations to the Commission of Inquiry, the Interchurch World Movement*. New York: Bureau of Industrial Research, 1919.

McKanan, Dan. "The Implicit Religion of Radicalism: Socialist Party Theology, 1900–1934." *Journal of the American Academy of Religion* 78, no. 3 (Sept. 1, 2010): 750–89.

McKee, William Finley. "The Social Gospel and the New Social Order, 1919–1929." PhD diss., University of Wisconsin, 1961.

McMath, Robert. *American Populism: A Social History, 1877–1898*. New York: Hill and Wang, 1993.

Messer-Kruse, Timothy. *The Yankee International: Marxism and the American Reform Tradition, 1848–1876*. Chapel Hill: University of North Carolina Press, 1998.

Meyer, Donald. *The Protestant Search for Political Realism, 1919–1941*. Berkeley: University of California Press, 1960.

Michels, Tony. *A Fire in Their Hearts: Yiddish Socialists in New York*. Cambridge, MA: Harvard University Press, 2005.

Michelson, Grant. "The Role of Workplace Chaplains in Industrial Relations: Evidence from Australia." *British Journal of Industrial Relations* 44, no. 4 (Dec. 2006): 677–96.

Miller, Sally M. "For White Men Only: The Socialist Party of America and Issues of Gender, Ethnicity and Race." *Journal of the Gilded Age and Progressive Era* 2, no. Special Issue 3 (2003): 283–302.

Miller, Sally M., ed. *Race, Ethnicity and Gender in Early Twentieth Century American Socialism*. New York: Garland Publishing, 1996.

Mirola, William. "Asking for Bread, Receiving a Stone: The Rise and Fall of Religious Ideologies in Chicago's Eight-Hour Movement." *Social Problems* 50, no. 2 (May 2003): 273–93.

Montgomery, David. *The Fall of the House of Labor: The Workplace, the State, and American Labor Activism, 1865–1925*. New York: Cambridge University Press, 1987.

Montgomery, David. "The 'New Unionism' and the Transformation of Workers' Consciousness in America, 1909–1922." *Journal of Social History* 7, no. 4 (Summer 1974): 509–29.

Moreton, Bethany. *To Serve God and Walmart: The Making of Christian Free Enterprise*. Cambridge, MA: Harvard University Press, 2009.

Murphy, Laura. "An 'Indestructible Right': John Ryan and the Catholic Origins of the U.S. Living Wage Movement, 1906–1938." *Labor* 6, no. 1 (Mar. 20, 2009): 57–86.

Nash, George. "Charles Stelzle: Apostle to Labor." *Labor History* 11, no. 2 (Spring 1970): 151–74.

Nelson, Bruce. "Religion and Upheaval: Religion, Irreligion, and Chicago's Working Class in 1886." *Journal of Social History* 25 (Winter 1991): 233–53.

Nelson, Phyllis Ann. "George D. Herron and the Socialist Clergy, 1890–1914." PhD diss., University of Iowa, 1953.

Neusse, Joseph. "Henry George and 'Rerum Novarum': Evidence Is Scant That the American Economist was a Target of Leo XIII's Classical Encyclical." *American Journal of Economics and Sociology* 44, no. 2 (Apr. 1985): 241–54.

Oberdeck, Kathryn. *The Evangelist and the Impresario: Religion, Entertainment, and Cultural Politics in America, 1884–1914*. Baltimore: Johns Hopkins Press, 1999.

Orsi, Robert. *The Madonna of 115th St: Faith and Community in Italian Harlem, 1880–1950*. 3rd ed, New Haven: Yale University Press, 2010.

Pernicone, Nunzio. *Carlo Tresca: Portrait of A Rebel*. ReadHowYouWant.com, 2011.

Phillips, Paul T. *A Kingdom on Earth: Anglo-American Social Christianity, 1880–1940*. University Park: Penn State University Press, 1996.

Pittenger, Mark. *American Socialists and Evolutionary Thought, 1870–1920*. Madison: University of Wisconsin Press, 1993.

Polland, Annie. "Working for the Sabbath: Sabbath in the Jewish Immigrant Neighborhoods of New York." *Labor* 6, no. 1 (Mar. 20, 2009): 33–56.

Pope, Liston. *Millhands and Preachers*. New Haven: Yale University Press, 1942.

Postel, Charles. *The Populist Vision*. New York: Oxford University Press, 2009.

Preston, William. *Aliens and Dissenters: Federal Suppression of Radicals, 1903–1933*. Urbana: University of Illinois Press, 1994.

Putney, Clifford. *Muscular Christianity: Manhood and Sports in Protestant America, 1880–1920*. Cambridge, MA: Harvard University Press, 2001.

Quandt, Jean. "Religion and Social Thought: The Secularization of Postmillenialism." *American Quarterly* 25, no. 4 (1973): 390–409.

Quint, Howard H. *The Forging of American Socialism: Origins of the Modern Movement*. Indianapolis: Bobbs-Merrill, 1964.

Reeve, Carl, and Ann Barton Reeve. *James Connolly and the United States: The Road to the 1916 Irish Rebellion*. Atlantic Highlands, NJ: Humanities Press, 1978.

Reid, Fred. "Socialist Sunday Schools in Great Britain, 1892–1939." *International Review of Social History* 11 (1966): 18–47.

Roll, Jarod. *Spirit of Rebellion: Labor and Religion in the New Cotton South*. Urbana: University of Illinois Press, 2010.

Ruotsila, Markku. *John Spargo and American Socialism*. New York: Palgrave Macmillan, 2006.

Salvatore, Nick. *Eugene Debs: Citizen and Socialist*. Urbana: University of Illinois Press, 1982.

Sanders, Elisabeth. *Roots of Reform: Farmers, Workers, and the American State, 1877–1917*. Chicago: University of Chicago Press, 1999.

Saxton, Alexander. *Religion and the Human Prospect*. New York: Monthly Review Press, 2006.

Schneirov, Richard. "New Perspectives on Socialism I: The Socialist Party Revisited." *Journal of the Gilded Age and Progressive Era* 2, no. Special Issue 3 (2003): 245–52.

Scibilia, Dominic. "The Christological Character of Labor: A Theological Rehabilitation of Mother Jones." *US Catholic Historian* 13, no. 3 (Summer 1995): 49–61.

Sehat, David. *The Myth of Religious Freedom*. New York: Oxford University Press, 2011.

Schmidt, Jean Miller. *Souls or the Social Order: The Two Party System in American Protestantism*. New York: Carlson, 1991.

Sellers, Charles. *The Market Revolution: Jacksonian America, 1815–1846*. New York: Oxford University Press, 1991.

Shore, Elliot. *Talkin Socialism: J.A. Wayland and the Role of the Press in American Radicalism, 1890–1912*. Lawrence: University Press of Kansas, 1988.

Sklar, Kathryn Kish. *Florence Kelley and the Nation's Work: The Rise of Women's Political Culture, 1830–1900*. New Haven: Yale University Press, 1995.

Smith, Gary Scott. *The Search for Social Salvation: Social Christianity and America, 1880–1925*. Lexington Books, 2000.

Smith, Timothy. *Revivalism and Social Reform in Mid-Nineteenth Century America*. New York: Abington Press, 1957.

Soden, Dale. *Outsiders in a Promised Land: Religious Activists in Pacific Northwest History*. Corvallis: Oregon State University Press, 2015.

Stansell, Christine. *American Moderns: Bohemian New York and the Creation of a New Century*. New York: Macmillan, 2001.

Stephens, Randall. "Assessing the Roots of Pentecostalism: A Historiographic Essay." *American Religious Experience*, April 2000. https://web.archive.org/web/20230130221253/http://are.as.wvu.edu/pentroot.htm (accessed June 22, 2023).

Stephens, Randall. *The Fire Spreads: Holiness and Pentecostalism in the American South*. Cambridge, MA: Harvard University Press, 2008.

Stout, Harry S., and D. G. Hart. *New Directions in American Religious History*. New York: Oxford University Press, 1998.

Stromquist, Shelton. *Reinventing "The People": The Progressive Movement, the Class Problem, and the Origins of Modern Liberalism*. Urbana: University of Illinois Press, 2006.

Synan, Vinson. *The Holiness-Pentecostal Movement in the United States*. Grand Rapids: Eerdman's, 1971.

Taiz, Lillian. *Hallelujah Lads and Lasses: Remaking the Salvation Army in America, 1880–1930*. Chapel Hill: University of North Carolina Press, 2000.

Tawney, R. H. *Religion and the Rise of Capitalism: A Historical Study*. London: Murray, 1926.

Tax, Meredith. *Rising of the Women*. New York: Monthly Review Press, 1980.

Taylor, Barbara. *Eve and the New Jerusalem: Socialism and Feminism in the Nineteenth Century*. Cambridge, MA: Harvard University Press, 1993.

Thompson, E. P. *The Making of the English Working Class*. New York: Vintage Books, 1963.

Thompson, E. P. "The Moral Economy of the English Crowd in the Eighteenth Century." *Past and Present* 50, no. 1 (1971): 76–136.

Tomasi, Silvano. *Piety and Power: The Role of Italian Parishes in the New York Metropolitan Area, 1880–1930*. Staten Island: Center for Migration Studies, 1975.

Turkstra, Melissa. "Constructing a Labour Gospel: Labor and Religion in Early 20th Century Ontario." *Labour / Le Travail*, Spring 2006, 93–130.

Valeri, Mark. *Heavenly Merchandize: How Religion Shaped Commerce in Puritan America*. Princeton, NJ: Princeton University Press, 2010.

Wacker, Grant. *Heaven Below: Early Pentecostals and American Culture*. Cambridge, MA: Harvard University Press, 2001.

Watson, Bruce. *Bread and Roses: Mills, Migrants, and the Struggle for the American Dream*. New York: Penguin, 2006.

Weber, Max. *The Protestant Ethic and the Spirit of Capitalism*. Trans. Stephen Kalberg. New York: Oxford University Press, 2010.

Weinstein, James. *The Decline of Socialism in America, 1912–1925*. New Brunswick, NJ: Rutgers University Press, 1984.

Weir, Robert. *Beyond Labor's Veil: The Culture of the Knights of Labor*. State College: Pennsylvania State University Press, 1996.

Weston, William. *Presbyterian Pluralism: Competition in a Protestant House*. Knoxville: University of Tennessee Press, 1997.

Wharton, Leslie. "Herbert N. Casson and the American Labor Church, 1893–1898." *Essex Institute Historical Collections* 117, no. 2 (1981): 119–37.

White, Ronald. *The Social Gospel: Religion and Reform in Changing America.* Philadelphia: Temple University Press, 1975.

Wiebe, Robert H. *The Search for Order, 1877–1920.* New York: Hill and Wang, 1966.

Wilentz, Sean. *Chants Democratic: New York City and the Rise of the American Working Class, 1788–1850.* New York: Oxford University Press, 1984.

Winter, Thomas. *Making Men, Making Class: The YMCA and Workingmen, 1877–1920.* Chicago: University of Chicago Press, 2002.

Index

For the benefit of digital users, indexed terms that span two pages (e.g., 52–53) may, on occasion, appear on only one of those pages.

Tables and figures are indicated by *t* and *f* following the page number